THE LITERATURE of THE BIBLE

THE
LITERATURE
of
THE BIBLE

Leland Ryken

Wheaton College
Wheaton, Illinois

ZONDERVAN
PUBLISHING HOUSE
OF THE ZONDERVAN CORPORATION | GRAND RAPIDS, MICHIGAN 49506

ISBN 0-310-32411-4

Grateful acknowledgment is made to the National
Council of Churches for permission to quote exten-
sively from the *Revised Standard Version*. Copyright
© 1952 and 1971 by the Division of Christian Education, National Council of the Churches of Christ
in the United States of America.

Frontispiece and photos on pages 11, 31, 43, 199, 215, 231, and 315,
courtesy of Levant Photo Service.

Photos on pages 79, 93, 119, 241, 259, 271, and 299,
courtesy of Matson Photo Service.

Photo on page 107, courtesy of Ewing Galloway.

Photo on page 333, courtesy of
Radio Times Holton Picture Library, London.

Printed in the United States of America

83 84 85 86 87 88 — 10 9 8

To My Students

Contents

Preface

Christianity is the most literary religion in the world and the one in which the word has a special sanctity. The clearest evidence of this literary emphasis is the Bible, which is not only the repository of Hebraic-Christian belief but is also a book in which literary form is of overriding importance.

This book is a work of literary criticism on the literature of the Bible and grows out of a college course on biblical literature that I have been privileged to teach. I have written for readers of the Bible who wish to understand and enjoy the literary dimension of the Bible and who wish to fit biblical literature into their experience of literature generally.

Anyone who writes on this topic must choose among a variety of approaches. I wish to make clear at the outset some of the assumptions that I have chosen to follow in my study of biblical literature. For one thing, I write as a literary critic and have not tried to duplicate the type of scholarship done by specialists in biblical studies. I hope that biblical and theological specialists will find something of value in my study, just as I am greatly indebted to their work. It is abundantly evident, however, that the biblical scholar and the literary critic tend to use different terminology in their approaches to the biblical text. Even when they use identical terms, such as "literary criticism" or "literary form," they often give those terms a different content. While there is a wealth of specialized biblical scholarship, there continues to be a great need for books written by literary critics for general readers of the Bible.

Since my intention is to help readers of the Bible fit their reading of Scripture into their broader experience of literature in general, I have related biblical literature to the familiar works of Western literature. While biblical scholarship has contributed much to our understanding of the Bible by placing it in the context of other ancient Near Eastern literature, this rather esoteric field of study has remained the province of the specialist.

I have chosen to use the tools of literary criticism that are in vogue today. I do not believe that it is anomalous to use modern critical terms in talking about ancient literature. Indeed, the anomaly would be not to employ the best critical equipment that is presently available. In using a modern critical vocabulary, I make no claim, of course, that biblical writers were consciously aware of writing works that conform to the literary categories I employ. Surely it is not surprising that biblical writers could have written tragedies or satires or encomia or parodies without calling their works by these names.

It will be apparent at once that my own critical approach is eclectic, as I believe the best criticism always is. I have used the critical tools that I think most useful to the enjoyment and understanding of biblical literature, whether those tools come from literary criticism or biblical scholarship, and from ancient or modern times.

My assumption at every point has been that the person who reads this book will also have read the works of biblical literature that I discuss. I have therefore avoided summarizing the content of the works themselves.

All quotations from the Bible have been taken from the *Revised Standard Version*. In particular, I have found *The Harper Study Bible*, edited by Harold Lindsell (Grand Rapids: Zondervan Publishing House), to be the most useful and satisfactory edition of the Bible presently available for readers and students of the Bible.

I have provided a glossary of literary terms on pages 359 to 362.

My book is indebted to the help of others. I have learned much from the comments of my students. I have benefited from countless insights offered by my colleagues in the Bible Department at Wheaton College, especially Professors Ralph Alexander, Gordon Fee, Alan Johnson, and Donald Lake. My writing of the book was facilitated by a grant from the Wheaton College Alumni Association. I owe the most to the encouragement of my colleague Professor Joe McClatchey and to the assistance of my wife Mary, who has been in every way my co-laborer in this project.

Wheaton College, Illinois
April, 1974

This arch over the entrance to the garden at Jacob's Well is symbolic of the riches awaiting the reader of biblical literature.

An Introduction
to Biblical
Literature

1

The necessary point of departure for a discussion of the literature of the Bible is the question "What is literature?" There is perhaps no area of literature where careful definition is as important as in the study of biblical literature, and a common failing in books and academic courses on the literature of the Bible is lack of precise definition. It is inaccurate to assume that everything in the Bible is literary in nature or intention.

To begin, literature is experiential. This means that the subject matter of literature is human experience. The approach to human experience, moreover, is concrete rather than abstract. Literature does not, for example, discourse about virtue but instead shows a virtuous person acting. We might say that literature does not tell *about* characters and actions and concepts but *presents* characters in action.

Literature not only presents experience but also interprets it. The writer of literature selects and molds his material according to discernible viewpoints. Human experience is presented in such a way as to express, whether explicitly or by implication, a world view.

Finally, literature is an interpretive presentation of experience *in an artistic form*. That is, the content of a work of literature is presented in the form of a novel, play, short story, poem, and so forth. Each of these literary kinds exhibits additional elements of artistic form, such as pattern or design, unity, theme or centrality, balance, contrast, recurrence, variation, intricacy or complexity, and progression. All of this is to say that when a writer sits down to write, he asks not only, What do I want to say? but also, How do I wish to say it? What kind of artifact do I desire to make? By the same token, the reader must be ready to respond to the artistic elements of literature. In general, beauty of form is as essential to literature as is truthfulness of content.

A working definition of literature, then, is that it is an interpretive presentation of experience in an artistic form. This means that there are two criteria that must be insisted on if we are to distinguish between the literary and nonliterary parts of the Bible: (1) literature is experiential rather than abstract, and (2) literature is artistic, manifesting elements of artistic form. It is of course true that much writing falls somewhere between the poles of literary and nonliterary writing, but the two criteria that I have cited remain the discernible ingredients of the literature of the Bible. These two criteria encompass not only the main literary forms, such as narrative, lyric, and drama, but also such traditional forms as the epistle and oratory. The latter forms are experiential and concrete by virtue of the writer's dramatic address to an audience; they are artistic by virtue of their eloquence and possession of rhetorical techniques.

There are two reasons why some parts of the Bible call for a literary approach. First, since some parts of the Bible are literary in form, a literary approach is necessary in order to understand what is being said. Any phenomenon has to be understood in terms appropriate to what it is. If parts of the Bible are literary, they must be approached with literary expectations and by asking the questions that we ask of literature. Secondly, a literary approach is necessary because it is the only approach that is genuinely concerned with the artistic beauty of the Bible. The artistic beauty of the Bible exists for the reader's enjoyment and artistic enrichment. To ignore this aspect of biblical literature is to distort the Bible as a written document.

II

 Biblical literature is a collection or anthology of works written by a variety of writers over the span of many centuries.[1] The very title "Bible" means "little books." Biblical literature is a small library containing a survey of Hebraic-Christian literature as it was written over a long period of time, just as we speak of a survey of English or American literature. Not only is the literature of the Bible a collection at various hands, but it is itself part of a larger collection that includes expository as well as literary writing. The literary parts of the Bible appear side by side with history, theological exposition, legal writing, and letters. This will explain why biblical literature is always shading off into history, theology, and civil law, and why the literature of the Bible is difficult to define and set off from nonliterary writing.

The fact that biblical literature is an anthology results in a remarkable variety of forms and styles. Literary forms represented in the Bible

---

[1] When I use the term "biblical literature," I mean those parts of the Bible that are literary and which are discussed subsequently in this book. Most of my generalizations apply equally to the other parts of the Bible, but in the present discussion I intend my focus to be on the literary parts of the Bible.

include the story of origins, heroic narrative, epic, parody, tragedy, lyric, epithalamion, encomium, wisdom literature, proverb, parable, pastoral, satire, prophecy, gospel, epistle, oratory, and apocalypse.

Comprehensiveness of subject matter also results from the Bible's *Comp.* status as a collection of different works. There is no aspect of human experience that is not presented within the pages of biblical literature. It is worthy of note, too, that biblical literature shows a tendency to portray what is elemental and enduring in human experience — God, nature, love, social relationships, death, evil, guilt, salvation, family life, judgment, and forgiveness.

Since biblical literature is both comprehensive and written by a *comple* variety of authors, it preserves the complexities and polarities of human experience to an unusual degree. The paradoxes of human life are held in tension in what can be called the most balanced book ever written. Divine sovereignty and human responsiveness, justice and mercy, law and freedom, man's simultaneous smallness and greatness, the claims of the individual and of society, the worth of both earth and heaven — these paradoxes are affirmed throughout biblical literature and constitute the poles between which God and man operate.

Because the individual parts of biblical literature are interdependent, no single work can be regarded as a totally self-contained unit. The meaning of an individual work is deepened and modified by other works. The portrait of God, for example, is built up by a brushstroke here and a brushstroke there, with each story or lyric poem contributing a small part to the total effect. Similarly, no single work is likely to give full scope to the biblical view of man, just as one could not deduce the biblical attitude toward romantic love by reading only the Song of Solomon. A related principle that must guide the reading of biblical literature is that the literary parts of the Bible will often be clarified by reference to what is contained in the expository parts.

Although biblical literature is a collection of diverse works, it *Unity* must also be regarded as possessing a high degree of unity. There is unity of national authorship, with only two books in the whole Bible (Luke and Acts) not having been written by Jews. There is unity of subject matter, consisting most broadly of God's ways with people and the relationship of people to God and fellow humans. There is a unity of world view and general theological outlook from book to book. There is unity of purpose underlying all biblical literature — the purpose of revealing God to people so that they might know how to order their lives. There is, finally, a unity of literary texture based on allusion. Various biblical writers allude to earlier works in the same canon, or to the same historical events, or to the same religious

15

beliefs and experiences, or to the same cultural context. The resulting unity of reference is immediately evident when one consults a modern Bible containing cross references in the marginal notes. No other anthology of literature possesses the unified texture of allusions that biblical literature displays.

It is at once apparent that biblical literature is essentially religious literature. It is pervaded by a consciousness of God, and human experience is constantly viewed in its religious dimension. This religious identity manifests itself in the purpose of the writers, who display a strong didactic impulse. Probably no work of literature in the Bible exists only for the sake of artistic pleasure or entertainment. As C. S. Lewis has well stated, the Bible is "not merely a sacred book but a book so remorselessly and continuously sacred that it does not invite, it excludes or repels, the merely aesthetic approach."[2] In biblical literature the artistic impulse is everywhere combined with the intention to teach something about God or man. Indeed, the didactic tendency is always ready to overshadow the development of a story or poem, as when the Epic of the Exodus is interrupted by long passages containing civil laws. The serious religious concern of biblical literature explains why there is little comedy and humor (as distinct from joy) in its pages. There is little in biblical literature to make the reader laugh.

Closely related to its status as religious literature is the matter of world view in biblical literature. A world view can be defined as a set of beliefs in which there is a central value and integrating principle for all areas of experience. In literature a world view can be identified by observing the identity of the literary characters, by identifying the nature of their experiment in living, and by noting the outcome of their experience. Biblical literature consistently affirms a God-centered world view. This means that God is not only the supreme value, but that He also gives identity to all other aspects of experience. For example, He determines what man is (God's creature, made in His image), what history is (the outworking of God's purpose), what knowledge is (the truth that God reveals), what the state is (a divinely ordained social order), what goodness is (obedience to God's will), what nature is (God's creation), and so forth.[3] In biblical literature this kind of Godward allegiance is pervasive. It is less a matter of the writers' trying to inculcate a truth than it is evidence of their habitual way of looking at reality.

(margin annotation: Essentially Religious)

(margin annotation: God-centered world view)

---

[2] "The Literary Impact of the Authorized Version," in *They Asked for a Paper* (London: Geoffrey Bles, 1962), p. 49.

[3] My concept of world view is based on the discussion of Richard Stevens and Thomas J. Musial, *Reading, Discussing, and Writing about the Great Books* (Boston: Houghton Mifflin Company, 1970), pp. 109-122.

16

Biblical literature shows a constant tendency to move from the particular event to the spiritual meaning or spiritual reality behind the event. We might call it the transcendental stance of biblical literature. By this I mean that biblical writers display an awareness of the spiritual significance behind human and natural occurrences. What in most literature would be considered a purely natural event — the birth of a baby, a shower of rain, the daily course of the sun — is regarded in biblical literature as being rooted in a divine reality beyond the natural world. There is a continual interpenetration of the supernatural into the earthly order, and God is a continual actor in human affairs. One effect of this is that life becomes filled with meaning, since every event takes on spiritual significance.

The supernatural orientation in biblical literature often takes the form of what might be called the theme of the two worlds. The underlying premise of biblical literature is that there are two planes of reality — the physical world, perceived through the senses, and the supernatural world, invisible to ordinary human view. Both worlds are objectively real, but whereas one order can be demonstrated empirically, the spiritual order of values must usually be accepted on faith. The constant appeal made by biblical writers is for people to order their lives by the unseen spiritual realities, even though doing so usually contradicts earthly or material or human standards.

From a literary point of view, the transcendental stance of biblical literature and its theme of the two worlds make it preeminently the literature of mystery, or the literature of wonder. It is a literature of mystery not in the sense that it mystifies the reader, or hides things from him, or maintains an aura of secrecy, but in the sense that it repeatedly confronts the reader with evidence that what he is inclined to treat as a purely natural event cannot be adequately explained in such terms. It is a literature of mystery not because it conceals the spiritual but for the opposite reason. It reveals the supernatural and shows that there is something that transcends the immediate earthly context. The constant occurrences of miracles in biblical narratives, for example, keep alive a sense of the mystery of supernatural power, just as the closing chapters of Job evoke a sense of human inadequacy to understand completely the God of nature, whose ways remain mysterious. The mysterious presence of spiritual reality in the ordinary earthly cycle of activities is captured when Moses sees a burning bush that is not consumed and takes off his shoes because he is on holy ground, or when Jacob awakens from a vision of God and declares, "Surely the Lord is in this place; and I did not know it.... How awesome is this place!" (Gen. 28:16-17). By refusing to allow reality to be conceived solely in terms of known, observable experience, biblical literature transforms the mundane into something with sacred significance and evokes a sense of the mystery of the divine.

Biblical literature claims to be a revelation. Its authors repeatedly picture themselves as being the spokesmen for God and the agents by which supernatural truth is communicated to men. As C. S. Lewis has stated in contrasting biblical and nonbiblical literature, "In most parts of the Bible everything is implicitly or explicitly introduced with 'Thus saith the Lord.' "[4] The Bible's status as a supernatural revelation results in a conviction about the unassailable truth of its content that is without an exact parallel in other literature. In the words of Erich Auerbach, "The Bible's claim to truth is not only far more urgent than Homer's, it is tyrannical — it excludes all other claims."[5]

The fact that biblical literature claims to be a revelation of events that are often transcendental in nature means that its interpretation frequently depends on an awareness of the principle of accommodation. We must understand that the depiction of God and supernatural occurrences has been accommodated to human understanding by being reduced to images that the human mind can grasp. Biblical writers knew that God is a spirit, not a localized person with a physical body. They were well aware that God transcends complete human understanding. Isaiah wrote, "For my thoughts are not your thoughts, neither are your ways my ways, says the Lord. For as the heavens are higher than the earth, so are my ways higher than your ways and my thoughts than your thoughts" (Isa. 55:8-9). Similarly, characters in the story of Job give expression to commonplace sentiment when they assert that man cannot "find out the deep things of God" (Job 11:7) and that concerning "the Almighty — we cannot find him" (37:23).

Yet biblical writers do not hesitate to portray God as possessing such human characteristics as a face, a hand, ears, eyes, and feet.[6] Similarly, even though God was held to be invisible, Isaiah depicts a vision of "the Lord sitting upon a throne" (Isa. 6:1-5). Although God is not subject to bodily limitations, the very anthropomorphic God of Genesis 1 and 2 is described as resting on the seventh day, and the writer of Exodus adds that God was refreshed by His rest after the six days of creative work (Exod. 31:17). The principle that resolves the apparent contradiction between God's acknowledged transcendence and His depiction in anthropomorphic images is the principle of accommodation. The biblical writers are unafraid to use

---

[4] Lewis, p. 49.

[5] *Mimesis: The Representation of Reality in Western Literature,* trans. Willard Trask (Princeton: Princeton University Press, 1953), p. 14.

[6] For illustration, see, respectively, Exodus 33:11; I Samuel 5:11; Nehemiah 1:6; Job 28:10; Nahum 1:3.

anthropomorphism, not because they lack a clear conception of God's spirituality and transcendence, but because they know that this wholly "Other" can be known and depicted in literature only by using the analogies of human experience.

Another characteristic of biblical literature is that it displays a vivid consciousness of values. Some conception of right and wrong underlies most literature, but in the Bible this conception is more sharply defined and more strongly held than elsewhere. For biblical writers the issue of what is good and what is evil is more important than anything else. Biblical authors are constantly saying, "This, not that." Biblical literature is similarly pervaded by a conviction that some things matter more than others, and that ultimately the value of anything depends on its spiritual status before a holy God. Value does not reside inherently in anything independently of its relationship to God, nor can human endeavor be regarded as ultimately valuable apart from obedience to God. All of this means that a prerequisite for reading biblical literature with understanding and enjoyment is a conviction that good and evil are realities and are ultimately the most important issues in life.

The vivid consciousness of values in biblical literature accounts in part for the subjective stance of the narrator that is found there. Biblical writers do not maintain an objective viewpoint. They are always taking sides. Author intrusion is common, with writers making didactic comments and clarifying the motives of God or other characters. Descriptions of events or characters tend to be evaluative, often in terms of the moral categories of right and wrong. The subjective narrative voice is not unique to biblical literature. It is the older way of storytelling. Homer, for example, often tells us that Odysseus is clever and Penelope worthy, just as Virgil insists that Aeneas is pious and Dido guilty of fury. It is in the same vein that a biblical writer will describe Joseph as being "handsome and good-looking" (Gen. 39:6), or state that Saul's visiting the witch at Endor was an evil act for which God judged him (1 Chron. 10:13-14).

Biblical literature is firmly embedded in historical reality. It constantly claims to be history and has repeatedly been authenticated as history by modern archaeology. The history of biblical literature is not simply factual but is, as Roland Frye has well stated, "always kept within a framework of interpretive significance."[7] One result of this historical emphasis is that a usual staple of literature, fiction, is nearly absent from biblical literature. Another result is that the freedom of biblical writers to invent details in a story was eliminated.

Presents a value system

Subjective

Embedded in historical reality

---

[7] "Introduction" to The Bible: Selections from the King James Version for Study as Literature (Boston: Houghton Mifflin Company, 1965), p. ix.

Biblical writers resist the tendency found elsewhere in ancient literature to embellish their stories with imagined details. The book of
Job, with its highly embellished poetic style and symmetrical arrangement of speeches, is the exception, not the rule. The fact that the
events themselves, and even the order of the events, were already
determined means that the creativity of biblical writers is not seen
primarily in their fictional inventiveness. Rather, their conscious
artistry is to be found in their selection of material according to
unifying themes and with a sense of artistic proportion. It is a
different kind of challenge but for most writers not an easier way
to be creative.

The literature of the Bible, like that of other ancient cultures,
often takes its impulse from the desire to embody in character and
story the values and conflicts that were central to the cultural experience. In keeping with this somewhat didactic intention, writers of
biblical literature select their material by the two criteria of idealism
and realism. On the one hand, they present idealized characters and
acts which constitute models and display the normative values that
the writer's society espoused. On the other hand, writers combine
realism with this idealizing tendency. They tell stories about characters who exhibit common human failings. Along with idealized characters and actions there are ignoble characters who teach by way of
negative example. In short, biblical literature, like ancient literature
generally, combines realism and idealism for purposes of instruction.
It presents models of virtue for the reader to emulate and depicts
examples of depravity for the reader to avoid.

The dramatic instinct for dialogue pervades biblical literature.
Strictly speaking, there is no pure drama in the Bible, and Hebrew
culture produced no theater. Most biblical writers, however, display
a strong tendency to achieve concreteness of presentation through the
use of dialogue. Most biblical stories depend heavily on dialogue
rather than summarized narrative as a way of describing the action.
The book of Job, although it is a narrative told by a narrator, is
structured like a play. And many lyric poems in the Bible are dramatic in structure, with the speaker addressing a mute but implied
listener.

Several things account for the prevalence of dialogue in biblical
literature. It is evidence of the literary impulse to be concrete in
presentation. When a writer gives the actual words of characters, it
is obvious that he is not simply offering an abstract summary about
an event but is actually presenting the event in all its experiential
immediacy. Secondly, the prominence of dialogue reflects the fact
that originally much of the Bible existed as oral literature. When
literature is chiefly spoken rather than written, storytellers or poets

naturally have a high regard for uttered speech, and it is not surprising that their literary works would make frequent use of speech patterns. Finally, the frequent use of dialogue is rooted in the biblical view of man and God. In biblical literature man achieves full meaning only in relationship — relationship to God and the human community. Similarly, the God of the Bible is the God who communicates — who speaks, calls, and invites human response. Dialogue is the natural and inevitable rhetorical mode for this view of man and God, for dialogue is the language of relationship and encounter. It is small wonder, therefore, that biblical literature is full of voices speaking and replying.

The concept of encounter goes far to explain what happens to the reader of biblical literature. There is an important sense in which the reader of biblical literature is its subject and center of reference.[8] Biblical writers, motivated by a consciously didactic purpose, intend to tell the reader something about himself. From this perspective, biblical literature exhibits two patterns — the reader's humiliation and his education. That is, biblical literature exposes the human inclination toward evil and shows how obedience to God provides an answer to man's plight. The reader who assimilates this twofold lesson will have participated in something more than a literary experience. In the final analysis the reading of biblical literature is an encounter with God. A belligerent critic of Milton's *Paradise Lost* once grumbled, "With the best will in the world, we cannot avoid Milton's God or refuse to react to him."[9] Precisely — and this is even truer of biblical literature, which presupposes response as a condition of reading. What Amos Wilder describes as an essential feature of the New Testament gospels is equally true of biblical literature as a whole: "It is as though God says to men one by one: 'Look me in the eye.' "[10]

Biblical literature paradoxically calls for both a naive and a sophisticated literary response. On the one hand, much biblical literature, especially the narrative parts, is popular or folk literature. Its appeal is to the unsophisticated literary taste. Anyone who has been privileged to hear the Bible stories as a child can look back on his early responses to the stories and realize that his childhood responses were usually the right ones. To read biblical literature with delight requires an intuitive response to what is being presented.

At the same time, biblical literature asks of us a sophisticated

---

[8] The approach that I take to the role of the reader in biblical literature is modeled on the approach of Stanley Eugene Fish to Milton's *Paradise Lost,* in *Surprised by Sin: The Reader in Paradise Lost* (New York: St. Martin's Press, 1967), especially pages 88-91.

[9] A. J. A. Waldock, *Paradise Lost and Its Critics* (Gloucester, Mass.: Peter Smith, 1959), p. 100.

[10] *Early Christian Rhetoric* (Cambridge: Harvard University Press, 1971), p. 54.

literary response. It does so in the sense that biblical writers wrote as craftsmen whose works display a grasp of literary forms and conventions. Biblical writers asked, whether consciously or instinctively, What form shall I use to express my vision? What kind of literary object do I wish to make? It is evident that biblical writers knew how to tell stories that were unified by the principle of tragedy or satire or heroism. Biblical poets knew that a psalm of lament had five main units and that a psalm of praise should have a three-part structure. They knew the art of inventing apt metaphors and similes. One result of this awareness of literary forms is that the most significant grouping of biblical literature is not by author but by literary kind. In other words, the greatest degree of similarity exists not among works written by the same writer but rather among works belonging to the same literary family.[11]

No introduction to biblical literature is complete without insisting on the archetypal content of the Bible. An archetype is a symbol, character type, or plot motif that has recurred throughout literature. One critic speaks of archetypes as "any of the immemorial patterns of response to the human situation in its permanent aspects."[12] These archetypes carry the same or very similar meanings for a large portion of mankind and appeal to what is most elemental in human experience.

Archetypal criticism is one of the most fruitful approaches to biblical literature because the Bible is *the* great repository of archetypes in Western literature. Northrop Frye calls the Bible "the major informing influence on literary symbolism" and believes that familiarity with the Bible is the prerequisite for understanding literature as a whole because of its archetypal content.[13]

Of particular importance is the overall archetypal pattern of literature. If one takes all of literature and charts it on a single model,

---

[11] Some readers of this paragraph will be inclined to conclude that I have claimed too much conscious artistry for biblical writers. Actually, the degree of conscious or unconscious artistry of the writers of the Bible is a purely speculative question on which there is no conclusive proof. My own concern is much less with the process by which the writers composed than with the product. To the detriment of a genuine appreciation of the artistic dimension of biblical literature has been the too facile assumption that biblical writers were unlettered, unsophisticated, and without literary intentions, and that therefore their works cannot possess a high degree of artistry.

[12] Leslie Fiedler, "Archetype and Signature: A Study of the Relationship between Biography and Poetry," in *An Introduction to Literary Criticism*, ed. Marlies K. Danzinger and W. Stacy Johnson (Boston: D. C. Heath and Company, 1961), p. 268.

[13] *Anatomy of Criticism* (Princeton: Princeton University Press, 1957), pp. 315-16; and *The Educated Imagination* (Bloomington: Indiana University Press, 1964), p. 110.

he finds that it will form a composite narrative that has appropriately been called "the monomyth." This composite narrative is cyclic in structure and possesses four phases. It corresponds to some common cycles of familiar experience, such as dawn-zenith-sunset-darkness, spring-summer-autumn-winter, and birth-triumph-death-dissolution.[14] If we universalize this pattern so that it forms a model that will encompass all of literature, we end up with the following monomyth:

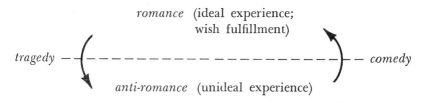

romance (ideal experience;
wish fulfillment)

tragedy — comedy

anti-romance (unideal experience)

Romance is literature that describes an idealized picture of human experience. It satisfies our desire for wish fulfillment. Its opposite, anti-romance, presents a world of complete bondage and the absence of anything ideal. A story in which the action descends from romance to catastrophe is a tragedy, and an upward movement from bondage to freedom is comedy. These are the four possible kinds of literary plots, and together they form the circular monomyth that unifies all of literature.

There are also more particularized manifestations of the general cyclic pattern of the monomyth. One example is the journey motif, in which the hero's story and character development are built around a journey. Another example is the quest, in which the hero departs from his homeland, undertakes the ordeal of a long journey that tests his powers and temporarily defeats him, and finally overcomes the obstacles, returning to his kingdom and (frequently) marrying a princess. The death-rebirth motif involves a hero who endures death or a deathlike experience and returns to life and security. In an initiation story the hero undergoes a series of ordeals as he passes from ignorance and immaturity to social and spiritual adulthood. The initiation motif, like the quest story and death-rebirth story, consists of three stages — separation, transformation through ordeal, and return. A fifth common plot is the scapegoat motif, in which a character with whom the welfare of the people is identified must die in order to atone for the sins of the people.

There are appropriate archetypal images for various phases of the monomyth and the particular versions of it discussed in the preceding paragraph. Generally archetypal images can be divided into two

---

[14] These illustrations come from Northrop Frye, "The Archetypes of Literature," in *Kenyon Review,* XIII (1951), 92-110.

groups — the ideal and the unideal, or the comic and the tragic, or the apocalyptic and demonic. The following list, based on the critical system of Northrop Frye, catalogs most of the archetypes of literature.

The Archetypes of Ideal Experience

The human world: the community or city; images of symposium, communion, order, unity, friendship, love; the marriage; the feast, meal, or supper; food staples, such as bread, milk, and meat; and food luxuries, such as wine and honey.

The animal world: a community of domesticated animals, usually a flock of sheep; a lamb, or one of the gentler birds, often a dove; a group of singing birds.

The vegetable world: a garden, grove, or park; a tree of life; the rose.

The inorganic world: a city, or one building or temple (for example, heaven portrayed as one house with many mansions) ; images of jewels and precious stones, often glowing and fiery; fire and brilliant light; burning that purifies and refines.

Water imagery: a river or stream; a spring of water; showers of rain; flowing water of any sort.

The forces of nature: the breeze or wind; calm after storm; the spring and summer seasons; the sun, or the lesser light of the moon and stars; light, sunrise, day.

Miscellaneous: images of ascent or rising; the mountaintop, or other images of height; images of birth and rebirth; images of motion (as opposed to stagnation) ; images of freedom; musical harmony, or singing.

The Archetypes of Unideal Experience

The human world: tyranny or anarchy; isolation among people; the harlot, witch, and similar creatures; images of cannibalism, torture, mutilation (the cross, the stake, the scaffold, gallows, stocks, etc.) ; slavery and bondage; images of disease and deformity; sleeplessness or nightmare, often related to guilt of conscience.

The animal world: monsters or beasts of prey; the wolf (traditional enemy of the sheep) , the tiger, the vulture, the cold and earthbound serpent, dragons, and the like.

The vegetable world: the sinister forest, often enchanted and in control of demonic forces; the heath or wilderness or wasteland, which is always barren and may be either a tropical place of great heat or a place of ice and intense cold.

The inorganic world: either the inorganic world in its unworked form of deserts, rocks, and wilderness, or its civilized form of cities of destruction and violence; the prison or dungeon; malignant fire that destroys and tortures instead of purifying.

Water imagery: the sea and all that it contains (sea beasts and water monsters).

The forces of nature: the storm or tempest; the autumn and winter seasons; sunset, darkness, night.

Miscellaneous: images of descent; the valley; the underground cave or tomb; death; dry dust or ashes; images of rust and decay; images of stagnation or immobility; discordant sounds, or cacophony.

What significance does all this have for the study of biblical literature? The composite archetypal narrative called the monomyth unifies biblical literature as a whole. It provides a general outline where every individual story or poem, as well as the imagery and symbolism of a given passage, take their place. Although biblical literature appears at first glance to be a heterogeneous collection of fragments, it turns out to be a single, composite whole.

The archetypal content of the Bible gives it not only unity but universality as well. Archetypes express what is most common and elemental in human experience. In Northrop Frye's words, "Some symbols are images of things common to all men, and therefore have a communicable power which is potentially unlimited."[15] Since archetypes belong not only to the Bible but are the basic constituent elements of literature itself, the archetypes of biblical literature allow us to relate it to other literature. This is true even when biblical literature reverses or inverts the usual meaning of an archetype. For example, although the wilderness usually carries its archetypal negative meaning in biblical literature, the Bible differs significantly from the conventional pattern by making the wilderness the place of blessing and the context for God's activity. One thinks of the encounter at Sinai in the Old Testament, or Christ's defeat of Satan in the wilderness temptation, or John the Baptist's ministry in the wilderness. This deviation from the archetypal norm does not negate the importance of the archetypal scheme I have outlined. Both the uniqueness and conventionality of biblical literature depend on an awareness of the archetypal structure of literature as a whole.

Generally speaking, biblical literature, like other ancient literature, is at the opposite pole from modern literature by being explicit in its archetypal content. Whereas modern literature tends to disguise its archetypal images and patterns with originality and realistic description, the older kind of literature tended to depict archetypal patterns in their explicit and undisplaced form.

---

[15] *Anatomy of Criticism*, p. 99.

III

If we define plot in its usual terms as a series of events arranged around a central conflict and possessing a unified development, biblical literature must be regarded as having an overriding plot of which the individual works constitute the various segments. The plot of biblical literature centers in the great spiritual conflict between good and evil.

A host of details comprises this conflict. There is character conflict between God and Satan, God and His rebellious human creatures, God's angels and the fallen angels (also called demons and evil spirits), and good and evil people. There is the scenic conflict between heaven and hell (prominent in the New Testament, though not in the Old Testament). There is inner human conflict between the claims of God and the claims of evil. On the level of action, the events of biblical literature illustrate either obedience or disobedience to God's will.

Almost every incident in biblical literature turns out to be in some sense a reenactment of this archetypal plot conflict between good and evil. Every act, and every mental attitude, shows God's creatures engaged in some type of movement, whether slight or momentous, toward God or away from Him. In this way the form of biblical literature — a structure of contrasts — embodies its meaning — the fact of spiritual conflict between good and evil.

The presence of the great spiritual conflict makes choice necessary on the part of biblical characters. Every area of human experience is claimed by God and counterclaimed by Satan and the forces of evil. There is no neutral ground. Every human event shows an allegiance toward or against God. The plot of biblical literature has the motif of choice built into its very structure and results in what we might call the drama of the soul's choice. A survey of biblical literature is from this point of view a series of great moral dilemmas and choices. Again and again, characters in biblical literature assume great magnitude as they make the great moral decisions.

In biblical literature decisive action consists of a person's response to external reality and does not reside in external reality itself. Man's problems do not stem from outward events or the hostility of the environment. In contrast to Platonic thought, the material world is not regarded as the great threat to human welfare. Biblical literature instead makes man's moral choices in history the crucial issue. The plot of biblical literature is thus a spiritual plot in which external events provide the *occasion* for significant moral action, good or bad. Given this view of history and human experience, everything that happens to a person is important, representing an opportunity to serve God or rebel against Him.

Plot must have progression as well as conflict. One element of progression in the biblical story is the unfolding of God's purposes throughout history. In this story God is the central character, or the protagonist. As Roland Frye has said, "The characterization of God may indeed be said to be the central literary concern of the Bible, and it is pursued from beginning to end."[16] From this perspective, the underlying plot of biblical literature is the record of God's acts — in history, in nature, and in the lives of people.

Aristotle formulated the progressive nature of plot in memorable terms when he said that a story must have "a beginning, middle, and end." The biblical view of history adheres to this pattern and provides unity of plot. Underlying biblical literature is a sequence that unfolds as follows: eternity, creation and life before the fall, ordinary human history, the end of history, and the eternal existence of good and evil creatures. This plot unity is reinforced by the fact that the Bible begins with an account of creation and life before the fall and concludes with a description of the consummation of history. Between the beginning and the end stretches history, which is viewed in biblical literature as redemptive for all who accept the salvation of God.

Unity of plot is achieved not only by the recurrent conflict between good and evil, the motif of God's unfolding purposes, and the biblical pattern of history, but also by the use of archetypes. Every individual segment of biblical literature can be plotted on the overall model of the monomyth. Both the plot motifs and the image patterns are continual reenactments of the unifying archetypal story of biblical literature as a whole. Northrop Frye correctly calls the Bible "a single archetypal structure extending from creation to apocalypse."[17]

IV

The subject of literature is human experience, and it is partly for this reason that the view of man that emerges from a work of literature is of overriding literary concern. There are several things about the biblical view of man that are worthy of note.

The Bible affirms individualism. It proclaims the worth and dignity of the individual and implies that value resides in some significant way in the principle of individuality. Thus biblical writers tend to write about real, historical people because they regard real persons

---

[16] Roland Frye, *The Bible: Selections*, p. xvi.
[17] *Anatomy of Criticism*, p. 315.

as being important enough to choose as a literary subject. The authors of the Bible ordinarily place their characters in a matter-of-fact historical setting, differing in this respect from other ancient literature, which tends to depict fictional settings. A glance at the civil and moral laws of the Bible will also show at once the high value that the Bible places on the individual. Similarly, in biblical thinking salvation is a personal matter, and it is individuals who are welcomed into heaven, where, according to Revelation 2:17, they will be given a new name that only they and God will know throughout eternity.

Important as the individual is, however, in the biblical view he never achieves full meaning apart from relationship to God and to the human community. This leads, on the one hand, to an emphasis on the individual's spiritual relationship to God. In fact, a major theme of biblical literature is the theme of the divine-human relationship, by which I mean the writers' sustained awareness of man's inescapable connections with God, and of God's unavoidable connections with man. The emphasis on relationship to the human community leads biblical writers to insist that man assumes completeness only in terms of his communal responsibility. Everywhere in biblical literature there is a preoccupation with ethics and man's duties toward his fellow man. Jesus summarized the biblical emphasis on relationship to God and man when He said that the whole law and the prophets (most of the Old Testament, in other words) depended on the principle of a person's love to God and to his fellow humans (Matt. 22:37-40).

In biblical literature man is viewed as both a physical and a spiritual creature of God. His corporality and spirituality are both affirmed as being good. Man's physical nature is said to have been created by God and to be good in principle. Hence the Bible's positive attitude toward the legitimate satisfaction of physical appetites and its praise of sexual love when carried out within its God-ordained confines. Biblical writers are horrified at the perversion of the appetites, not because they have a low view of them, but for precisely the opposite reason — because they have such an exalted view of the appetites in their good manifestations. By contrast, pagan mythology is full of stories of illicit sexual acts and orgies among the gods because the pagan cultures had no high view of the body in the first place (see especially Plato in this regard).

The Bible assumes a threefold view of man. In Adam man was once a perfect creature. Through Adam's fall and through his own evil acts, he is a fallen creature, prone by his evil nature to disobey God. Fallen man, however, can be restored to his original state through God's redemptive grace. The balance inherent in this view of man is obvious. It avoids humanistic optimism by virtue of its realistic assessment of man's incapacity to do what is good and right. It also avoids the pessimism that believes man's depravity to be the whole truth about the human condition.

Above all, in the biblical view man is significant, whether for good or evil. His choice for or against God is always treated in biblical literature as a momentous choice. In classical, humanistic literature, man can rise to the rational level or sink to the level of the beast, within a wholly temporal context. In biblical literature the possibilities reach farther. Man can attain the glory of heaven or be lost in hell, within a context of unending eternity.

V

Biblical writers share a core of common assumptions about God. For the most part they do not argue or explain these ideas. Instead they allude to them as beliefs that both they and their audience presuppose in any discussion of God.

Biblical writers accept as an axiom the eternal existence of God. God is a spiritual being, although He may assume human or visible form on given occasions. His attributes declare Him to be divine and include omnipotence (God is all-powerful), omniscience (God knows all things), omnipresence (God is everywhere-present), immutability, and infinity. God is sovereign, the one who controls and directs all things. As the sovereign God He is the ultimate source of everything that exists, including the physical world, truth, beauty, and goodness.

This sovereign God is a moral being. He is assumed by biblical writers to be holy, perfect, just, and loving. He is a God of truth and righteousness. He has compassion for the oppressed and is angry with those who perpetrate evil. His mercy is seen in His readiness to forgive erring persons.

The authors of the Bible refer to a number of roles that God fills. He is the creator of the world and the sustainer of His creation. God is also the sovereign judge who evaluates the spiritual status of His moral creatures, punishing the evil and rewarding the righteous. He often appears in the role of the deliverer who rescues people and nations in times of crisis. He is the redeemer who forgives people's sins and gives them a new spiritual nature. Elsewhere He is a lawgiver, a guide, a friend, a ruler, the object of spiritual devotion, and the revealer of future events.

God's character includes paradoxes. He is both transcendent and immanent. As a transcendent God He is a spiritual being who lives in heaven and is above earthly reality in both nature and value. His simultaneous immanence allows Him to be active in the world, in history, and in nature. In His transcendence God is awesome and terrifying; as a God who is immanent in His creation, He is personal and close to His creatures.

Of particular importance is God's status as a covenant God. This means that He is a God who enters into relationship with people, with families, with His Church, and, in the case of Israel, with a nation. The covenant God of the Bible establishes an agreement in which He promises to be a God to His covenant people, who are expected to reciprocate by obeying and worshiping Him. The very titles "Old Testament" and "New Testament," which could equally well be translated "Old Covenant" and "New Covenant," suggest how important the concept of the covenant God is in biblical theology.

Modern readers generally place literary characters on trial in any work they read. It is not sufficient to be told that a character is good or bad. The writer must show rather than tell. This expectation must be discounted when a reader turns to the portrayal of God in the Bible. Biblical writers uniformly assume that God is perfect in all that He does and is. They may protest that God's goodness or justice is not evident at the moment, but that very protest draws its urgency from the prior assumption that God is a God of perfect qualities and that therefore His perfection should be evident in history or in their personal lives.

"For lo, He who forms the mountains, and creates the wind, and declares to man what is His thought . . . and treads on the heights of the earth—the Lord, the God of hosts, is His name!" (Amos 4:13 RSV). View west to Arabah from the vicinity of Mt. Hor.

The Story
of Origins

2

The first three chapters of Genesis comprise a self-contained story in which creation is balanced by the fall, God's creativity by Satan's destructiveness. Together these chapters are a story of origins, explaining how life as we know it began. Chapters 1 and 2 describe the world that God made, while chapter 3 describes how that world was altered.

The story told in early Genesis stands at the beginning of biblical literature as a whole and lays the foundation for much that follows. If one accepts Aristotle's definition of a story as a sequence of events having a beginning, middle, and end, it is evident that Genesis 1-3 is the beginning, Revelation and other prophecies the end, and all other events the middle.

The parallels between Genesis and Revelation are an important part of the artistic unity of the Bible. Both stories stand at the transition point of time and eternity, with Genesis describing how time began and Revelation predicting how it will end. Both early Genesis and Revelation speak of matters that lie beyond the horizon of our present experience. Events in both stories are for us inaccessible in a direct way. In this sense both the beginning and conclusion of the biblical story are an apocalypse, or unveiling. Both stories have a sense of mystery, for there is always an element of mystery where time and eternity touch each other.

Genesis 1 is the Bible's creation story. The only chief character is God. In fact, the story is mainly a catalog of the mighty acts of God, a theme that will recur throughout the Bible. As the protagonist of the creation story, God is shown to have several leading traits. He is sovereign and divine, majestic in His transcendence. He stands outside the cosmos and controls it with His mighty Word. He is both the creator, calling things into being, and a craftsman, giving things beautiful form (vs. 2). He is also the sustainer and provider for what He has made.

The physical setting of the story is unlocalized and general. The temporal setting, far in the distant past, reinforces the elemental atmosphere. The plot of the story is simple in its outline, consisting of a chronological catalog of God's acts. Because Genesis 1 describes

God's great artistic act, it calls for a form that is consciously artistic. This is exactly what the storyteller gives us.

One element of artistic form that pervades the story is recurrence. The action of the story falls into six days of activity, each of which follows a similar pattern. Furthermore, the accounts of the days of creation begin and end with a repeated formula ("And God said, let..."; "And there was evening and there was morning..."). This repetition creates a ritualistic effect.[1] Other repeated phrases include, "Let there be ...," "God called ...," "and it was so," and "God saw that it was good."

Order and design are evident in the story in the arrangement by days and the fixed pattern within each day. The fixed pattern is as follows: announcement ("And God said..."), command ("Let there be..."; "let it be gathered..."; or "let it bring forth..."), report ("And it was so," or "And God made..."), evaluation ("And God saw that it was good"), and placement in a temporal frame ("And there was evening and there was morning, a ... day").[2]

Unified progression is a third element of artistic form present in the story. The creation begins with a basic phenomenon, light. Each subsequent thing builds upon what has preceded. For example, land and sea are the necessary predecessors of plants and animals. The creation of light precedes the creation of light bearers. There is also movement toward a climax, since man, created last, is the apex of the whole creation.

One evidence of artistic balance in the story is the presence of three balanced pairs of events, as follows: light is created on the first day and light bearers on the fourth; the firmament or sky is separated from the sea on the second day, and birds and sea creatures are made on the fifth; dry land and vegetation appear on the third day, and land animals and man on the sixth. The emphasis on three in this scheme is simply the first of many references in biblical literature to this number, just as the seven days of creation initiate a repeated use of the number seven in the Bible.

The principle of balance achieves even more significance in the inclusion of both the image of order and the image of energy in the creation account. Throughout human history two great poles of human experience have been rule and energy, reason and emotion, order and impulse. The story told in Genesis 1 fuses both qualities.

---

[1] Claus Westermann, in his book *The Genesis Accounts of Creation*, trans. Norman E. Wagner (Philadelphia: Fortress Press, 1964), p. 6, writes that "the first chapter of the Bible strikes one ... like a mysterious song, like a festal celebration — one could almost say, like a heavenly liturgy.... It affects one as a litany."

[2] The fixed pattern that I cite here is based on Westermann, *Genesis Accounts of Creation*, p. 7.

Here they complement each other, whereas in fallen human experience they are often opposites that clash.

On the one hand, creation is described as an instantaneous act of God's word and as an ordering process. We might call it "the creating word" technique. For example, we read, "And God said, 'Let there be light'; and there was light" (Gen. 1:3). Similarly, "And God said, 'Let the waters under the heavens be gathered together into one place, and let the dry land appear'" (vs. 9; see also vss. 6-7, 14-15). The image of order is further established when various events of creation are described as an ordering or dividing process. Thus God is said to have "separated the light from the darkness" (vs. 3) and to have "made the firmament and separated the waters which were under the firmament from the waters which were above the firmament" (vs. 7). Similarly, on the fourth day God created heavenly luminaries "to separate the day from the night" (vs. 14), and in verses 16 to 18 the sun and moon are three times said "to rule" the day and night, implying a law-bound cosmos.

Complementing these descriptions of the creative act are passages that describe creation as an act of biological generation. The emphasis here is on living organisms producing other organisms in biological fashion. The imagery and terminology are physical rather than intellectual, and the language stresses energy and vitality rather than rule and order. For example, in verses 10 to 12 we read about "plants yielding seed" and "fruit trees bearing fruit in which is their seed," as well as that "the earth brought forth vegetation." This picture of biological fertility is continued in the description of the fifth day of creation, where the waters are said to "bring forth swarms of living creatures" (vs. 20) and to "swarm" with creatures (vs. 21). God issues a command to these creatures to "be fruitful and multiply and fill the waters in the seas, and let birds multiply on the earth" (vs. 22). Such images of overflowing generative energy complement the passages that describe creation as an ordering process brought about by the instantaneous word of God.

The opening of the creation story, which states that "in the beginning God created the heavens and the earth," is an example of the tendency found in Hebraic literature to begin with a generalization and then move to particulars. The opening statement also identifies the story at once as belonging to the literary family that we might call the story of origins. There are parallels in other ancient literature, but upon scrutiny the parallels turn out to be not very exact. C. S. Lewis comments on the matter thus: "I suspect that many people assume that some clear doctrine of creation underlies all religions: that in Paganism the gods, or one of the gods, usually created the world; even that religions normally begin by answering the question,

'Who made the world?' In reality, creation, in any unambiguous sense, seems to be a surprisingly rare doctrine."[3]

The analogues to early Genesis normally begin with an original substance already in existence. Many of these stories are not really creation stories but theogonies — stories about the origins of gods. In Genesis 1 we find no theogony, no biography of God, no apology for His existence. God is simply assumed to exist prior to the visible creation. He is above all things, not the product of some primal chaos. Unlike pagan stories, the creation story of the Bible does not describe a host of gods who were somehow immanent in the universe, but one God who stands apart from it and is beyond it. And in contrast to other pagan narratives that relate the origin of the world to a great battle among the gods, early Genesis describes the creation of the world as the act of an almighty God through a process that, as we have seen, is the very epitome of harmony and order.

God's speeches in the story of Genesis 1 are often phrased as commands, which are followed by the obedience of various forces of nature. Already an important theme of biblical literature is being established, namely, the productiveness of obedience to God. In the creation story the obedience of nature to God's will results in a beautiful order and creativity.

The creation of man on the sixth day implies man's uniqueness. God is recorded as saying, "Let us make man in our image, after our likeness" (vs. 26). None of the other creatures is said to bear such a close resemblance to God Himself. Even within the context of Genesis 1, the statement about God's making man in His image has a rich meaning, for God has been depicted as possessing eternity, power, creativity, wisdom, and intelligence. God is also recorded as saying that man is to "have dominion ... over all the earth" (vs. 26), thereby establishing man's position of authority and implying that some kind of hierarchy exists in God's creation. The command for man to have dominion over the earth has been called the creation mandate and is, by extension, a cultural mandate as well. That is, the earth is ordained by God as man's proper sphere of activity, and human endeavor within that sphere is affirmed as being good when it is governed by the desire to glorify God.

The goodness of the created order is made explicit in the story when five of the days of creation are accompanied by the statement that God saw that His creation "was good." The last verse of Genesis 1 brings this motif of the good creation to a climax with the statement

---

[3] *Reflections on the Psalms* (New York: Harcourt, Brace & World, 1958), pp. 78-80. Analogues to the biblical creation story are collected by James B. Pritchard, ed., *Ancient Near Eastern Texts Relating to the Old Testament* (Princeton: Princeton University Press, 1950).

that "God saw everything that he had made, and behold, it was very good." The first three verses of Genesis 2, describing God's rest on the seventh day, are also climactic in the creation story, since they conclude the account on a note of rest after labor and evoke a sense of celebration after the protagonist's successful completion of His mighty feat.

Genesis 2:4-24 continues the creation account. This passage is a close-up after the panorama of Genesis 1. It stresses the creation of man and the beginning of his life in the garden. There are three main actors in this part of the story — God, Adam, and Eve. The addition of human characters to the story means that Genesis 2 is particularly concerned with relationships within God's created order. Accordingly, instead of abstract divine commands, as in Genesis 1, we get an abundance of dialogue, and instead of miraculous events we get an emphasis on relationships.

God's role in Chapter 2 is fourfold: (1) He is the creator — the one who forms and plants and arranges; (2) He is the one who establishes the conditions of reality; (3) He is the covenant God — the infinite personal God who enters into a relationship with man, His creature; (4) He is the God of providence — the God who sustains His creatures and provides for their needs. Whereas Genesis 1 stresses God's cosmic transcendence, Genesis 2 adds to the characterization of God by depicting His immanence, personal nearness, and involvement in the earthly scene.

Adam and Eve are portrayed as prototypes of humanity. They are man and woman, not individualized but generalized and typical. They are shown as having three roles: a marital role toward each other, a role involving worship toward God, and a role of dominion over the creation.

The action of Genesis 2 begins with God's placing man in the earthly paradise. Verse 8 tells us simply, "And the Lord God planted a garden in Eden, in the east; and there he put the man whom he had formed." These words capture in eloquent simplicity a phenomenon that has seized the human imagination and consciousness through the centuries. It can be called the paradisal ideal, and it is an archetypal human longing. As C. S. Lewis expresses it, paradise is "a region of the mind which does exist and which should be visited often."[4]

Descriptions of the earthly paradise in literature have always had certain conventions. The place of perfection is always remembered as a garden. As such, it has been a place of profuse vegetation and fragrance. Verse 9 of Genesis 2 briefly attributes sensuous richness and pleasure to the Garden of Eden when it states that "out of the

---

[4] *The Allegory of Love* (New York: Oxford University Press, 1936), p. 352.

ground the Lord God made to grow every tree that is pleasant to the sight and good for food." It is important to note the way in which a description such as this arouses our own picture of paradise without imposing its own detailed conception upon us.

Paradise has archetypally been a realm removed from ordinary existence and impossible to return to in the flesh. It is a condition always placed somewhere and sometime outside normal human experience. The remoteness of the Garden of Eden in the Genesis account is evident in the fact that although it is given a geographic location ("Eden" means a definite geographic area), it has never been precisely located. Verses 10 to 14 capture the paradoxical nature of paradise as being both real and inaccessible. These verses seem to place paradise in an identifiable geographic locale, but for us even this precise localization has been lost. Why the remoteness? we might ask. According to early Genesis, paradise is remote from our experience because it was lost. Since paradise is presented as being both real and lost, it combines the themes of yearning and nonpossession, or desire and inaccessibility.

Paradise has been conventionally described as both a place and a way of life. As a way of life it is a place of rest, pleasure, contentment, virtue, beauty, closeness to nature, youthfulness, harmony, and freedom. Because of the extreme brevity of the story told in Genesis 2, these motifs are left largely undeveloped. Once again the reader is left to imagine the details of the paradisal way of life.

Paradise has ordinarily been characterized by an absence of civilization, and it has that identity in early Genesis. Virtue is displayed negatively, as the absence of ordinary fallen human experience. Since the life described is one of natural simplicity, there is an almost total lack of the complex social roles that we experience. The self-enclosed nature of the garden makes its existence one in which the ordinary actions of men are absent. It is a world that existed before men sailed the seas or built cities.

The paradise of Genesis 2 is conventional in all these ways. There are a few additional traits peculiar to the Hebraic version of the paradisal garden. In the biblical account, it is made clear that the garden was planted by God. This implies two important principles: nature is God's art, manifesting His creative craftsmanship, and nature is God's provision for His creatures, especially man. A second major distinction of the biblical description of paradise is that, in contrast to pagan myths, it was not a place of inviolable retirement but was from the beginning a place of trial. This means that the Garden of Eden is depicted as a place and condition of perfection, but with a potential for change.

When God put man into the Garden of Eden, He established some basic conditions of reality. The fact that He put man "in the garden of Eden to till it and keep it" (Gen. 2:15) shows that work was part of God's ideal for people and that life in paradise was not idle but purposeful. God also placed within the garden a prohibited tree (vss. 16-17), the fruit of which could not be eaten without penalty of death. The forbidden tree is important for several reasons. It is evidence of God's provision for man because it provided man the opportunity to demonstrate his love and gratitude to God in action as well as word. It also shows that the universe God created is a law-bound universe that operates according to moral and spiritual laws as well as physical laws. Finally, the forbidden tree establishes the conditional nature of prelapsarian perfection and makes moral choice an essential part of human existence.

After the first seventeen verses of Genesis 2 have established Adam's relationship to God, the remainder of the chapter depicts his relationship to Eve. The story in which Adam names the animals in paradise and then discovers that there is no suitable companion for him (vss. 19-20) dramatizes Adam's awareness of his incompleteness. After the creation of Eve, Adam expresses his attitude toward her in poetic form (vs. 23):

> This at last is bone of my bones
>   and flesh of my flesh;
> she shall be called Woman,
>   because she was taken out of Man.

Adam's emphasis on the fact that woman shares his identity does more than assert that Eve is a human companion "at last," after the animals have been declared unsuitable for his fellowship (vs. 20). Adam's statement establishes woman's equality with man in being and worth. Man and woman are shown in Genesis 2 to have the same nature and the same capacity for good or evil. Woman's subordinate role in marriage, insisted on in other parts of the Bible, is not a matter of her being inferior as a person but is rather a way of achieving the mutually desired goal of domestic order.

Verse 24, which states, "Therefore a man leaves his father and his mother and cleaves to his wife, and they become one flesh," is an important part of this story of origins. It describes the origin of the basic unit of human society, the family. Within the context of Genesis 2, marriage is God-ordained, involves a relationship of trust and love (man and wife cleave to each other), involves physical, sexual union as an expression of love (man and wife become "one flesh"), and is God's provision for human companionship and completeness. The detail about Adam and Eve's unashamed nakedness (vs. 25) is part of the absence of civilization present in paradise. It is also a measure of the difference between life before the fall and life after the fall, a symbol of the freedom man enjoyed in his state of innocence, and an index to the beauty of the physical body in its God-given state.

The story of the fall, as narrated in Genesis 3, belongs to several narrative families. It is a tragedy — a fall from bliss to catastrophe. It is a temptation story in which an agent of temptation lures an innocent person into evil. And it is a story of initiation in which characters pass for the first time from innocence to evil. The complex weaving of these three motifs into a single brief plot accounts in part for the artistry of the story.

There are three main characters in the fall itself — a snake, Eve, and Adam. After the fall a fourth character, God the Judge, becomes important. Nowhere in the story is the serpent identified as Satan; that identification is made in Revelation 12:9 and 20:2.

The plot of a temptation story centers in the encounter between the agent of temptation and the person being tempted, and great interest attaches to the way in which the tempter manipulates the victim. Accordingly, the character of the satanic serpent is important in Genesis 3. The first verse of the chapter makes subtlety the chief trait of the snake. This quality is not inherently bad, but in the story it is perverted to a bad use, just as the serpent's use of dialogue perverts to an evil end something that God had earlier used for the good purpose of establishing relationship with Adam and Eve. The subtlety of the serpent is first seen in his questioning of God's command (vs. 2), a questioning that implies the unreasonableness of God's prohibition. Having planted the seed of doubt in Eve's mind, the serpent goes on to contradict God's statement that the forbidden fruit could not be eaten without penalty of death (vss. 4-5). The serpent, or Satan, is shown here in his characteristic pose, contradicting God and misleading people through his lies.

Eve's eating of the forbidden fruit is a complex act. Its essential identity is disobedience — doing what God had forbidden. But other sins also enter, as though the original sin is a composite act, summing up a number of particular sins. For example, the fact that Eve saw that "the tree was to be desired to make one wise" (vs. 6) not only suggests that Eve was deluded by Satan's fraudulent claim that eating the fruit would confer the power of godlike knowledge (vs. 5), but also that she was guilty of pride in her desire to go beyond human limitations and "be like God" (vs. 5). Other motivations for eating the forbidden fruit include its good taste and its visual beauty (vs. 6). We must understand these details clearly. Biblical literature does not share the uneasiness or hostility that classical literature and philosophy display toward the physical appetites. There was nothing wrong with Eve's eating when she was hungry, or enjoying the beauty of the garden, or desiring knowledge. These things become wrong in the story of the fall only when they violate the supreme value — obedience to God.

The rest of Genesis 3 is devoted to the effects of the fall. The immediate result is Adam and Eve's shame over their nakedness, which had previously been good (vs. 7). It is symbolic of a basic change that has occurred. The hiding of Adam and Eve from God amplifies the extent of their fall by dramatizing their awareness of guilt and alienation from God. In the accompanying dialogue, Adam's evasion of responsibility (vs. 12) is a mark of his fallen nature and contrasts unfavorably with Eve's straightforward acceptance of responsibility for her actions (vs. 13). The curses pronounced by God on the serpent and on Adam and Eve (vss. 14-19) show that the fall was cosmic in its effects, influencing the whole created order and the human descendants of the first parents.

Although the story of Genesis 3 is mainly tragic, it contains a note of comfort as well. Verse 15, containing God's words to the satanic serpent, is central to the meaning of biblical literature as a whole. It states,

> I will put enmity between you and the woman,
>   and between your seed and her seed;
> he shall bruise your head,
>   and you shall bruise his heel.

Here begins the great plot of the Bible — the endless spiritual warfare between good and evil, God and Satan. Equally important is the promise of God's eventual triumph over evil, as symbolized by the bruising of the serpent's head and the less injurious bruising of the heel of the woman's seed. The prediction that the seed of the woman would conquer the serpent is the first promise in biblical literature of Christ, the Redeemer. Restoration also becomes an element in the story of the fall when God "made for Adam and for his wife garments of skins, and clothed them" (vs. 21). A final act of God's provision is His preventing man from eating of the tree of life (vss. 22-23), lest man doom himself to a life of endless misery in a fallen world.

There is a sense in which the story told in Genesis 1-3 fulfills the expectations of great narrative better than any other story in literature. More than other stories, this one concludes with things where they did not begin. It records the calling into existence of everything that exists, and it tells about a single, irreversible event in the history of the world. The story leaves the reader with the impression that some unique event has occurred, an event that effected permanent changes and which cannot be repeated in exactly the same way in subsequent history. The fact that the pattern of the fall is reenacted in human experience only serves to reinforce the idea that the story told in Genesis 3 did, in fact, leave things where it did not find them.

The story of origins told in Genesis 1-3 embodies a number of important themes. It establishes many principles that are essential to an understanding of the Judeo-Christian view of reality. Since the narrative is so brief, one would expect the storyteller to state some of his ideas in abstract, propositional form. This is exactly what he refuses to do. Any thematic principle that emerges from the story must be deduced from the actual events or dialogue. It is an amazing instance of theme being perfectly incarnated in narrative form.

I wish to conclude this discussion of the story of origins by listing some of the important themes. The story asserts that God exists and is the ground of all being. God is transcendent, the "wholly other" apart from everything else. God is also immanent in His creation, with which He has a personal relationship and from which He never relinquishes His connection. External reality was created by God. The physical and human world was created good and is good in principle; man's troubles are not inherent in the external world but stem from his wrong choices. The story shows that good and evil are realities and that moral choice is an unavoidable condition of life. Reality is shown to be law-bound, orderly, and intelligible. Evil effected a permanent change in the physical and human world, so that it is no longer simply good. There is something wrong with the status quo, something that needs restoration and reorientation toward God. Man is both great and terrible. God created man to a life of fulfillment and purpose; after the fall such fulfillment is achieved through great effort (as evidenced, for example, by woman's pain in childbirth and man's sweat as he labors for a living). The story of origins suggests that man achieves meaning through relationship to God and to fellow humans. Happiness can be found through obedience to God's perfect will, while human disobedience and rebellion bring misery. Finally, God's grace is available to restore fallen man.

Detail from the Mosque of Abraham at Hebron, commemorating one of the Old Testament's great heroes of the faith.

Heroic
Narrative

3

I

Heroic narrative is a branch of narrative literature in which the story is built around the life and exploits of the protagonist, or hero. Heroic narrative springs from one of the most ancient and persistent impulses of literary art, namely, the desire to embody accepted norms of thought and action in the story of a protagonist whose destiny is regarded as being representative or exemplary. The following definition of a literary hero explains the concept more fully: "A traditional ... hero must be more than merely the leading figure or protagonist of a literary work. The true hero expresses an accepted social and moral norm; his experience reenacts the important conflicts of the community which produces him; he is endowed with qualities that capture the popular imagination. It must also be remarked that the hero is able to act, and to act for good. Most important of all, the narrative of his experience suggests that life has both a significant pattern and an end."[1]

Since the story of the hero is designed to embody the philosophical views of the culture producing it, the following issues are of particular importance:

1. The view of man: What kind of being is man? How can man achieve meaning in life? What is man's proper end or goal? What is man's origin, and what is his destination?

2. The religious view: Does the work postulate a transcendental realm? What is its nature? How is the other world related to this world?

3. The view of society: What is the nature of the human community? What is the individual's role in society? What is the nature of the individual's obligations to his fellow humans?

---

[1] Walter Houghton and G. Robert Stange, ed., *Victorian Poetry and Poetics* (Boston: Houghton Mifflin Company, 1968), p. xxiii.

4. The question of values: What does the story postulate as the highest value in life? Is the highest value a person (God, self, some individual, man in general), an institution (state, church, home), or an abstract quality (love, truth, beauty, order, reason, emotion, etc.)?

Since heroic narrative is constructed around the hero, the plot consists of the conflicts he encounters. Because of the prominence of the protagonist in the story, the usual considerations of literary characterization take on special significance. The central identity of the hero is important. His identity might be established by the narrator in the story, dramatized by his thoughts and actions, or implied by other characters' responses to him. Related to the question of the hero's identity are the matters of his response to situations, his motivation, and the use of foils (characters that provide a parallel and/or contrast to the hero, thereby accentuating the hero's traits). Great importance must be attached to the nature of the hero's actions — to his experiment in living. The question of the roles filled by the hero in the story is always relevant, as is the nature of his development during the course of the story.

II

The genre of heroic narrative governs a great deal of the Old Testament and begins with the story of Abraham (Genesis 11:27–25:11). There are at least four structural principles that give shape to the story of Abraham. One is biographical chronology, as suggested by the fact that the story begins with a genealogy of Abraham's ancestors and concludes with an account of his death. The journey motif, with constant movement from one region to another, also gives the story a pattern. The story is, thirdly, a quest story in which Abraham searches for both land and descendants. Finally, the story is organized on the principle of God's progressive revelation of His covenant to Abraham.

Plot conflict springs partly from the hero's conflict with natural forces, chiefly famine, and with various characters, including Pharaoh, Lot, Ishmael, and Abimelech. The main conflict in the story is psychological and spiritual in nature and occurs between faith in God's word and the ethic of expediency.

The setting of the story is largely generalized in its descriptions. There are references to geographic regions, and to plains, wilderness, and mountains. These references lend a primitive, elemental quality to the story, an effect heightened by descriptions of such elemental activities as finding water and preparing food.

There are two main dimensions to Abraham as a heroic character.

The narrator's constant concern with Abraham's spiritual condition suggests that a major part of Abraham's heroism is spiritual in nature. As a spiritual hero Abraham is essentially a man of faith in God and of obedience to God's will. We repeatedly see Abraham worshiping and revering God.

Abraham is also a domestic hero. We usually see him in his domestic roles — husband, uncle, father, head of a household, owner of possessions (as in *The Odyssey,* "home" means land and possessions as well as family), promised head of nations (as the customary epithet "patriarch" implies), and, in a special sense, head of the messianic line. It is worthy of note that military heroism, so prominent elsewhere in ancient literature, is virtually absent from the image of the hero that emerges from the story of Abraham.

God is a leading character in the story. On the one hand, He is depicted as a transcendent and sovereign God. He is not made in man's image, as the pagan deities usually are. His "otherness" is stressed. At the same time, God is very much an agent in human and earthly affairs. He is the friend of Abraham and converses with Abraham as one man does with another. He is the covenant God, entering into a relationship with His people. He is both generous, showering blessings on Abraham simply because He loves him, and demanding, insisting on supreme allegiance to Himself and a way of life that is holy.

Erich Auerbach's comparison of the storytelling technique in Homer and Genesis is a classic work of literary criticism.[2] It is Auerbach's contention that in Homer character and events are scrupulously externalized and described. Nothing remains hidden or unexpressed. By contrast, the writer of Genesis externalizes only as much as is necessary for the purpose of the story. Much is left unexpressed and calls for interpretation. In Auerbach's words, the story of Abraham is "fraught with background"; that is, characters and events have a meaning that goes beyond the external surface of the story and must be supplied by our inferences or by details found elsewhere in the story.

The opening of the story of Abraham (Gen. 12) illustrates Auerbach's thesis. The story begins abruptly with the statement, "Now the Lord said to Abram, 'Go from your country and your kindred and your father's house to the land that I will show you.'" When did God speak? Where did He confront Abraham? What does God look like, and how does He speak to Abraham? We are told none of these things. The whole event is surrounded by mystery. Why does God

---

[2] "Odysseus' Scar," in *Mimesis: The Representation of Reality in Western Literature,* trans. W. R. Trask (Princeton: Princeton University Press, 1946), pp. 3-23.

command Abraham to move? Again there is no explicit answer, but we can interpret the event, to use Auerbach's formula. God commands Abraham to move because He has chosen Abraham as the agent through whom He will establish a nation and bequeath a promised land.

Abraham's response to God's call likewise illustrates the story-teller's technique of giving minimal information and forcing the reader to infer some of the details. Abraham's first act is an act of obedience, as summarized in the statement "So Abram went, as the Lord had told him" (vs. 4). What went on in his mind? We can only guess, for in the story only the event is described. Why did Abraham obey an indefinite command to travel to a land that God would show him? Again we are compelled to interpret: Abraham obeyed God because of his faith in the character and word of God.

The opening lines of the story are important for other reasons as well. God commands a journey, thereby setting up the quest story that follows. The goal of the quest is indefinite, not even tied to a specific locale. This means that the pursuit of the goal is undertaken in faith. The command is accompanied by a blessing (Gen. 12:2-4) and represents the first time that God establishes His covenant with Abraham. God's covenant is simply the relationship that He enters into with His people. It is a relationship involving promises and requiring man's acceptance of responsibility, which takes the form of obedience. God promises Abraham both personal prosperity and the assurance that he will be an agent of blessing for other people. In its most general terms, God's covenant is based on the promise that He will be a God to believers and their families (see especially Gen. 17:7-8).

From this point in the story, the renewal of the covenant punctuates the narrative at key points. Generally there is a progressive principle at work, with God revealing more details and promising further blessings as the story progresses. For example, when Abraham first arrives in the land of Canaan, God promises descendants and "this land" (Gen. 12:7), with both details advancing the content of the first revelation. After Abraham chooses Hebron as his dwelling place in deference to Lot, God amplifies the covenant promise by promising a *huge* line of descendants (Gen. 13:14-17).

Subsequent reestablishments of the covenant make the promises increasingly specific and detailed. The entire fifteenth chapter is devoted to God's renewal of the covenant. On this occasion God tells Abraham that his own son will be his heir (Gen. 15:4) and that his descendants will be oppressed slaves in a foreign land for 400 years, after which they will claim the land of Canaan as their own (Gen. 15:13-21). The motif of the covenant, which by this point in the story has become intertwined with the quest for a son, is extended further in chapter 17, another complete chapter devoted to the covenant promises of God. Several things make this revelation of the covenant climactic: Abram's name is changed to "Abraham," meaning "father of a multitude"; Sarai's name is changed to "Sarah," meaning "princess"; circumcision is established as a visible sign of the covenant relationship; and the birth of a son, who is to be called "Isaac," is predicted as occurring a year later. In the following chapter Abraham entertains three angelic visitors, who repeat the promise of the birth of a son.

The final scene in which God reveals His covenant blessing to Abraham comes at the climax of the whole story, Abraham's offering of his son Isaac on Mt. Moriah. On this occasion God not only pronounces a blessing (Gen. 22:16-18), but makes it clear that His blessing exists because Abraham has lived up to his covenant responsibility — "because you have obeyed my voice" (Gen. 22:18). The regularity with which God repeats and further reveals His covenant with Abraham shows that this theme is a major concern of the story and a leading structural principle in the narrative.

The most important plot conflict is the inner struggle between faith in God and the ethic of expediency. This conflict is established early in the story when a famine forces Abraham to Egypt (Gen. 12:10-20). As an alien married to an attractive woman, Abraham was in a precarious position. Fearful for his life, he did what seemed expedient instead of trusting God to protect his life. He commanded Sarah to pose as his sister, ignoring the consequences that this would have for Sarah and others. The ethic of expediency worked well for another hero of ancient literature, Odysseus. In fact, Abraham would seem to deserve the epithet so often attached to Odysseus, namely, "clever Abraham." In contrast to the story of Odysseus, the ethic of expediency gets Abraham into difficulty. God sends a plague on the house of Pharaoh after the king has taken Sarah into his house, and the king, grasping the situation, sends Abraham and his household away. The episode thus dramatizes God's protection of Sarah and Abraham, for it is God's intervention that preserves their marriage. Abraham's lack of faith has been exposed, and God's grace has been manifested.

A second event that shows Abraham succumbing to the ethic of expediency involves the decision to have a child by his maid Hagar (Gen. 16). Having been promised a son, and receiving no children from his wife Sarah, Abraham, with the agreement of his wife, resorts to expediency and fails to trust God. The story's negative attitude toward Abraham's decision to have a child by his maid is made clear when family discord is shown to be the immediate result. In fact, the descendants of Hagar's child Ishmael became the national foe of the Israelites, and God's promise to Hagar that He would "so greatly multiply your descendants that they cannot be numbered for multitude" (Gen. 16:10) is an inversion and parody of the covenant promise to Abraham.

Yet another instance of Abraham's struggle between faith and expediency occurs when he is brought into contact with Abimelech, king of Gerar (Gen. 20). Abraham, a slow learner, tries the ethic of expediency once more by telling Sarah to pose again as his sister. Again God intervenes by appearing to Abimelech in a dream, thereby rescuing Abraham from his plight.

These moral lapses should not be interpreted as evidence that Abraham is mainly deficient in faith. They are simply evidence that biblical writers select their material from two criteria — realism as well as idealism. They describe the human failings of the hero as well as portraying his superiority. Abraham is mainly an idealized hero, as a summary of the story will suggest. When God calls him to leave his land, Abraham responds at once with faith and obedience (Gen. 12:4-5). When conflict with nature precipitates disagreement with his nephew Lot (Gen. 13:5-7), Abraham allows Lot to choose the more fertile area in which to settle. In fact, a main function of Lot in the story of Abraham is to act as a foil to the character of Abraham. Lot chooses on the basis of tangible, material benefits, while Abraham usually operates on faith in God's word, without tangible proofs. On one of the occasions when God promises descendants to Abraham, Abraham's faith is described in words that sum up his whole character — "And he believed the Lord" (Gen. 15:6).

Abraham's chief venture in faith is his willingness to sacrifice his son Isaac (Gen. 22). The narrative makes it clear that the call to sacrifice Isaac is a test of Abraham's faith (vs. 1). Abraham responds with obedience, thereby demonstrating his faith in God.[3] Archetypal patterns in the story include, in addition to the test of the hero, the scapegoat motif, the death-rebirth motif, the journey whose chief significance is the inner development of the hero, and the hero's encounter with the divine on a mountaintop. The whole episode is parabolic or symbolic as well as actual. It summarizes man's duty to God, which is obedience and faith. God also uses the event to reveal what He does for man. In pagan religions children were offered in sacrifice as an appeasement to the gods.[4] God here teaches Abraham that this is wrong and that peace with God comes through a sub-

---

[3] According to Hebrews 11:19, Abraham "considered that God was able to raise men even from the dead."

[4] For biblical references to the practice and evidence that God never sanctioned human sacrifice, see 2 Kings 3:27; 16:1-4; Jeremiah 7:30-31; 19:3-9.

stitutionary atonement that God Himself provides. The sacrificial lamb that God provides as a substitute for human life points forward to the ceremonial laws that God was to give on Sinai, and beyond them to the substitutionary atonement of Christ, who in Scripture is called the Lamb of God.

Abraham's domestic role is as much a part of his story as is his spiritual role. The story of Lot, for example, not only functions as a foil to Abraham's piety, but also demonstrates the importance of family relations. Thus Abraham's military deliverance of Lot when the latter is captured by an enemy (Gen. 14:1-16) is motivated by a sense of familial obligation, as suggested by the narrator's statement that Abraham gathered his band of trained soldiers when he "heard that his kinsman had been taken captive" (vs. 14). Similarly, the rather long account of God's sparing of Lot's family from the destruction of Sodom and Gomorrah (Gen. 18:16–19:29) is not, as it first appears, a digression from the story of Abraham. At the completion of the story, the event is tied to the domestic life of Abraham when the narrator comments, "So it was that, when God destroyed the cities of the valley, God remembered Abraham, and sent Lot out of the midst of the overthrow" (Gen. 19:29).

The scene in which Abraham entertains three angelic visitors (Gen. 18) also shows the hero in a domestic role. Hebrews 13:2, which cites the event as an example of "hospitality to strangers," is an adequate gloss on the story. Mystery pervades this drama in miniature. The visitors are not identified and their purpose is not disclosed until after the meal. The strenuous efforts of Abraham and Sarah to provide for the needs of their guests have many parallels elsewhere in ancient literature, especially Homer's *Odyssey,* which, like the story of Abraham, celebrates domestic values. The scene of hospitality in Genesis 18 will be reenacted in the reception that Abraham's servant receives from the household of Laban (Gen. 24:15-33). Abraham's actions in the scene follow two patterns.[5] In the presence of his guests, he puts on a nonchalant air, using understatement as he offers them "a little water" (Gen. 18:4) and "a morsel of bread" (vs. 5). He also stands by disinterestedly under a tree while the guests eat (vs. 8). Behind the scenes, though, Abraham exerts himself strenuously. When he first sees the strangers, he runs to meet them and bows himself to the earth (vs. 2). Subsequently we read that he "ran to the herd" and "hastened to prepare" a calf (vs. 7). The "morsel of bread" turns out to be several cakes (made from "fine meal," no less) and a whole calf (vss. 6-7).

The part of Abraham's story that recounts the marriage of Isaac

---

[5] These two motifs have been noted by Norman C. Habel, *Literary Criticism of the Old Testament* (Philadelphia: Fortress Press, 1971), p. 45.

(Gen. 24) is likewise an extension of the domestic identity of Abraham. It shows Abraham in the role of a father who believes that the marriage of his son is not simply a naturalistic event but must be placed in a context of obedience to God's will. It is in this vein that he sends a servant to find a wife from his God-fearing kinsmen instead of the pagan Canaanites. The story of romantic love told in this chapter dramatizes several important aspects of the biblical view of marriage. Marriage is shown to occur between two persons who believe in God, to be based on consent, despite the parents' actions in arranging it (verse 58 stresses the element of consent), and to occur between persons who love each other (verse 67 declares not only that Rebekah became Isaac's wife but also that "he loved her").

Before concluding this consideration of the story of Abraham, we would do well to return to the definition of a literary hero. The experience of a literary hero reenacts the important conflicts of the culture that produces him. Abraham experiences conflict with the natural environment. There is a constant struggle for existence, and perpetual journeying as a means of survival. All of this reflects the nomadic culture of the day. There are also conflicts with alien peoples, and Abraham is distinctly a nomad and sojourner after he leaves Haran. Above all, there is spiritual and psychological conflict between trusting God's promises for the future and the urge to take matters into one's own hands. It is the tension, central to the Hebraic-Christian experience, between living on a supernatural basis and living on a purely naturalistic basis.

A literary hero also embodies the values of the age producing him, and again Abraham fits the convention. His character embodies qualities of obedience to God, integrity of character, and allegiance to home, which includes family, relatives, descendants, possessions, and land.

According to the definition, the hero's story suggests that life has a significant pattern. Abraham's life is patterned on the covenant relationship with God. God's relationship with man gives meaning and coherence to Abraham's life, as evidenced by the way in which the renewal of the covenant punctuates the stages of action and provides one element of organization in the story. The story of this hero suggests that obedience to God gives life an adequate basis.

The story embodies a world view that is theocentric in nature. Faith and obedience to God are the governing factors in Abraham's existence. So far as the view of man is concerned, the story indicates that man is a flawed being, but capable of great accomplishments through faith in God and obedience to His Word. He is also a social being for whom social obligations are a matter of overriding importance.

The story of Jacob (Genesis 25:19 through chapter 35) differs from the usual heroic story in being less consciously built around a hero who embodies normative values. In fact, many details in the story constitute a satiric exposure of Jacob's character flaws. The literary focus is not on the definition of heroism but the action of the story itself — a story replete with conflict, intrigue, suspense, dramatic irony, scenes of surprised discovery, and a tense reconciliation scene.

Jacob's story has a circular, three-part movement: the early life in the parental home, a twenty-year exile in Haran, and a return to the land of the hero's birth. Further pattern emerges when we observe that a divine encounter introduces each phase of the story. The prophetic oracle to Rebekah (Gen. 25:23) predicts the sibling conflict and triumph of Jacob that dominate the early action. The vision at Bethel (Gen. 28:11-17), where Jacob receives the covenant promise, initiates a phase in which God blesses Jacob despite his ignominious behavior. And Jacob's wrestling with the angel of God (Gen. 32:22-31), from whom he receives the covenant name "Israel," transforms him into the more sympathetic character about whom we read subsequently in Genesis.

The main plot conflicts in the story involve family discord, especially the sibling rivalry between Jacob and Esau that begins even before their birth. We are told that during Rebekah's pregnancy "the children struggled together within her" (Gen. 25:22). The struggle is amplified when God tells Rebekah that the conflict will eventuate in hostility between the descendants of the two brothers. Jacob's very name, which means "he takes by the heel," or "he supplants," captures the central identity of Jacob. He is the one who struggles with others and overcomes them. The sibling conflict between Jacob and Esau is described as a contrast between two temperaments. We are told that "Esau was a skilful hunter, a man of the field, while Jacob was a quiet man, dwelling in tents" (vs. 27). This contrast between children is broadened into parental conflict, for "Isaac loved Esau, because he ate of his game; but Rebekah loved Jacob" (vs. 28).

The first event in the story where the conflict between the brothers becomes acute involves Esau's selling of his birthright for a mess of pottage (Gen. 25:29-34). Jacob shows himself a schemer from the beginning by taking advantage of Esau's hunger and bargaining with Esau instead of generously giving him some food. Esau is even more blameworthy in the episode, for he lightly regards his birthright, which carried with it spiritual significance (the line of God's covenant promise would be perpetuated through the son holding the birthright). Esau's impiety and perverse scale of values (he lives only for the moment and has no instinct for spiritual realities) are made clear by the narrator's comment, "Thus Esau despised his birthright" (vs. 34).[6]

The conflict between the brothers over the birthright or blessing reaches its climax in the story of the stolen blessing (Gen. 27). The main ingredients in this exciting narrative are intense conflict, intrigue, suspense, dramatic irony (in the form of mistaken identity), and sudden discovery. The conflict involves two pairs of characters — Isaac and Esau, and Rebekah and Jacob. Jacob again shows himself a schemer (as does his mother) and is morally reprehensible for seizing the blessing through dishonesty instead of trusting God to provide him with the birthright. The episode involves elaborate intrigue as Rebekah puts Esau's clothes on Jacob and wraps goatskins around his arms and neck. Dramatic irony, a narrative technique in which the reader has more information than some of the characters in the story, occurs when the blind Isaac is tricked by the disguise of Jacob. Suspense underlies the whole dialogue between Jacob and his father because of the threat that at any moment Isaac might perceive the true identity of his son. The suspense is increased when Isaac is repeatedly doubtful that the son is, in fact, Esau. When Esau arrives on the scene, too late, the episode reaches its climax in the sudden discovery of both father and son. The emotional scene is realized with vivid detail — Isaac is said to have "trembled violently" (vs. 33) and Esau "cried out with an exceedingly great and bitter cry" (vs. 34). As Esau correctly states (vs. 36), the event has demonstrated the appropriateness of Jacob's name, for he has now supplanted Esau twice. The conflict between the two brothers is intensified and extended beyond this occasion when Esau begins to plot the murder of Jacob (vs. 41).

The next phase of Jacob's story, in which he flees for his life, belongs to a familiar archetype. It is the initiation motif, with the young hero setting out, usually secretly and by night, on a perilous journey that will lead to his initiation into adulthood. Telemachos, Aeneas, Young Goodman Brown, and Huckleberry Finn belong to the same archetype. Jacob's journey takes the form of a quest for his ancestral home, Haran. Before he reaches the goal of his quest, Jacob has a highly significant encounter with God (Gen. 28:10-17). By night he dreams of a ladder reaching from earth to heaven. As so often in literature, a dream becomes the vehicle for a spiritual revela-

---

[6] Hebrews 12:16-17 cites Esau as an example of an "immoral and irreligious" person "who sold his birthright for a single meal" and then was unable "to inherit the blessing . . . though he sought it with tears."

tion. The ladder, with angels ascending and descending on it, symbolizes the communication and spiritual rapport between God and Jacob. God and man are united, with angels serving as intermediaries.

The dream has a deeper and more specific meaning as well. God speaks from the top of the ladder and repeats the familiar promises of the covenant which had first been made with Abraham and were later renewed with Isaac. God promises Jacob descendants through whom all nations will be blessed and who will one day possess the land on which Jacob is resting (vss. 13-14). More generally, God promises, "Behold, I am with you and will keep you wherever you go" (vs. 15). God is again shown to be a loving, covenant God, and Jacob has now been authenticated as the heir of the covenant line and promises. The hero has been initiated into spiritual adulthood in a significant way. Jacob's response (vss. 16-17) captures both the mystery and the closeness of God, who is again pictured as being both transcendent and immanent: "Then Jacob awoke from his sleep and said, 'Surely the Lord is in this place; and I did not know it.' And he was afraid, and said, 'How awesome is this place! This is none other than the house of God, and this is the gate of heaven.'" Jacob's building of an altar (vs. 18) reflects his sense of the sanctity of any occasion when God invades a person's life, and his vow to give God a tenth of his possessions (vs. 22) shows his readiness to accept his covenant responsibilities before a loving God.

The account of Jacob's twenty-year stay in Haran (Gen. 29-31) is devoted to his domestic life and the development of his character. Plot conflict in this part of the story centers in the domestic strife within Jacob's family and the continuing struggle between Jacob and Laban. The incident of the substitute bride (Gen. 29:23-35) is an example of the narrative device known as poetic justice, since Jacob's earlier deceit with his father is now repaid. The sibling rivalry between Leah and Rachel is also a foil to earlier events in the story. Jacob's identity as a schemer with economic motivations is confirmed in the incident in which he places striped tree branches before the goats in an attempt to induce the conception of striped and spotted goats (Gen. 30:37-43). His subsequent dream in which an angel informs him that the birth of striped and spotted goats was actually due to God's activity on Jacob's behalf (Gen. 31:10-12) is both a sign of God's favor toward Jacob and a rebuke to Jacob, who had attributed his success to his own schemes. The twenty-year interlude ends much as the first phase of Jacob's life ended, with the hero again fleeing from a relative whom he has antagonized.

The story of sibling rivalry reaches its final development when Jacob returns to his original home (Gen. 32-33). It is chiefly a story of suspense, in which Esau's response to his brother is in doubt, and of climax, as we move inexorably toward the encounter between the brothers. The conflict is established when Jacob learns that Esau is coming to meet him with a band of 400 men (Gen. 32:6). Jacob's division of his family and flocks into two groups so that one part might escape if the other was destroyed shows the desperate extent of his plight (vss. 7-8).

As he faces his greatest crisis, Jacob's character undergoes significant development. His prayer in which he humbles himself before God's goodness (Gen. 32:9-10) shows an instinctively aggressive and grasping personality that has finally come to the end of itself and to the beginning of dependence on God. Equally important is the fact that Jacob's claim upon God's protection is based on the covenant promise that God had made to Jacob (vs. 12).

Jacob's wrestling with God at the brook Jabbok (Gen. 32:22-32) is one of the great moments in world literature. The nighttime setting of the encounter (vs. 22) adds to the mood of danger and urgency. By sending his family and "everything that he had" across the stream (vs. 23), Jacob is reduced to essential humanity, being "left alone," as the narrator states (vs. 24). This is the context of Jacob's encounter with a divine wrestler. Mystery pervades the unexplained presence and identity of a man who wrestles with Jacob until daybreak. Jacob's equally strange insistence that he will not let the stranger go unless he blesses Jacob is the type of event that calls for interpretation, in Auerbach's terms. The request is made because the mysterious wrestler is God. Jacob's new name, Israel, means "he who strives with God" and signifies a new relationship with God. It also confirms the identity of Jacob as the one who strives. The stranger is never explicitly identified as God, but that identification is implied when Jacob names the place "Peniel," saying, "For I have seen God face to face, and yet my life is preserved" (vs. 30). The rising of the sun (vs. 31) is a fitting symbol for the beginning of a new era in Jacob's spiritual existence, and the limping due to the disjointed thigh (vss. 25, 31) is a permanent reminder of the significance of the event.

Reconciliation scenes, when handled well, are a high point in narrative art. The reunion of Esau and Jacob (Gen. 33) is a good example. There is a brief prelude (vss. 1-3) in which the scene is visualized, as in a play. On one side we see Esau approaching with his 400 men. On the other side we see Jacob busily arranging his family, with "Rachel and Joseph last of all," in typical Jacobian fashion. As the two groups approach each other we can see Jacob "bowing himself to the ground seven times."

The climax comes with great emotional force: "But Esau ran to meet him, and embraced him, and fell on his neck and kissed him, and they wept" (vs. 4). The reconciliation reverses the expectation of a hostile meeting and gives the story of family antagonism a comic ending in which the previous discord is resolved.

The remainder of Jacob's story is intermingled with the story of Joseph, where Jacob is mainly the patriarch of the family — a necessary figure in the story but not the center of the action. Jacob emerges from the pages of Genesis as a strong, aggressive character who precipitates conflict wherever he goes. The fact that he is preeminently the man who supplants and strives explains why he is such a colorful and memorable literary character.

IV

The story of Joseph (Gen. 37, 39-46, 50) involves two separate threads of action that become fused late in the story. One part of the story involves Joseph's relations with his family. The second strand of action concerns his life in Egypt. In the final stages of the narrative, the two stories become related, because the famine forces the sons of Jacob to Egypt, where Joseph's relations with them again become important. It is possible to summarize the main stages of the action simply by observing the roles that Joseph plays as the story progresses. He is, in turn, the family outcast, the keeper of Potiphar's estate, the prisoner, the interpreter of dreams, and the political administrator of Pharaoh. The plot structure is that of comedy — a U-shaped plot in which events descend into various kinds of catastrophe but end in happiness.

With Joseph we are introduced to a conception of heroism that will run as a major theme through the whole Bible. It is the suffering servant motif. In such a story the protagonist undergoes suffering, usually undeserved, and through that suffering is able to bring about great good for other people. Joseph is just such an innocent sufferer who becomes a savior of mankind.

One important theme that emerges from the story of the suffering servant is the idea that human suffering is meaningful. It is meaningful because God uses the evil and suffering of people to bring about a greater good. Joseph himself stresses this twice after his ordeal is over. In the first instance Joseph tells his brothers that God's victory has overshadowed the human tragedy of his life: "And now do not be distressed, or angry with yourselves, because you sold me here; for God sent me before you to preserve life.... And God sent me before you to preserve for you a remnant on earth, and to keep alive for you many survivors. So it was not you who sent me here, but God" (Gen. 45:5, 7-8). After the death of Jacob, Joseph's brothers fear that Joseph will requite them for the evil they had done, but Joseph again affirms the positive purpose of his suffering: "As for you, you meant evil against me; but God meant it for good, to bring it about that many people should be kept alive, as they are today" (Gen. 50:20). In keeping with this theme of purposive suffering, Joseph's life is a life of destiny. Its end is perceptible in the dreams predicting a significant future that he receives already in his youthful years. Joseph, in short, lives out his life in accordance with God's redemptive purposes for mankind.

The story is full of pattern and symmetry. On four separate occasions Joseph rises to a position of dominance: over his brothers (Gen. 37), the servants in Potiphar's house (Gen. 39:4-6), his fellow prisoners (vss. 21-23), and the land of Egypt (Gen. 41:39-41). A symbolic garment stands at the transition point between these phases: the brothers disrobe Joseph before casting him into the pit (Gen. 37:23), Potiphar's wife seizes his garment and uses it to convict him (Gen. 39:12-18), Joseph "changed his clothes" upon leaving the dungeon to meet Pharaoh (Gen. 41:14), and upon his rise to power in Egypt he was arrayed "in garments of fine linen" (vs. 42). And in each phase Joseph undergoes an imprisonment that is symbolic of both persecution and preservation: the pit, the prison, and the land of Egypt.

The exposition of the story (Gen. 37:1-11) idealizes the hero and pictures him as the innocent sufferer whose virtue initiates conflict with less noble persons. The ill report that Joseph brings to his father about his brothers (vs. 2) is evidence of his moral sensitivity to the evil doings of his brothers. The favoritism that Joseph's father shows toward him is an index to the desirability and attractiveness of the young hero, with the stigma for the favoritism belonging to the father rather than to Joseph.

Joseph's dreams are also an important part of the exposition of the story. The dreams show Joseph's heroic status as God's agent of prophetic revelation. The narrator interprets Joseph's disclosure of his two dreams not as an act of boasting on Joseph's part but rather as the occasion for the hatred and jealousy of other family members to show themselves (vss. 8, 10-11). The function of the dreams in the story as a whole is to intensify the plot conflict between Joseph and his brothers, to prefigure the success that the hero will eventually achieve, and to endow Joseph's life with a sense of destiny from the very beginning. The dreams themselves, like those later in the story, draw upon the world of nature for their substance. The mode is symbolism, and the details in the dreams must be translated into their human meanings.

Joseph's early life resembles that of his father Jacob, with family discord the main feature of his youthful existence. The story of sibling hatred reaches its culmination when Joseph's brothers cast him into a pit and then sell him into slavery (Gen. 37:12-36). The pastoral world, usually idealized, here becomes the setting for in-human, monstrous evil — a kind of anti-pastoral. The selling of Joseph into slavery makes the story a reenactment of the familiar archetype of the young hero who undertakes a dangerous journey that will initiate him into spiritual and social adulthood.

Other archetypal patterns emerge in the story of Joseph's foreign career. The events in Egypt fall into the same U-shaped, comic structure that Joseph's life as a whole does. His initial success as the manager of Potiphar's estate is followed by his imprisonment, after which he returns to prosperity as Pharaoh's administrator. The temptation motif is present when Potiphar's wife tries to seduce the handsome young hero (Gen. 39:6-18). Joseph's refusal of the wife's solicitation further idealizes him by showing his loyalty to his master (vss. 8-9) and his horror at the thought of sinning against God (vs. 9). When the wife's lie makes Joseph the innocent sufferer, we are reminded of yet another archetype, the suffering servant.

The extended series of events in which Joseph's brothers negotiate with him for grain (Gen. 42-45) is a notable instance of dramatic irony. Joseph's brothers do not realize, as the reader does, who Joseph is. There is dramatic irony of another kind when Joseph claims to be testing the brothers' honesty about not being spies when he is actually testing their characters to determine whether they have changed for the better in the intervening years. The story is a prolonged test for the brothers. The testing shows their loyalty to their father, their acknowledgment of guilt in having sold Joseph (Gen. 42:21-22), their lack of envy when Benjamin receives a larger portion at the table (Gen. 43:34), and, in the case of Judah (who had earlier pro-posed selling Joseph), their willingness to act as a surety for Benjamin (Gen. 44:33). Suspense stems from the fact that Joseph must feign emotional distance from those he loves.

The story moves gradually to a great climax. The bowing down of Joseph's brothers several times is climactic, both because it is a reversal of earlier events and because it fulfills Joseph's early dreams. The final climax comes with the disclosure of Joseph's identity to his brothers and the happy reunion of the family.

The story of David spans several Old Testament books (for repre-sentative episodes, see 1 Sam. 16-17; 2 Sam. 5-19). The story is a less consciously artistic performance than the other heroic narratives of the Old Testament. It lacks close unity and overall design, resembling a historical chronicle in its fragmented structure. The story is important to literature, however, because of its picture of the hero. David is the biblical parallel to Achilles and Odysseus and Aeneas and King Arthur. He is a political figure comparable to the conventional hero of ancient literature.

David is in every way one of the most complex characters in biblical literature. His complexity is rivaled in ancient literature only by Odysseus. He is a hero of complex roles, including shepherd, poet, warrior, subject, king, friend, husband, father, and religious leader. He is also a man of complex personal qualities. He is a man of both action and contemplation; the narratives of his life capture the first trait, while his psalms reflect the second quality. The psalms show him to be a man of strong emotions, either in the pit of depression or in the ecstasy of praise. He sometimes displays great self-restraint, as when he twice refuses a ready-made opportunity to kill his enemy Saul, while on other occasions he shows an equally unexplained tendency to give in to his passions, as when he commits adultery with Bathsheba and orders the innocent Uriah murdered in battle. Through all his tragedies and triumphs, the spiritual dimension is never absent from David's life. When he sins, it is recognized as sin against God. When he triumphs, he turns in praise to the God who has given him the victory. All of this bespeaks a man for whom all of life is God's.

The story of David combines two sets of values usually thought to be antithetical — the pastoral and the heroic values. Ordinarily, pastoral writers despise courtly, heroic values and show how much vice can be avoided by living the simple life of a shepherd. David begins his life as the humble shepherd, the rustic, the sweet singer of Israel (2 Sam. 23:1), the man of spiritual introspection. But he becomes the leader of a nation, the man of heroic action, the courageous warrior defeating enemies on the battlefield. David's dual identity is captured at one point in his story when God says regarding him, "I took you from the pasture, from following the sheep, that you should be prince over my people Israel" (2 Sam. 7:8).

David first enters the heroic world of kingship when Samuel anoints him king over Israel (1 Sam. 16). The story of the anointing is an example of the archetype of the unlikely hero, or the Cinderella motif. In fact, David, the youngest son of Jesse, is so obscure that he must be fetched from the sheep when the anointing takes place (vs. 11). The motif of the unlikely choice is used here to exemplify a major theme of biblical literature, the unreliability of human standards in comparison with God's perspective. This theme is made explicit when "the Lord said to Samuel, ... the Lord sees not as man sees; man looks on the outward appearance, but the Lord looks on the heart" (vs. 7). The opening chapter of the story idealizes the future hero: he is described as being "skilful in playing, a man of valor, a man of war, prudent in speech, and a man of good presence; and the Lord is with him" (vs. 18). We also read regarding the boy hero that he "was ruddy, and had beautiful eyes, and was handsome" (vs. 12).

The story of David and Goliath (1 Sam. 17) is a favorite with children, and no wonder — its appeal is to the most naive and least sophisticated of literary tastes. It has all the ingredients of a good story. There is vivid conflict, involving the pagan bully against the children of God, in a war setting. The single combat simply heightens the sense of conflict by concentrating it in a single event. The conflict is between obvious right and obvious wrong, making it compelling. From the point of view of David and the narrator, the issue at stake is nothing less than "that all the earth may know that there is a God in Israel" (vs. 46). The struggle between two competing sets of values is made even clearer when David says to the giant, "You come to me with a sword and with a spear and with a javelin; but I come to you in the name of the Lord of hosts, . . . whom you have defied" (vs. 45). The story also possesses a villain — a giant, no less, who evokes instinctive feelings of horror and moral revulsion when he defies the armies of God. The narrative features a boy hero, a homespun underdog who does in the proud enemy of God. It appeals to the romantic strain in us — to our instinct for wish fulfillment, even though we realize that life is tragic as well as comic. There is concreteness of presentation; we can hear the giant defying Israel and see David picking up five smooth stones and visualize him running to meet Goliath. Finally, the story displays a firm sense of structure. The storyteller does not clutter the narrative with too many details. He begins with an exposition of background information, conveys a sense of rising action, constructs his story around a single climax, and, once the climax has been reached, quickly brings the story to a conclusion.

David's kingship is the major concern of his heroic narrative. The account of his reign begins in 2 Samuel 5, which stresses his role as the new king (vss. 1-12), his domestic role (vss. 13-16), and his military success against foreign enemies (vss. 17-25). Kingdom, home, war — these will be the dominant notes in his story. David's heroic status is clearly identified as a gift from God; the narrator asserts that "David became greater and greater, for the Lord, the God of hosts, was with him" (vs. 10). The way in which David inquires of God regarding his battle plans (vss. 19, 23-25) conforms to a common pattern of heroic narrative in which a divine force aids the hero.

Chapters 6 and 7 of 2 Samuel develop the religious identity of the hero. David's dancing with abandon before the ark of God (2 Sam. 6:14) shows him to be a man of strong religious emotions. His desire to build a temple for God (2 Sam. 7:1-3) further establishes his piety, as does his prayer after God has rejected him as the one to build the temple (vss. 18-29). God's words about what he has done and will do for David (vss. 4-17) are sometimes called the Davidic covenant, and they, too, serve to establish David's favor with God.

Battlefield action is a staple in ancient heroic literature, as embodied in classical epic and perpetuated in medieval romance. It is also prominent in the story of David (see, for example, 2 Sam. 8, 10). It makes David the clearest biblical parallel to the conquering heroes of classical epic and the old heroic code. In the conventional heroic formula, the hero wins fame for himself through prowess on the battlefield. This convention is illustrated in David's story when we read, "And David won a name for himself" (8:13). The added biblical dimension is well summarized in the statement, "And the Lord gave victory to David wherever he went" (vs. 14).

2 Samuel 11, the story of David's adultery with Bathsheba, is the first of several chapters dealing with the personal and domestic life of the hero. It shows David to be a man of strong passions and depicts the tragedy that engulfs him when he fails to control his sexual desire for a beautiful woman. The episode also exemplifies the way in which one sin leads to another in an attempt to conceal the original sin. In this case the sin of adultery quickly leads to the premeditated murder in battle of Bathsheba's husband, Uriah. David's message to the captain ("Do not let this matter trouble you, for the sword devours now one and now another" — vs. 25) shows his inhuman callousness toward the murder.

David is not the only hero of ancient literature who is diverted from his pursuits by sexual relations with a beautiful woman. Odysseus, whose fidelity to home and wife is unquestioned, has sexual relations with both Calypso and Circe. Unlike David, however, he is not morally reprehensible within the logic of the story because his relations are involuntary relations with goddesses, whose advances he could not disregard without harm. His sexual infidelity to his wife is not even considered objectionable by the narrator or his wife Penelope. In this regard the real contrast between the stories of Odysseus and David is not between the two heroes, but rather between the conceptions of deity that emerge from the two stories. In the biblical account, the holy God is displeased with the sin of adultery, as evidenced by the narrator's statement that "the thing that David had done displeased the Lord" (2 Sam. 11:27). The underlying principle is clear: adultery is horrible because it is a perversion of something God-ordained and sacred, namely, faithful wedded love. The stories in classical mythology that depict gods and goddesses (such as Calypso and Circe in *The Odyssey*) engaging in promiscuous sexual relations with each other and with humans reflect a low view of the gods, who are made in man's image, and a low view of the sanctity of wedded love, the perversion of which is not notable because the thing itself is not regarded highly in the first place.[7]

The contrast between David and Aeneas is also instructive. The relationship between Aeneas and Dido constitutes a diversion from the hero's duty to found the Roman Empire. It is an act that displeases Jupiter, and in this it resembles the story of David. But why does it displease Jupiter? It displeases him because the love affair diverts Aeneas from his political task. By contrast, God is displeased with David because he has committed an immoral act of sin — a violation of God's moral law. Similarly, the essential nature of Aeneas' sin is that he has allowed passion to conquer his reason, while David's act is disobedience to a personal, holy God. The resolution of Aeneas' sin lies simply in his allowing the light of reason to dispel the dark passions that have momentarily gained control of his sense of duty. David's restoration, however, involves his coming to terms with the past act. He cannot simply walk away from the act by a resolve to reform. His sin needs forgiveness from a holy and forgiving God, as is made particularly clear in Psalm 51, written on the occasion of David's sin with Bathsheba.

The story of David's adultery reaches its climax when the prophet Nathan tells a parable that convicts David of his sin (2 Sam. 12:1-15). There are several noteworthy features about the parable involving a rich man who steals the only lamb of a poor man. The parable draws upon a rural metaphor. It concentrates on the vast difference between the rich and poor men, rendering the rich man's action inexcusable. David's own response to the monstrous inhumanity of the rich man is horror at the rich man's lack of pity (vs. 6). The parable serves the persuasive purpose of exposing David's sin and leading him to repentance. This rhetorical purpose is gained by approaching David's sin in an indirect manner. The king is led to think that he is judging a civil case, whereas the story is really told with a view toward transferring its meaning to another level. The parable's effectiveness is evident from the fact that David confesses his sin against God (vs. 13) and receives God's forgiveness as a result (vs. 13).

David's sin results in family consequences, as Nathan had predicted (2 Sam. 12:11). In fact, the story of David, like that of Shakespeare's *King Lear,* presents an action as it occurs on several levels at once,

---

[7] For comment on the unidealized view of romantic love in classical antiquity, see C. S. Lewis, *The Allegory of Love* (New York: Oxford University Press, 1936), pp. 4-8.

namely, the personal, familial, and civil. Thus the moral disorder within David, the father and king, quickly branches out and produces moral disintegration in both the family and state. For example, the incest of David's son Amnon (2 Sam. 13:1-19) and his murder at the hand of his brother Absalom (vss. 20-29) reenact David's two heinous sins of sexual perversion and murder. The effect is that of a subplot.

With the story of Absalom's revolt (2 Sam. 15-19), the moral disorder moves outward from the individual and family into the state. These chapters are a self-contained story, cyclic in structure. They begin with the king fleeing for his life and conclude with his return as king. On a social and political level, disintegration and fragmentation of the state are balanced by restoration of unity. Absalom is a tragic figure and belongs to the archetype of the usurper. The political intrigue that he initiates represents an evil act of rebellion against God-ordained and legitimate authority.

David's flight (2 Sam. 15:13—16:14) uses the procession motif to bring together a series of personal encounters, within a context of war. The series of character vignettes begins with Ittai, who remains a loyal follower of the king even though it involves unnecessary risk on his part (2 Sam. 15:19-23). The Levites are an example of the religious officials who are bewildered and forced to comply with strange happenings with the coming of war (vss. 24-29). Ahithophel plays the part of the traitor (vs. 31), while Hushai becomes the person willing to risk his life for the rightful cause (vss. 32-37). Ziba is the opportunist, using war and treachery as a means of obtaining personal gain (2 Sam. 16:1-4). And Shimei is simply the enemy, glad for the misfortune that has engulfed the legitimate ruler (vss. 5-14).

The flight of the king involves not only personal encounters but the use of vivid narrative detail as well. The following scene, for example, gains its power through specific detail and depiction of innocent suffering: "But David went up the ascent of the Mount of Olives, weeping as he went, barefoot and with his head covered; and all the people who were with him covered their heads, and they went up, weeping as they went" (2 Sam. 15:30). Similarly, Shimei's antagonism is captured not only by his curses ("Begone, begone, you man of blood, you worthless fellow!" — 2 Sam. 16:7), but also by the picture of him walking along the hillside opposite David, cursing as he went and throwing stones and flinging dust at David (vs. 13). David's ideal behavior, a variation of the suffering servant motif, is accentuated by the remarkable restraint that he displays when his servants offer to make an end of Shimei, only to have David reject their offer (vss. 9-12).

The story of David is incomplete without his lyric poems, which give an added dimension to his characterization that is lacking in pure narrative. His lyric poems, which appear mostly in the Psalms, take us inside the hero in a way that narrative by itself cannot do. In an important way these poems show us the psychological and spiritual reality behind the activities that made up David's busy life.

What, then, is the significance of the heroic narrative of David? As I have said, the story of David is perhaps the closest parallel in biblical literature to the heroic narratives of classical epic and medieval romance. His military heroism, aptly summed up in the shout of the crowds, "David [has slain] his ten thousands" (1 Sam. 18:7), puts him in a large group of ancient literary heroes and makes him an example of the conventional heroic formula that regards political kingship as the ultimate earthly reward and the battlefield as the scene of the decisive events of history.

The story of David's heroic exploits enacts the important conflicts of the culture producing the story. The conflicts in David's story are chiefly political in nature and involve both external threats (mainly the Philistines) and internal threats (especially the civil war instigated by Absalom). David's domestic role is also stressed and accounts for several family conflicts. If we remember that a king was, in the older way of thinking, a representative figure, we will be in a position to understand how the ills afflicting David's family were intended to serve as models of what ordinary people ought to do and ought to avoid in the domestic ordering of their own lives. In terms of values, this heroic narrative affirms the importance of national security, civil order, domestic tranquility, obedience to God, and forgiveness of sins. A great deal of the didactic purpose is realized negatively, by presenting examples of sin and disorder that the reader is encouraged to avoid.

#

The story of Gideon (Judges 6-8) illustrates a concept of heroism similar to that exemplified by David. Gideon, too, is a military hero who leads his nation to success on the battlefield against foreign oppressors. Like David, he is God's appointed leader. There are two ingredients to his heroism — God's presence, and manly fortitude. This is summarized by the angel's initial statement, "The Lord is with you, you mighty man of valor" (Judg. 6:12). The same dual emphasis occurs when the Lord commissions Gideon with the words, "Go in this might of yours . . . ; do not I send you?" (vs. 14).

Gideon is largely an idealized hero. His first act of heroism consists of combating idolatry in his own family and can be called the heroism of godly worship (Judg. 6:25-27). His heroism is next tested in the arena of international conflict when he leads Israel to victory over the invading Midianites. The shout of the Jewish soldiers, "For the Lord and for Gideon" (Judg. 7:18), again shows a concept of heroism in which God and man are harmoniously joined.

As is true of much biblical narrative, there is a minor note of tragedy in the story of this godly hero. After his military conquests, Gideon collects from the soldiers their earrings and makes of them "an ephod" (Judg. 8:27), apparently some kind of image. In subsequent history the ephod became the object of idolatrous worship, so that "it became a snare to Gideon and to his family" (vs. 27). The inclusion of this detail is a good index to the realism of the Bible, which never spares its characters by passing over their bad qualities. It is also a reminder that not everything included in biblical narratives should be interpreted as being good or normative action.

Despite the adherence of the story of Gideon to the familiar image of the military hero, the full meaning of the story becomes apparent only when it is seen partly as a foil to the conventional story of military heroism as contained in classical epic and medieval romance. The usual military hero is a study in self-reliance. His chief assets are physical strength and courage. He fights at least partly to gain honor for himself, and this honor, in turn, is won through prowess on the battlefield. The conventional hero utters boastful speeches and calls attention to his own abilities.

The story of Gideon, like the story of Joshua's conquest of Jericho (Josh. 6), inverts the characteristics of conventional heroic narrative. Instead of praising human strength, the story of Gideon depicts the small place that human effort plays in the victory over Midian. In fact, God allows an army of only 300 soldiers to undertake the battle, "lest Israel vaunt themselves against me, saying, 'My own hand has delivered me' " (Judg. 7:2). Whereas the conventional military hero is of royal blood or even (as in the case of Aeneas) the offspring of a god or goddess, Gideon describes himself as coming from the weakest clan in his tribe and as being the least in his family (Judg. 6:15). Without external claim to heroism, he has nothing but God's sustaining power to make him heroic. Whereas the conventional heroic narrative celebrates the deliverance brought about by great and strong armies, the story of Gideon emphasizes the military inadequacy of the Jewish forces, thereby extolling the divine nature of the deliverance. The conventional hero, relying on his own abilities, wins victory through heroic action and is rewarded with fame and a political kingdom. Gideon, by contrast, relies on God's help, and when offered a kingdom refuses it on the ground that God, the real deliverer, is worthy to rule (Judg. 8:22-23). Thus in yet another way God is given the honor usually accorded the hero. To sum up, whereas conventional heroic narrative glorifies man, the story of Gideon glorifies God.

It soon becomes evident that the stories of Gideon and Joshua at Jericho are the biblical version of something common in modern literature, the anti-hero (the protagonist who displays a lack of the traits of the conventional hero). Gideon is an anti-hero in his lack of self-reliance, in his lack of any achievement that he can call his own, and in his unwillingness to aggrandize himself through assuming political leadership. However, while the modern anti-hero pales into a state of nihilistic nonachievement, Gideon and Joshua, in relinquishing the claims of conventional heroism, achieve much more than is humanly possible. Their weakness becomes divine strength, and their antiheroism becomes an expression of the heroism of trust in God.

VII

Like the other Old Testament narratives, the story of Daniel (Dan. 1-6) is firmly established in a historical setting. The events that are narrated occur during the exile of Judah after the nation had been carried into captivity by the Babylonians.

The plot of the story is not structured as a single climax but as a series of ordeals. Each chapter is a separate action, as follows: the testing of the four Hebrew youths, Daniel's interpretation of Nebuchadnezzar's dream, the fiery furnace ordeal, Nebuchadnezzar's account of his fall and restoration, Belshazzar's feast, and the ordeal of Daniel in the lions' den. The conflicts in this plot occur both on an individual and on a national level. On the individual level, Daniel, the protagonist, encounters a number of antagonists, including kings, a pagan life style, the threat of losing his Jewish identity, jealous colleagues, and hungry lions. But Daniel's personal conflicts occur in a broader context of international conflict between the Jewish nation, with a strong religious identity, and the Babylonians, with an equally strong pagan orientation.

A characteristic feature of the style is the elaborate repetition of phrases and speeches. In fact, the story of Daniel has a style that is more clearly reminiscent of oral epic than any other Old Testament narrative.

There are several important dimensions to Daniel's heroism. As a hero, Daniel, whose name means either "God is judge" or "God is my judge," is wholly idealized. As in the story of Joseph, the narrator selects details that idealize the hero and describe him in superlatives. In effect, such literature holds up a model of virtue as a goal toward which the reader can aim. Daniel is a nationalistic hero, as evidenced, for example, when he refuses to compromise on the question of the ceremonial laws regarding the preparation of food, something that set the Jewish nation apart from other nations. Daniel is also a hero of ability and integrity. He is valedictorian of his class, admired and befriended by one pagan king after another despite his strong religious convictions. Above all, Daniel is depicted as a religious hero. His life revolves around God. His religious intensity is what impresses the pagans around him, some of whom speak of "the God of Daniel." He is preeminently the man of God who does not allow his high position in society to lead him to compromise his faith.

There are some noteworthy features of the "world" of the story. It is a supernatural world in which there is constant acknowledgment of the existence of a spiritual world and frequent interpenetration of the supernatural world into the visible order of reality. The atmosphere is oriental, full of spiritual awareness. All of this produces a sense of mystery. There are many dreams, mysterious and having great importance in the lives of people. There are many astrologers and interpreters of dreams around the court.

The world of the story is, secondly, a political world. The courts of great and powerful rulers form the setting for the action. The personal story of Daniel takes place against a background of rising and falling kings. Dreams usually have a political significance in the story. The hero himself is a statesman — an adviser to rulers.

Finally, the world of the story is a world in which God is sovereign. Repeatedly God is shown to be the one who is in control of events on earth and in the lives of individuals. He is the still point of stability in a world of change, and He is the only one who can reveal the truth in a world replete with mystery.

Chapter 1 describes the testing of the religious faith of Daniel and his three young Hebrew friends. The conflict is a struggle between contrasting life styles. Life in the king's palace where the four youths are educated is characterized by excessive luxury, as suggested by the images of "rich food" and wine (Dan. 1:5). Daniel's life style is virtually pastoral in its simplicity, with his diet consisting of "vegetables to eat and water to drink" (Dan. 1:12). The very presence of two sets of names for the youths (Dan. 1:6-7) suggests a conflict between two ways of life.

The crisis faced by the youths involves more than a threat to their life style. Although it is not stated explicitly in the text, we can infer that the king's feasts would have used food that had first been dedicated to the gods. To eat such food would be an act of honor and worship to the pagan gods. This will explain why Daniel believed that to participate in the king's banquet would be to "defile himself"

(Dan. 1:8). Faced with this test of loyalty to God, Daniel initiates a test.

The outcome of the test, along with other descriptions of the youths in this episode, illustrates a common tendency of heroic literature — the search for superlatives. For example, the youths are said to be "without blemish, handsome and skilful in all wisdom, endowed with knowledge, understanding learning, and competent to serve in the king's palace" (Dan. 1:4). In other words, they were the best of their kind. Similarly, after the test has been passed we read, "As for these four youths, God gave them learning and skill in all letters and wisdom" (Dan. 1:17). Again, "In every matter of wisdom and understanding concerning which the king inquired of them, he found them ten times better than all the magicians and enchanters that were in all his kingdom" (Dan. 1:20).

The episode involving Nebuchadnezzar's dream (Dan. 2) is a test of Daniel's ability to tell and interpret dreams. As in the testing of the four youths, the event serves to exalt God's sovereignty. The statement of the Chaldeans that "there is not a man on earth who can meet the king's demand" (Dan. 2:10) is an interesting comment on human inadequacy and functions as a foil that heightens the greatness of God, who *can* meet the king's demand. Faced with the crisis of interpreting the dream, Daniel turns naturally to prayer (Dan. 2:17-18), which is followed by God's revelation in answer to the prayer (vs. 19) and by Daniel's lyric poem praising God as the revealer of mysteries (vss. 19-23). The final element in the pattern is testimony, which occurs when Daniel testifies to the king regarding the power of God to reveal dreams (vss. 27-30).

The king's dream about a figure that is crushed by a stone is given a political interpretation (Dan. 2:36-45), reinforcing the political preoccupation of the story. The figure in the dream is comprised of several minerals, arranged in a descending hierarchy of value. The mode is symbolism, with the minerals representing political empires. The historical sequence of empires culminates in an apocalyptic vision of the kingdom that God will establish forever (Dan. 2:44). Characteristically, it is God's kingdom, rather than the kingdoms of men, that is given prominence in the story. Daniel's exaltation (Dan. 2:46-49), accompanied by Nebuchadnezzar's acknowledgment of God's glory, evokes the artistic pleasure appropriate to comedy.

The ordeal of the fiery furnace (Dan. 3) combines the motifs of testing and miraculous rescue. The threat to Daniel's three friends again involves their loyalty to God and comes in the form of compulsory emperor worship. The episode is one of many great moral dilemmas found in the pages of biblical literature, and the three friends, like many another biblical hero, assume grandeur as they choose for God (Dan. 3:16-18). Nebuchadnezzar is an interesting study in overreaction and runs true to form by ordering that the furnace of punishment be "heated seven times more than it was wont to be heated" (Dan. 3:19). Like the lions' den, it is an image evoking the instinctive feeling of terror that we associate with a child's response. The intrusion of the supernatural into the earthly scene, a pervasive feature of the story of Daniel, here takes the form of a mysterious fourth person walking with the unhurt men in the fiery furnace. The fourth figure, one "like a son of the gods" (Dan. 3:25), represents a theophany, or appearance of God.

With the fourth chapter the point of view shifts, as Nebuchadnezzar becomes the narrator. His purpose is to relate God's mighty acts, as evidenced by his statement that "it seemed good to me to show the signs and wonders that the Most High God has wrought toward me" (Dan. 4:2). The impact is heightened by the fact that a pagan king is the one to give such a testimony. King Nebuchadnezzar is punished by God for his sin of hubris, or excessive pride, similar to that which afflicts the heroes of Greek tragedy. His pride is dramatized when he describes how he walked in his palace and said, "Is not this great Babylon, which I have built by my mighty power as a royal residence and for the glory of my majesty?" (Dan. 4:30). God's judgment falls at once, and the story becomes a death-rebirth story, similar in its archetypal pattern to the fiery furnace ordeal and the experience of Daniel in the lions' den. The main lesson that Nebuchadnezzar draws from his experience is the reality of God's sovereignty, as summarized in his conclusion that God "does according to his will in the host of heaven and among the inhabitants of the earth; and none can stay his hand or say to him, 'What doest thou?'" (Dan. 4:35).

Chapter 5 shifts the scene to one of the memorable events in biblical literature, Belshazzar's feast and the handwriting on the wall. The banquet is a scene of luxury and intemperance, climaxed by the irreverent act of using the captured vessels from the temple of Jerusalem (vss. 1-4). Into this context of carousing and sacrilege comes the mysterious appearance of a man's hand writing on the wall, evoking feelings of horror. The terror is made vivid in the description of how "the king's color changed, and his thoughts alarmed him; his limbs gave way, and his knees knocked together" (vs. 6). As is typical of the entire story of Daniel, the words written on the wall have a political significance and involve God's judgment against evil. The elaborate reward that Daniel receives from the king after interpreting the words (vs. 29) is ironic, since the reward is inappropriate to a message of doom and because being named ruler over a third of the kingdom is of little value when the kingdom itself will fall within a few hours.

Daniel's position as one of three presidents in the kingdom of Darius (Dan. 6) is the final chapter in the life of a great statesman who was trusted by one king after another. The statement that "an excellent spirit was in him" (vs. 3) is an apt summary of Daniel's ability, which impressed everyone around him. The fact that Daniel's jealous associates realized that they could find no complaint against him "unless we find it in connection with the law of his God" (vs. 5) is an index to his inviolable loyalty to God. Again the test takes the form of compulsory emperor worship, with the den of lions introducing the same element of horror as was earlier represented by the fiery furnace. The heroism of uncompromising faith in God is vividly depicted in the account of how Daniel, when he "knew that the document had been signed, . . . went to his house where he had windows in his upper chamber open toward Jerusalem; and he got down upon his knees three times a day and prayed and gave thanks before his God, as he had done previously" (vs. 10).

The characterization of Darius is also important in the story of the lions' den. His distress when he sees the results of his edict about worship (vs. 14) dramatizes his inner conflict between law and personal conscience. His extreme concern for Daniel, evidenced by his wish that God would deliver Daniel (vs. 16) and his night of fasting (vs. 18), is an indirect way of depicting Daniel's ideal character. The inner conflict of Darius is also evident when on the following morning he "cried out in a tone of anguish" (vs. 20) to inquire about Daniel's safety. The story of miraculous deliverance from the lions' den becomes another example of God's vindication of those who are pure in heart before Him (vs. 22). Poetic justice takes the form of the casting of the accusers into the den of lions and the praise that the pagan Darius gives to God.

VIII

The story of Ruth is a narrative of idyllic romance, if we use the dictionary definition of an idyl as "a short poem or prose work describing a simple, pleasant aspect of rural, pastoral, or domestic life." The story is a love story revolving around the heroine for whom the book is named. Ruth is above all a domestic heroine. She is twice married, devoted to her mother-in-law, the lady of the romance who occupies the center of the story, a mother in the royal line of David and a member of the messianic line. It is impossible to separate the domestic from the religious heroine. Indeed, the domestic heroine draws much of her identity from her religious strength. The basis of her appeal as a woman is nowhere said to be stunning beauty but rather her gentleness and strength of character. Ruth's religious commitment, seen in her early choice to serve God, makes her one of the few examples in Old Testament history of foreigners who were successfully assimilated into Hebrew society.

The story of Ruth has an elemental quality. It depicts such basic human experiences as death, religious devotion, romantic love, family ties, and motherhood. In the background of the human actions and relationships are references to the natural world of famine and harvest, with the result that the domestic concerns of the story are broadened beyond family relations to include the whole domestic realm of making a living and sustaining life. Even the love between Ruth and Boaz is partly romantic and partly a matter of fulfilling familial obligations. The allusions to the rural cycle of seasons also have the effect of making romantic love something that is part of the natural order of things. It is not a discordant force in human experience, as so often in literature, but something that corresponds to the natural flow of events and is in harmony with social norms as well. In keeping with this emphasis, the idealized love depicted in the story finds its natural culmination in the socially sanctioned institution of marriage.

The plot of the story is comic, beginning in tragedy but moving steadily toward a happy conclusion as various obstacles are overcome. The main characters begin in isolation from their society and gradually become assimilated into it, the usual pattern in comedy. The triumph at the end of the story is the customary one for a comic plot, consisting of a marriage. The story, for all its simplicity, is skillfully constructed in such a way as to build toward the climactic nighttime meeting between Ruth and Boaz at the threshing floor. Each of the four chapters contributes a phase to the action, according to the following sequence: background to the story, early stages of romance between Ruth and Boaz, the climactic confrontation on the threshing floor, and the denouement (tying up of loose ends).

A carefully designed story is often said by literary critics to possess a "well-made plot." Although the elements of such a plot differ from one critic to another, a widely accepted formulation is the following: exposition (background information), inciting moment (or inciting force), rising action, turning point (at which time the reader can begin to see how the conflict will be resolved), further complication, climax, and denouement. The story of Ruth falls into such a pattern, probably reflecting the conscious artistry of the storyteller. The exposition consists of the tragic sojourn in Moab. The inciting force is the return to Bethlehem, and the rising action is the emerging romance of Ruth and Boaz. The turning point comes when Naomi arranges the night meeting between the two lovers, and further complication is described briefly when Ruth carries out her mother-in-law's instructions. The climactic meeting is followed by the fulfillment of legal requirements and the subsequent marriage.

Chapter 1 is expository in nature and narrates the tragic background to the story of love. It describes the crucible of suffering and loss out of which the story of love springs. The opening chapter also establishes domestic relations as a main concern of the story. Naomi's parting blessing to her two daughters-in-law, for example, reinforces the domestic theme: "The Lord grant that you may find a home, each of you in the house of her husband!" (Ruth 1:9). Ruth's clinging to her mother-in-law also dramatizes the importance of family relationships. Ruth's steadfastness and loyalty to her mother-in-law are expressed in terms that have become memorable to Western culture and which achieve their eloquence through elaborate balance and parallelism: "Entreat me not to leave you or to return from following you; for where you go I will go, and where you lodge I will lodge; your people shall be my people, and your God my God; where you die I will die, and there will I be buried" (vss. 16-17). The fact that Ruth here chooses Naomi's God shows her choice to be a religious as well as domestic one and explains why Milton, in his ninth sonnet, cites Ruth (along with Mary) as an example of a woman who chose "the better part," that is, spiritual over material values.

The second chapter of Ruth depicts romantic courtship in a rustic or pastoral setting. As in other pastoral literature, the rural setting provides an idealized atmosphere in which an idealized love takes root and grows. In keeping with the pastoral context, the lady of the romance is a gleaner of grain, and her lover is a farmer. In a story of pastoral romance, the courtship is always conducted in terms appropriate to the rustic milieu; this is exactly what happens in the story when the favor of Boaz is expressed by his inviting Ruth to glean with his own maidens (2:8) and drink the water of his workers (vs. 9), as well as by his command to his workers to allow Ruth to glean among the sheaves and even to "pull out some from the bundles for her" (vs. 16).

The climax of the love story comes with the encounter between Ruth and Boaz on the threshing floor (Ruth 3). Naomi's plan for Ruth to lie down at the feet of Boaz was apparently an accepted way of showing love, since she tells Ruth that Boaz "will tell you what to do" (vs. 4). Ruth's proposal that Boaz marry her (vs. 9) and Boaz's acceptance of the proposal bring the courtship to its conclusion.

The final chapter of the romance reinforces the domestic emphasis of the story in several ways. Boaz's meticulous fulfillment of all legal requirements shows that the marriage is conducted according to well-defined social regulations and has full social sanction. The sanction of society is also evident when the townspeople pronounce their blessing on the marriage with the words, "May the Lord make the woman, who is coming into your house, like Rachel and Leah, who together built up the house of Israel" (4:11). In classical literature, as C. S. Lewis has observed, romantic love "seldom rises above the levels of merry sensuality or domestic comfort, except to be treated as a tragic madness ... which plunges otherwise sane people (usually women) into crime and disgrace. Such is the love of Medea, of Phaedra, of Dido...."[8] The biblical stories of love stand in beautiful contrast. Motherhood is the final dimension to the story of this domestic heroine (vss. 13-16), and the related theme of the continuity of generations becomes a concluding note in the harmony of the story (vss. 17-22).

IX

Esther, whose story is told in the biblical book by that name, is above all a national heroine. Her importance as a person is completely subordinated to her status as a representative of the Jewish people. The emphasis is not on the religious dimension of the heroine. The name of God does not appear in the story, and the whole interest of the narrator is in Esther as a symbol of the Jewish people. Not too much should be made of the absence of an explicitly religious focus. After all, to be a Jew was to be part of a religious community, a fact implied though not explicitly stated in the story.

The triumph of the work lies in its narrative technique. For one thing, there is an abundance of narrative conflict. On the personal level there is a skirmish between King Ahasuerus and Queen Vashti and a prolonged campaign between Haman and Mordecai. The issue becomes much bigger, however, and is enlarged to include Haman's Persian army and the Jewish nation. Seldom has a plot conflict done a better job of involving the emotions of the reader in the outcome of the plot. Haman is so obviously a villain, and the Jews so obviously the innocent victims in great danger, that the reader's emotional response is intense. The story also attains a high degree of suspense. Step by step the plight of the Jews becomes hopeless. There are various obstacles to overcoming the forces of evil, and the climax is delayed, increasing the suspense.

The plot is a full-fledged comic plot and evokes all the aesthetic pleasures appropriate to its kind. The heroine's story begins with prosperity, descends into potentially tragic events, and quickly rises

---

[8] *Allegory of Love*, p. 4.

to a happy ending. Tension is built up and released, as in all complete comedies. The plot unfolds in three stages, which we might call prelude, struggle, and aftermath. Chapters 1 and 2, recounting the king's rejection of Vashti and marrying of Esther, are simply part of the necessary background to the conflict between Haman and the Jews. Chapters 3 to 7 narrate, step by step, how Haman plotted against Mordecai and the Jews, and how the latter developed a counterplot. Chapters 8 to 10 describe the aftermath of the struggle.

The social setting of Esther is very different from that in the pastoral idyl of Ruth. It is an aristocratic world of court life, replete with royal banquets, courtly officials, and court customs and protocol.

The storyteller employs narrative as a way of establishing the necessary background information. The extended description of regal splendor and celebration in the king's palace (1:1-9) provides a contrast to the poor Jewish nation and probably would have evoked a hostile response from the Jewish audience. The first power struggle in a story replete with such struggles occurs when Queen Vashti refuses the king's summons to make a public display of her beauty (vs. 12). The king's advisors take this act as a threat to masculine authority and respond with the defensive act of removing Queen Vashti from her royal position (vss. 16-22).

Esther's being made queen (2:1-18) is also part of the background. The heroine of the story is introduced in idealized fashion as being "beautiful and lovely" (vs. 7) and the most pleasing to the king of all the women at the court (vs. 17). Esther's Jewish identity, although concealed from the king, is twice mentioned in the exposition (vss. 10, 20).

A final strand in the background action is the story of how Mordecai uncovered a plot against the king's life (2:19-23). This puts the king in a position of indebtedness to Mordecai and will become important later in the story. The fact that Mordecai's act "was recorded in the Book of the Chronicles in the presence of the king" (vs. 23) will also assume significance at a climactic point in the story (6:1-11) and serves the narrative function of foreshadowing.

The chief conflict in the plot begins as a personal grievance of Haman when Mordecai refuses to do obeisance to him. Mordecai's refusal to bow is due to either religious conviction, national antagonism, or personal revulsion against the ignobility of Haman. The personal conflict quickly broadens into a nationalistic conflict when "Haman sought to destroy all the Jews" (3:6). This plot conflict becomes greatly intensified when, through court intrigue, Haman issues an edict that all Jews are to be annihilated (vs. 13).

The rising action of the story consists of an account of how various obstacles to the deliverance of the Jews are overcome. Mordecai's first hurdle is enlisting the help of Esther. Her hesitation is finally conquered when Mordecai convinces her that she, too, will be killed in the slaughter of the Jews (4:13), and when he challenges her with the thought, "Who knows whether you have not come to the kingdom for such a time as this?" (vs. 14). Another obstacle is the inaccessibility of the king, who has not called for Esther in thirty days and into whose presence one could not go without consent (vs. 11).

The turning point of the plot comes with Esther's decisive choice to confront the king, knowing that she might perish by her violation of the law (4:16). At the moment of crisis, her heroism becomes dramatically evident, like that of other biblical heroines and heroes.

Further complication in the plot consists of Esther's indirect and gradual approach to the king, which delays the climax and greatly heightens the suspense of the plot. In her first conversation with the king, she merely invites him and Haman to a dinner (5:4). When the king asks at the banquet, "What is your petition?" (vs. 6), Esther evades the issue again by inviting the two men to a second dinner (vss. 7-8). With the second dinner Esther finally makes her appeal for her nation (7:3-4), and the climax then comes speedily.

The climax of the story achieves much of its emotional impact through the presence of poetic justice, of which there are three notable examples. One instance occurs in chapter 6 when, after the king has just discovered from the historical chronicles his indebtedness to Mordecai, Haman enters the king's presence and is asked, "What shall be done to the man whom the king delights to honor?" (6:6). Trapped by his own conceit, Haman prescribes a public ceremony honoring the man who delights the king, only to find himself conferring the honor on his enemy Mordecai instead of receiving it himself. The picture of Haman hurrying to his house, "mourning and with his head covered" (vs. 12), completes the poetic justice. The second example concerns the high gallows that Haman constructed for Mordecai but on which he himself is finally hanged (7:10). A final important occurrence of poetic justice consists of Mordecai's becoming next in political rank to the king (10:3) and receiving the king's signet ring, "which he had taken from Haman, and gave ... to Mordecai" (8:2).

If we can trust the tastes of readers of literature through the centuries of Western civilization, the story of Esther contains many of the ingredients that have been viewed as making up a good story. These elements include a beautiful and courageous heroine, scenes of luxurious banqueting, romantic love, intrigue, intense conflict, a villain, suspense, decisive moral choice, climax, and battle. The story is a notable instance of the Cinderella motif — a story built around a deprived girl (an orphan and a member of an enslaved nation) who becomes queen, and a story of romantic love. At the national level the story belongs to an equally popular archetype — the rescue story. Indeed, the Bible is so full of rescue stories that it emerges as a great anthology of rescue stories.

The conscious artistry of the storyteller is reflected in the fact that his story, like the story of Ruth, can be outlined in terms of the well-made plot. This design focuses attention on the heroine, since the turning point is Esther's decision to confront the king with her appeal, and the climax comes with her disclosure of the Jews' plight.

X

Several important conclusions can be drawn from this survey of selected Old Testament narratives. One cannot fail to be impressed by the large amount of the Bible that consists of stories. As Amos Wilder has written, "The narrative mode is uniquely important in Christianity."[9] For one thing, the popularity of the story as a biblical form is evidence of the universal human interest in narrative. One of the most pervasive human impulses can be summed up in the four words "Tell me a story."

The prominence of narrative as a biblical form arises from the Bible's view of God. The God of the Bible is, above all, the God who acts. He acts not simply in the inner consciousness of people but in the arena of history. Historical narrative is the inevitable mode for writing about the God who acts in history. As Wilder has stated so well, "A Christian can confess his faith wherever he is, and without his Bible, just by telling a story or a series of stories. . . . God is an active and purposeful God and his action with and for men has a beginning, a middle and an end like any other story."[10]

It is evident that the story form is uniquely suited to the task of embodying the main outlines of biblical truth. By bringing human characters into interaction with God and with each other, biblical narrative is able to explore the dynamics of relationship that is so central to the biblical view of man. By presenting a double plot in which spiritual and earthly levels of action occur simultaneously, biblical narrative illuminates the spiritual reality that is always the context for human experience. Because narrative is a progression of events moving toward a goal, it is uniquely suited to depicting the dynamic, growing nature of religious experience. And by virtue of

[9] *Early Christian Rhetoric* (Cambridge: Harvard University Press, 1971), p. 56.
[10] Ibid.

its focus on plot conflict, biblical narrative expresses the nature of the continuing struggle between good and evil.

A survey of heroic narrative in the Old Testament illustrates the manysidedness of religious experience in the Bible. The image of the hero varies greatly from one story to another. The character differences between the staunch patriarch Abraham and the youthful Joseph, or between the strong willed Jacob and the gentle Ruth, or between the deeply flawed David and the wholly idealized Daniel are plain to see. This variety affirms the importance of individualism, since the distinctiveness of each protagonist is implied to be uniquely significant before God. In the midst of diversity, however, we can also observe the theocentric emphasis of biblical narrative. Biblical stories repeatedly attribute to God the worth and glory that humanistic literature assigns to human heroes.

Since history rather than fiction is the chief subject of biblical narrative, the reader is encouraged to look closely at the inner dynamics of narrative form. Fictional inventiveness is not the primary ingredient of narrative, as a modern reader may be inclined to think. The essence of a story is plot — a unified and meaningful sequence of events. The focus of interest is in the unfolding dynamics of the action. The important consideration for the storyteller is the selection of material according to unifying principles and with a sense of the proportion of the individual parts in relation to each other and the whole.

Biblical narrative reveals the literary impulse of many of its writers. The contrast between the historical chronicles of the Old Testament (books such as Joshua, Judges, 1 and 2 Kings, and 1 and 2 Chronicles) and the heroic narratives is instructive. At one end of the spectrum of historical narrative is the documentary impulse of the historian to write down anything that is important in a given era. The result is a collection of fragments, usually brief, dealing with a comprehensive assortment of events and persons. At the other end of the spectrum is literary narrative, based on the premise that literature is an artistic distillation of experience, not a comprehensive recording of the raw data of experience. Biblical narrative contains abundant examples of the whole spectrum. The purpose of my discussion is to show the high degree of literary mastery that many of the stories in the Bible possess.

Looking north from Jebel Mousa (Mt. Sinai), scene of one of the most stirring episodes in the Exodus wanderings.

The Epic
of the Exodus

4

I

Epic is a particular species within the class of heroic narrative. To begin, epic is long narrative. It is an encyclopedic form — a story with a proliferation of episodes. In fact, epic is so expansive, embodying so many important themes and values, that it can be said to sum up a whole age. Epic has traditionally had a strong nationalistic interest and contains many historical references. In terms of structure, the episodic plot of epic is unified around a central hero who is a political leader. Epic has a strong didactic impulse. It makes much use of what the Renaissance and eighteenth century called "supernatural machinery" — divine beings who participate in the affairs on earth. Many epics have been structured as a quest. And in addition to these characteristics of content, epic has traditionally included certain stylistic techniques that have made it distinctive. These include a high style — a consciously exalted mode of expression that removes the language from the commonplace through the use of epithets (titles for persons or things), pleonasm, repeated formulae, epic similes, epic catalogs, and allusions.

With the traditional features of epic providing the standard, it becomes evident that there is only one biblical story that is in the running for consideration as an epic. It is what I shall call the Epic of the Exodus, which occupies parts of the biblical books of Exodus, Leviticus, Numbers, and Deuteronomy. The main narrative sections are as follows: Exodus 1-20, 32-34; Numbers 10-14, 16-17, 20-24; Deuteronomy 32-34. With traditional epic as a measuring stick, it is easy to see to what extent the Epic of the Exodus is conventional.

The story of the exodus from Egypt to Canaan meets the test of long narrative. The story is nationalistic in emphasis, recording the formation of Israel as a nation and depicting the decisive event in the early history of the nation. A great deal of the story is devoted to describing the values and doctrine that can be said to sum up the Hebrew spirit. The story is set in history and is filled with historical allusions. It is unified partly by a normative hero and partly by the quest for the promised land. The Epic of the Exodus displays a strong didactic impulse, and the presence of divine beings is pervasive. The only major way in which the Epic of the Exodus fails to meet the definition of epic is in the area of stylistics. There is virtually a total absence of the high style typical of epic. Instead of poetry there is prose. There is little pleonasm, little use of epithets or epic formulae.

Of all the famous epics, *The Aeneid* of Virgil is the clearest parallel to the Epic of the Exodus. Both epics tell about the formation of an empire and are a call to its readers to contemplate the early history of their nation. Both are quest stories in which a group of people travel from one geographic area to another in order to establish a stable nation in a promised land. Both stories are unified around a hero who is a leader of people and who embodies the normative values of the story. Both epics are religious epics, filled with references to the proper worship of deity. Both epics embody and praise the virtues accepted as being normative in the society from which the epics arose.

The parallels between the Epic of the Exodus and other epics should not be allowed to obscure the important way in which the biblical epic differs from traditional epic. Conventional epic is humanistic in the sense that it exists to praise and glorify a human hero. The conventional epic hero is godlike in his accomplishments; indeed, he may even be of divine parentage, as Aeneas is. Heroes like Aeneas or Achilles or Beowulf merit praise by virtue of their own superhuman deeds. Traditional epics focus on human endeavor and show man accomplishing heroic feats. Their stories are essentially stories of human merit. As John Steadman puts it, "Whatever praise the epic poet might incidentally bestow on the gods, his primary object was to praise men by recounting their laudable achievements."[1]

With this brief survey of the heroic value structure of traditional epic before us, it is at once apparent that the Epic of the Exodus is, like Milton's epics, an anti-epic. Everywhere we find the traditional epic values inverted. For the praise of men, the writer has substituted the glory of God. Instead of depicting human strength, this epic depicts human frailty and sinfulness. Instead of a story in which a human warrior leads his nation to victory through superhuman feats on the battlefield, this narrative attributes the mighty acts of

---

[1] *Milton and the Renaissance Hero* (Oxford: Oxford University Press, 1967), p. 196.

deliverance to God. Indeed, the human warriors are usually passive spectators of the mighty acts of God. Instead of a human leader who depends on his own qualities of greatness, the storyteller here depicts a reluctant leader who is unsure of his own claims to leadership, inarticulate, of obscure origin, and meek. Instead of exalting the nation about whom the epic is written, this epic continually stresses the imperfections of the Israelites — their rebelliousness, their lack of faith, their tendency to complain. Whereas the traditional epic stresses physical warfare, the Epic of the Exodus places even more emphasis on spiritual conflict. Moral rebellion against God frequently replaces the conventional theme of armed conflict between nations. The usual epic formulae and virtues are attributed to God rather than to a human hero.

A brief look at some key events will document what I have said about the anti-epic. The hero's hesitancy to assume leadership (Exod. 4) is an example of the theme of human inadequacy. Moses' claim that he is "not eloquent" (Exod. 4:10) makes him a contrast to other epic heroes, who are unfailingly eloquent. Similarly, his fear that others "will not believe me or listen to my voice" (Exod. 4:1) is unconventional. Unlike other epic leaders, Moses is without external claim to prominence, being the son of a slave. His only real credential for leadership is that he has been called and equipped by God.

The events leading to the exodus from Egypt, and especially the ten plagues, are solely the result of God's activity. The Israelites themselves remain inactive spectators of the mighty acts of God. At the conclusion of the ten plagues, we read regarding the Jews, "Thus they despoiled the Egyptians" (Exod. 12:36). This is the usual formula in heroic epic, but the usual expectations are completely denied. The conquest has not been won on the battlefield through human effort but has been given to the Israelites by God's miraculous intervention.

The speech of Moses to the people shortly after the departure from Egypt (Exod. 13:3-16) is replete with statements that attribute the epic acts to God rather than a human hero. This anti-epic note comes out in statements such as these: "by strength of hand the Lord brought you out from this place" (Exod. 13:3); "when the Lord brings you into the land of the Canaanites..." (Exod. 13:5, 11); "and you shall tell your son on that day, 'It is because of what the Lord did for me when I came out of Egypt'" (Exod. 13:8); "by strength of hand the Lord brought us out of Egypt" (Exod. 13:14); "the Lord slew all the first-born in the land of Egypt" (Exod. 13:15). In short, the storyteller reserves his praise for God instead of a human hero.

God is also the epic hero in the events surrounding the deliverance at the Red Sea. In fact, He moves Pharaoh to pursue the Israelites for the purpose of getting "glory over Pharaoh and all his host; and the Egyptians shall know that I am the Lord" (Exod. 14:4). When the Hebrew people are terrified by the approaching Egyptian army, Moses points to their divine deliverer with the words, "Fear not, stand firm, and see the salvation of the Lord, which he will work for you today.... The Lord will fight for you, and you have only to be still" (Exod. 14:13, 14). Subsequently we read about how "the Lord routed the Egyptians in the midst of the sea" (Exod. 14:27), how "the Lord saved Israel that day from the hand of the Egyptians" (Exod. 14:30), and how "Israel saw the great work which the Lord did against the Egyptians" (Exod. 14:31). It is small wonder that Moses, instead of singing a song exalting a human warrior in the manner of classical epic, leads the people in a song that praises God (Exod. 15). It is also interesting that God appears in the role of epic warrior, as indicated by the statement, "The Lord is a man of war" (Exod. 15:3).

The great disparity between God and man is emphasized not only by exalting God but also by exposing the unworthiness of the Israelites. The latter are depicted in the story as chronic complainers. When the Egyptian army approaches, they say to Moses, "Is it because there are no graves in Egypt that you have taken us away to die in the wilderness? What have you done to us, in bringing us out of Egypt?... For it would have been better for us to serve the Egyptians than to die in the wilderness" (Exod. 14:11-12). When they discover the bitter waters at Marah, they are said to have "murmured against Moses" (Exod. 15:24). Lacking meat, they "murmured against Moses and Aaron" and hankered after "the fleshpots" of Egypt (Exod. 16:2-3). When they lack water at Rephidim, they are reported to have "found fault with Moses" (Exod. 17:2). On another occasion they wept and said, "O that we had meat to eat! We remember the fish we ate in Egypt for nothing, the cucumbers, the melons, the leeks, the onions, and the garlic" (Num. 11:4-5). In short, the Israelites respond to physical hardship by displaying a lack of contentment with what God has sent, inability to live without luxuries, a complaining spirit, and unwillingness to postpone gratification until they reach the promised land.

The consistently unflattering view of the narrator's own nation involves specifically spiritual sins as well as their complaining spirit. When God sends quail and manna, making it a test of obedience (Exod. 16:4-5), the people fail the test by showing themselves guilty of greed (Exod. 16:20) and desecration of the sabbath (Exod. 16:25-29). When Moses' return from the mountain is delayed, the Israelites resort to idolatry (Exod. 32). There are rebellions against legitimate authority, led by Miriam and Aaron on one occasion

(Num. 12) and by Korah, Dathan, and Abiram on another occasion (Num. 16). The Israelites' supreme venture in shameful behavior occurs when they display a lack of faith by accepting the report of the ten spies who advise against entering the promised land (Num. 13-14). Even Moses, the highly idealized epic leader, is guilty of pride, impatience, and disobedience when he strikes the rock at Meribah instead of speaking to it (Num. 20:2-13).

As this survey of events suggests, the human record in the Epic of the Exodus is almost uniformly disastrous. At one point God speaks of how the people "have put me to the proof these ten times and have not hearkened to my voice" (Num. 14:22). If one goes back over the story, he will discover ten occasions when the Israelites as a whole are said to murmur against God, against God's chosen leaders, or against the circumstances into which God has brought them. It turns out to be a list of most of the key events that have been recorded.[2] Whatever glory there is in the epic belongs to God, who repeatedly contends with human sinfulness and leads the Israelites to Canaan in spite of themselves. This anti-epic theme reaches its culmination in the song that Moses sings shortly before his death (Deut. 32), a song that praises God's faithfulness and dispraises Israel's waywardness. The song has the whole weight of the previous story behind it and is the logical terminus of the anti-epic motif in the Epic of the Exodus.

The Epic of the Exodus opens on a note of international conflict (Exod. 1). The conflict is precipitated by several things, including the death of Joseph, the ascent of a new Egyptian king, and remarkable growth in the Jewish population. The conventional epic theme of conflict between rival nations takes the form of villainous taskmasters, an oppressed minority, and a monstrous plan of genocide. The midwives' refusal to kill the male Jewish babies is the earliest record of legitimate civil disobedience in biblical literature, and the statement that "God dealt well with the midwives" (Exod. 1:20) alerts us to the fact that from the beginning God is the chief character in the epic.

---

[2] The incidents are as follows: the oppression by the slavemasters in response to Moses' early activity (Exod. 5:20-21); the Red Sea crisis (Exod. 14:10-12); the bitter waters of Marah (Exod. 15:24); the lack of food near Elim (Exod. 16:2-3); the disobedience regarding the gathering of manna (Exod. 16:20, 27); the lack of water at Rephidim (Exod. 17:2-3); the golden calf incident (Exod. 32); the complaining at Taberah (Num. 11:1); the craving for meat (Num. 11:4-5); and the unbelief of the ten spies (Num. 13-14).

The birth and early life of the hero are also part of the exposition of the plot. The death-rebirth story surrounding Moses' infancy (Exod. 2:1-10) is the first archetype in a story replete with archetypes.[3] To dramatize the early identity of the hero, the storyteller has chosen two representative incidents — Moses' killing of an Egyptian who was beating a Hebrew (Exod. 2:11-15) and his coming to the aid of the shepherdesses who were mistreated by domineering shepherds (Exod. 2:15-22). These two episodes show the epic protagonist to be a man of decisive action and a champion of oppressed people.

God's call and equipping of Moses (Exod. 3-4) complete the preliminary phase of the action. The appearance of God in a burning bush dramatizes both his immanence and his transcendent holiness (Exod. 3:1-6). The goal of the epic quest is clearly established when God states that he will bring the Israelites out of Egypt "to a good and broad land, a land flowing with milk and honey" (Exod. 3:8; cf. also vs. 17). Scattered references throughout the story to a promised land flowing with milk and honey keep the goal of the quest in the consciousness of the reader. The reluctance of the epic hero to undertake a role of leadership and his total reliance on God invert the usual epic concept of the self-reliant hero. The prominence of God is reinforced by his assertions of authority, such as "I will send you" (Exod. 3:10) and "I will be with you" (Exod 3:12), and by the use of exalted epithets, or titles, such as "The Lord, the God of your fathers, the God of Abraham, the God of Isaac, and the God of Jacob" (Exod. 3:15; 4:5). God's self designation, "I AM WHO I AM" (Exod. 3:14), keeps alive a sense of His transcendence and mystery.

The crossing of the Red Sea (Exod. 14) is the first major event of the journey and in a number of ways epitomizes the entire trip to Canaan. The episode is centered in a crisis, consisting of the Israelites' precarious position between the Red Sea and the approaching Egyptian army. Faced with a test of their faith, the Israelites fail the test miserably, as they always do, by complaining to Moses. Moses, in turn, calls on God, who effects a miraculous deliverance. This pattern of crisis–complaint–divine deliverance will recur throughout the remainder of the story.

Following the initiation into the rigors of the journey and God's miraculous deliverance at the Red Sea, the story follows the journey motif until the Israelites reach Mt. Sinai. The journey of the Israelites has many similarities to the stories of journeying people in such epics as *The Odyssey* and *The Aeneid*. There are conflicts with the natural environment, with antagonistic countries or tribes, and with elements

---

[3] Other stories of infants rescued from the water are cited by Theodor H. Gaster, *Myth, Legend, and Custom in the Old Testament* (New York: Harper and Row, 1969), pp. 225-29.

of rebellion within the traveling community itself. Monotony is the great narrative pitfall that a storyteller must avoid in this kind of story, and the writer of the Epic of the Exodus succeeds magnificently in providing variety of adventure. There are moments of suffering interspersed with moments of relief. Some episodes are narrated briefly, while others are developed more leisurely and in greater detail. Above all, there is the repeated interpenetration of the divine world into the human, earthly realm. All in all, we might say that the journey presents the epic spectacle of man confronting certain elemental aspects of his experience.

The series of crises that comprise the journey illustrates the pervasive theme of biblical literature that man's responses to historical events are the basic issue of his life. Every external crisis presents the Israelites with an opportunity to complain against their predicament or trust God to deliver them. Sadly, in all of the recorded incidents the Israelites repudiate God and resort to complaint. If we keep in mind that biblical writers intend to present the reader with evidence of his own moral tendencies, we will realize that the failure of the Israelites is a comment on fallen human nature.

The incident involving the bitter waters of Marah (Exod. 15:22-26) illustrates these generalizations. The crisis is very dire — not simply disappointment but disappointment after the triumph of the Red Sea deliverance, and not simply the deprivation of water but the presence of water that tantalizes by not being drinkable. The people use the crisis only as an opportunity to repudiate God and Moses, whereas God intended it as an occasion for revelation. The revelation occurs when God makes the waters sweet, after which we read, "There the Lord . . . proved them, saying, 'If you will diligently hearken to the voice of the Lord your God . . . I will put none of the diseases upon you which I put upon the Egyptians; for I am the Lord, your healer' " (Exod. 15:25-26). These words establish God's willingness to save, the conditional nature of His salvation, the necessity for obedience, and the status of life as a test. The tragedy is that the Israelites fail to measure up to these realities.

The manna that God sends as bread to the Israelites has symbolic as well as literal significance. As God's provision for the daily physical needs of His people, it symbolizes His providential concern for His earthly creatures. But there is another level of symbolism as well. The manna tasted "like wafers made with honey" (Exod. 16:31). The symbolism becomes apparent when we are also told that "they ate the manna, till they came to the border of the land of Canaan" (Exod. 16:35). The manna was an anticipation which pointed forward to the promised land flowing with milk and honey.

When the Israelites reach Mt. Sinai, the epic is interrupted and all but swallowed up with descriptions of various civil, ceremonial, and moral laws, and the rules governing the tabernacle. This break in the narrative flow is an index to how biblical epic differs from traditional literary epic. For one thing, biblical epic has a far stronger didactic impulse. All epics have some desire to teach and inform, but the Epic of the Exodus carries this all out of proportion, both from the standpoint of traditional epic and narrative unity. Moreover, the mass of space devoted to the giving of the law reveals the essentially religious nature and purpose of biblical literature. The Bible is above all a religious book. Its literary portions represent literature governed by a religious purpose. Nowhere is a biblical writer bound by what are literary considerations. His devotion is first of all to his religious intention. This explains, I believe, why we find so much obviously religious, nonliterary material embedded in the middle of the Epic of the Exodus.

The experience at Sinai is essentially an encounter with God, and God's appearance is impressive. The people are told to consecrate themselves and wash their garments in awe of God's appearance (Exod. 19:10, 14). God's descent to the top of the mountain occurs initially on the climactic third day (Exod. 19:11). There is a death penalty for touching the mountain (Exod. 19:12-13). The appearance of God is associated with the awesome aspects of nature — thunder, lightning, fire, and earthquake (Exod. 19:16). There is a thick cloud on the mountain (Exod. 19:16), which is also wrapped in smoke (Exod. 19:18), thereby veiling God and distancing Him from direct view. God is also distanced when He tells Moses, "You cannot see my face; for man shall not see me and live. . . . Behold, there is a place by me where you shall stand upon the rock; and while my glory passes by I will put you in a cleft of the rock, and I will cover you with my hand until I have passed by" (Exod. 33:20-22). And when Moses comes down after talking to God on the mountain, his face shines (Exod. 34:29-35). These and other details maintain God's mysterious and awesome transcendence.

Although most of the Mosaic laws are recorded in expository form, the Ten Commandments (Exod. 20:1-17) are written in a highly artistic form.[4] One might well ask, Why have the Ten Commandments been remembered through the centuries, while the mass of Mosaic laws have failed to become embedded in our cultural and

---

[4] In addition to the elements of literary form that I discuss, the Ten Commandments display a similarity to the form of international suzerainty treaty, or vassal treaty, found in the ancient Near East. For a complete discussion, see Meredith G. Kline, *Treaty of the Great King* (Grand Rapids: Eerdmans Publishing Company, 1963), pp. 13-26.

religious consciousness in the same way? One answer is that the Ten Commandments are literary in a way the other rules usually are not.

The Ten Commandments are replete with such elements of artistic form as ordered recurrence, variation, balance, pattern, contrast, and centrality. Recurrence according to a discernible order is evident in the series of ten main commandments, each phrased as a command and eight of the ten beginning with the repeated formula, "You shall not." Variation is played off against this recurrence by the interspersing of long and short commands (1 is short, 2 is long, 3 is short, 4 is long, 5-9 are short, 10 is long). Balance is present by virtue of the fact that there are four commands dealing with man's relationship to God and six dealing with man's relationship to his fellow man. Pattern can be seen in the way in which the negative and positive statements unfold in an A-B-A sequence (1 to 3 are negative, 4 and 5 are positive, 6 to 10 are negative). The fact that there is a total of ten commandments conveys a sense of completeness. Contrast is also present, since for each command there is an implied contrast between the pattern of conduct described in the command and its opposite. Each command sets up the possibility for choice between two ways of life. The Decalogue employs the artistic device of centrality, much as a painting does, with the concept of law the focal point around which the individual parts are arranged.

There are several important themes in the Decalogue as a whole. One of these is the sovereignty of God. God is the one who gives the laws and who speaks all of the words. The commandments bear the imprint of God's moral character and are a concrete expression of what He is like. The Ten Commandments are presented as a summary of God's will for human life, and they accordingly begin with a call to God-centered living.

A second overriding theme is the moral responsibility of man. The Decalogue is a call to righteous living before both God and society. It is a testimony to the fact that man, in the biblical view, is a moral creature. The Decalogue, moreover, sets up the unavoidable state of human life — a choice between good and evil, which is at the same time a choice for or against God. It is a variation of the great theme of the Bible — the spiritual warfare between darkness and light.

A third theme is what I shall call the beauty of order. The Ten Commandments affirm that life, as it was meant to be lived, is a law-bound life. There are certain spiritual and moral rules inherent in the universe, just as there are physical laws. Personal and social freedom are gained only as man recognizes the moral order that exists and is violated with such miserable results. The very form of the Decalogue, with its clear design and firm sense of structure, embodies the concept of order.

The Ten Commandments are also unified by the theme of love — love to God and love to man. Jesus himself gave this summary of the Old Testament law (including the Ten Commandments) when He said that the "great commandment" is this: "You shall love the Lord your God with all your heart, and with all your soul, and with all your mind. This is the great and first commandment. And a second is like it, You shall love your neighbor as yourself. On these two commandments depend all the law and the prophets" (Matt. 22:37-40).

It is important to realize that the commandments are not presented as the means by which man can be justified before God. They are the response, made in love, to what God has done for His people. The prologue (Exod. 20:2) makes this clear. In it God calls attention to His status as the God of His people and as the one who has already delivered them. This is the context for what follows. Gratitude, not self-justification, is the keynote of the Decalogue.

As is true of most biblical literature, the Ten Commandments display a thrust outward from the particular to the general, from the event or act to a spiritual meaning behind it. Thus, although each commandment speaks directly to a specific act, it implies a general principle that can be applied to any area of life. Like literature generally, it combines the particular and the universal. Thus if one goes down the list of ten commandments, he will find the following principles expressed in shorthand fashion: (1) God's uniqueness and supremacy (the specific command is "no other gods"); (2) God's spirituality and concern for proper worship (no graven image); (3) the dignity of God's name and being (not taking His name in vain); (4) God's claim to the creature's time and His concern with the sabbath as a sign of His covenant relationship (keeping the sabbath day holy);[5] (5) recognition of legitimate authority (honoring of parents); (6) reverence for life (no murder); (7) the sanctity of marriage, the home, and human sexuality (no adultery); (8) respect for property (no stealing); (9) honesty (no false witness); (10) contentment (avoidance of covetousness). The movement from the particular to the general is also evident in the fact that although the commandments are first of all matters of personal living, they have a communal application and are the foundation for a whole society of people as well as for the individual.

---

[5] The following Old Testament passages stress that sabbath observance was a sign of God's covenant relationship with the believing community: "Wherefore the people of Israel shall keep the sabbath, observing the sabbath throughout their generations, a perpetual covenant" (Exod. 31:16); "Moreover I gave them my sabbaths, as a sign between me and them, that they might know that I the Lord sanctify them" (Ezek. 20:12); ". . . hallow my sabbaths that they may be a sign between me and you, that you may know that I the Lord am your God" (Ezek. 20:20).

Moses' ascent to the mountain to receive supernatural revelation is full of archetypal significance. The mountaintop as a place of encounter with the supernatural is apparently based on the principle that physically a mountain is the point at which earth touches heaven. Other examples of the archetype in the Bible include Abraham's act of obedience on Mt. Moriah (Gen. 22), the deaths of Aaron (Num. 20:28) and Moses (Deut. 34:1-6) on a mountain, Samuel's sacrifice on "the high place" (1 Sam. 9:11-14), God's sending of fire on Mt. Carmel and Elijah's ascent to the mountaintop to pray after the event (1 Kings 18:19-42), Elijah's meeting with God on a mountain (1 Kings 19:9-12), the building of the temple on "Mt. Zion," Christ's transfiguration on "a high mountain" (Matt. 17:1-8), and Christ's ascension into heaven from the Mount of Olives (Acts 1:6-12). The initiation of the epic hero into a supernatural realm of experience, from which he returns instructed and equipped to fulfill his mission as leader, is also an archetype. Parallels include Odysseus' journey to Hades, Aeneas' similar journey to the underworld, Dante's journey through the realm of the dead, Red Cross Knight's interlude in the House of Holiness (Spenser's *Faerie Queene*), and Adam's vision of fallen history before his expulsion from the Garden of Eden in Milton's *Paradise Lost*.

The golden calf incident (Exod. 32-34) draws together a number of important concerns in the epic. Moses' delay in returning from the mountain is another in the series of crises that the Israelites experience. In typical fashion they use the crisis as an opportunity to repudiate God. Special irony stems from the fact that when the people resort to idolatry they violate the very law that Moses is in the process of receiving. Moses' intercession for the people before God confirms his role as mediator between the people and God, much as his breaking of the tables of stone captures in a vivid portrait his impetuousness against spiritual disorder. Aaron, by giving in to the people's evil demand for an idol (Exod. 32:22), emerges as a foil to Moses, the strong leader willing to take an unpopular stand. Finally, the episode shows again God's judgment against evil and His willingness to forgive sins and renew His covenant relationship (Exod. 32:25–33:6).

After a prolonged break in the narrative, the journey motif again comes to dominate the story, beginning in Numbers 10. The rebellion of Miriam and Aaron against the authority of Moses (Num. 12) not only shows God's judgment against a refusal to submit to legitimate authority but is also important to the characterization of Moses. The narrator asserts that "the man Moses was very meek, more than all men that were on the face of the earth" (Num. 12:3). Meekness would seem on the surface to be incompatible with the fact that Moses is so obviously an authority figure who withstands all challenges to his leadership and destroys the forces of evil. The paradox is resolved by the fact that Moses in himself is meek, even retiring, but bold in carrying out God's will and the obligations of his office. God's statement that He speaks with Moses "mouth to mouth, clearly, and not in dark speech" (Num. 12:8) shows Moses' spiritual rapport with God and is an authentication of his heroism.

The sending of the twelve spies into Canaan (Num. 13-14) precipitates yet another crisis of faith. The worthiness of the epic quest is verified when the spies return with the report that "we came to the land to which you sent us; it flows with milk and honey, and this is its fruit" (Num. 13:27). The ten spies who advise against invasion reduce the venture to a physical, military level and ignore their spiritual resources. Thus they conclude, "The people who dwell in the land are strong, and the cities are fortified and very large" (Num. 13:28). A contrast is provided by Joshua and Caleb, who exercise faith in God and realize their supernatural resources: "If the Lord delights in us, he will bring us into this land and give it to us ... the Lord is with us; do not fear them" (Num. 14:8-9). God's past acts of deliverance are the standard by which the unbelief of the people is exposed, as God Himself makes clear when He says to Moses, "And how long will they not believe in me, in spite of all the signs which I have wrought among them?" (Num. 14:11).

The archetypal death-rebirth pattern comes to dominate the epic when God punishes the unbelieving Israelites by forcing them to wander in the wilderness for forty years (Num. 14:26-35). From the death of a past nation rises the birth of a new nation, spiritually qualified to enter the promised land. The same motif of a nation reborn appears in Virgil's *Aeneid*.

The Epic of the Exodus, which began with an account of the hero's birth and early life, concludes with the story of his death (Deut. 32-34). Moses is allowed to see the promised land with his eyes but does not enter it because of his disobedience at Meribah (Num. 20:2-13). Like the hero in Virgil's *Aeneid,* Moses does not experience the attainment of the quest.

With the death of Moses, the Epic of the Exodus concludes. Its story has been unified by the life of its hero and by the single action of the journey from Egypt to Canaan. The conquest of the promised land, recounted in the book of Joshua, brings the quest to its fulfillment. Strictly considered, though, it is not part of the epic, which is the self-contained story of a journey and the life of a central hero. The story told in Joshua is additional to this unified narrative, and it has the more fragmented structure of a historical chronicle.

The city of Gaza looking west toward the sea, scene of one of Samson's great triumphs.

Biblical
Tragedy

5

I

Tragedy can be defined as a narrative form that depicts a movement from prosperity to catastrophe. Tragedy presents a fall — a change of fortune — and must be differentiated from anti-romance, which also deals with misery but does not present a movement from ideal experience to disaster. In tragedy the focus is on the tragic protagonist, who in premodern tragedy is a person of high social standing. Such a conventional tragic hero, usually a king, is greater than common humanity but subject to the natural order and to moral criticism. The important element in his high public position is not simply social eliteness but representative status. Ordinarily a tragic hero possesses something that can be called greatness of spirit. He is usually a good man with some weakness of character, and he is always to some extent sympathetic.

When we shift our attention from character to plot, it is at once evident that tragedy centers around the action that the tragic protagonist undertakes. If the protagonist is a passive victim, the result is pathos, not tragedy. Usually the tragic action begins with the protagonist facing a dilemma. He is drawn in two or more directions and must make a moral choice. This means that a tragic hero is always responsible for his downfall, since he has made the tragic choice. Usually the tragic hero is also deserving of his catastrophe, with his fall stemming from some frailty of character. Some tragic protagonists are more deserving of their fall than others, but all are responsible for it by reason of their having acted in moral choice.

The protagonist's tragedy is usually related to the tragic world in which he operates. His tragic act may even be a good one in another set of circumstances. This emphasis on the tragic world means that the tragedy is a combination of free choice and cosmic determinism. The hero acts freely, at least initially, but the consequences of his actions bind him. He often acts in ignorance of the real nature of the forces at work in the tragic world and in ignorance of the consequences of his actions. The tragic hero is thus both an agent and a victim of his tragedy. In the catastrophe that follows his defeat the tragic hero often attains a kind of victory, usually consisting of moral or intellectual perception on his part.

To summarize, tragedies tend to unfold according to the following tragic pattern of action: dilemma–choice–catastrophe–suffering–perception–death. A given tragedy may omit one or more of these phases, but the pattern is remarkably consistent. Tragedy can be defined as a narrative form of literature in which a protagonist of high degree and greatness of spirit undertakes an action (makes a choice) within a given tragic world and as a result inevitably falls from prosperity to a state of physical and spiritual suffering, sometimes attaining perception.

Biblical tragedy begins with Genesis 3, the story of the fall. This story is, in fact, the archetypal tragedy — the source and model of all later tragedies. As a model, it contains virtually all the ingredients of later biblical tragedies. The characters, Adam and Eve, are prominent and representative figures. They operate in a world that demands moral choice, which is a choice to obey or disobey God. The issues are clearly defined before the test comes. The tragic choice consists of disobedience to God, with the tragic protagonist being both responsible for and deserving of his downfall. The tragic choice sets into motion tragic consequences, controlled by a sovereign God and involving big cosmic forces that overwhelm the tragic hero. Finally, here as elsewhere in biblical tragedy, the reader is left with the feeling that the tragic hero is thoroughly the agent of his own downfall and does not achieve grandeur in his fall.

II

The tragedy of Saul (1 Sam. 8-11; 13:8-15; 15-16; 18; 24; 26; 28; 31) follows the customary tragic pattern. The fact that the story does not occupy a consecutive series of chapters in 1 Samuel is not evidence that the story is something other than a tragedy. The tragedy of Saul is mingled with the ascent of David, whose story occupies the intervening chapters. The details dealing with Saul have been selected by the storyteller on the basis of tragic form. Saul, being a king, has both social prominence and representative status. He is a man of dual allegiance — toward faith in God and a tendency to take things into his own power in the immediacy of the moment. His tragedy has a prelude in which his dual tendency is established and is then concentrated in a single moment of choice (ch. 15), which is invested with the character of a test. At root, Saul's tragedy is a tragedy of disobedience and rebellion against God.

Saul's story begins with the idealization of the tragic protagonist. His exalted status is partly a matter of impressive appearance, as evidenced by the statement that Saul was "a handsome young man. There was not a man among the people of Israel more handsome than he; from his shoulders upward he was taller than any of the people" (9:2). Saul's spiritual endowment by God complements his physical prominence. He is anointed by Samuel (10:1), after which he was "turned into another man" (10:6). Elsewhere we read that "God gave him another heart" (10:9) and that "the spirit of God came mightily upon Saul" (11:6). The incident of Saul's hiding among the baggage to avoid the attention he would receive on the occasion of his crowning completes his characterization by establishing his modesty as a person.

The first recorded act of wickedness in Saul's story is his intrusion of himself into the priestly office by offering the burnt offering instead of waiting for Samuel to arrive and perform the act (13:8-15). When Samuel arrives on the scene, he rebukes Saul with the statement, "You have done foolishly; you have not kept the commandment of the Lord your God, which he commanded you" (13:13). Samuel here identifies the essential nature of Saul's act as disobedience to God. In terms of the overall design of the tragic story, this incident is part of the background of the tragedy. It gives the reader his first glimpse into the tragic flaw of character that constitutes the deficiency of the hero and which will figure in his eventual downfall. Already here there is a conflict within Saul between expediency and obedience to God. Saul is faced with the option of acting in obedience to a spiritual set of values or doing what seems most immediately expedient. Pulled in these two directions, he makes the wrong choice.

The tragic choice of Saul is narrated in 1 Samuel 15 and concerns his disobedience of God's command to destroy everything belonging to the Amalekites. As always in biblical tragedy, the proper mode of behavior is clearly defined for the protagonist, making his wrong choice inexcusable. Samuel tells Saul, "Now go and smite Amalek, and utterly destroy all that they have; do not spare them, but kill both man and woman, infant and suckling, ox and sheep, camel and ass" (vs. 3). Having been characterized earlier as a man of piety and expediency, Saul now chooses the wrong set of values and spares the best of the spoils. There is even a touch of hubris (overweening pride) in Saul's act of setting up "a monument for himself" (vs. 12). Like many another tragic protagonist, Saul begins to lose touch with reality as his character disintegrates. He greets Samuel with the words, "I have performed the commandment of the Lord" (vs. 13).

97

Although the earlier action has made it clear that "Saul and the people" spared the best of the animals (vs. 9), Saul attempts to shift the blame by saying, "They have brought them from the Amalekites; for the people spared the best of the sheep and of the oxen" (v. 15). Samuel summarizes in poetic form the tragic norm by which the action of Saul is blameworthy (15:22-23):

> *Behold, to obey is better than sacrifice,*
> *   and to hearken than the fat of rams.*
> *For rebellion is as the sin of divination,*
> *   and stubbornness is as iniquity and idolatry.*
> *Because you have rejected the word of the Lord,*
> *   he has also rejected you from being king.*

The decline of Saul is given a spiritual dimension, just as his earlier prosperity had been defined in terms of God's spiritual endowment. We read that "the Spirit of the Lord departed from Saul, and an evil spirit from the Lord tormented him" (16:14). This is the effect of Saul's tragic choice, the outworking of his rejection of God. It constitutes the huge cosmic force that begins to overpower the tragic hero. The same motif appears again when the spirit of Samuel tells Saul at Endor, "The Lord has turned from you and become your enemy.... Because you did not obey the voice of the Lord,... therefore the Lord has done this thing to you this day" (28:16, 18). The tragic hero's downfall is initiated by choice but comes to involve overpowering supernatural forces as well.

Saul's disintegration of character is displayed mainly in his insane jealousy of David. David's refusal to kill Saul on two occasions serves as a foil to Saul's tragic decay, and David's unwillingness to do the expedient thing contrasts with Saul's earlier succumbing to the ethic of expediency. Saul's visit to the witch at Endor (28:3-19) shows the degeneration and perversion of his spiritual sense, and his disguising himself (28:8) becomes an external symbol of his loss of his earlier identity. Saul's end, when he commits suicide, is as pathetic as that of any biblical character (31:4) and his body is fastened to a wall in an enemy city (31:10).

Another biblical tragedy that fits the typical pattern is the story of Solomon (1 Kings 2-4, 7-11). As a king, Solomon is a representative figure for the culture in which he lived. He possesses character traits that make him capable of developing in two different ways. On the one hand, he is a man of superhuman wisdom, piety, obedience to

God, and prayer. But from the beginning he marries pagan wives, loves material splendor, and tolerates idolatrous modes of worship. Over a lifetime Solomon gradually slips into a life dominated by the second set of qualities, and therein lies his tragedy.

Solomon is characterized early in his story as a complex mixture of good and bad qualities. The negative note includes his marriage to a daughter of King Pharaoh in violation of God's command (3:1) and his practice of sacrificing at the high places, a pagan practice (3:3). The positive aspect of his character is summarized by the statement that "Solomon loved the Lord, walking in the statutes of David his father" (3:3).

The idealization of the tragic hero is seen most clearly in the story of Solomon's choice of what he desires from God (3:5-14). In this dream encounter with God, the king chooses "an understanding mind" (vs. 9). The story dramatizes a scale of values, with wisdom shown to be superior to wealth, long life, and conquest. Poetic justice occurs when God rewards Solomon's virtue in choosing understanding by also giving him the things for which he did not ask. The climax of this important event in the protagonist's life comes when God outlines the alternatives open to Solomon. God tells Solomon, "If you will walk in my ways, keeping my statutes and my commandments, as your father David walked, then I will lengthen your days" (3:14). Solomon's wisdom is dramatized by the famous story of how he determined the true mother of a disputed baby by suggesting that the baby be cut in half (3:16-28).

The history of Solomon's life is described by the narrator in generally positive terms. His political prominence (4:1-28) is a mark of his success as a ruler. His wisdom, a gift from God, is also part of his heroic status (4:29-34). His piety emerges from his building of God's temple (chs. 5–7) and his impressive prayer when the temple is dedicated (ch. 8). Solomon's prosperity appears at its greatest when he is visited by the queen of Sheba (10:1-13), who is led to exclaim, "Behold, the half was not told me; your wisdom and prosperity surpass the report which I heard" (10:7). And yet Solomon's life ends in tragedy. By concentrating so much attention on the good qualities of the tragic hero, the narrator arouses the reader's interest in the causes of his unlikely tragedy.

Solomon's tragic choice is unusual on several counts. It is more complex than is true of most tragedies, consisting of his love of many wives (11:3), a perversion of the intimacy of married love; his marriage of foreign women (11:1), a deliberate violation of God's injunction against marrying pagan wives (11:2); and his sacrifice of the pure worship of God to the idolatrous paganism of his wives (11:4-8). The tragedy is also atypical in that it is not an instantaneous, temporally localized choice. We read that "when Solomon was old" he turned against God (11:4). Combined with earlier details in the story, we can infer a picture of gradual acquiescence with evil. The writer of the tragedy of Solomon does not present the tragedy as an isolated act of the will. He is interested not in the moment of sensuality and materialism and idolatry but in the lifelong habit of weakness for women, love of splendor, and idolatry. It is a vision different from that of most tragedians but no less profound.

The tragic consequences in the story of Solomon involve, as we expect, God's exercise of His moral justice. We read that "the Lord was angry with Solomon, because his heart had turned away from the Lord ..., who had appeared to him twice, and had commanded him concerning this thing, that he should not go after other gods" (11: 9-10). Appropriate to Solomon's political status, his tragic end involves the ascent of political adversaries and the disintegration of his kingdom (11:13-25).

IV

The story of Samson (Judges 13–16) is one of the most complex stories in biblical literature. It is both a tragedy and a heroic folk narrative. The hero is both criticized and celebrated. The result is that most of the episodes in the story have an ambivalent interpretation, depending on whether the event is viewed from the perspective of Samson as a tragic figure or a folk hero. Samson's tragedy centers in his repeated violation of his Nazirite vow to God. The story of his heroism centers in his superhuman strength, which makes him a deliverer of his nation from the enemy Philistines.

Like other tragic heroes of biblical literature, Samson has as great a potential as can be imagined. His birth is foretold by an angel (13:3) and he is a Nazirite to God from birth (13:5). The prohibitions prescribed for a Nazirite (13:4) set Samson apart from his society. As is typical of tragic protagonists, Samson is greater than ordinary humanity. His prominence, like that of Saul, has a strongly spiritual identity, as evidenced by the statements that "the boy grew, and the Lord blessed him" (13:24) and "the Spirit of the Lord began to stir him" (13:25).

The first recorded event in Samson's life, his marriage to the Philistine woman of Timnah (14:1-4), illustrates the ambivalence that pervades the entire story. The tragic element in Samson's command to his parents to get the Philistine woman as his wife, "for she pleases me well" (14:3), resides in the fact that he allows his personal, sexual desire for a pagan woman to overcome God's command to keep himself separate from spiritual perversion. Furthermore, when Samson gives in to his wife's tears and entreaties by telling her the answer to the riddle he posed at the wedding feast (14:17), he already exhibits the tragic weakness that will eventually destroy him. But from the perspective of heroic narrative, the event is a positive one, since it led to the destruction of thirty enemies after Samson's riddle was guessed (14:10-19). It is because God used the marriage for the deliverance from the Philistines that the narrator counters the objections of Samson's parents to the marriage with the statement that "his father and mother did not know that it was from the Lord" (14:4).

A similar ambiguity is present in other events in the story. Samson's use of three hundred foxes to burn the fields of the Philistines (15:4-8) is an abuse of his strength in an act of ignoble personal vengeance. But when put into the context of international warfare between the Philistines and Israelites, the event becomes another example of military deliverance by a national hero. Samson's tragic flaw of sensuality is seen in his promiscuity with the harlot at Gaza (16:1), but the tragic aspect of the episode is again balanced by the heroic act of Samson's carrying off the heavy gates of the city (16:3).

The central event in the tragedy of Samson is his love for Delilah and the accompanying disclosure of the secret of his strength (16:4-17). The episode gains added force because it so closely parallels the earlier story of his marriage to the woman of Timnah. The temptation that ends finally in Samson's tragedy unfolds in four episodes, each following a common pattern: Delilah pleads with Samson (vss. 6, 10, 13, 15); Samson responds (vss. 7, 11, 13, 17); Delilah betrays Samson (vss. 8, 12, 14, 19); Samson exerts himself (vss. 9, 12, 14, and omitted in the last episode). The essence of the tragedy is that by divulging the secret of his strength Samson violates his Nazirite vow, which prescribed that "no razor shall come upon his head" (13:5). The catastrophe occurs when God leaves Samson (16:20), and the tragic suffering takes the form of Samson's having his eyes gouged out and being made a slave in the mill (vs. 21).

In literature generally a tragedy is likely to conclude on a dualistic note, with the hero's fall counterbalanced to a degree by some kind of moral or intellectual victory that he seizes from his experience. Biblical tragedy tends to break this pattern, since the tragic hero is not ennobled by his suffering. The tragedy of Samson is an exception. Its conclusion preserves the ambivalence found elsewhere in the story by making the final event both a tragedy and a triumph. On the physical plane, the tragic hero is defeated, being brought to a premature death by pulling the temple of Dagon upon himself. But as a national hero Samson achieves his greatest victory, since "the dead whom he slew at his death were more than those whom he had slain during his life" (16:30). The triumph is spiritual as well as military, for it is an answer to Samson's prayer (16:28) and demonstrates his renewed rapport with God.

There are few characters in biblical literature as paradoxical as Samson. He is the archetypal example of the strong man who uses his strength for personal ends and whose sensual appetites and weakness for bad women are appalling. But he is also one of the great folk heroes of Hebrew literature, renowned for using his strength in God's service and listed in the honor roll of the heroes of faith in Hebrews 11 (vs. 32).

V

There has been widespread discussion among literary critics on the question of whether Christian tragedy can exist. A thorough survey of the issue is beyond the scope of this discussion, but I wish to emphasize that the example of biblical literature is a main and neglected repository of literary theory that will answer this and other questions about literature. The debate about Christian tragedy has tended, in my view, to be largely unsatisfactory, chiefly because critics have seized upon a limited aspect of tragedy or Christianity instead of taking a broad and flexible view.

A majority of critics deny that Christian tragedy is possible. Thus we read that "the chance of being saved destroys the tragic sense" and therefore "no genuinely Christian tragedy can exist,"[1] that "the least touch of any theology which has a compensating Heaven to offer the tragic hero is fatal,"[2] and that "it is a frank contradiction in terms to equate religious with tragic experience."[3] Other representative critics write that "the religion of the Bible is inimical to Tragedy,"[4] that "Christianity reverses the tragic view and makes tragedy impossible,"[5] and that "Christianity is intransigent to tragedy."[6]

---

[1] Karl Jaspers, *Tragedy Is Not Enough* (Boston: The Beacon Press, 1952), p. 38.

[2] I. A. Richards, *Principles of Literary Criticism* (New York: Harcourt, Brace and Company, 1934), p. 246.

[3] Una Ellis-Fermor, *The Frontiers of Drama* (London: Methuen and Company, 1945), pp. 17-18.

[4] D. D. Raphael, *The Paradox of Tragedy* (Bloomington: Indiana University Press, 1961), p. 51.

[5] Richard B. Sewall, *The Vision of Tragedy* (New Haven: Yale University Press, 1962), p. 50.

[6] Laurence Michel, "The Possibility of a Christian Tragedy," in *Thought* (1956), 427. Critics who argue for the possibility of Christian tragedy include Preston Roberts, "A Christian Theory of Dramatic Tragedy," in *The Journal of Religion*, XXXI (1951), 1-20; and Roger L. Cox, *Between Earth and Heaven:*

The partial vision inherent in these statements is obvious. It is true that Christianity is a message of redemption and hope. But for whom? Not for everyone, surely, nor even for the majority of mankind. In the biblical view, history is redemptive only for those who believe in God's forgiveness. Christianity is a religion of both redemption and judgment. It sets up the possibility for triumph through belief, but it does not make such triumph a universal fact. The Gospel's witness regarding Jesus is that "he who believes in the Son has eternal life; he who does not obey the Son shall not see life, but the wrath of God rests upon him" (John 3:36).

The question of whether tragedy is compatible with Christianity falls into two overriding questions. One is, "Is tragedy compatible with a Christian view of reality?" The second, more limited question is, "Can tragedy befall a redeemed believer in God?"

The question of whether tragedy is compatible with the Christian world view is immediately answerable in the affirmative by the presence of tragic narratives in the Bible. Christ himself told many tragic parables, a fact that by itself should have forestalled much of the debate about Christian tragedy. Such parables as those about the unprofitable servant whose sloth led him to be cast into outer darkness, the five foolish virgins whose lack of preparedness led to their exclusion from the messianic banquet, the wicked tenants who were thrust out of the vineyard, and the improperly dressed guest whose attendance at a wedding ended in his being cast into outer darkness clearly show the importance of the tragic vision to Christianity.[7] The stories of such figures as Adam and Eve, Saul, Solomon, Samson, Judas Iscariot, and many Old Testament kings lead to the same conclusion.

A consideration of the basic outlines of biblical doctrine likewise illuminates the issues. Tragedy presupposes a causal relationship between a character's actions and his destiny. The underlying principle of biblical teaching is that people can choose life or death, God or evil, and that events will depend on their moral choices. Paul summarizes the biblical principle that human choice determines human destiny when he writes, "whatever a man sows, that he will also reap" (Gal. 6:7). This principle opens the way for either a comic or tragic destiny. Jesus expressed a generally tragic view of human experience when He observed, "The gate is wide and the way is easy, that leads to destruction, and those who enter by it are many.

Shakespeare, Dostoevsky, and the Meaning of Christian Tragedy (New York: Holt, Rinehart and Winston, 1969), pp. 1-26.

[7] For a literary analysis of the tragic principles at work in some of the parables, see Dan Otto Via, Jr., *The Parables: Their Literary and Existential Dimension* (Philadelphia: Fortress Press, 1967), pp. 110-144.

For the gate is narrow and the way is hard, that leads to life, and those who find it are few" (Matt. 7:13-14) .

The possibility of redemption and glorification in heaven does not mitigate the fact of tragedy — on the contrary, it heightens the tragic effect in biblical tragedy. As Martin Jarrett-Kerr has said, "Only in a world where real tragedy is possible is redemption also possible. Perhaps the reverse is also true: only in a world where redemption — and therefore damnation too — is possible, is tragedy also possible."[8] Nonbiblical tragedy laments the physical death of its tragic heroes; Christian tragedy deepens the tragedy by lamenting the spiritual as well as the physical death of its protagonists. In the words of Jesus, "Do not fear those who kill the body but cannot kill the soul; rather fear him who can destroy both soul and body in hell" (Matt. 10:28) .

We have yet to ask, Can tragedy befall a redeemed believer? In an ultimate sense, it cannot. A recurrent emphasis of biblical teaching is that suffering is the gateway to victory, though it is doubtful whether suffering that is caused by moral error necessarily leads to glory. The assurance for the believer is that "we know that in everything God works for good with those who love him" (Rom. 8:28) .

In the short view, however, tragedy is certainly a part of the believer's experience. Although David was forgiven by God, his adultery with Bathsheba and murder of Uriah led to tragic consequences during his lifetime. The prodigal son of Christ's parable was restored to his father's favor, but he did not recover his squandered inheritance. Adam and Eve experienced God's restoration, but they were exiled from the Garden of Eden to endure the hardships of fallen reality. Moses continued to be God's chosen leader after his sin at Kadesh, but he did not enter the promised land. Samson ended his life in a state of renewed rapport with God, but his life also ended on a tragic note of premature death. The eventual victory of a tragic hero does not imply that his temporal tragedy is less than tragic. As Oscar Mandel states in his book *A Definition of Tragedy*, "The tragic situation is not necessarily the whole work of art. . . . It may occur as only one section of a larger piece." Despite ultimate redemption in Christian tragedies, "these stories are tragic; that is to say, the tragedy is consummated, regardless of what follows after."[9]

On both counts, then, Christian tragedy is possible, as seen from both biblical example and biblical doctrine. Christianity presupposes a possibility of either ultimate tragedy or ultimate victory, and it illustrates the possibility of temporal tragedy within a context of eventual salvation.

---

[8] *Studies in Literature and Belief* (London: Rockliff, 1954), p. 63.

[9] *A Definition of Tragedy* (New York: New York University Press, 1961), pp. 99, 160.

VI

Unfortunately the theoretic question of whether Christian tragedy is possible has obscured the more appropriate question, What is distinctive about biblical or Christian tragedy? To begin, biblical tragedy always has a strongly spiritual dimension. The tragic heroes begin not simply as prominent figures but also as spiritually outstanding characters. Their fall also takes on a spiritual meaning. If Greek tragedy presents variations on the common theme of hubris (pride), biblical tragedy can similarly be related to a single root issue, disobedience to the will and commands of God. This means that the tragic heroes of biblical literature are both responsible for and deserving of their fate. Their catastrophe does not seem disproportionate, since they have rebelled against a perfect God.

Greek tragedy is often said to be the tragedy of fate. The reader is left with the impression that the hero in Greek tragedy has been an unfortunate victim, either of the gods or of ignorance. In biblical tragedy the responsibility falls completely on the tragic protagonist. The issues are always clearly defined beforehand, so that the tragic hero knows what choice he should make. Circumstances may test the hero and make it understandable how he came to make his wrong choice. But in biblical tragedy the enemy is within and does not reside in the tragic world. Moral choice, not external constraint or ignorance, is the crux of the matter.

In biblical tragedy the tragic consequences differ greatly from the same phase of the tragic action elsewhere in literature. In Greek tragedy the hero is brought to defeat by some impersonal cosmic force that his tragic choice sets in motion. In biblical tragedy, the hero's tragic error brings him under the judgment of God, who administers a cosmic moral order. In Greek and Elizabethan literature, the powerlessness of the tragic hero as he struggles against overpowering odds generates a great deal of sympathy for him. The reader sympathizes with the suffering hero as opposed to the forces arrayed against him. In biblical tragedy, because a righteous God is the one who administers justice, this kind of sympathy for the suffering hero vanishes. The tragic heroes of biblical literature do not assume grandeur as they struggle against inevitable defeat. They disintegrate as characters as the Spirit of God departs from them. Biblical tragedy, in short, never allows us to forget that people who evoke our human pity for their plight can at the same time demand our moral judgment for their repudiation of God.

In Greek tragedy the ways of the gods often remain mysterious, and the hero is shown to have made his tragic choice without full awareness of the issues involved. In biblical tragedy the issues are clearly defined.[10] The tragic hero is inexcusable for his wrong choice because he violates clearly established commands of God. The impression left by classical tragedy is a pessimistic fear to do anything, since the gods might destroy a person for it. Biblical tragedy does not encourage such passivity, but is rather a challenge to obey God and choose His ways.

Perhaps the distinction between biblical and nonbiblical tragedy can be summed up by saying that in nonbiblical tragedy the tragic hero is, above all, the sympathetic tragic victim, while in biblical tragedy he is the unsympathetic sinner. The appropriate response in the first case is, Isn't it too bad that all this happened to the tragic hero? The appropriate response to biblical tragedy is, Isn't it too bad that he disobeyed God, when it might have been otherwise?[11]

---

[10] As Roberts states, in Christian tragedy "the tragic hero's problem is not primarily one of knowledge" ("Christian Theory of Dramatic Tragedy," p. 12).
[11] W. H. Auden, in "The Christian Tragic Hero," writes, "Greek tragedy is the tragedy of necessity; i.e., the feeling aroused in the spectator is 'What a pity it had to be this way'; Christian tragedy is the tragedy of possibility, 'What a pity it was this way when it might have been otherwise.' " — *Tragedy: Vision and Form,* ed. Robert W. Corrigan (San Francisco: Chandler Publishing Company, 1965), p. 143.

Part of Job's riches included "3000 camels" (Job 1:3).

The Book
of Job

6

I

The book of Job has been variously classified as wisdom literature, drama, and tragedy. Strictly speaking, it is none of these things. Although the speakers in the dialogue speak in poetry that sometimes draws upon conventional formulae of the wisdom literature tradition, the continuous narrative sweep of the work makes it much different from the collections of proverbs that constitute wisdom literature. Since much of the story consists of dialogue, there can be no doubt that it has a strong dramatic element, but it is not a drama. It is told by a narrator and was not intended for the stage. This makes it a narrative instead of a play. Much of the story is devoted to the tragic details in the life of Job, but the work as a whole is not a tragedy. The sequence of events makes up a comic plot, in the usual definition of that term (a U-shaped plot in which events begin in prosperity, descend into tragedy, and rise suddenly to a happy conclusion). The story also has a high incidence of lyric passages, in which various characters give an outpouring of personal emotion or reflection. And there is much use of descriptive poetry, especially in the form of portraits of various character types. To sum up, Job is a comic narrative comprised of elements of wisdom, drama, lyric, and tragedy.

The structure of the work can be looked at from several points of view. One element of structure is the comic, U-shaped plot. The story gives more attention to the tragedy than many comedies do. The usual comic pattern is to concentrate on the gradual conquest of obstacles to social integration and the gradual integration of the protagonist into his society. A comedy can, however, show the entire movement from prosperity through tragedy to restoration, and that is what the book of Job does.

The story is also structured like a modern problem play. A problem of philosophical nature is posed and various characters offer their solutions to the problem. At the end a definitive answer is established.

The plot is carefully and artistically structured, as follows:

Prologue (chapters 1-2)
Dialogue or debate (3-31)
  Job's lament (3)

Cycle 1 (4-14)	Cycle 2 (15-21)	Cycle 3 (22-27)
Eliphaz (4-5)	Eliphaz (15)	Eliphaz (22)
Job's reply (6-7)	Job's reply (16-17)	Job's reply (23-24)
Bildad (8)	Bildad (18)	Bildad (25)
Job's reply (9-10)	Job's reply (19)	Job's reply (26-27)
Zophar (11)	Zophar (20)	————
Job's reply (12-14)	Job's reply (21)	————

  Job's concluding monologue (28-31)
Elihu's speeches (32-37)
Confrontation between God and Job (38-42:6)
Epilogue (42:7-17)

There are several plot conflicts that assume importance. The assault of Satan against Job initiates the action. The conflict between Job and his friends accounts for the character conflict in the plot. There is a sense, too, in which early in the work Job is in conflict with God, protesting that God has mistreated him.

The setting of the story is generalized, so much so that its precise geographic location (the land of Uz) cannot be determined with certainty. Presumably, much of the dialogue occurs outdoors, where Job is pictured as sitting on the ash pile. Job is depicted as living both in the country (1:3, 13-17; 31:8, 20, 31, 38-40) and the city (29:7). There is reference to both house (1:4; 19:15; 42:11) and tent (31:31). The most logical conclusion is not that the story is a patch-work of earlier narratives but that Job is a seminomad, living in a walled city during some seasons of the year and migrating with his herds at other seasons.

The best approach to the theme of the work is to state the questions raised in the story and then use an inductive method of following the progress that the story makes in answering the questions. Three issues seem central to the story. (1) Why do the righteous suffer? (2) Is disinterested religion possible? Will man serve God "for naught" (i.e., without tangible, earthly, material benefits)? (3) What is God like? Is He just? sovereign? loving? From a philosophic point of view the work is a theodicy — a work that attempts to reconcile God's goodness and sovereignty with the existence of evil and suffering in the world. The usual tendency of theodicies is to vitiate either God's goodness or His sovereignty. To do either of these things is to violate the attributes of God as depicted in the Bible.

In terms of style, the story is not told with rapid narrative movement. Its pace is leisurely. There is little action, since the work consists mainly of philosophic dialogue. The style is poetically embellished. Parallelism pervades the poetic parts of the work, with most speakers repeating their statements, saying the same thing in different ways. To the detriment of an appreciation of this poem is most readers' desire to move quickly through the story, reading to get a glimpse of the main events in the plot. The writer obviously expects us to respect a leisurely pace and to relish the poetry rather than the sequence of events.

II

The story begins with an idealized description of the protagonist (1:1-5). There is no hint of anything negative in the account of this man who "was blameless and upright, one who feared God, and turned away from evil" (vs. 1). Job's care to sacrifice on behalf of his children, lest they had sinned "in their hearts" (vs. 5), shows his concern for inner holiness as well as outward righteousness, and the fact that he practiced his religion "continually" (vs. 5) further attests his good character. Job is also placed in a domestic setting in the opening paragraph. He is pictured as having a family and vast possessions. The description does more than establish Job's social prominence. To an audience accustomed to viewing God's reward of the righteous in very tangible terms the emphasis on family and possessions would be an outward sign of Job's spiritual integrity.

Following the introduction of the protagonist of the story, a supernatural context is established for the narrative by the dialogue in heaven between God and Satan. From one point of view God initiates the testing of Job by holding him up as a model of virtue (1:8). Satan's question, "Does Job fear God for nought?" (1:9), is an implied attack on the character of Job and God. It denies the reality of Job's faith in God, which is implied to be a way of buying God's favor, and it suggests that God cannot evoke genuine response from His creatures on the basis of His character but must buy their loyalty. Satan's challenge to God to destroy Job's domestic prosperity (1:11) lends suspense to the plot by raising the question of how Job will respond to the test. The fact that God prevents Satan from harming Job himself (1:12) shows that God does not relinquish His control of the universe but rather permits the suffering to occur.

In a memorable scene, Job's domestic world disintegrates (1:13-19). The scene unfolds visually, like a drama in miniature. It has four phases, like four hammer blows, as each of four messengers appears to describe an episode of woe. Job's response is to place his adversity in a supernatural context, even though he does not know all that has taken place in heaven: "Naked I came from my mother's womb, and naked shall I return; the Lord gave, and the Lord has taken away; blessed be the name of the Lord" (1:21).

The assault of Satan on Job and Job's patient acceptance of adversity are reinforced by a second episode (2:1-9) that virtually repeats the events of chapter 1. The conflict is intensified by virtue of the fact that the suffering is now extended to Job's body (vss. 4-5). Again God retains some control over the suffering of Job, as evidenced by His command to Satan to "spare his life" (vs. 6). This time Job's wife emerges in the story and serves as a foil. Her advice to "curse God and die" (vs. 9) makes her the kind of person who fits Satan's estimate of human nature.[1] Job's response to his wife is significant: "Shall we receive good at the hand of God, and shall we not receive evil?" (2:10). Job again insists that his experience comes from God, and he shows that he does not harbor any illusions about what life in a fallen world is like. The narrator's summary that "in all this Job did not sin with his lips" (2:10) is important because it continues the idealization of Job. As a result, the precise nature of the philosophic question of the work is well defined as concerning why *the righteous* suffer.

The prose prologue has been constructed on the principle of recurrence, which is evident in the repeated speeches and situations (including the dialogue in heaven, the testing of Job, and the patient response of Job). There has been much use of dialogue and descriptive detail as a means of achieving concreteness, and there has been significant interpenetration of the supernatural and earthly realms. So far as the overall design of the plot is concerned, the prologue sets up a leading narrative device that is present in the rest of the story, namely, dramatic irony, which stems from the fact that the reader now knows certain things of which the characters in the story are ignorant.

The greatest importance of the prologue, however, is the fact that it provides some answers to the problems raised in the work. The main question of the whole story is already given one answer: Job suffers because God is testing his faith. This means that Job's suffering has a purpose. Perhaps a second answer also emerges: Job suffers because God permits Satan to bring suffering into his life. This makes the permissive theory of evil (God allows suffering but is not its source) a basic principle underlying the whole story. By beginning the action in heaven, the prologue also alerts us to the fact that the problem of human suffering cannot be understood in a purely earthly or naturalistic context. Another theme is that God is in control of

---

[1] The advice of Job's wife is based on Leviticus 24:10-16, which prescribes death as the penalty for cursing God.

His world. Even evil can occur only within the broader context of His providence, and He never completely relinquishes His protection of Job. The prologue denies at the very outset of the story that suffering is necessarily a result of sin or a punishment for wrongdoing. The punitive concept of suffering does not apply to Job's situation, because the dialogue in heaven has established the fact of Job's innocence before God.

The dialogue that occupies most of the book is too lengthy to allow for detailed explication here. A few generalizations are important, however. The whole dialogue, which quickly turns into a debate, is conducted in ignorance of what has happened in the council in heaven. That council is part of the reader's conceptual background against which he measures the speeches, with the discrepancy resulting in dramatic irony. Job's friends, as well as Elihu (who speaks later), repeat a few common themes: suffering is a punishment that evil people bring upon themselves, Job has sinned and must repent if he wishes to be restored, God is just and cannot be blamed for man's suffering. The friends completely miss the question to which the book of Job calls such significant attention: why do *the righteous* suffer? They misconceive the question as being simply, Why do people suffer? The obtuseness of the friends means that we should not attach too much importance to their statements. Their monotonous and misguided arguments are merely the static background against which the development of Job stands out more clearly. The significant plot revolves around Job, and the speeches of the friends, which become increasingly hostile, only serve to elicit the growing perception of Job.

If we trace Job's development through the three cycles of the dialogue, we can see a clear and significant path of development. His opening lament (ch. 3) exhibits the utter despair in which he begins his philosophic quest for an answer to the problem of suffering. In the first cycle of speeches Job displays a negative view of the afterlife, which is regarded as threatening man with oblivion (3:17-19; 10:20-22; 14:7-22). God's transcendence and superiority to man are a source of despair, since they seem to Job to prove God's lack of concern for His creatures (ch. 9). Perhaps the main theme in Job's first series of speeches is his desire to be shown his sins: "Make me understand how I have erred" (6:24); "I desire to argue my case with God" (13:3); "Make me know my transgression and my sin" (13:23). An important question is whether Job does not evince a kind of pride and belligerence in protesting his innocence before God. In view of Job's repentance at the end of the story, it would appear that we are justified in regarding some of his early speeches in an unfavorable light. For example, on one occasion Job charges

that God's connection with man is a malignant thing and that
man would be better off with a God who pays no attention to him
(7:11-12, 17-20):

> *I will complain in the bitterness of my soul.*
> *Am I the sea, or a sea monster,*
> * that thou settest a guard over me?*
> *... What is man, that thou dost make so much of him,*
> * and that thou dost set thy mind upon him,*
> *dost visit him every morning,*
> * and test him every moment?*
> *How long wilt thou not look away from me. ...*
> *If I sin, what do I do to thee, thou watcher of men?*
> *Why hast thou made me thy mark?*

On another occasion Job charges God with cruelty when he says,
"Does it seem good to thee to oppress, to despise the work of thy
hands?" (10:3).

In the second cycle of speeches Job continues to display a partly
inadequate view of God. For example, we know from the prologue
that Job is wrong in charging that God has torn Job in His wrath
and hated him (16:9). In other ways, however, Job makes some
significant advances in the second phase of the dialogue. For one
thing, in chapter 21 Job completely dissociates suffering from the
fact of sin on the part of the sufferer. He appeals to experience to
support the idea that calamity and prosperity do not always come as
an automatic result of evil or goodness. This destroys one inaccurate
concept of the meaning of suffering.

The key passage in the second cycle is the following affirmation,
which begins with an exalted prelude in which Job expresses a desire
for the permanence of the mighty statement he is about to utter
(19:23-27):

> *Oh that my words were written!*
> * Oh that they were inscribed in a book!*
> *Oh that with an iron pen and lead*
> * they were graven in the rock for ever!*
> *For I know that my Redeemer lives,*
> * and at last he will stand upon the earth;*
> *and after my skin has been thus destroyed,*
> * then without my flesh I shall see God,*
> *whom I shall see on my side,*
> * and my eyes shall behold, and not another.*

One commentator has appropriately called this "Job's supreme venture of faith."[2] The main thrust of Job's affirmation is that in an

---

[2] Edgar Jones, *The Triumph of Job* (Naperville, Ill.: SCM Book Club, 1966),

afterlife with God he will be vindicated by God. Job does not know all the details, but he has attained a blessed hope. Throughout the first half of the story Job's conviction has been that God's justice must be discernible in history. No theodicy is very successful as long as it remains earthbound, because the truth is that God's justice is not always evident in history. By lifting his gaze beyond history, Job is making a most significant advance in his thinking and is providing a foreshadowing of the climactic appearance of God, who resolves the question of His justice by revealing Himself as the one who transcends the merely earthly and temporal.

In the last cycle of speeches the negative view of God is almost totally absent from the statements of Job, who now constantly calls upon God and wishes to be drawn close to Him. The sequence of increasing intimacy with God that underlies the development of Job dramatizes a main theme of the story — that suffering draws the believer into closer fellowship with God. Job now manifests a new humility before God and a new faith in the integrity of God's character (23:5, 7, 10):

> I would learn what he would answer me,
>   and understand what he would say to me. . . .
> There an upright man could reason with him,
>   and I should be acquitted for ever by my judge. . . .
> But he knows the way that I take;
>   when he has tried me, I shall come forth as gold.

Job concludes the third cycle of speeches with two impressive oratorical performances. One is the hymn to wisdom (ch. 28), an independent poem which in the context of the story is part of the final affirmation of Job and an anticipation of his encounter with God. In the poem Job lists a series of natural phenomena whose hidden source can be discovered by man (vss. 1-11). He then introduces a contrast by asserting that the hidden source of wisdom cannot be found by man. Instead, it resides with God: "it is not found in the land of the living" (vs. 13), being "hid from the eyes of all living" (vs. 21). On the positive side, "God understands the way to it, and he knows its place" (vs. 23). Job is here asserting that true wisdom and, by implication, the final answer to his philosophic questions about suffering come from a supernatural source. Moreover, when Job asserts the proposition that "the fear of the Lord, that is wisdom" (vs. 28), he foreshadows what he will experience concretely in the final encounter with God.

---

p. 89. I have found this book the most helpful commentary on Job, and my entire discussion is indebted to it.

Job's other triumph of eloquence is his great oath of innocence (ch. 31). An overpowering sense of climax is built up as an identical formula occurs fifteen times. The formula consists of an initial clause to this effect: "If I have done this evil...," and concludes with a curse to this effect: "...let this calamity befall me." The oath of innocence amounts to a description of the ethical standard by which Job has lived and includes his integrity in the areas of sexual purity (vss. 1, 9-10), honest dealing (vs. 7), treatment of servants (vs. 13), benevolence to the poor (vss. 16-23), use of money (vss. 24-25), idolatry (vss. 26-28), attitude toward enemies (vss. 29-30), hospitality (vss. 31-32), and confession of sins (vss. 33-34).

The climax of the book comes with the two speeches that God utters to Job (chs. 38-41). The first speech (38-39) is a series of rhetorical questions. The list has several noteworthy characteristics. It draws upon concrete images and pictures, mainly from nature. In chapter 39, for example, there are vignettes of the mountain goat (vss. 1-4), the wild ass (vss. 5-8), the wild ox (vss. 9-12), the ostrich (vss. 13-18), the horse (vss. 19-25), and the hawk (vss. 26-30). There is much figurative speech, as when the creation of the world is described in terms of architecture and construction (38:4-6) or clouds and darkness are viewed as a garment for the sea (38:9). The list concentrates on the mysterious aspects of nature, thereby conveying a sense of the mystery of God's transcendent ways. The result is that God's superior wisdom and understanding emerge, just as His second speech will describe His superior power. The real theme of the speech, conveyed by indirection, is the mighty acts of God. The focus shifts from Job, who ceases to be the center of the world of the story. Although Job has expressed a wish to bring God to trial, when God finally appears He takes the initiative in questioning Job, who is silent. There is also a remarkable reversal of expectation in the fact that God says nothing about Job's righteousness or lack of it, and the problem of Job's suffering is not even mentioned. We should also note that the topic of God's speech is not nature but the God of nature. Some readers have supposed that Job's consolation is a kind of mystical confrontation with nature. Nothing could be farther from the truth. His confrontation is with the God who is revealed in nature.

The second speech of God (chs. 40-41) is similar to the first in its use of nature as a means of suggesting God's transcendence. The two sections are a description of Behemoth, or the hippopotamus (40:15-24), and Leviathan, either a crocodile or a mythological sea beast (ch. 41).

On the surface, God's final speeches are irrelevant to the main concern of the story. They provide no apparent explanation to the problem of suffering. Instead they confront Job with a miscellany of facts. But by indirection they say a great deal about the main problem that has been raised. God's words from the whirlwind prove that He has used Job's suffering, not as a means of punishment, but as the occasion for a fuller revelation of Himself. Job has been drawn into a fuller experience with God and has received a new revelation of God's wisdom and power. The fact that God does not answer Job directly suggests yet another major theme: God's ways transcend man's ways, so that man cannot know everything. What he can do is exercise faith in God's character, knowing that God's understanding transcends his own.

The responses of Job to God's speeches bring to a conclusion his development as a character. His response to God's first speech is a humble submission to God's superior knowledge (40:4-5):

> Behold, I am of small account; what shall I answer thee?
> I lay my hand on my mouth.
> I have spoken once, and I will not answer;
> twice, but I will proceed no further.

Job's response to God's second speech carries his progress even further. There is now a note of repentance, which is understandable if we remember the belligerence of his early speeches: "I have uttered what I did not understand, things too wonderful for me, which I did not know" (42:3). Job's deepened experience of God is conveyed through the image of the greater reality of a visual scene over a sound that is heard: "I had heard of thee by the hearing of the ear, but now my eye sees thee" (42:5). The last statement that Job makes is, "I despise myself, and repent in dust and ashes" (42:6). What, we might ask, necessitates this repentance on the part of Job? The answer is that Job does not repent for a specific moral sin but because his view of God had been inadequate.

The epilogue (42:7-17) provides a comic conclusion to the story by showing Job's fortunes restored. This conclusion has been much abused and misunderstood. It comes as an anticlimax, and that is precisely its significance. The important thing in Job's life is his faith in God. His faith is shown to be capable of surviving both calamity and prosperity, and neither of these things is the really significant issue. Many commentators complain that the ending destroys the theme that disinterested religion is possible, but that theme has already been established as fully as it could be. The comic ending confirms the character of God, who is shown again to be a loving God who blesses His servants. After all, the whole idea of tormenting Job had been Satan's idea.

What answers has the work provided to the three main questions that it raises? The story has established several truths about the problem of why the righteous suffer. It shows that man cannot completely understand the meaning of suffering in the lives of blameless people. What he can know is that there is a transcendent God whose purposes, though inscrutable, can be trusted. Within this framework of limited knowledge, man can rest upon several certainties when he suffers. The book of Job shows that God uses suffering to draw His creatures into closer fellowship with Himself and as the occasion for a fuller revelation of Himself. God uses and controls suffering for His own purposes, which include the testing and purifying of His creatures' faith. Suffering in the story of Job is shown to test what a person really is.

Is disinterested religion possible? The book of Job demonstrates that religion without tangible, material benefits is gloriously possible. People can remain faithful to God on the basis of what He is and what He promises in the future life.

What, finally, is God like? He is both loving and powerful. He does not relinquish His control over His universe, nor does He desert those who call on Him. Suffering in the life of a person is not evidence that God's providence has ceased. Above all, God is worthy of confidence and love, since in the long run He will vindicate those who have faith in Him.

An important interpretation of the book of Job holds that the book provides no propositional or philosophic answers but instead resolves the question of suffering in an existentialist manner, with Job experiencing God rather than having his questions answered. The foregoing discussion will have implied that, while I respect the importance of the existentialist interpretation of the story, I cannot agree that the story provides no propositional answers to its questions. It is true that the themes of the work are embodied in the narrative and conveyed by indirection instead of by direct statement. But this is the normal procedure in literature. A number of ideas can be formulated on the basis of the prologue to the story of Job alone. The same is true of the conclusion, which is certainly an experiential encounter with God but which, like any piece of literature, embodies and implies certain propositions.

Many of the Psalms come from David's experience as a shepherd.

The Lyric Poetry
of the Psalms

7

I

A complete study of the Psalms would involve at least five different types of scholarship. One is textual scholarship, with its concern to establish a reliable version of the original manuscript and to render the original understandable in a reader's contemporary language. There is also source criticism, with its attempt to describe the origin of the Psalms — their dates, authorship, and cultural milieu. Biblical theology is concerned with providing an exposition of the theological content of the Psalms, while liturgical history shows how the Psalms have been used in worship. Literary criticism, finally, concerns itself with explaining the Psalms as lyric poems.

A good starting point for literary criticism of the Psalms is the statement by C. S. Lewis that "the Psalms must be read as poems; as lyrics, with all the licenses and all the formalities, the hyperboles, the emotional rather than logical connections, which are proper to lyric poetry."[1] The Psalms are first of all poems. Poetry, like the rest of literature, is the interpretive presentation of human experience in an artistic form. It differs from other literary types by being a more concentrated form of discourse and a more consciously artistic object than other types. Concentration is achieved through the use of images, symbols, allusions, metaphors, similes, emotive vocabulary, and multiple meanings. The fact that poetry is artistic means that as an object of beauty a poem will display in fuller measure and with greater frequency the components of artistic form, including pattern or design, unity, theme or centrality, balance, harmony, contrast, unified progression, recurrence, and variation. One cannot read far in the Psalms without sensing, as Moulton has said, "that the Psalms are not versified diaries of the saints: every line proclaims them the work of poets — not the less saints for being poets."[2] The writers of

---

[1] *Reflections on the Psalms* (New York: Harcourt, Brace & World, 1958), p. 3.
[2] Richard G. Moulton, *The Modern Reader's Bible* (New York: The Macmillan Company, 1966; originally published 1895), p. 1437.

the Psalms were imaginative, creative, lovers of poetry as well as lovers of God, and people who regarded the artistry of their poems as something important.

The chief formal characteristic of the Psalms, their most obvious element of pattern, is something that survives in translation. It is called parallelism and is the basic poetic technique of Hebrew poetry. The most frequently used kind of parallelism is synonymous parallelism, which consists of saying the same thing twice in different words but with the same grammatical structure:

> *He who sits in the heavens laughs;*
> *the Lord has them in derision (2:4).*

> *Therefore the wicked will not stand in the judgment,*
> *nor sinners in the congregation of the righteous (1:5).*

As Lewis comments, "If this is not recognized as pattern, the reader will either find mares' nests (as some of the older preachers did) in his effort to get a different meaning out of each half of the verse or else feel that it is rather silly."[3] Antithetic parallelism occurs when the second member states the truth of the first in a negative way or introduces a contrast:

> *For the Lord knows the way of the righteous,*
> *but the way of the wicked will perish (1:6).*

In climactic parallelism the second lines completes the first by repeating one member of the first line and adding to it:

> *Ascribe to the Lord, O heavenly beings,*
> *ascribe to the Lord glory and strength (29:1).*

One important thing about parallelism is that, unlike meter, it does not disappear when a work is translated into different languages.

There are three main elements that require attention in an individual lyric poem. The point of departure for understanding a poem is to grasp its topic, which can eventually be amplified into a statement of theme (a complete sentence, not simply a concept). Ordinarily a poem is also carefully structured. There is both a sequential structure (the organization of the poem as one reads from beginning to end) and an underlying contrast or set of contrasts. The third ingredient is the poetic texture, consisting of the smaller elements of poetry such as figures of speech, connotations or multiple meanings of words, imagery, tone, and allusion.

The Psalms are not simply poems but lyric poems. A lyric poem

---

[3] Lewis, *Reflections on the Psalms,* page 3.

can be defined as a short poem, originally meant to be sung, expressing the thoughts and especially the feelings of a single speaker. The salient characteristics of a lyric poem, then, are four: it is musical, subjective or personal, emotional, and brief.

Originally lyric poems, including the Psalms, were sung or recited orally to the accompaniment of the lyre. This is the tradition from which the Hebrew Psalms arise, and it accounts for the many references to musical instruments that we find in the Psalms.

The lyric is preeminently an utterance that is overheard. The lyric poet usually speaks in his own voice, using the "I" form of the pronoun. The significant aspect of the poem is the expression of the speaker, who in the Psalms is often in the act of addressing God directly. In large measure we can say that whereas the prophet's utterance is the words of God to man, the Psalms contain the thoughts and feelings of man addressed to God. Even if the speaking voice in a psalm is plural ("we," "us"), it is important to remember that the poem was written by a single person, expressing sentiments that were first of all his own. There is no such thing as a communal emotion; there is instead a group of individuals who have the same personal feelings. If the sentiments expressed in a lyric poem are so obviously the private feelings of the poet, we might ask how we should read the Psalms. The answer is that we should read them as giving expression to a shared religious experience. It is an example of the commonplace that the poet is a spokesman and representative, saying what others want said and saying it better than they could. Like a public prayer, the psalmists' outpourings of religious thought and feeling are at once private and public: they are spoken by a single person but express what an entire group feels.

The emotional element in a lyric poem is often considered its chief identifying trait — its differentia. Although a lyric poem may contain thought or reflection, it is above all an utterance of intense emotion. It is not easy to convey emotion in poetry. The means of doing so include the use of an exclamatory idiom, the use of hyperbole (conscious exaggeration for the sake of communicating strong feeling), the use of emotive words, and the vivid description of the stimulus to the emotion (thereby evoking a similar feeling in the reader). Mainly, however, the psalmists make religious feelings the subject matter of their poetry. Praise, adoration, awe, joy, sorrow, depression — these are the emotional subjects that recur throughout the Psalms. As a result, we should come to the Psalms with the expectation of finding there the expression of religious feelings. We should not expect to find an account of historical events, since ordinarily a lyric poem will make use only of so much history or narrative as is necessary to make clear the nature and source of the emotion being presented. Nor should we expect to find an exposition of theological doctrine. Theological doctrine can be deduced from the Psalms, but that is not their main business. The Psalms, being lyric poetry, exist primarily to give expression to the emotional side of religious experience.

The Psalms are also brief. Since a lyric poem often expresses a single feeling at the moment of greatest intensity, it is necessarily brief. It is impossible to prolong an emotional pitch indefinitely. The fact that the Psalms were intended as songs to be sung is perhaps another reason for their relative brevity. Because of their brevity, the Psalms must be regarded as self-contained units. They are not chapters in a continuing sequence but are complete entities, separate from the psalms that precede and follow them. Lyrics usually have a single controlling topic or theme. Unless one is aware of the unifying theme, an individual psalm has a tendency to remain a series of fragments, a kind of misreading somewhat fostered by the conventional division of the Psalms into verses. The unifying theme may be a thought or an emotion that controls all of the details in the poem and unifies them into a single whole. The unifying theme is usually stated early in the poem, functioning as the stimulus or point of departure and exercising a formative influence on the development of the poem.

A broad survey of lyric poems will reveal that frequently they are constructed on a three-part structure: (1) statement of theme, or presentation of the lyric stimulus; (2) development of the thoughts or emotions of the speaker; (3) resolution of the reflection or emotion into a concluding thought, mental resolution, or attitude.[4] The first task of a lyric poet is to get the original cause of his thoughts and feelings before the reader. The methods of presenting the stimulus are many, including an invocation, a description, an address to a second character, or the statement of an idea that has stirred the poet to sing. The development of the reflection or emotional sequence can likewise consist of several different types of material, such as repetition of the theme in different terms or images, movement from the original topic to related topics (as when a psalm moves from praise of God's acts to praise of His character), and development by describing the opposite emotion or thought (as when dispraise of idols becomes a way of praising God). In the third part of a lyric poem, the emotion or reflection is finally resolved into a note of finality. In a well-constructed lyric the process of the poem illustrates the natural transition from the initial stimulus to the concluding resolution.

As poetry, the Psalms are very conventional. Like a Renaissance

---

[4] This three-part lyric structure was first noted by John Erskine, *The Elizabethan Lyric* (New York: The Macmillan Company, 1903), p. 17.

love sonnet, for example, they are virtually anonymous. There is nothing to distinguish the style of one writer from that of another. All of the poets use parallelism and take their imagery from conventional sources, such as nature, religious worship, hunting, war, farming, and family life. The significant grouping of the Psalms is by kind, chiefly lament and praise, not by author.

How can we unify our experience of the Psalms and avoid seeing them as a collection of fragments? I would suggest that we fit them into the generalizations made about biblical literature as a whole in the introductory chapter. We might begin by looking at the individual psalms as chapters in the plot of the Bible.

Virtually every poem in the Psalter contributes in some way to the overall plot conflict between good and evil. The writers of the Psalms are caught in some kind of stance relating to this pervasive conflict. There are two categories of people in the world of the Psalms — good and evil, the godly and the godless. Most of the Psalms show the speaker dramatizing some kind of choice. These lyrics capture the poet at a single moment of thought or feeling, and virtually every poem shows the poet's choice for God. Being subjective in nature, the Psalms provide a good opportunity for the poet to align himself with the cause of God. If biblical literature generally can be regarded as the drama of the soul's choice, this is preeminently true of the Psalms, where the speakers habitually are shown in the act of turning to God.

If the plot of biblical literature is regarded as the unfolding of God's purposes throughout history, the Psalms can be viewed as episodes in that plot. They constantly present for praise and contemplation the acts of God — in history, in nature and creation, in the lives of people.

The Psalms also constantly reenact the essential movements of the monomyth that unifies all of literature. Any individual psalm can be plotted on the archetypal monomyth, and a unity of reference occurs at once. This unity is increased by the presence of many archetypal images and symbols, which give a unity of poetic texture to the Psalter as a whole. The archetypal pattern that recurs most frequently in the Psalms is well summarized in Psalm 30:5: "Weeping may tarry for the night, but joy comes with the morning." This comic movement from misery to happiness occurs throughout the psalms of lament and praise. Even the imagery in the quoted verse is archetypal, consisting of darkness and light, night and morning.

The Psalms are an anthology of lyric poems in which the principles of selection are much the same as those that unify biblical literature as a whole. There is unity of national authorship (the Jewish community), of subject matter (religious experience), of theological out-

125

look, and of purpose (to give expression to the feelings and reflections of religious experience). There is a unifying world view, which is solidly theocentric.

In other ways, too, the Psalms are unified by the generalizations that unify biblical literature generally. The Psalms show a tendency to move from the particular event to the general meaning or reality behind the event. External historical events and internal psychic events are usually related to some kind of spiritual reality beyond them, with the divine world constantly being brought into the flow of ordinary reality. There is no better example than the Psalms in all biblical literature of the vivid consciousness of values. Finally, since the Psalms are subjective, they naturally illustrate the subjective stance of the narrator that is characteristic of biblical literature.

II

Psalm 1 is both an appropriate preface to the Psalter as a whole and a good illustration of the generalizations that I have made about the Psalms as lyric poems. As an introduction to the Psalter, it puts into focus at once what is ultimately valuable in life, namely, godliness. It also asserts the basic condition of human existence — moral choice between opposing ways of life. The remainder of the Psalter will present endless variations of these central themes. From a literary point of view, Psalm 1 also exemplifies the two leading criteria of literature — concreteness of presentation and artistry.

Artistic form involves patterned recurrence, and Psalm 1 is carefully structured as a sequence of alternating positive and negative statements. The poet begins with a description of what the godly man does not do (vs. 1):

> Blessed is the man
> who walks not in the counsel of the wicked,
> nor stands in the way of sinners,
> nor sits in the seat of scoffers.

This negative description is balanced in verse 2 by a positive description:

> but his delight is in the law of the Lord,
> and on his law he meditates day and night.

Verse 3 contains a sequence of positive-negative-positive statements:

> He is like a tree
> planted by streams of water,

> *that yields its fruit in its season,*
> *and its leaf does not wither.*
> *In all that he does, he prospers.*

Verse 4 has a negative-positive pattern:

> *The wicked are not so,*
> *but are like chaff which the wind drives away.*

This is followed in verse 5 by a negative description:

> *Therefore the wicked will not stand in the judgment,*
> *nor sinners in the congregation of the righteous.*

Verse 6 culminates the pattern of alternating statements by describing the positive results of godliness and the negative results of wickedness:

> *for the Lord knows the way of the righteous,*
> *but the way of the wicked will perish.*

This alternation between positive and negative statements satisfies our artistic instinct for order and shapeliness and design.

The most pervasive artistic pattern in the Psalms, parallelism, is much in evidence in Psalm 1. An example of synonymous parallelism is the statement that the godly man "walks not in the counsel of the wicked, nor stands in the way of sinners, nor sits in the seat of scoffers" (vs. 1). Similarly, "the wicked will not stand in the judgment, nor sinners in the congregation of the righteous" (vs. 5). An example of antithetic parallelism is the statement "the Lord knows the way of the righteous, but the way of the wicked will perish" (vs. 6). The function of such parallelism is artistic; it presents a pleasing pattern without asking that every statement add to the logical content.

A final aspect of the artistic form of the poem is its unified progression. Verses 1 and 2 describe two types of persons, verses 3 and 4 describe, through the use of two similes, what happens to the two persons (one attains fulfillment, the other does not), and verses 5 and 6 describe the final verdict and end of the two persons, with the verb tense shifting from present to future as the poem ends climactically with an account of future judgment.

It would appear that the writer of Psalm 1 not only had something he wanted to say but also was concerned with saying it in an artistic way. He asked, whether consciously or instinctively, What kind of poem do I want to make?

The second leading characteristic of literature is that it presents experience concretely rather than abstractly. The content of Psalm 1 can be stated in the form of two or three propositions, as follows: life presents people with a choice between two ways of life — the godly and the wicked; the choice that a person makes is a significant choice; the ultimately valuable thing in life is godliness. The poet, however, does not state these ideas in propositional form. He does not give a theological definition of godliness, nor does he tell the reader about godliness as a concept. Instead, he describes how a godly person acts.

One literary device that the poet uses to make his presentation of godliness experiential is story, or action. This is surprising, because Psalm 1 is not a narrative poem but a lyric poem. Yet verse 1 tells us what the godly person does. It describes actions and events. Similarly, in verses 2 and 3 we read that the godly man meditates and yields fruit and prospers in all that he does. To some small extent, at least, the poet has used this story as a way of conveying his idea of godliness.

The main technique that the poet uses is a structure of contrasts. Underlying the whole poem is a prolonged contrast between the two ways. It is significant that the poet nowhere states abstractly, "Life presents us with a choice." Instead, he contrasts two ways of life, indirectly conveying the idea that this is the option open to people and indirectly asserting that the godly life is a conflict with its opposite, wickedness. The poet presents us with the conflict; he does not tell us *about* it.

Verse 3 uses simile, or comparison, to achieve experiential concreteness and immediacy. It compares the godly man to a tree. The main point of the comparison is productiveness. A healthy tree lives and grows and produces as it was intended to do. The poet compared godliness to a tree because he wished to make his statement experiential. The Psalms were written by and for a nation of farmers in a geographic area where drought was a threat. To compare the godly man to a tree growing next to a stream was, for the psalmist, to make his point with much greater force than if he had left the concept an abstraction. The verse illustrates the nature of the poetic imagination. The imagination sees the relationships among things. It leads a person to say, "Godliness is like a tree down by the river." The imagination unifies and synthesizes experience and is the opposite of the analytic faculty, which divides and categorizes experience.

Psalm 23 is also an example par excellence of great lyric poetry.

The personal element in the poem is pervasive, with seventeen instances of the first person pronoun. It is an utterance that is overheard, as we witness the speaker engaged in a reflective process. The poet addresses God directly in verses 4 and 5 and communes with himself elsewhere. The theme of the poem is God's providence, a theme that the speaker develops by listing the acts of provision that God performs in his life.

The poem is not highly emotional in tone. Instead the poet lists the things that constitute the stimulus for such feelings as contentment, peace of mind, thankfulness, trust, and confidence for the future. These emotions are very much a part of the experience of reading the poem but are left implicit in the psalm itself, which focuses on God and His acts.

The poem is simply structured. The main principle of organization is a catalog of God's acts of provision in the life of the poet. A secondary structural element is the journey along a path, mainly the daily movement of the sheep between sheepfold and pasture, with a hint in verse 4 of seasonal movement between the winter sheepfold and the summer grazing areas in the mountains.

The opening statement of the poem, "The Lord is my shepherd," introduces the controlling image or metaphor that will appear throughout the poem — the figure of a shepherd's relationship to his sheep. This metaphor recurs throughout the Bible in descriptions of the believer's relationship to God. In Psalm 23 the poet compares God's providence to the shepherd's care over a flock of sheep. The great advantage that the poet secures by using the pastoral symbol is universality. Pastoral poetry is an open-ended metaphor. One half of the comparison is the shepherd's situation; the other half is the experience of any reader. A reader can walk into a poem such as this and make it his own, something he could not do if David had made his utterance directly autobiographical.

Since the poet conveys his experience indirectly through metaphor, we cannot understand what he is saying about God's providence without first knowing something about the conditions of shepherding in ancient Palestine. The shepherd had to find narrow strips of green grass and springs of water in the middle of the drought of summer. The sheep had to be protected from attack by wild animals, as evidenced by David's account in 1 Samuel 17:34-36 of how he killed a lion and bear that had attacked his flock. The narrow paths among rocky ledges also constituted dangers for the sheep as they moved from one locale to another. If we understand these conditions and the total dependence of the sheep on their shepherd for their sustenance, we will be able to grasp what the poet is saying about his own relationship to God.

The exact extent to which the pastoral metaphor is present throughout the poem is not completely clear. It is easy to see the allusions to the shepherd's life in the first two verses and in the reference to the shepherd's rod and staff. In the interpretation that follows, I wish to suggest that the entire poem can be understood in terms of the pastoral metaphor, though some images and terms have multiple references and can be given a human as well as animal meaning.[5]

Out of several possible thoughts and feelings inherent in the image of the shepherd and his sheep, the poet singles out the shepherd's provision as his theme, as indicated by the statement "I shall not want." The scope of the provision is very general. As the subsequent lines show, the poet receives both physical and spiritual provision, and God's providence will be said to include not only food and water but also such qualities as comfort, goodness, and mercy. By saying that he does not lack any necessity, the poet makes it clear that he is talking about the satisfaction of basic needs. This is consistent with the pastoral imagery of the poem; the speaker is comparing himself to sheep, which are not creatures of luxury.

Verse 2 is also pastoral in its references. The poet declares, "He makes me lie down in green pastures. / He leads me beside still waters." This statement continues the catalog of God's acts. Although the provision seems at first glance to involve food, this is probably not the primary meaning of the verse. It is true that water and herbage are the two things necessary for the sustaining of the life of sheep, but the sheep are here pictured as lying down in the green pasture and walking beside the water. The key concept is rest and refreshment, and the scene is a kind of oasis. In the background is the custom of starting a flock of sheep on rough herbage early in the day, leading the sheep to the richer, sweeter grasses as the morning progresses, and finally coming to a shady place for the noontime rest in lush, green pasture. The emphasis on "still" waters is appropriate not only because the image contributes to an atmosphere of peaceful rest but also because sheep will not drink from a fast-flowing stream.

The picture of green pastures and still waters is the first of a number of images in the poem that are not only rooted in the conditions of shepherding but also have a direct meaning on the human level. In all places and at all times, apparently, people have pictured perfection and contentment as a pastoral world — a green world

---

[5] For background information that explains many of the pastoral allusions in the psalm, see William A. Knight, *The Song of Our Syrian Guest* (Boston: The Tudor Press, 1907); and James K. Wallace, "The Basque Sheepherder and the Shepherd Psalm," *Reader's Digest*, LXXVII (July, 1960), 179-184. The latter article contains the interpretation of a Basque shepherd who claims access to an oral tradition lost to the modern reader.

where the grass is profuse, where the water flows gently and pleasantly, where the shade is cool and inviting, and where all is rest and quiet. It is a universal human longing and affects the human soul and imagination in deep and profound ways. With a few masterful words the poet of Psalm 23 evokes our own picture of this rural world of bliss.

Verse 3 continues the catalog of God's acts of provision:

> *he restores my soul.*
> *He leads me in paths of righteousness*
> *for his name's sake.*

The first line speaks of restoration, or bringing back to a previous condition. The reference to "soul" would seem to indicate that the figure of the sheep has been dropped and that the poet is now talking in human terms. As elsewhere in the poem, however, the term in question can be understood in pastoral as well as human terms, since the word translated "soul" carries the force of "life" and refers to physical vitality. The effect of using the pastoral image is to make its human reference open-ended. The restoration can refer to physical restoration, mental or emotional recovery, spiritual reconciliation with God after a specific sin, or the act of salvation by which a sinner is restored by God from his fallen human condition.

The statement that God leads in "paths of righteousness" also looks like a human reference, inasmuch as the moral quality of righteousness is inappropriate for an animal. There is no reason to question that one of the meanings of the verse is that God provides for man's spiritual and moral needs, chiefly through His revealed law, which gives man moral guidance. There is also a literal meaning to the statement on the pastoral level. A literal translation of the phrase would be "right paths" or "straight paths." On this, the primary level of description, the poet is referring to the shepherd's guidance of his sheep on the right paths, as opposed to paths that are dangerous, as he leads his flock between the sheepfold and the places of grazing. The image of the path is the first clear evidence in the poem that the poet is using as a structural principle one of the oldest of all literary motifs, the journey. The statement that the shepherd leads his sheep in right paths "for his name's sake" alludes to an idea important in ancient cultures, namely, the necessity for a person to live up to the obligations of his name or role. A parallel statement in the Psalms is that God "saved them for his name's sake" (106:8).

Verse 4 is based on the journey motif: "Even though I walk through the valley of the shadow of death, / I fear no evil." Centuries of Christian experience have fixed the meaning of the phrase "the valley of the shadow of death" as a reference to human death. While this is one of the figurative meanings of the verse, a literal rendition of the text would be "the valley of deep darkness" (RSV footnote). The literal image is that of a very dark valley, where the fear of sheep would be at its greatest. The valley and darkness are both archetypal images of evil and danger. This is one of the few places in the poem where the speaker makes his emotional response explicit, as he asserts, "I fear no evil." It is part of the realism of the poem that the speaker implicitly acknowledges the inevitability of adverse experiences. What the poet claims is freedom from fear, not freedom from evil. He bases his assurance on the abiding presence of God, as evidenced by the clause "for thou art with me." The latter statement marks the point in the poem where the poet ceases to speak of God in the third person ("the Lord," "he") and turns to direct address. Generally it is legitimate to attribute significance to a deviation from an established poetic pattern. In the present instance, the mention of darkness and danger perhaps evokes a strong sense of helplessness in the speaker and moves him, maybe unconsciously, to cast himself on his divine shepherd in a more direct and personal way than elsewhere in the psalm.

The personal address to God continues in the next clause: "thy rod and thy staff, / they comfort me" (vs. 4). This is an obvious reference to actual conditions of shepherding. The rod of the shepherd was the familiar crook, used for rescuing sheep from gullies or placing over the backs of the sheep to count them as they entered the sheepfold (Leviticus 27:32 contains a reference to "whatever passes under the rod"). The staff was more of a protective weapon, being a kind of club used to ward off attacking animals. These pastoral images symbolize God's protection, and again the poet makes his emotional response (comfort) explicit.[6]

---

[6] The Basque shepherd, *Reader's Digest*, LXXVII, 183-184, gives this explanation of verse 4: "There is an actual Valley of the Shadow of Death in Palestine, and every sheepherder from Spain to Dalmatia knows of it. It is south of the Jericho Road leading from Jerusalem to the Dead Sea, and it is a narrow defile through a mountain range. Climatic and grazing conditions make it necessary for the sheep to be moved through this valley for seasonal feeding each year. . . . Travel through the valley is dangerous because its floor has gullies seven or eight feet deep. Actual footing on solid rock is so narrow in many places that a sheep cannot turn around, and it is an unwritten law of shepherds that flocks must go up the valley in the morning hours and down toward the eventide, lest flocks meet in the defile. About halfway through the valley the walk crosses from one side to the other at a place where the path is cut in two by an eight-foot gully. One side of the gully is about 11 inches higher than the other; the sheep must jump across it. The shepherd stands at this break and coaxes or forces the sheep to make the leap. If a sheep slips and lands in the gully, the shepherd's rod is

According to many commentators, the figure of speech shifts in verse 5 to the image of a host making provision for a human guest:

> Thou preparest a table before me
> in the presence of my enemies;
> thou anointest my head with oil,
> my cup overflows.

It is thoroughly plausible to read this verse, as well as the last one, as referring to human hospitality. In all interpretations of the passage it is agreed that the nature of the provision is physical care. The anointing of the head with oil is probably not a reference to ritual anointing but rather to a customary act of hospitality to travelers in the Near East. The description of how the speaker's physical needs are met despite the efforts of enemies to destroy him may well be an allusion to a specific event in David's life.

There are other interpretations of the last two verses that do a better job of preserving the unity of the poem. One of these interpretations takes its cue from that statement about the receipt of hospitality in the presence of enemies and relates the description to the desert law of hospitality.[7] According to the desert code of revenge, a fugitive from blood vengeance was safe from his pursuers if he entered someone's tent before his pursuers caught him. Within the tent he would be received with hospitality by his host and would be safe from his avengers. There was a limit of two days and one night to this immunity. After the period of safety the person would have to face the avengers. Perhaps the writer of Psalm 23 is comparing God's provision to the security and hospitality represented by this desert code. If so, the verse is unified with the rest of the poem because, although the image shifts from that of a shepherd and his sheep to that of a host and his guest, the pastoral world continues to be the frame of reference.

Even more unity is present if we interpret the fifth verse as referring to the activities of a shepherd as he cares for his sheep. Paradoxically, whereas earlier the poet uses animal imagery to refer to something human, he now uses a human situation to picture the circumstances of sheep. In finding grass for his sheep, the shepherd would figuratively prepare for them a table, where they might eat in

---

brought into play. The old-style crook circles a large sheep's neck or a small sheep's chest, and the animal is lifted to safety. . . . Many wild dogs lurk in the shadows of the valley, looking for prey. The shepherd, skilled in throwing his staff, uses it as a weapon."

[7] For more on this interpretation, see John Paterson, *The Praises of Israel* (New York: Charles Scribner's Sons, 1950), pp. 113-14.

the presence of animal enemies and, perhaps, also poisonous plants.[8]
The act of anointing with oil is readily understandable if one is
familiar with the conditions of shepherding. Each night as the sheep
entered the sheepfold the shepherd examined them for injuries. The
shepherd would then anoint the scratches of injured sheep with olive
oil. In each sheepfold there was a large vessel filled with water. From
this the shepherd would fill a large two-handled cup, from which the
sheep would drink and into which a fevered sheep might sink its
nose. The image of the overflowing cup makes most sense at this
level, because when applied at a human level it evokes the picture of
a sloppy host.

It is also possible to interpret the last verse of the psalm as referring
to the conditions of shepherding. It states,

> *Surely goodness and mercy shall follow me*
> *all the days of my life;*
> *and I shall dwell in the house of the Lord*
> *for ever.*

If in the earlier verse human images have been used to describe the
care of a shepherd for his sheep, the house could here be taken to
refer to the sheepfold. Alternately or simultaneously, the speaker
could here be comparing his experience of God's provision to the
security represented by a home. The word translated "for ever"
means "as long as I live," being parallel in meaning to the earlier
phrase "all the days of my life." It is important to note that the
poem ends by pointing outward. The verbs of the last verse are in
the future tense, suggesting confidence on the part of the speaker
and giving the conclusion a note of finality. The resolution of this
lyric is not so much an end as a beginning. The thrust is outward,
beyond the present moment.

No other psalm is as well-known as this one. Several things account
for its power. For one thing, the thoughts and feelings expressed by
the poet are those which people most long for. The psalm speaks of
peace, comfort, security, provision, freedom, hope. These are the
things for which the human heart longs. They are basic and universal
needs, as understandable to a child as to an adult. A second reason
for the attractiveness of the psalm is the pastoral convention to which
it belongs. The picture of a green world of rest and contentment has
always appealed strongly to the human soul. It touches people deeply,
universally, and unconsciously as well as consciously. Thirdly, the
psalm is very inclusive, despite its simplicity. It speaks of both rest
and movement along a path, both sunshine and shadow, both green

---

[8] For the details on which this interpretation is based, see Knight, pp. 20-22;
and Wallace, p. 184.

meadows and dark and dangerous valleys, both present and future, both physical and spiritual provision. It does not evade the shadows but swallows them up in the victory of God's provision. Finally, the literary excellence of the poem is obvious — its metaphoric richness, its multiplicity of meanings, its concreteness and realism, its unity, and its balance.

IV

Poetry is the most concentrated form of writing. Whereas the basic unit in a story is the episode or scene, the basic unit of poetry is usually said to be the image. A narrative writer, for example, might describe the blessedness of a godly person by telling about some representative events in the life of such a person. By contrast, the writer of Psalm 1 is able to picture the vitality, fulfillment, and stability of the godly person through the single image of a tree planted by a stream of water. Because of its concentration, poetry often says several things at the same time. The result can be called ambiguity or multiple meaning. Sometimes a poem achieves this complexity and compression by being laminated (consisting of two or more levels of meaning). For example, Psalm 23 is on one level a description of the shepherd's relationship to his sheep, but throughout the poem there is also a second, human set of meanings. Similarly, the story told in Genesis 3 is simultaneously a tragedy, a temptation story, and an initiation.

Psalm 46 is a multilayered poem that illustrates both the complexity and the artistry of which poetry is capable. The sequential structure of the poem falls into three well-proportioned sections, the last two ending with a repeated refrain. The organization is as follows: God's presence in the midst of natural upheavals (vss. 1-3), God's presence in the midst of military threats (vss. 4-7), and God's assertion of His authority against warring nations (vss. 8-11). The poem is also structured on some basic conflicts — God vs. forces of disruption, the stability of God's presence vs. instability and chaos in other areas of life, and (on the psychological level) peace of mind vs. the things that would induce fear.

The imagery of the first section comes mainly from the world of nature and pictures the dissolution of the natural order (vss. 1-3):

> *God is our refuge and strength,*
> *a very present help in trouble.*
> *Therefore we will not fear though the earth should change,*
> *though the mountains shake in the heart of the sea;*

> *though its waters roar and foam,*
> *though the mountains tremble with its tumult.*

The reference to the change of the earth (vs. 2) is probably an allusion to earthquakes or erosion. The shaking of the mountains in the sea, accompanied by the roaring and foaming of the water, also describes, on the naturalistic level, the occurrence of an earthquake.

The beginning of the second section at once strikes a new note of calm (vss. 4-5):

> *There is a river whose streams make glad the city of God,*
> *the holy habitation of the Most High.*
> *God is in the midst of her, she shall not be moved;*
> *God will help her right early.*

This stability is all the more remarkable because it occurs at a time when events elsewhere on the earth are chaotic: "The nations rage, the kingdoms totter; / he utters his voice, the earth melts" (vs. 6).

In the third part of the poem, the action takes place in a political and military world, as God brings an end to human warfare and asserts His own kingship (vss. 8-10):

> *Come, behold the works of the Lord,*
> *how he has wrought desolations in the earth.*
> *He makes wars cease to the end of the earth;*
> *he breaks the bow, and shatters the spear,*
> *he burns the chariots with fire!*
> *"Be still, and know that I am God.*
> *I am exalted among the nations,*
> *I am exalted in the earth!"*

It is when we move from describing the poem to interpreting or explaining it that several complementary readings emerge. On one level of meaning the poem is a song of Zion, a category of Psalms that grew out of the worship experience in Jerusalem. Viewed in this way, the center of the poem, thematically as well as structurally, occurs in verses 4 and 5, where the poet speaks of the presence of God in His temple at Jerusalem. The references to "the city of God" and "the holy habitation of the Most High" (vs. 4) are clearly allusions to Jerusalem and the temple. The beginning and end of the psalm, in which the poet asserts his faith in the protecting presence of God, express the confidence that stems from having experienced the reality of God's presence in the temple. The temple experience is shown to pervade all of life.

To read the psalm in this way necessitates a symbolic reading of the landscape described in verse 4. Jerusalem had no river running through it, and the city's water was supplied by aqueducts (Isa. 7:3 alludes to the conduit that supplied the city with water). The river that gladdens the city of God is symbolic of God's grace and presence, as it is elsewhere in biblical literature. For example, Isaiah describes Israel's future restoration with the words, "Look upon Zion, the city of our appointed feasts! . . . there the Lord in majesty will be for us a place of broad rivers and streams" (Isa. 33:20-21). The prophet is clearly not speaking of a literal river but of God's presence, which is symbolized by the picture of a stream. Another prophet, Joel, uses the same image in an obviously symbolic passage (Joel 3:18):

> *And in that day*
> *the mountains shall drip sweet wine,*
>   *and the hills shall flow with milk,*
> *. . . and a fountain shall come forth from the house of the Lord. . . .*

A similar instance of a river flowing from the temple in Jerusalem occurs in Ezekiel 47:1-12. The river of Psalm 46 would thus appear to be a symbol of God's presence, especially as experienced in the worship of God at His temple in Jerusalem.

The entire poem can also be read as a celebration of God's intervening protection in times of military and political threats to His people. As such it belongs to the category of Old Testament lyric known as the song of victory. As in other psalms of this type, God appears in the role of military hero. He is a military "refuge" and a "strength" in battle. He makes wars to cease and destroys the weapons of His opponents. He is a Lord "of hosts" (that is, hosts of warriors), and after winning the battle He asserts himself as ruler over the earth He has subdued.

The imagery of the opening section of the poem depicts cataclysmic upheavals in nature that might seem at first glance incapable of a military interpretation. The poet, however, is again using a symbolic mode in which the images must be regarded as representing something beyond themselves. In the writings of the Old Testament prophets, the attacks of armies were sometimes depicted in images of natural catastrophe. For example, Isaiah predicted the military destruction of Babylon with the words "Therefore I will make the heavens tremble, / and the earth will be shaken out of its place" (Isa. 13:13). Elsewhere the invasion of Judah by the Assyrian army is predicted in images that also echo those of Psalm 46: "They roar like the roaring of mighty waters / The nations roar like the roaring of many waters" (Isa. 17:12-13). On one level of meaning, then, Psalm 46:1-3 describes in a symbolic mode the agitation of Israel's military foes that is described directly later in the poem.

The psalm can also be given an eschatalogical or apocalyptic interpretation. In the Olivet Discourse (Matt. 24-25), Jesus answered His disciples' questions about what it would be like at the time of His coming and the close of the age by describing the last times as a period of immense chaos on earth: "You will hear of wars and rumors of wars.... For nation will rise against nation, and kingdom against kingdom, and there will be famines and earthquakes in various places.... Immediately after the tribulation of those days the sun will be darkened, and the moon will not give its light, and the stars will fall from heaven, and the powers of the heavens will be shaken; then will appear the sign of the Son of man in heaven, and then all the tribes of the earth ... will see the Son of man coming ..." (Matt. 24:6-7; 29-30). This passage describes the last days as a time of international chaos and cataclysmic upheavals in nature, followed by the appearance of Christ. Psalm 46 follows an identical movement. The reference to the melting of the earth in verse 6 of the psalm can likewise be understood in the context of the New Testament apocalyptic prediction that in the "coming of the day of God ... the elements will melt with fire" (2 Pet. 3:12).

An apocalyptic interpretation of the city (vss. 4-5) is also possible. In Revelation heaven is called "the holy city, new Jerusalem" (Rev. 21:2). God is pictured as being in the midst of the city, as He is in Psalm 46, and there is a river flowing through the holy city of Revelation as there is through the city of God in Psalm 46: "Then he showed me the river of the water of life, bright as crystal, flowing from the throne of God and of the Lamb through the middle of the street of the city" (Rev. 22:1-2).

We might well ask, What is the most accurate description of Psalm 46? Is it a hymn of Zion, a song of victory, or an apocalyptic vision? It can legitimately be viewed as being all three at the same time. It is one of the triumphs of poetry to be able to be many things simultaneously. As the preceding explication has shown, poetry is able to achieve such complexity because it speaks a symbolic language in which images possess not a single meaning but a cluster of different meanings.

The most significant grouping of psalms is by kind, not by author. The category that comprises the greatest number of psalms is the lament, which comprises approximately one-third of the Psalter. In terms of formal structure, the private and communal lament consists of the following elements, in a variety of sequences: (1) the invocation or introductory cry to God, with the address sometimes expanded by the addition of honorific epithets; (2) the lament or complaint; a definition of the distress or description of the crisis; the stimulus to the lament; (3) petition or supplication; (4) statement of confidence in God; (5) vow to praise God. The stimulus to lament in the Psalms is varied, consisting of such calamities as bad harvests, drought, epidemics, attack from enemies, disease, mockery by enemies, doubt, and the burden of sin. Because the form of the lament is so fixed, one of the pleasures that we should expect and respond to when reading such a poem is to observe the poet in the act of satisfying our sense of the order and design that belong to this kind of poem. In this regard the reader should respond as he does when reading a sonnet or epic or elegy.

Psalm 10 illustrates the typical traits of the private lament. Like other laments, it possesses a vigorous plot conflict. In this case, the wicked oppressor is pitted against the helpless poor. The poet not only dramatizes his own response to this conflict but evokes an identical response from the reader.

The invocation (vs. 1) implies an obligation on God's part to act: "Why dost thou stand afar off, O Lord? / Why dost thou hide thyself in times of trouble?" The reason for these questions emerges from the description that follows, in which the poet defines the crisis as involving the oppression of the poor (vss. 2-11). He employs a barrage of techniques in describing the situation. The overriding device is the character — a brief descriptive sketch of a moral type. The poet first uses hunting metaphors to describe the oppression of the poor: "In arrogance the wicked hotly pursue the poor; / let them be caught in the schemes which they have devised" (vs. 2). The wicked person is next described in terms of his typical actions: "For the wicked boasts of the desires of his heart, / and the man greedy for gain curses and renounces the Lord" (vs. 3). There is psychological realism as we enter the consciousness of the wicked: "All his thoughts are, 'There is no God'" (vs. 4); "He thinks in his heart, 'I shall not be moved'" (vs. 6). Verse 8 uses hyperbole to evoke the anger of the reader against the wicked oppressor: "He sits in ambush in the villages; / in hiding places he murders the innocent." The imagery here refers either to robbers or hunters, and although the oppression of the wicked is not likely to involve literal murder, the imagery is appropriate to the economic and social oppression of the poor. Elsewhere the oppressor is both an animal, lurking "in secret like a lion" (vs. 9), and a hunter, drawing the poor "into his net" (vs. 9). After the reader has finished reading the description, he is left with the impression that the poet's imagination is overflowing with poetic devices as he defines the problem and evokes an appropriate response.

The resolution to the lyric comes in the final phase (vss. 12-18), which combines petition and confidence. The supernatural perspective, established by the poet's statement "Thou dost see" (vs. 14), offers the only consolation in the face of social injustice. The call for justice is just as vivid and particularized as the description of the oppression has been: "Break thou the arm of the wicked and evil-doer" (vs. 15).

As this poem illustrates, psalms of lament assume two things — that there is a right and a wrong, and that God can be trusted to vindicate the cause of the righteous. Usually a third assumption is also present — the speaker himself belongs to the godly cause.

Psalm 35 is one of many personal laments arising out of David's conflicts with political enemies. It is a poem of vivid conflict in which even the opening invocation draws upon military imagery. God is described as a warrior and is invoked to join the battle of the speaker against his enemies (vss. 1-3):

> Contend, O Lord, with those who contend with me;
> fight against those who fight against me!
> Take hold of shield and buckler,
> and rise for my help!
> Draw the spear and javelin
> against my pursuers!

The exclamatory idiom in such a passage conveys the emotional intensity that the poet feels.

Psalm 35 places the petition before the definition of the crisis. In the supplication the speaker asks for retribution in both abstract terms ("shame," "dishonor," "confounded") and particular images ("like chaff before the wind," a "dark and slippery" path). The situation out of which the prayer arises — the treachery of the enemy — is established through the use of hunting metaphors: "For without cause they hid their net for me; / without cause they dug a pit for my life" (vs. 7). Elsewhere the poet uses vivid descriptive detail in picturing his foes as gathering in glee as he stumbles (vs. 15) and "gnashing at me with their teeth" (vs. 16). He also dramatizes their animosity: "Aha, aha! our eyes have seen it!" (vs. 21); "Aha, we have our heart's desire!" (vs. 25).

Although Psalm 35 has the ingredients of the conventional lament, it mingles these elements together in a disorganized and random manner. As one moves through the poem sequentially, he finds the following arrangement of parts: petition (vss. 1-6), complaint (vss. 7-8), petition (vs. 8), vow to praise (vss. 9-10), complaint (vss. 11-16), petition (vs. 17), vow to praise (vs. 18), petition (vs. 19), complaint (vss. 20-21), petition (vss. 22-27), and vow to praise (vs. 28). The structure is psychological, following the movement of the speaker's mind, whereas the usual lament has an established logical pattern, with one step leading expectedly to the next. The effect of a psalm such as Psalm 35 is that of emotional intensity overcoming a logical and artistic pattern. Experience proves stronger than theory in such a poem. Even so, the effect of an unstructured lament depends on the reader's knowledge of the conventional form, which becomes the background by which the unstructured poem is seen to be unstructured.

In Psalm 38 the enemy is not an external foe but the internal, spiritual effects of sin. Correspondingly, the invocation is a prayer for forgiveness: "O Lord, rebuke me not in thy anger, / nor chasten me in thy wrath!" (vs. 1). In the description of the crisis, the poet uses a series of vivid images and metaphors to depict the reality of his guilt. God's disapproval of his sin is compared to someone shooting arrows and pushing a person down: "thy arrows have sunk into me, / and thy hand has come down on me" (vs. 2). Sin is like a torrent of water ("my iniquities have gone over my head" — vs. 4) and like a burden ("they weigh like a burden too heavy for me" — vs. 4). The most prolonged figure that the poet employs is his comparison of his guilt-induced isolation to a disease, probably leprosy (vss. 5-8, 11). His oblivion to external reality as he becomes obsessed with inner guilt is conveyed by similes comparing the sinner to a deaf man and a dumb man (vs. 13). The lament concludes with the statement of confidence (vss. 15-16), another lament (vss. 17-20), and a final prayer for forgiveness (vss. 21-22). As one looks back over the poem, he discovers that it is structured on the principle of A-B-C-B-A, with confidence in God at the center of the configuration (petition, lament, confidence, lament, petition).

Most lament psalms are occasional poems, arising from a particular occasion in the poet's life. Psalm 51 is a typical example. According to the headnote in the manuscript, the poem was written on the occasion of Nathan's exposure of David's sin of adultery with Bathsheba. The poem begins with a cry to God in which the speaker seeks relief not from physical suffering but from the guilt of sin (vss. 1-2):

> *Have mercy on me, O God,*
> *   according to thy steadfast love;*
> *according to thy abundant mercy blot out my transgressions.*
> *Wash me thoroughly from my iniquity,*
> *   and cleanse me from my sin!*

The appeal is to God's love and mercy, with no evidence of the protestation of innocence found so often elsewhere in the Psalms.

The lament or definition of crisis is here a confession of sin: "For I know my transgressions, / and my sin is ever before me" (vs. 3).

In keeping with the theocentric emphasis found everywhere in the Psalms, the poet defines his sin not as a social sin but as an act against God: "Against thee, thee only, have I sinned" (vs. 4). Sin leads to an awareness of what God is like: "thou art justified in thy sentence / and blameless in thy judgment" (vs. 4). Sin also leads to the speaker's awareness of what man is like, namely, constitutionally evil: "I was brought forth in iniquity" (vs. 5).

Corresponding to the internal nature of the enemy (guilt), the petition (vss. 6-12) likewise stresses inner spiritual qualities. The poet acknowledges, "Behold, thou desirest truth in the inward being; / therefore teach me wisdom in my secret heart" (vs. 6). Similarly, the speaker's request is for "a clean heart" and "a new and right spirit within me" (vs. 10).

The vow to witness about God's forgiveness occurs in verses 13-17. In keeping with the spiritual nature of the psalm, even the concept of sacrifice is given an inner, spiritual meaning: "The sacrifice acceptable to God is a broken spirit; / a broken and contrite heart, O God, thou wilt not despise" (vs. 17).

The customary song of lament can be viewed as containing a strategy for consolation. Faced with a crisis, the speaker undertakes a quest for relief, which usually comes through appealing to God, exercising trust in God's character, and acting on such trust by making a vow to praise God for the deliverance that He is sure to bring. Psalm 77 illustrates how a strategy for consolation underlies the typical lament poem. The psalm falls into two distinct sections, with verses 1-10 describing the speaker's distress and verses 11-20 containing a recollection of God's former acts. Distress is equally balanced with confidence in God's goodness. Many verbs in the poem emphasize that it is a meditative lyric, not a dramatic address to God: "I think...," "I meditate...," "I consider...," "I remember...," "I commune...," "I will meditate...and muse...," etc.

Psalms of lament can describe the distress in either precise detail or very general terms. Psalm 77 uses the latter technique, with the poet describing his emotional depression without making clear the stimulus for his feeling (vss. 2-3):

> *In the day of my trouble I seek the Lord;*
> *in the night my hand is stretched out without wearying;*
> *my soul refuses to be comforted.*
> *I think of God, and I moan;*
> *I meditate, and my spirit faints.*

At one point the speaker's distress is shown to involve God's past acts of deliverance and His present lack of activity, so that the poet is led to ask, "Will the Lord...never again be favorable?" (vs. 7).

The speaker's strategy for consolation consists of his taking refuge in the past acts of God, as evidenced by his statement, "I will remember thy wonders of old" (vs. 11). The poet develops this thought by first describing what God *means* to him. The language is correspondingly theological, with God depicted as one who is "holy" and "great" (vs. 13), who "workest wonders" and "hast manifested thy might among the peoples" (vs. 14). This abstract rendition of God is then balanced by a concrete description of God's activity. The description is a composite picture, combining a thunderstorm, the deliverance of Israel at the Red Sea, and God's guidance of Israel through the wilderness. These elements are combined to form a single epiphany or appearance of God (vss. 16-20):

> *When the waters saw thee, O God,*
> *   when the waters saw thee, they were afraid,*
> *   yea, the deep trembled.*
> *The clouds poured out water;*
> *   the skies gave forth thunder;*
> *   thy arrows flashed on every side.*
> *The crash of thy thunder was in the whirlwind;*
> *   thy lightnings lighted up the world;*
> *   the earth trembled and shook.*
> *Thy way was through the sea,*
> *   thy path through the great waters;*
> *   yet thy footprints were unseen.*
> *Thou didst lead thy people like a flock*
> *   by the hand of Moses and Aaron.*

The poem suggests that an adequate strategy for consolation consists not simply of an adequate theology but also an experiential awareness of God's presence in the world.

Like many another lyric poem, Psalm 77 is based on an intricate system of balanced opposites. In the present instance, distress is balanced by confidence, present doubt by God's past acts, the abstract description of God by the concrete appearance, and God's revelation in human history by His revelation in nature.

Although most lament poems in the Psalter are personal statements, there is also a category of communal laments. These differ from the private lament only in the fact that the crisis is one that affects the entire community instead of an individual. Psalm 74 is an example. This psalm is an occasional poem, the occasion being the destruction of Jerusalem and the temple. The opening cry to God gives the situation in summary form (vss. 1-3):

> *O God, why dost thou cast us off for ever?*
> *   Why does thy anger smoke against the sheep of thy pasture?*
> *Remember thy congregation, which thou hast gotten of old,*

143

which thou hast redeemed to be the tribe of thy heritage!
Remember Mount Zion, where thou hast dwelt.
Direct thy steps to the perpetual ruins;
the enemy has destroyed everything in the sanctuary!

The lament itself occurs in verses 4-11 and is a minute description of the wrecking of the temple.

The most memorable part of the psalm is the statement of confidence (vss. 12-17), which consists of a comprehensive catalog of the different areas in which God works. The poet begins with a generalization, asserting that God works "salvation in the midst of the earth" (vs. 12). The catalog itself begins with a historical allusion to the exodus: "Thou didst divide the sea by thy might" (vs. 13). This is followed by an account of God's might as seen in the imaginative world of dragons and monsters (vss. 13-14):

thou didst break the heads of the dragons on the waters.
Thou didst crush the heads of Leviathan,
thou didst give him as food for the creatures of the wilderness.

These references to the worlds of history and human imagination are complemented by a description of God's activity in nature: "Thou didst cleave open springs and brooks; / thou didst dry up ever-flowing streams" (vs. 15). There is, finally, an allusion to God's act of creating the world (vss. 16-17):

Thine is the day, thine also the night;
thou hast established the luminaries and the sun.
Thou hast fixed all the bounds of the earth;
thou hast made summer and winter.

Several conclusions emerge from a survey of the lament psalms. The lament is probably the most fixed form in the Psalter. Its effect diminishes if one reads many laments consecutively, since monotony is inevitable. Within the fixed form, most writers of laments achieve originality, not by virtue of their subject matter, but by an amazing variety in imagery, metaphor, and descriptive technique. Finally, the regularity with which the five elements of the lament appear in these poems suggests some degree of conscious craftsmanship on the part of the poets. There was undoubtedly some understanding of what constituted a lament, and writing such a poem must have been partly a self-conscious attempt to make the poem according to certain assumptions of what it should include. Nothing else will account for the constancy of the form and the unexpected regularity with which the statement of confidence and vow to praise God are included, since these elements cannot be considered inevitable when a poet writes a complaint.

VI

The second major grouping of psalms is the psalm of praise. The English word "to praise" originally meant "to set a price on; to appraise." From this came the idea that to praise means "to commend the worth of; to express approval or admiration of." Praise is a response; it is stimulated by someone or something. The Psalms, being theocentric in emphasis, always direct the praise to God. While praise may remain unexpressed, it usually proceeds from a feeling or attitude to an act, whether verbal or involving worship.

There are two main categories of praise in the Psalms. Declarative praise extols God's activity on a particular occasion. Its main thrust is that God *has done* such and such on this precise occasion. Descriptive praise describes God's qualities or the acts that He does perpetually. Its thrust is that God *is* this or that and that He habitually *does* these things. Descriptive praise is not occasional in the way that declarative praise is. Both types of praise can be either a private or public utterance.

There are several elements that are always present in praise. One of these is the elevation of the person or thing being praised. A second element is the direction of the praiser's whole being away from himself toward the object of praise. A third ingredient of much praise is testimony. That is, praise has a communal dimension to it, with the praise occurring in a group of people and serving as the speaker's testimony to the worth of someone or something. It is evident that praise in the Psalms moves on both a vertical plane (directed toward God) and a horizontal plane (directed toward fellow believers or the nations of the world).

The psalm of praise has a fixed form, just as the lament has. There is almost always an introduction to the praise. The introduction regularly consists of one or more of the following elements: (1) an exhortation to sing to the Lord, to praise, to exalt; (2) the naming of the person or group to whom the exhortation is directed; (3) mention of the mode of praise. Psalm 149:1-3 is an introduction possessing all three elements. The second main part is the development of the theme of praise. It ordinarily begins with a motivatory section in which the poet gives the reason for the call to praise. The most important part of the psalm of praise is the poet's listing of the praiseworthy acts or qualities of God. In the conclusion of the typical psalm of praise, the poet reaches some kind of resolution, which often takes the form of a brief prayer or wish.

Psalm 18 illustrates the distinctive features of the psalm of praise. It is a psalm of declarative praise, with some descriptive praise late in the poem. The speaker is David, in his public role as military hero. According to the inscription, it is "A Psalm of David, the servant of the Lord, who addressed the words of this song to the Lord on the day when the Lord delivered him. . . ." This makes the lyric an example of a category of Old Testament lyric known as the song of victory. The emphasis in such a poem is on the immediate, battle-field response to God's deliverance.

The introductory section of the psalm directs the praise toward God, who is pictured with military imagery as the strong deliverer (vss. 1-3) :

> I love thee, O Lord, my strength.
> The Lord is my rock, and my fortress, and my deliverer,
>   my God, my rock, in whom I take refuge,
>   my shield, and the horn of my salvation, my stronghold.
> I call upon the Lord, who is worthy to be praised,
>   and I am saved from my enemies.

The epithets (titles for God) in such a passage are not only a way of exalting God but also of directing attention to the specific role for which He is being praised. In terms of lyric strategy, this opening section establishes the stimulus to the poet's emotional response.

The second section of the poem, verses 4-19, is a narrative account of the military danger of the speaker and of God's miraculous rescue of him. The poet uses a variety of metaphors in evoking a sense of the terror that was his in the face of threatened death. Death is successively a strangler who encompasses his victims with cords (vs. 4), a river that assails objects in its path (vs. 4), a hunter who throws nets over his victims (vs. 5), and a hunter who sets traps (vs. 5). The imagined picture of God's intervention is equally impressive, as God's activity is associated with the awesome aspects of nature (vss. 7-9) :

> Then the earth reeled and rocked;
>   the foundations also of the mountains trembled
>   and quaked, because he was angry.
> Smoke went up from his nostrils,
>   and devouring fire from his mouth;
>   glowing coals flamed forth from him.
> He bowed the heavens, and came down;
>   thick darkness was under his feet.

The actual rescue (vss. 16-19) is also described figuratively as a rescue from "many waters" (vs. 16), an earlier symbol for the threat of death. The speaker also pictures himself as being placed on "a broad place" (vs. 19).

In verses 20 to 30 the poet asserts his righteousness, taking the view that God has "rewarded me according to my righteousness" (vs. 20). This does not negate the idea that the deliverance has been an act of God's mercy. Rather, the protestation of innocence is part of the poet's praise of God as a God who is faithful to His covenant promises. The essential element in the covenant was the principle of reciprocity: "With the loyal thou dost show thyself loyal" (vs. 25). In order to establish God's faithfulness to His covenant promise, the poet must first demonstrate that he has feared and obeyed God. He summarizes his point in verse 30 with the statement "the promise of the Lord proves true." The exaltation that the poet feels is evident in his hyperbolic statement "by thee I can crush a troop; / and by my God I can leap over a wall" (vs. 29).

In verses 31 to 48 of the psalm, David praises God as the one who strengthens the king. This section is mostly descriptive praise, describing what God does habitually or has done many times, and David speaks as a single person, though in his public role as king. The passage is in part a parody of a conventional motif in heroic poetry, the arming of the hero. Usually the military hero is praised for his own strength, of which his armor becomes a symbol. By contrast, David here makes his arming by God an occasion for praising God as the one who is responsible for his triumphs. An example of how the motif of the arming of the hero is used to praise God is the following passage (vss. 32-35):

> . . . the God who girded me with strength,
>   and made my way safe.
> He made my feet like hinds' feet,
>   and set me secure on the heights.
> He trains my hands for war,
>   so that my arms can bend a bow of bronze.
> Thou hast given me the shield of thy salvation,
>   and thy right hand supported me,
>   and thy help made me great.

The poem concludes in customary fashion with a kind of summary statement and an expression of the poet's conviction that God's acts will continue in the future (vss. 49-50):

> For this I will extol thee, O Lord, among the nations,
>   and sing praises to thy name.
> Great triumphs he gives to his king,

and shows steadfast love to his anointed,
to David and his descendants for ever.

The vow to praise God "among the nations" makes it clear that David has not only directed his praise toward God but has intended it as a testimony to others as well.

A number of psalms of praise can appropriately be linked to the psalms of lament. They are a response to God's answer to an earlier lament. The lament and the song of praise stand on opposite sides of the crisis, which forms the context for both of them. Both the lament and the song of praise allude to a specific event, in these instances. These psalms of praise contain an introduction, a report of the crisis and deliverance, and a conclusion. Throughout the poems, the emphasis is on God, not on the psychological relief of the speaker over his escape from distress.

Psalm 30 is representative of this category of poems. Verse 1 gives the stimulus that moves the poet to sing: "I will extol thee, O Lord, for thou hast drawn me up, / and hast not let my foes rejoice over me." Verses 2-10 amplify the event by giving a retrospective summary of the crisis, even including the words of the speaker's earlier lament (vss. 8-10). The last two verses briefly allude to God's deliverance and to the poet's feeling of thanks.

Psalm 65 is another declarative psalm of praise. It is a public rather than private utterance. The event that occasioned the poem can be inferred to be an abundant harvest at the end of a summer during which drought had threatened the crops and God had answered the people's prayer for rain. This will explain the opening statement that "praise is due" to God. Praise is due because God has answered prayers. The same thing is implied by the epithet "thou who hearest prayer" (vs. 2), and by the mention of an obligation to perform vows that had been made in the time of distress (vs. 1).

Like many another communal psalm of praise, Psalm 65 places the praise in the context of worshiping God at the temple in Jerusalem. Thus the praise is said to be due God "in Zion" (vs. 1). Similarly, the poet states, "We shall be satisfied with the goodness of thy house, thy holy temple" (vs. 4).

Before praising God for His particular act, the poet devotes a section of his poem to descriptive praise of what God does generally in the world of nature (vss. 5-8). The imagery in this section evokes an impression of elemental nature with the mention of such phenomena as "the earth," "the farthest seas," "the mountains," "the roaring of the seas," and "the morning and the evening."

The poem concludes with a declaration of God's sending of rain and enabling the crops to grow (vss. 9-13). The passage begins with a minute description, based on observation of nature, of how rain falls on a cultivated field (vss. 9-10):

> *Thou visitest the earth and waterest it,*
> *thou greatly enrichest it;*
> *the river of God is full of water;*
> *thou providest their grain,*
> *for so thou hast prepared it.*
> *Thou waterest its furrows abundantly,*
> *settling its ridges,*
> *softening it with showers,*
> *and blessing its growth.*

This is followed by a descriptive passage that makes brilliant use of metaphor. There is a generalization in which the poet summarizes in general terms the event for which he is praising God: "Thou crownest the year with thy bounty" (vs. 11). Having used the imagery of royalty, the poet continues this motif in the next line to evoke an impression of abundance: "the tracks of thy chariot drip with fatness" (vs. 11). In the final scene, the poet personifies nature and pictures nature as dressing herself for a festal celebration (vss. 12-13):

> *the hills gird themselves with joy,*
> *the meadows clothe themselves with flocks,*
> *the valleys deck themselves with grain,*
> *they shout and sing together for joy.*

This memorable vignette is notable for several reasons: as a celebration scene it conveys the joy appropriate to the harvest occasion, as a description of nature it keeps the focus of the poem on the theme of God's provision in nature, and by personifying nature in human terms the poet domesticates nature, reminding us that as a farmer he is concerned about the usefulness or submission of nature to human needs.

Psalm 66 illustrates several important facets of praise in the Psalms. The call to "come and see what God has done" (vs. 5) might well be said to be the leading motif of all the songs of praise, which constantly call the reader to contemplate the God who acts. The statement that "he turned the sea into dry land; / men passed through the river on foot" (vs. 6) reminds us of the way in which the appeal in the psalms of praise is often to Jewish history, one of the biggest arenas in which God is shown to act. That true praise does not idealistically refuse to admit adversity becomes clear in the poet's description of how God has tested and afflicted His people (vss. 10-12). Another important feature is that the verbal praise expressed in the psalm occurs along with the fulfillment of a vow in the performance of sacrifice (vss. 13-15):

> *I will come into thy house with burnt offerings;*
> *I will pay thee my vows. . . .*
> *I will offer to thee burnt offerings of fatlings,*
> *with the smoke of the sacrifice of rams;*
> *I will make an offering of bulls and goats.*

Such a passage lends support to the view of Westermann that "the vow of praise originally was connected with a vow to offer sacrifice" and that "praise is not a substitute for sacrifice, but had its own original meaning alongside of sacrifice."[9] Finally, the status of praise as testimony before others is captured in the poet's statement, "Come and hear, all you who fear God, / and I will tell what he has done for me" (vs. 16).

Psalm 96 is a typical psalm of descriptive praise, extolling God for what He is. Whereas many of the psalms call the believing community to praise God, this one belongs to the category in which the call to praise is extended to the whole world (vss. 1-3):

> *O sing to the Lord a new song;*
> *sing to the Lord, all the earth!*
> *Sing to the Lord, bless his name;*
> *tell of his salvation from day to day.*
> *Declare his glory among the nations,*
> *his marvelous works among all the peoples!*

The apostrophes (addresses to people who are absent but treated as though they were present) and the imperative commands convey a sense of excitement, as though emotional intensity were overpowering the speaker's sense of decorum.

The motivatory section praises the qualities of God. He is "great" (vs. 4) and "above all gods" (vs. 4). He is the creator who "made the heavens" (vs. 5), and He possesses "honor and majesty," "strength and beauty" (vs. 6). All of these are conventional motifs in the psalms of praise. After a second call to praise (vss. 7-9), God is praised in His role as judge of the earth (vss. 10-13). This, too, is an important theme of the Psalms, appearing more frequently than poems praising God as king or creator. Many of the Psalms personify nature by commanding various natural forces to join in the praise of God. Psalm 96 contains a typical example (vss. 11-12):

---

[9] Claus Westermann, *The Praise of God in the Psalms*, trans. Keith R. Crim (Richmond: John Knox Press, 1961), p. 76.

Let the heavens be glad, and let the earth rejoice;
let the sea roar, and all that fills it;
let the field exult, and everything in it!
Then shall all the trees of the wood sing for joy....

Psalm 97 illustrates not only the characteristic structure of the psalm of praise but also the three-part structure that is inherent in lyric poetry. The opening statement of the poem is the thought that stimulates the lyric response of the poet: "The Lord reigns; let the earth rejoice; / let the many coastlands be glad!" (vs. 1).

The poet develops his theme by describing God as king of the earth and of other gods. By picturing God as surrounded by "clouds and thick darkness" (vs. 2), the poet veils God from direct view, distancing Him and evoking a sense of His transcendence. Conceptual images also prevent our visualizing God and His throne in ordinary earthly terms: "righteousness and justice are the foundation of his throne" (vs. 2). Yet another descriptive technique is the association of God with the terrifying and powerful aspects of nature (vss. 3-5):

Fire goes before him,
and burns up his adversaries round about.
His lightnings lighten the world;
the earth sees and trembles.
The mountains melt like wax before the Lord,
before the Lord of all the earth.

Even while using the images of nature, the poet here creates a picture that goes beyond the events that normally occur. Praise of something can take the form of dispraise of its opposite. This psalm is representative of a number in which the speaker dispraises pagan idols as a way of praising the supremacy of God: "All worshipers of images are put to shame...; all gods bow down before him" (vs. 7).

The poet resolves his poem of praise by joining the side of God in the great spiritual conflict (vss. 10-12):

The Lord loves those who hate evil;
he preserves the lives of his saints;
he delivers them from the hand of the wicked.
Light dawns for the righteous,
and joy for the upright in heart.
Rejoice in the Lord, O you righteous,
and give thanks to his holy name!

The world of this psalm, as indeed of the entire Psalter, is clearly divided into moral categories of good and evil. There are the saints and the wicked. By means of his subjective stance, the poet is able to dramatize his own commitment to God, thereby praising Him in yet another way.

The Psalms are rather consistently political and military in reference. Psalm 124, a public psalm of declarative praise, can be taken as representative of a number of psalms that celebrate God's goodness in delivering Israel from a political enemy. Verses 1-5 describe the national danger, verses 6-7 picture God's deliverance, and verse 8 makes a final comment. The underlying conflicts that structure the poem occur between Israel and her enemies and between man's helplessness and God's protective power.

The poem employs a negative approach to God's goodness by picturing what would have happened to Israel without God's intervention (vss. 1-5). As so often in the Psalms, the poet uses a kaleidoscopic variety of images to evoke a sense of the terror of the enemy. The enemy is first pictured as a group of sea monsters who, except for God's deliverance, "would have swallowed us up alive" (vs. 3). Their anger was like a fire that was "kindled against us" (vs. 3). The climactic image of horror pictures the onslaught of the enemy as a flood of raging waters (vss. 4-5):

> then the flood would have swept us away,
>   the torrent would have gone over us;
> then over us would have gone
>   the raging waters.

Even the section that praises God's intervention keeps the dread of the enemy before the reader. The deliverance is compared to the rescue of a victim from a wild beast: "Blessed be the Lord, / who has not given us as prey to their teeth" (vs. 6). The enemies are also like fowlers who capture birds (vs. 7):

> We have escaped as a bird
>   from the snare of the fowlers;
> the snare is broken,
>   and we have escaped!

The concluding attitude that the poet voices in this praise of God's deliverance is a humble affirmation of trust: "Our help is in the name of the Lord, / who made heaven and earth" (vs. 8).

Psalm 136 is the most elaborate of the antiphonal hymns. The first half of each verse was undoubtedly sung by a priest or priestly chorus, with the fixed refrain in the second half uttered by the congregation. After an introductory call to praise (vss. 1-3), the poem catalogs the works of God that manifest His worthiness to be praised.

The acts of God move from the area of nature (vss. 4-9) to history (vss. 10-22) to God's providential care in the personal lives of His people (vss. 23-25). The historical section (vss. 10-22) illustrates the way in which a mere recital of history became, for the Old Testament believer, a statement of theology. History proved that God is the God who acts and who governs history in such a way that it becomes redemptive for those who follow Him.

As even this very selective survey of psalms of praise indicates, praise was a way of life for the psalmists and the believing community. What are we to make of this poetry of praise? The best comments on the subject have been made by C. S. Lewis.[10] Lewis observes that "all enjoyment spontaneously overflows into praise" — that, in fact, enjoyment is incomplete until it issues forth in praise. Praise, writes Lewis, is "inner health made audible." And just as people praise what they value, they urge other people to join in their praise. Also excellent is Westermann's observation that praise belongs to life and that life without praise is inconceivable.[11] This is so because to praise means to extol, and everyone extols one thing or another. In the Psalms the praise is directed by the believer to God.

VII

Any discussion of the artistry of the Psalms must include mention of the acrostic psalms. These are poems in which the successive units (either half verses, verses, or groups of verses) begin with the successive letters of the Hebrew alphabet. In Psalms 9, 10, 25, 34, and 145 the verses begin with words whose first letters are, consecutively, the letters of the Hebrew alphabet. In Psalm 37 the opening letters of alternate verses are arranged according to the sequence of the alphabet. Another variation occurs in Psalm 111, where each line (rather than each verse) begins with the successive letters of the Hebrew alphabet.

The most elaborate acrostic poem in the Psalter is Psalm 119. This artistically shaped poem consists of twenty-two sections, each comprised of eight verses. These units feature, in order, the twenty-two letters of the Hebrew alphabet, with all eight verses of a given unit beginning with the same letter of the alphabet. This orderliness reinforces the meaning of the poem, which is the law of God. The poem thus illustrates on an artistic level the beauty of order that it declares to exist on the moral level.

---

[10] "A Word about Praising," in *Reflections on the Psalms*, pp. 90-98.
[11] Westermann, *Praise of God*, pp. 158-161.

VIII

A collection of lyric poems such as the Psalms gives a picture of a cultural milieu and its values just as fully as does an epic poem. We can legitimately ask, therefore, What kind of "world" emerges from the Psalms? What sort of people were the Old Testament Hebrews?

The Jews were religious people — worshipers of God and having a strong sense of moral right and wrong. They did not feel apologetic about regarding themselves as the people of God as opposed to wicked unbelievers. They were people of strong emotions, which find their expression in the greatest anthology of lyric poetry ever produced. The Hebrews lived close to nature and were for the most part a nation of farmers, living in the country rather than the city. At the same time, the Jews had a strong nationalistic loyalty. Patriotism was a dominant strand in the national consciousness as captured in the Psalms. They were warriors who carried out their military endeavors in an awareness of religious commitment. In fact, a reading of the Psalms suggests that their military experiences had a way of casting them upon God in especially intense and meaningful ways. Finally, we should not overlook that the Hebrews enjoyed good poetry. The Psalms were known and recited as a shared cultural experience as perhaps no other body of poetry has ever been.

The creative power of God is lauded in Psalm 139.

God, Worship, and Nature in the Psalms

I

What is God like? To this question the psalmists give a variety of answers. Their answers must be studied within the framework of lyric poetry rather than systematic theology for the obvious reason that they wrote lyric poems, not theological treatises. They were less concerned to convey information about God than to write about their own experience of God and of their response to Him. Their utterances, moreover, are poetic in form, having all the characteristics of lyric poetry and asking to be understood and enjoyed in those terms.

Psalm 139 is an ode that illustrates how a lyric poet communicates his experience of God. An ode is a lyric poem that treats a lofty subject in an exalted style. It is usually a celebration of the subject, and it is the loftiest and gravest kind of lyric, just as epic is in the narrative family. Psalm 139 is a prayer addressed to God. The sequential structure of the poem is clear and firm: praise of God's omniscience (vss. 1-6), praise of God's omnipresence (vss. 7-12), praise of God's omnificence (vss. 13-18), and dispraise of all who oppose God (vss. 19-24).

The focus of the poem is paradoxically on both God and the speaker, as it is in many of the psalms of praise. On the one hand, the opening invocation, "O Lord," can be said to introduce the topic of the entire poem. In fact, there are thirty-six references to God in the poem. At the same time, the personal element is evident from the way in which the great attributes of God are discussed as they are experienced in the life of the poet. God's omniscience, for example, is not an abstract principle but is experienced in God's knowledge of "me." Similarly, God's omnipresence means that "I" cannot flee from His presence, and His creative power is seen in His creation of "me." Complementing the thirty-six references to God are forty-five references to the speaker. This emphasis on a "thou-I" situation forces attention on the centrality of relationship in this description of what God is like.

The first section of the poem deals with God's omniscience, beginning with a generalization and then naming specific details that support and illustrate it (vss. 1-6):

> *O Lord, thou hast searched me and known me!*
> *Thou knowest when I sit down and when I rise up;*
> *thou discernest my thoughts from afar.*
> *Thou searchest out my path and my lying down,*
> *and art acquainted with all my ways.*
> *Even before a word is on my tongue,*
> *lo, O Lord, thou knowest it altogether.*
> *Thou dost beset me behind and before,*
> *and layest thy hand upon me.*
> *Such knowledge is too wonderful for me;*
> *it is high, I cannot attain it.*

The verbs in this passage keep the focus on God's knowledge: "searched . . . and known," "knowest," "discernest," "searchest out," "art acquainted," "knowest . . . altogether," "beset . . . behind and before." Accordingly, it is God's "knowledge" that is said to be "wonderful" to the poet.

The opening section already illustrates the poet's tendency to embellish his utterance in a poetic manner. Parallelism of clauses and thoughts pervades the passage. Balance and antithesis are evident in several lines: "when I sit down and when I rise up"; "my path and my lying down"; "behind and before." Chiasmus ("crossing"), a poetic device in which a pair of items appears twice in two successive lines, but with the order reversed in the second line, occurs in verses 2 and 3, where the activities of reclining and walking are repeated in the reverse order ("my path and my lying down"). In verse 5 the poet uses a spatial metaphor when he compares God's all-encompassing knowledge to something that boxes him in, overhead as well as around: "Thou dost beset me behind and before, / and layest thy hand upon me."

Verse 7 provides a transition from God's omniscience to His omnipresence by posing a question that subsequent verses will answer: "Whither shall I go from thy Spirit? / Or whither shall I flee from thy presence?" In answering this question, the poet pictures himself as attempting to escape from God's presence. It is a variation of the quest motif. Parallelism pervades the passage, as it does other sections of the psalm. The poet first pictures escape upward: "If I ascend to heaven, thou art there!" (vs. 8). This is balanced by downward escape: "If I make my bed in Sheol, thou art there!" (vs. 8). Yet a third possibility is described, namely, outward movement in a horizontal direction (vss. 9-10):

> If I take the wings of the morning
>   and dwell in the uttermost parts of the sea,
> even there thy hand shall lead me,
>   and thy right hand shall hold me.

Having exhausted the possibilities of escape in space, the poet next turns to darkness, the archetypal agent of secrecy, and plays upon the antithesis of light and darkness (vss. 11-12):

> If I say, "Let only darkness cover me,
>   and the light about me be night,"
> even the darkness is not dark to thee,
>   the night is bright as the day;
> for darkness is as light with thee.

The wonder and emotional response of the poet are implied by his discovery that "even" there escape from God is impossible.

The poet's third point in his development of the theme of God's greatness is that God is omnificent, or all-creating. It is not God's creation of the world that occupies the speaker. In keeping with the earlier emphasis on God's personal concern for the individual, the poet concentrates on God's creative activity in forming the poet himself (vss. 13-16):

> For thou didst form my inward parts,
>   thou didst knit me together in my mother's womb.
> I praise thee, for thou art fearful and wonderful.
>   Wonderful are thy works!
> Thou knowest me right well;
>   my frame was not hidden from thee,
> when I was being made in secret,
>   intricately wrought in the depths of the earth.
> Thy eyes beheld my unformed substance;
>   in thy book were written, every one of them,
> the days that were formed for me,
>   when as yet there was none of them.

Several metaphors convey the poet's meaning. God's intimate control of the developing fetus is suggested by the images of forming, knitting, and observing with eyes. The poet compares the mysterious growth of the fetus in the womb to the ancient myth that the feminine earth was the mother of all living things, which were produced in the middle of the earth. Yet another figurative expression is the "book" of God, a biblical archetype that sometimes refers, as it does here, to the divine plan by which God orders the destiny of His creatures.

Verses 17 and 18 are simply a lyric interlude containing the emotional response to the God whose qualities the poet is praising:

> *How precious to me are thy thoughts, O God!*
> *How vast is the sum of them!*
> *If I would count them, they are more than the sand.*
> *When I awake, I am still with thee.*

The last statement shows that from the earlier motif of flight away from God, the poet has moved to a celebration of his union with God.

As we have observed in other psalms, lyric poets often develop their theme by introducing a contrast into their development. Psalm 139 illustrates this mode of development. Beginning with verse 19, the poet moves from praise of God to dispraise of people who hate God (vss. 19-24). This transition is not at all illogical. As a chapter in the overriding plot of the Bible, the poet here aligns himself on the side of God in the spiritual struggle between good and evil. It is not for his own enemies that he wishes destruction. His conflict is rather with the enemies of God. It is the vivid consciousness of values that prompts the psalmist to despise evildoers as the counterpart of loving God.

The ode concludes on a quiet note in which the poet asks God to search and purify him (vss. 23-24):

> *Search me, O God, and know my heart!*
> *Try me and know my thoughts!*
> *And see if there be any wicked way in me,*
> *and lead me in the way everlasting!*

These lines are a unified part of the last movement of the poem. Having asked for the destruction of any evil that stands opposed to the God whose greatness has been praised, the speaker applies the principle to himself. He places himself under the same scrutiny that prompted him in the preceding verses to request the punishment of the wicked. The conclusion of the poem also balances the opening. By asking for God to search him, the speaker acquiesces in his opening declaration that God is the one who searches and knows him perfectly.

Psalm 139 is one of the most exalted lyrics in the Psalter. Psalm 103, another ode, is similar in scope. Its subject is the mighty acts of God, a recurrent theme in the Psalms. The structure is based on a catalog that describes God's acts, and its poetic texture is rich. The poem is an introspective meditation in which the poet addresses one of his faculties, the soul (vss. 1-2):

> Bless the Lord, O my soul;
>> and all that is within me, bless his holy name!
> Bless the Lord, O my soul,
>> and forget not all his benefits.

The reflective process of the speaker commences with a consideration of his own personal experience of God's grace. In a series of parallel clauses, the poet continues to apostrophize his own soul (vss. 3-5):

> ... who forgives all your iniquity,
>> who heals all your diseases,
> who redeems your life from the Pit,
>> who crowns you with steadfast love and mercy,
> who satisfies you with good as long as you live,
>> so that your youth is renewed like the eagle's.

The list begins with the forgiveness of sins, reflecting the priority of values in the Judeo-Christian world view. Since it is the spiritual or religious faculty that is being addressed, the statement about the healing of diseases should be taken as a metaphor, being parallel in meaning to the statement about forgiving iniquity. The passage is notable from a literary point of view for its careful parallelism, its choice of verbs overflowing with beautiful and positive connotations, and its use of metaphor (sin is a disease, spiritual calamity is a pit, love and mercy are a crown, revival of soul is like the vigor of a soaring eagle). In verse 5, just as the pattern of consecutive "who..." clauses threatens the series with monotony, the poet introduces a variation by making the last line grammatically different from the preceding lines. God is the subject of all the verbs, suggesting that, above all, God *acts*. The arena of His activity is here the personal life of the speaker, and the events are spiritual in nature. Another principle underlying the list is that every act of God involves His restoring or bringing back to a thriving condition.

In verses 6 to 18 the poet broadens his scope and describes God's grace as seen in national history and in the human community generally. There is movement outward from the speaker as a private person to the speaker as a spokesman for the community at large. The poet's first assertion is that history is a divine order, operating according to a principle of justice: "The Lord works vindication / and justice for all who are oppressed" (vs. 6). Even more far-reaching in implication is the statement that "He made known his ways to Moses, / his acts to the people of Israel" (vs. 7). God, in other words, is a God who reveals Himself and does so in history. The poet also praises God's forgiving nature (vss. 8-10), echoing in a communal context what he has earlier said about his personal experience. The idea is first stated in positive form: "The Lord is merciful and gracious, / slow to anger and abounding in steadfast love" (vs. 8). In the next verses the poet states the same truth in negative terms (vss. 9-10):

> *He will not always chide,*
> > *nor will he keep his anger for ever,*
> *He does not deal with us according to our sins,*
> > *nor requite us according to our iniquities.*

It is the artistic instinct that makes a writer balance one type of statement with its opposite. The speaker goes on to depict the nature of God's forgiveness through the use of two striking spatial images, one involving height and the other horizontal movement (vss. 11-12):

> *For as the heavens are high above the earth,*
> > *so great is his steadfast love toward those who fear him;*
> *as far as the east is from the west,*
> > *so far does he remove our transgressions from us.*

A third simile, drawn from the domestic world, evokes with great effectiveness a sense of God's personal relationship with His creatures: "As a father pities his children, / so the Lord pities those who fear him" (vs. 13).

In a subsequent movement of this song, the poet uses contrast as a way of praising God's love. He first describes man's transience (vss. 14-16) and contrasts it to the enduring nature of God's love: "But the steadfast love of the Lord is from everlasting to everlasting" (vs. 17). The poet is careful to define God's love within the context of His covenant relationship to His people; thus His love is said to extend "to those who keep his covenant and remember to do his commandments" (vs. 18).

The ode ends on a note of ecstasy with a series of apostrophes, which are also doxologies (calls to praise):

> *Bless the Lord, O you his angels,*
> > *you mighty ones who do his word,*
> > > *hearkening to the voice of his word!*
> *Bless the Lord, all his hosts,*
> > *his ministers that do his will!*
> *Bless the Lord, all his works,*
> > *in all places of his dominion.*
> *Bless the Lord, O my soul!*

The implication of the conclusion is clear: a God who does the acts that have been described evokes response and praise. The last line of the poem is a brilliant stroke. It repeats the opening line of the poem, giving the poem an envelope structure and a sense of completeness. By repeating the opening sentiment, the psalmist reminds us of how much ground the meditation has covered. Also, after the expansiveness and heightened emotions in the middle of the poem, we subside again into quiet, personal meditation at the end.

Psalm 107 is yet another ode that praises God, this time for His deliverance of people in need. The underlying contrast in the poem is between man's neediness and God's deliverance.

The main rhetorical feature of the psalm is a series of four short narratives, each of which unfolds according to a carefully designed pattern. The poet successively describes God's deliverance of people suffering in the desert (vss. 4-9), in prison (vss. 10-16), from disease (vss. 17-22), and from peril on the sea (vss. 23-32). Each section follows an identical sequence, beginning with a scene of desolation. The second phase of each narrative consists of a repeated refrain: "Then they cried to the Lord in their trouble, / and he delivered them from their distress" (vss. 6, 13, 19, 28). In the third section of each unit, the poet describes God's deliverance, using the imagery that had been used in the initial account of the people's plight. Each short narrative concludes with a call to thank God for His deliverance, beginning with a fixed refrain ("Let them thank the Lord for his steadfast love, / for his wonderful works to the sons of men!" — vss. 8, 15, 21, 31).

There is an ambiguity regarding the exact nature of the need in the descriptions. The scenes of disaster can plausibly be interpreted as being either literal or symbolic or both. For example, the wasteland images of the first passage might well be symbols for any kind of need that people experience, or it could be a fairly literal description of God's leading the Israelites through the wilderness to a promised land. Similarly, the prison imagery of the second account could be symbolic, since the same images are used elsewhere in Scripture to describe spiritual bondage (see Luke 4:17-21 for an example). The sickness in the third narrative could equally well be literal or symbolic, for although the ailments are realistic in symptom (vs. 18), they are also linked to the people's "sinful ways" and "iniquities" (vs. 17). However we interpret these images, it is certain that the poet manages to evoke elemental and archetypal associations of disaster with each of his sketches.

In a concluding section (vss. 33-43) the poem contrasts God's humiliation of the proud ("he pours contempt upon princes" — vs. 40) with His rescue of the poor ("but he raises up the needy out of affliction" — vs. 41). To describe the overthrow of the prosperous,

163

the poet uses demonic archetypes taken from the realm of nature (vss. 33-34):

> *He turns rivers into a desert,*
> *springs of water into thirsty ground,*
> *a fruitful land into a salty waste,*
> *because of the wickedness of its inhabitants.*

Balancing this is a scene that draws upon the archetypes of comedy and romance in picturing a golden age of bliss (vss. 35-38):

> *He turns a desert into pools of water,*
> *a parched land into springs of water.*
> *And there he lets the hungry dwell,*
> *and they establish a city to live in;*
> *they sow fields, and plant vineyards,*
> *and get a fruitful yield.*
> *By his blessing they multiply greatly;*
> *and he does not let their cattle decrease.*

The lyric concludes on a fitting note of finality by urging the reader to heed the truths that have been asserted: "Whoever is wise, let him give heed to these things; / let men consider the steadfast love of the Lord" (vs. 43).

Not all of the lyric treatments of the subject of God tune the lyre as high as the odes we have considered thus far. Many are simple meditations on a single quality or characteristic of God. A good example is Psalm 90, a reflection on the topic of God's eternity. As a structural principle the poet has used the contrast between God's eternity and man's transience.

The opening sentence announces the theme of the poem and identifies it as a prayer: "Lord, thou hast been our dwelling place / in all generations." The comparison of God to a dwelling place conveys a sense of God's protective care for His people, while the additional thought that He has been a refuge "in all generations" already suggests the enduring permanence of God.

The poem is an excellent example of the meditative lyric at its best. As it unfolds we witness a mind in action, moving from an initial reflection through a series of related thoughts. The sequence of ideas pushes constantly forward, and the effect maintained is that we are observing a speaker in the very process of thinking and reflecting.

The poet begins by observing that God is not simply old but older than the primordial act of creation (vs. 2):

> *Before the mountains were brought forth,*
> *or ever thou hadst formed the earth and the world,*
> *from everlasting to everlasting thou art God.*

164

The next verse adds the idea that God's permanence makes Him different from man as well as from the creation: "Thou turnest man back to the dust, / and sayest, 'Turn back, O children of men!' " (vs. 3). God's transcendence over time is then expressed by means of two similes (vs. 4) :

> *For a thousand years in thy sight*
> *are but as yesterday when it is past,*
> *or as a watch in the night.*

A metaphor and another simile repeat the idea of man's transience and insubstantiality when compared to God's sovereign eternity: "Thou dost sweep men away; they are like a dream" (vs. 5). An extended simile drawn from nature becomes the climactic statement of the theme of man's mortality (vss. 5-6) :

> *like grass which is renewed in the mornings*
> *in the morning it flourishes and is renewed;*
> *in the evening it fades and withers.*

Having completed the possibilities in the contrast between God's eternity and man's mortality, the speaker presses on to a related idea. God's permanence can also be contrasted to man's sinfulness, which is the ultimate cause of his mortality. This analysis makes man's difference from God not simply temporal but also spiritual, as suggested by the first two verses of this section (vss. 7-8) :

> *For we are consumed by thy anger;*
> *by thy wrath we are overwhelmed.*
> *Thou hast set our iniquities before thee,*
> *our secret sins in the light of thy countenance.*

Subsequent verses (9-10) repeat the idea that man's misery stems from God's judgment of his sin. A rhetorical question is used to comment on man's unawareness of the relationship between mortality and sin: "Who considers the power of thy anger, / and thy wrath according to the fear of thee?" (vs. 11). The concluding verse of this section voices a prayer to be delivered from such unawareness: "So teach us to number our days / that we may get a heart of wisdom" (vs. 12). The word "so" here refers to the previous sentence and is a request that people might number their days (that is, consider their mortality) in the light of the power of God's anger against their sinfulness.

The meditation, which began as a contemplation of God's eternity and has progressed into a sober reflection on human mortality and sinfulness, concludes with a series of petitions. There is mingled

165

optimism and pessimism in the muted passage, with the awareness of God's sovereign goodness balanced by the implied recognition of man's frailty and the misery of life (vss. 13-17) :

> Return, O Lord! How long?
>   Have pity on thy servants!
> Satisfy us in the morning with thy steadfast love,
>   that we may rejoice and be glad all our days.
> Make us glad as many days as thou hast afflicted us,
>   and as many years as we have seen evil.
> Let thy work be manifest to thy servants,
>   and thy glorious power to their children.
> Let the favor of the Lord our God be upon us,
>   and establish thou the work of our hands upon us,
>   yea, the work of our hands establish thou it.

Many of the overtones and nuances of meaning in these verses depend on our awareness of how the words have been used earlier in the poem. The prayer for God to satisfy "in the morning" cannot be divorced from the statement in verse 6 that although man is like grass that flourishes "in the morning," by evening the grass "fades and withers." The picture of rejoicing and being glad "all our days" (vs. 14) is subdued because of the earlier assertion that "all our days pass away under thy wrath" (vs. 9). And the wish for God's work to be manifest (vs. 16) cannot be made without recalling that part of God's work is to turn man back to dust (vs. 3) and sweep him away (vs. 5).

Poetry often makes its point indirectly instead of by direct statement. Psalm 91 is an example. It indirectly characterizes God as a God who protects those who trust in Him. The ostensible focus of the poem, however, is not on God but on the person who trusts God. God's character is viewed indirectly in terms of what happens in the life of the believer. The main technique used by the poet is a catalog of short, vivid illustrations and metaphors. For vigor of imagination, the poem ranks with the best in the Psalter.

The opening verses of the psalm picture the quiet assurance that belongs to the person who trusts in God (vss. 1-2) :

> He who dwells in the shelter of the Most High,
>   who abides in the shadow of the Almighty,
> will say to the Lord, "My refuge and my fortress;
>   my God, in whom I trust."

Trust in God is here shown to be a personal matter ("my refuge," "my fortress," "my God"). The epithets of the opening verse direct attention to the appropriate attribute of God, His sovereignty ("the

Most High," "the Almighty"). Metaphors picture God's protection as a building or cave that protects from outside threats and as a shadow that shields a person from the sun. The references to God as a refuge and fortress take us to yet a third area of experience, warfare.

The rest of the poem provides a rationale for the opening description of the calm assurance that belongs to the person who trusts God by listing the acts of God upon which such assurance is based. The statement that God "will deliver you from the snare of the fowler" (vs. 3) uses a metaphor from hunting, while the prediction of deliverance "from the deadly pestilence" shifts the focus to the medical world of plagues and illness. An analogy pictures God as a protective bird: "he will cover you with his pinions, / and under his wings you will find refuge" (vs. 4). By the time we reach the next line, the imagery has shifted to a military scene: "his faithfulness is a shield and buckler" (vs. 4). In each of the next two verses, deliverance at night is balanced by deliverance during the day (vss. 5-6) :

> *You will not fear the terror of the night,*
> *nor the arrow that flies by day,*
> *nor the pestilence that stalks in darkness,*
> *nor the destruction that wastes at noonday.*

The first line of the passage describes freedom from the archetypal fear of darkness and perhaps from nightmares. The phrase "the arrow that flies by day" could be a military reference, though in several Old Testament passages the judgment of God is pictured as arrows that inflict disaster (Ps. 38:2; Job 6:4; Lam. 3:13). In verse 6 pestilence is personified and vividly pictured as stalking a victim. It is probably a reference with multiple meanings. On two Old Testament occasions, God sent deadly pestilence by night (Exod. 11:4-5; Isa. 37:36), and the psalmist may here intend an allusion to these or similar historical events. It is also possible that the lines refer to early medical views that attributed the spread of plagues to bad air and evil smells, especially as encountered in an enclosed room. The "destruction that wastes at noonday" (vs. 6) is undoubtedly sunstroke.

Later verses in the psalm show the poet using hyperbole to depict events which, while not conveying literal truth, express emotional truth and state with power the confidence that any believer in God can experience. The first such statement involves a scene of warfare (vss. 7-8) :

> *A thousand may fall at your side,*
> *ten thousand at your right hand;*
> *but it will not come near you.*
> *You will only look with your eyes*
> *and see the recompense of the wicked.*

Similarly, the statement that "no evil shall befall you, / no scourge come near your tent" (vs. 10) is an exaggeration used to convey strong feeling. The same thing can be said of the pictures that follow (vss. 11-13):

> For he will give his angels charge of you
>   to guard you in all your ways.
> On their hands they will bear you up,
>   lest you dash your foot against a stone.
> You will tread on the lion and the adder,
>   the young lion and the serpent you will trample under foot.

These miraculous events are not the normal experience of believers, but that is beside the point in a lyric that is designed to communicate feeling, not fact.

The concluding speech in the poem is put into God's mouth. It asserts the same truth that has been presented from a human perspective earlier, namely, that God protects those who trust in Him (vss. 14-16):

> Because he cleaves to me in love, I will deliver him;
>   I will protect him, because he knows my name.
> When he calls to me, I will answer him;
>   I will be with him in trouble,
>   I will rescue him and honor him.
> With long life I will satisfy him,
>   and show him my salvation.

Psalm 32, like most lyric poems dealing with God, concentrates on a single aspect of God's character and work, His forgiveness. The whole poem is based on the tension between guilt and forgiveness. Careful parallelism underlies the poem, which begins with two beatitudes that state the theme, first in positive terms and then with a negative formula (vss. 1-2):

> Blessed is he whose transgression is forgiven.
>   whose sin is covered.
> Blessed is the man to whom the Lord imputes no iniquity,
>   and in whose spirit there is no deceit.

Lyric poetry is the voice of personal experience. The poet frequently validates his assertions by an appeal to his own observations and experience. Psalm 32 illustrates this tendency of lyric poetry. The poet proves his opening assertions, not by logical argument, but by narrating an event from his own life. He first paints a vivid picture of the effects of unrepented sin (vss. 3-4):

> *When I declared not my sin, my body wasted away*
> *through my groaning all day long.*
> *For day and night thy hand was heavy upon me;*
> *my strength was dried up as by the heat of summer.*

The description is either hyperbolic, conveying an emotional sense of the speaker's distress, or a literal account of a guilt-induced, psychosomatic ailment. The second phase of the story depicts the speaker's confession and restoration (vs. 5):

> *I acknowledged my sin to thee,*
> *and I did not hide my iniquity;*
> *then thou didst forgive the guilt of my sin.*
> *I said, "I will confess my transgressions to the Lord";*
> *then thou didst forgive the guilt of my sin.*

On the basis of his private experience, the poet moves to a generalization for all believers, using a metaphor from nature to embellish his thought (vs. 6):

> *Therefore let every one who is godly*
> *offer prayer to thee;*
> *at a time of distress, in the rush of great waters,*
> *they shall not reach him.*

What he asserts as a general principle for all believers the poet also applies to himself, expressing his conviction in terms taken from the military world (vs. 7):

> *Thou art a hiding place for me,*
> *thou preservest me from trouble;*
> *thou dost encompass me with deliverance.*

The poem ends on a didactic note, urging readers to heed the wisdom of what has been uttered and to rejoice in God's goodness (vss. 8-11).

The God of the Psalms is emphatically a God who is encountered in worship. Psalm 95 summarizes this thrust of the Psalter. Of most interest in the poem are the motivatory sections in which the poet gives the rationale for his calls to worship God. In effect the poet asserts that God is to be worshiped because of who He is: "For the Lord is a great God, / and a great King above all gods" (vs. 3). He amplifies this statement about God's universal kingship by describing the scope of His rule, using the balanced images of "the depths" and "the heights," and "the sea" and "the dry land" (vss. 4-5):

> *In his hand are the depths of the earth;*
> *the heights of the mountains are his also.*

> *The sea is his, for he made it;*
> *for his hands formed the dry land.*

Later in the poem a second rationale for worship is offered. The emphasis here is on God's covenant relationship with His own people, a relationship that is described in pastoral imagery (vs. 7):

> *For he is our God,*
> *and we are the people of his pasture,*
> *and the sheep of his hand.*

Several concluding generalizations can be made about the God of the Psalms. He is above all the God who acts. His acts are attested by the experiential statements of the psalmists themselves. God is both transcendent, far exalted above His creation, and immanent, very much a part of what happens in His creation. He is a moral God, always concerned with righteousness and evil. This concern has a dual manifestation, showing itself in angry judgment against sin and in mercy and forgiveness toward those who turn to Him in obedience.

Worship is another of the overriding concerns of the Psalms. The conventional title for the poems of worship is "songs of Zion." Zion emerged into historical record in the era of David. It was a Jebusite stronghold when David captured it from the Canaanites and made it his capital, calling it "the city of David" (2 Sam. 5:7). He brought the ark of the Lord to Zion, setting it "in its place" in the tent that he had pitched for it (2 Sam. 6:17). When Solomon's temple was built on Mt. Moriah (2 Chron. 3:1), the ark was brought in festal procession from the sacred tent and was housed permanently in the "most holy place" of the temple (1 Kings 8:1-6). Eventually the name "Zion" was understood as referring to the temple, the hill on which the temple stood, and Jerusalem as a city. In short, in the Psalms "Zion" is the designation for the Hebrew center of worship.

The background against which all the hymns of Zion must be viewed is the pervasive feeling of the Israelites that God dwelt in the temple. Psalm 11:4 states, "The Lord is in his holy temple." Similar statements abound: "O Lord, I love the habitation of thy house, and the place where thy glory dwells" (Ps. 26:8); "so I have looked upon thee in the sanctuary, beholding thy power and glory" (63:2); "for the Lord has chosen Zion; he has desired it for his habitation: 'This is my resting place for ever; here I will dwell'" (132:13-14).

Because of the presence of God in the temple, the Jews attached great importance to the place.

In the background of the Psalms of worship is yet another phenomenon, the existence of religious pilgrimages. Most of these journeys were made to the temple in Jerusalem. All males were required to go to Jerusalem three times annually, at the festival of unleavened bread (or the passover), the feast of weeks, and the feast of tabernacles (or feast of booths). The prevalence of such pilgrimages in Hebrew culture undoubtedly accounts for much of the emphasis on worship that we find in the Psalter. In fact, many of the songs were sung enroute to Jerusalem, and in important ways the Psalter can be called a temple collection, since it represents an anthology of songs eventually used in worship at the temple.

Several verses from Psalm 27 illustrate how the Hebrew worshiper experienced God in the temple. After expressing his trust in God (vss. 1-3), the speaker states a desire for perpetual communion with God. What is noteworthy is how he conceives of such perpetual union (vs. 4):

> One thing have I asked of the Lord,
>   that will I seek after;
> that I may dwell in the house of the Lord
>   all the days of my life,
> to behold the beauty of the Lord,
>   and to inquire in his temple.

To be united with God is to worship regularly in His temple at Jerusalem. The intensity of the poet's desire is conveyed by overstatement — "one thing have I asked," "all the days of my life." The reference to dwelling "in the house of the Lord" should not be interpreted literally, since no one actually lived in the sanctuary itself. The poet is rather expressing his desire for frequent worship of God in the temple, since this was his most tangible contact with God.

Psalms 42 and 43, printed separately but actually comprising a single poem, express a similar feeling about God's presence in the temple. The poem has a psychological structure in which the poet moves through a series of emotions, including longing for God, sorrow over absence from Zion, trust in God, hope for eventual return to the temple, and nostalgia over past pilgrimages. Underlying plot conflicts include past pilgrimages vs. present exile, longing for God vs. His actual absence, Jerusalem vs. the speaker's pagan environment, and sorrow vs. consolation. The poem moves between the poles of despair and hope, with the speaker's meditation moving gradually toward increasing confidence. Repetitive structure derives from the statement of a refrain three times (42:5, 11; 43:5).

The speaker's situation is implied in the poem. He is living in exile and is prevented from journeying to the temple as he once did. His sorrow is double: he is deprived of temple worship, and he is living in a hostile pagan environment.

The poem begins with a memorable simile in which the speaker expresses his intense longing for God's presence (42:1-2):

> *As a hart longs*
> *for flowing streams,*
> *so longs my soul*
> *for thee, O God.*
> *My soul thirsts for God,*
> *for the living God.*

The question that follows can be understood only in terms of the Hebrew attitude toward temple worship, as the speaker asks, "When shall I come and behold / the face of God?" (vs. 2). To behold the face of God was to worship in the temple in Jerusalem. The physical journey was also a spiritual quest for union with God. The poet's despair is conveyed by means of hyperbole: "My tears have been my food day and night" (vs. 3). The reason for the despair is said to be the taunts of the pagans, who ask, "Where is your God?" (vs. 3). Once again the answer of the psalmist is implied: his God is in Jerusalem, in the temple.

The speaker shifts suddenly from present despair to nostalgia over the past in this psychologically structured poem. He recalls earlier pilgrimages with the words (vs. 4),

> *These things I remember,*
> *as I pour out my soul:*
> *how I went with the throng,*
> *and led them in procession to the house of God,*
> *with glad shouts and songs of thanksgiving,*
> *a multitude keeping festival.*

The first occurrence of the refrain is a rebuke to the speaker's soul for its despairing attitude (vs. 5):

> *Why are you cast down, O my soul,*
> *and why are you disquieted within me?*
> *Hope in God; for I shall again praise him,*
> *my help and my God.*

The relief is only temporary, for in verse 6 the speaker begins a new cycle of despair. It is in this section that he pictures himself as living in "the land of Jordan and of Hermon" (vs. 6), in a foreign land. The poet also uses a new technique for conveying his despair, painting a symbolic landscape as a way of describing an internal mood (vs. 7) :

> *Deep calls to deep*
> *   at the thunder of thy cataracts;*
> *all thy waves and thy billows*
> *   have gone over me.*

The rest of this unit repeats earlier themes, including hope in God, despair over God's forgetting, the taunts of enemies, and the refrain expressing temporary comfort.

In the third movement of the poem (Ps. 43), the note of confidence becomes dominant. Whereas the previous sections have been largely introspective meditation, the last part is an extended prayer in which the focus is on God rather than the speaker. It is a plea that God will again allow the speaker to travel to Jerusalem. The most notable expression of this quest is verse 3, in which the speaker personifies the spiritual qualities of light and truth and pictures them as capable of guiding him to Mt. Zion:

> *Oh send out thy light and thy truth;*
> *   let them lead me,*
> *let them bring me to thy holy hill*
> *   and to thy dwelling!*

Worship at the temple, which had earlier been sorrowful reminiscence, now becomes joyous anticipation (vs. 4) :

> *Then I will go to the altar of God,*
> *   to God my exceeding joy;*
> *and I will praise thee with the lyre,*
> *   O God, my God.*

The refrain assumes a new meaning in its context at the conclusion of the poem. The poem has dramatized a movement from sorrow to hope, with the result that the final statement about hoping in God and being confident that "I shall again praise him" (vs. 5) conveys a new meaning of assurance and finality.

Psalm 48 praises God by praising His place of worship. It shows the close relationship between God and His temple in Jerusalem. In fact, the psalm can appropriately be called a Jerusalem poem. A plot sequence underlies the poem, as we move from the approach to Jerusalem to worship within the temple to a procession around the temple.

The first three verses of the poem praise Jerusalem and Mt. Zion, at the same time praising the God who dwells there. As we read these verses, we can infer the approach of a pilgrim to Jerusalem. Suddenly Mt. Zion towers before him, and he is led to say (vss. 1-2):

> Great is the Lord and greatly to be praised
>   in the city of our God!
> His holy mountain, beautiful in elevation,
>   is the joy of all the earth,
> Mount Zion, in the far north,
>   the city of the great King.

The second part of the poem, verses 3 to 8, praises God's protection of Zion:

> Within her citadels God
>   has shown himself a sure defense.
> For lo, the kings assembled,
>   they came on together,
> As soon as they saw it, they were astounded,
>   they were in panic, they took to flight;
> trembling took hold of them there,
>   anguish as of a woman in travail.
> By the east wind thou didst shatter the ships of Tarshish.
> As we have heard, so have we seen
>   in the city of the Lord of hosts,
> in the city of our God,
>   which God establishes for ever.

This vivid and dramatic story of God's defeat of pagan kings is either a symbolic picture of Zion's favored position or it is an attempt to capture the excitement of a historical deliverance, such as the defeat of Sennacherib (Isa. 36-37).

Verses 9 to 11 describe the thoughts evoked by the temple. They picture festal celebration within the temple. The meditation begins with a contemplation of God's love: "We have thought on thy steadfast love, O God, / in the midst of thy temple" (vs. 9). It then moves to the thought of the universality of God's influence: "As thy name, O God, / so thy praise reaches to the ends of the earth" (vs. 10). And it concludes with a recollection of God's mighty acts (vss. 10-11):

> Thy right hand is filled with victory;
>   let Mount Zion be glad!
> Let the daughters of Judah rejoice
>   because of thy judgments!

The poem concludes with a description of a procession around the temple. The speaker makes a mental note of all the details in the scene, showing the important role played by the physical surroundings in worship (vss. 12-14):

> *Walk about Zion, go round about her,*
> *number her towers,*
> *consider well her ramparts,*
> *go through her citadels;*
> *that you may tell the next generation*
> *that this is God,*
> *our God for ever and ever.*
> *He will be our guide for ever.*

As so often in lyric poetry, the poet conveys his emotion not by talking about his feeling but simply by describing concretely the sensations and experiences that stimulate his emotional response.

The poem has progressed just as we would expect a lyric to do. It began with a brief account of the stimulus to praise, the sight of the hills of Jerusalem. It has developed its theme of praise by talking about God's protection of Zion and by reenacting the experience of worshiping in the temple. And it concludes on a note of finality by pointing outward from the present moment and predicting God's faithfulness forever.

Psalm 84 is one of the high points in the songs of Zion. The poem is an occasional poem, taking its impetus from a pilgrimage to the temple. The poem is, therefore, a valuable index to the mood of the typical pilgrim. The outline of the poem is clear and firm: initial responses to the temple upon arrival (vss. 1-4), the joy of the journey (vss. 5-7), prayer uttered at the temple (vss. 8-9), and concluding feelings of the temple worshiper (vss. 10-12).

The poem begins with the pilgrim's cry of joy as he catches sight of the temple: "How lovely is thy dwelling place, O Lord of hosts" (vs. 1). The thing that initially impresses the pilgrim is the loveliness of the temple's appearance. It is a response that includes both aesthetic enjoyment and spiritual anticipation. "Lovely" means not only aesthetic beauty but also belongs to the language of love, suggesting that in the mind of the pilgrim the temple building was really inseparable from God's presence as experienced there.

The speaker proceeds to state his joy and longing for the temple experience (vs. 2):

> *My soul longs, yea, faints*
> *for the courts of the Lord;*
> *my heart and flesh sing for joy*
> *to the living God.*

Such longing for God is a recurrent motif in the Psalms. Two things are suggested by the statement that "my heart and flesh sing for joy to the living God." For one thing, the phrase "the living God" is parallel to the phrase "the courts of the Lord" in the preceding

175

sentence. The two are really indistinguishable. To enter "the courts of the Lord" is to experience "the living God." Secondly, the reference to heart and flesh may reflect the unity that the Old Testament worshiper felt. In his religious experience body and soul, the material and the spiritual, were combined.

Verse 3 is a masterstroke in which the poet describes the birds that nest in the temple:

> *Even the sparrow finds a home,*
> *and the swallow a nest for herself,*
> *where she may lay her young,*
> *at thy altars, O Lord of hosts,*
> *my king and my God.*

The poet here fuses the small and the great — a sparrow and God. Numerous psalms indicate that no part of God's creation is unimportant. In some psalms, for example, all creatures are said to praise God. In this psalm all creatures find their sanctuary in God. The very fact that the pilgrim would include this description in his account of noteworthy events at the temple shows the very real part that physical sensation and observation played in the religious experience of the Israelite. The most important thing about the image of the birds is its implied human meaning. The domestic associations of the image are greatly insisted on. The sparrow is said to find "a home"; the swallow not only builds a nest but is further pictured as raising her offspring there. The point is unmistakable: the temple is a home. Its associations are homey and domestic. God is not only awesome but also fatherly. The pilgrim, like the birds, finds a home and a refuge in the sanctuary of God.

Verse 4 is an outburst of emotional response to the arrival at the temple: "Blessed are those who dwell in thy house, / ever singing thy praise!" The privileged people who are said to "dwell" in the temple are either those who work and minister in the temple or those who worship there. In either case, the nature of God's house is certain — it is a house of praise.

Verses 5 to 7 shift the focus from arrival at the temple to the joy of the pilgrimage or journey:

> *Blessed are the men whose strength is in thee,*
> *in whose heart are the highways to Zion.*
> *As they go through the valley of Baca*
> *they make it a place of springs;*
> *the early rain also covers it with pools.*
> *They go from strength to strength;*
> *the God of gods will be seen in Zion.*

Palestine was a mountainous and thirsty land. The suffering involved in the journeys to Jerusalem was undoubtedly very real. This passage describes, metaphorically and/or literally, God's provision for the needs of the pilgrims as they made their trips through desert areas. The statement "They go from strength to strength" means that in each crisis God intervenes and strengthens. A similar statement is Isaiah's comment that "they who wait for the Lord shall renew their strength" (Isa. 40:31).

Verses 8 and 9 are a prayer uttered by the pilgrim upon reaching the temple:

> O Lord God of hosts, hear my prayer;
>   give ear, O God of Jacob!
> Behold our shield, O God;
>   look upon the face of thine anointed!

The prayer for favor on God's "anointed" is probably a prayer for the king, who was regarded as the representative of the nation and the channel of God's blessing upon His people.

The conclusion of the poem expresses the final feelings of the pilgrim regarding the temple experience. It gives a picture of the life-creating power of the temple experience. The speaker first expresses a preference for union with God in the temple over lesser values (vs. 10):

> For a day in thy courts is better
>   than a thousand elsewhere.
> I would rather be a doorkeeper in the house of my God
>   than dwell in the tents of wickedness.

The statement gains its eloquence and force partly through antithesis: one day vs. a thousand days, God's courts vs. other places, a door-keeper vs. an owner of tents, and the temple vs. luxurious dwellings. By choosing the smaller thing (one day, being a doorkeeper) over the larger (a thousand days, dwelling in tents), the poet startles us into feeling the strength of his conviction about what is truly valuable. The next sentence is an explanation of the reason for the speaker's unconventional scale of values: "For the Lord God is a sun and shield; / he bestows favor and honor" (vs. 11). This is followed by a statement that can be interpreted in alternate ways: "No good thing does the Lord withhold / from those who walk uprightly" (vs. 11). This either continues the hyperbolic tone of overstatement as a way of expressing strong feeling, or it is a literal statement in which the emphasis on "no *good* thing" implies that whatever God sends, whether prosperity or adversity, is for the good of the person

177

who trusts in Him. The poem concludes with an appropriate final resolution: "O Lord of hosts, / blessed is the man who trusts in thee!" (vs. 12).

Songs of religious worship are filled with epithets that exalt God and direct attention to his nature and roles. Psalm 84 is no exception. A catalog of its epithets reveals the following titles for God: "O Lord of hosts" (vss. 1, 3, 12); "the living God" (vs. 2); "my king and my God" (vs. 3); "the God of gods" (vs. 7); "O Lord God of hosts" (vs. 8); "O God of Jacob" (vs. 8); and "the Lord God" (vs. 11). These titles belong to the high style. They give a poem a dignity appropriate to a lofty subject and invest it with the character of praise simply through their presence.

Psalm 121 is part of a group of fifteen psalms (Psalms 120-134) which have a common heading, "A Song of Ascents." This heading indicates that the poems were pilgrim psalms, undoubtedly sung enroute to Jerusalem. As expected, these songs of Zion are filled with allusions to the experience of worshiping God in Jerusalem.

Psalm 121 epitomizes these songs of ascent. Its main structural principle is the contrast between the dangerous pilgrimage and the protection of God. It begins by evoking a brief picture of the beginning of the journey to Jerusalem. As the speaker contemplates the perilous journey through the mountains, he states, "I lift up my eyes to the hills" (vs. 1). On a more symbolic level, the statement is an apt summary of the Hebraic effort toward transcendence, since to lift one's eyes upward above the earthly terrain is to acknowledge one's dependence on a transcendent God. As he lifts up his eyes to the dangerous hills, the pilgrim contemplates the source of his confidence, using a question-answer technique (vss. 1-2):

> *From whence does my help come?*
> *My help comes from the Lord,*
> *who made heaven and earth.*

The fact that God created heaven and earth is just beneath the surface in the Psalms, which are full of allusions to God's role as creator. As the epithet in this passage makes clear, the doctrine of creation was not a bit of abstract theory for the Old Testament believer but was a reality that enabled him to master the situations of everyday life. Since God had made everything that exists, He was also the one who could control the circumstances of a person's life.

After the opening generalization that help comes from the Lord, the poet develops his lyric by listing the protecting acts of God. He begins with a reference to the perilous journey, replete with opportunities of slipping and losing one's footing: "He will not let your foot be moved" (vs. 3). The epithet "he who keeps you" (vs. 3) directs attention to the leading role of God in the poem, while the statement that God "will not slumber" (vs. 3) asserts the continuous nature of God's protective care. Verse 4 exists simply for the sake of emphasis: "Behold, he who keeps Israel / will neither slumber nor sleep." The additional phrase "nor sleep" does not add any cognitive meaning to the statement that God will not "slumber." Its function is emotional, or lyric, not intellectual.

Verse 5 repeats the identity that God has in this poem:

> *The Lord is your keeper;*
> *the Lord is your shade*
> *on your right hand.*

To call God "a shade" is to draw the picture of a tree that protects a traveler from the scorching heat of the sun. The additional thought that God is a shade on a person's "right hand" draws upon a second metaphor, namely, that God is like a warrior who accompanied his lord into battle and customarily stood on his right hand, holding his master's protective weapons in readiness.

The next verse returns to the literal rigors of the journey to Jerusalem. Protection from sunstroke and heat exhaustion is asserted by the statement, "The sun shall not smite you by day." Peril by day is balanced by a reference to peril by night: "nor the moon by night." This is an allusion to the ancient notion that viewed the moon as a cause of disease and to the persistent human association of the moon with mental disorders.[1]

The last two verses of the poem conclude the psalm on a general note of finality by broadening the scope from particular dangers of the trip to all types of calamity and from the present journey to all subsequent time (vss. 7-8):

> *The Lord will keep you from all evil:*
> *he will keep your life.*
> *The Lord will keep*
> *your going out and your coming in*
> *from this time forth and for evermore.*

On its primary level the psalm concerns the journey from the pilgrim's home to Jerusalem. On a metaphoric level it also talks about God's acts of deliverance on the archetypal journey of life.

Psalm 122 is a pilgrim's parting salutation to Jerusalem. It is, like

---

[1] For a biblical example of the latter belief, see Matthew 17:15, where the father of an epileptic boy tells Jesus that his son is a lunatic, that is, "moon-struck."

several other psalms, a Jerusalem poem. The poet begins with retrospective joy over the worship experience: "I was glad when they said
to me, / 'Let us go to the house of the Lord!' " (vs. 1). Now that he
has completed the sojourn in Jerusalem, the speaker is filled with
awe at the thought of what has transpired: "Our feet have been
standing / within your gates, O Jerusalem!" (vs. 2). The latter address is an example not only of personification but apostrophe (direct
address to someone absent as though he were present), which most
often appears in contexts of strong emotion.

The second part of the poem (vss. 3-5) is a meditation on what
Jerusalem means to the worshiper. It is both a symbol for the unity
of the worshiping community and the goal of the thankful heart
(vss. 3-4):

> Jerusalem, built as a city
> which is bound firmly together,
> to which the tribes go up,
> the tribes of the Lord,
> as was decreed for Israel,
> to give thanks to the name of the Lord.

Jerusalem is also the seat of earthly rule, an important consideration
for a nation in which religious and political or national interests
were combined: "There thrones for judgment were set, / the thrones
of the house of David" (vs. 5).

The last four verses of the poem are a prayer expressing the parting
wishes of the worshiper. It is a poetry of subdued but strong emotion
(vss. 6-9):

> Pray for the peace of Jerusalem!
> "May they prosper who love you!
> Peace be within your walls,
> and security within your towers!"
> For my brethren and companions' sake
> I will say, "Peace be within you!"
> For the sake of the house of the Lord our God,
> I will seek your good.

It is important to note how the concepts of city, peace, security,
brethren, temple, God, and good merge together in this passage.
This was exactly the kind of mixture of sentiments that constituted
the experience of traveling to Jerusalem to worship God in the temple.

Psalm 125, another of the songs of ascents, uses the temple experience as a symbol for various aspects of the religious life. The poet
allegorizes the scene with which he is familiar in Jerusalem. For
example, "Those who trust in the Lord are like Mount Zion, / which

cannot be moved, but abides for ever" (vs. 1). And again, "As the mountains are round about Jerusalem, / so the Lord is round about his people" (vs. 2). The temple experience has here become a source of poetic symbolism.

Psalm 137, written during the Babylonian exile, is one of the most intensely moving poems anywhere in literature. Its focal point is the temple of God, as the poet expresses such sentiments as despair over its destruction, continued love for it, and anger toward those who defied God in destroying it. It is a poem with vigorous plot conflict between the Hebrew exiles and their Babylonian captors.

Verses 1-3 describe with a few vivid brushstrokes the situation of the speaker. The experience occurs "by the waters of Babylon" (vs. 1), with the mention of Babylon evoking all kinds of negative associations as the dread conqueror of Israel. In this situation of exile the speaker and his fellow Hebrews are described as experiencing the sorrow that springs from nostalgia: "there we sat down and wept, / when we remembered Zion" (vs. 1). To remember Zion, of course, is to recall the reality and joy of God's presence as He was encountered in the temple. The scene of sorrow is continued with the poet's description of how "on the willows there / we hung up our lyres" (vs. 2). The archetypal connection between willow trees and weeping makes the willows a fitting symbol for the inner feelings of the speaker.

Vivid character conflict is introduced into the scene of sorrow and nostalgia (vs. 3):

> *For there our captors*
> *required of us songs,*
> *and our tormentors, mirth, saying,*
> *"Sing us one of the songs of Zion!"*

The epithets used to designate the Babylonians ("our captors," "our tormentors") effectively communicate their status as despised enemies. The Babylonians' request to hear "the songs of Zion" is an act of sacrilege and mockery, further establishing their spiritual degeneracy. The reference, of course, attests the well-known love of the Hebrews for the temple.

Once the situation has been established, the second part of the poem (vss. 4-6) asserts the poet's love of Jerusalem. The speaker begins with a rhetorical question: "How shall we sing the Lord's song / in a foreign land?" (vs. 4). The juxtaposition of "the Lord's song" with "a foreign land" keeps alive the reader's awareness of the plot conflict in the poem. The poet then calls down violent punishments upon himself if he forgets his love for Jerusalem, with the devices of apostrophe and personification further intensifying the speaker's emotional involvement (vss. 5-6):

> *If I forget you, O Jerusalem,*
>> *let my right hand wither!*
> *Let my tongue cleave to the roof of my mouth,*
>> *if I do not remember you,*
> *if I do not set Jerusalem*
>> *above my highest joy!*

This is not idolatry. For the Hebrew worshiper, Jerusalem meant communion with God. This is what the poet here asserts as his highest value.

The last movement of the poem is a prayer for God's judgment against the enemies who destroyed the temple (vss. 7-9):

> *Remember, O Lord, against the Edomites*
>> *the day of Jerusalem,*
> *how they said, "Rase it, rase it!*
>> *Down to its foundations!"*
> *O daughter of Babylon, you devastator!*
>> *Happy shall he be who requites you*
>> *with what you have done to us!*
> *Happy shall he be who takes your little ones*
>> *and dashes them against the rock!*

Once again the poet uses epithet combined with apostrophe ("O daughter of Babylon," "you devastator") as a way of evoking a strong negative response to the enemies. The word translated "happy" can also mean "blessed," carrying the meaning that the avengers of the Babylonians will be approved by God for having carried out His will against His enemies. What the poet asks for is punishment in the form of military conquest. It is the concreteness of his picture that troubles many readers.

These concluding verses belong to a category of psalms known as the imprecatory psalms — psalms in which the poet calls down bad fortune upon someone else. Much has been written about these psalms, which are usually considered a problem. Without attempting a full discussion of these psalms, I wish to make a few observations. These sentiments must be placed in the broad context of the great spiritual conflict between God and His evil enemies. The psalmists are not asking for personal revenge. They recognize that vengeance belongs to God, whose justice is perfect. To feel strongly opposed to evildoers is the logical outworking of the consciousness of moral values in the Psalms and biblical literature as a whole. If a reader does not share this moral view of the world, it is not only the Psalms that will offend. It is also important to remember that a lyric poem captures a speaker at a single moment of intense emotion. It does not ordinarily present a complete and reasoned exposition of a topic. Revulsion against evildoers is not the only biblically sanctioned attitude toward the ungodly. Desire for the punishment of those who hate God is balanced by a desire for their conversion to God. As for the supposed discrepancy between the imprecatory psalms and the ethical teaching of Christ in the New Testament, we should recall that Christ told His followers to love their own enemies, not the enemies of God or of mankind.

What can be said in conclusion about the concept of worship in the Psalms? For one thing, worship is adoration. That was the original meaning of the concept and that is what it means in the Psalms. The emphasis in this kind of worship is not on receiving but on giving. Worship in the Psalms is God-centered, not self-centered. Worship for the Hebrews involved going to a special place at a particular time, so that the worship experience often exhibits a feeling of festal celebration. Worship is both personal and corporate. It is shown to be enjoyable — something that the worshiper delights to do. Worship in the Psalms is, finally, emotional, finding its appropriate expression in a lyric mode.

Yet another leading topic in the Psalms is nature, and on this subject there is no introduction equal to C. S. Lewis's chapter on the topic, where he makes the following points.[2] Two factors determine the approach of the psalmists to nature. The first is that they were a nation of farmers. As such they had both a utilitarian and aesthetic appreciation of nature. Secondly, the Jews were unique in having a clear and thoroughgoing doctrine that a transcendent God had created nature. To view God as the creator of nature empties nature of deity in the sense that there is no trace of the pagan belief that various objects in nature are divine. God and nature are separate, and there is no attempt to populate the streams and trees with local deities. In another sense the Hebrew conception fills nature with God, making it a revelation or manifestation of God. In the Psalms there is also an appreciation of nature as an achievement or artistic product, since it has been made by God. Even more unique is the Hebrew appreciation for aspects of nature that are indifferent or hostile to man. This appreciation stems from an awareness that man

---

[2] *Reflections on the Psalms* (New York: Harcourt, Brace & World, 1958), pp. 76-89.

and all the rest of nature are fellow dependents, having been created by the same God.

Instead of looking at the references to nature that are scattered throughout the Psalms, I wish to concentrate on the handful of poems devoted wholly to the topic. These poems happen to be among the greatest in the Psalter.

Psalm 8 takes as its topic the glory of God as revealed in creation. The purpose of this nature poem is to express praise of God, a clear index to the theocentric stance that pervades all of the nature poetry in the Bible. Already in the opening statement of his theme, the poet directs attention away from his ostensible subject, nature, to his real subject, God: "O Lord, our Lord, / how majestic is thy name in all the earth!" (vs. 1). The opening exclamation, along with the double address to God, conveys the strong feeling of the speaker. The important aspect of his assertion is that nature reveals God's glory, not its own. The additional comment that the majesty is present "in all the earth" makes the point that the glory of God as seen in nature is a universal glory, not limited to any geographic locale.

Verses 3 to 8 define man's position in relationship to the natural creation. One-half of the poet's observation concentrates on the smallness of man when compared with the greatness of the natural universe (vss. 3-4):

> When I look at thy heavens, the work of thy fingers,
>   the moon and the stars which thou hast established;
> what is man that thou art mindful of him,
>   and the son of man that thou dost care for him?

These lines illustrate beautifully the Hebrew conviction that nature is a divine product, an artistic achievement that God has performed. God, in fact, is humanized and pictured in anthropomorphic terms as working with His hands to form the earth.

The subsequent passage balances the idea of man's smallness with a paradoxical assertion of his simultaneous greatness (vss. 5-6):

> Yet thou hast made him little less than God,
>   and dost crown him with glory and honor.
> Thou hast given him dominion over the works of thy hands;
>   thou hast put all things under his feet.

After thus declaring man's position of dominance over creation in general terms, the poet goes on to balance his statement by giving specific illustrations of such dominance (vss. 7-8):

> all sheep and oxen,
>   and also the beasts of the field,

> *the birds of the air, and the fish of the sea,*
> *whatever passes along the paths of the sea.*

The apparent contradiction between man's smallness and greatness is explainable on the basis of God's grace. Although man by himself and in comparison with the rest of creation is small, God has conferred on him a role of headship. This results in both humility and confidence. This passage, incidentally, can profitably be compared with the "Wonders of Man" speech in Sophocles' play "Antigone" (lines 331-370). That speech also catalogs the ways in which man is master over nature and becomes a magnificent expression of Greek humanism. In the psalm man's mastery of nature is not his own accomplishment but is said to be conferred upon him by God.

The poet does not conclude his poem on the note of man's greatness but turns his thoughts back to God, the starting point of his meditation: "O Lord, our Lord, / how majestic is thy name in all the earth!" (vs. 9). The envelope structure of the poem is more than a matter of artistry. It symbolizes how for the psalmist any meditation about nature and man must begin and end with God. The view of nature that emerges from the poem is significant. Nature is shown to be a declaration of what God is like, a universal witness to God's glory, a product of God's artistic creativity, and a system that is subject to man, implying a hierarchy in the created order.

Psalm 19 is the poem that Lewis declares to be "the greatest poem in the Psalter and one of the greatest lyrics in the world."[3] Once again the main theme is not nature but the excellence of God's revelation of Himself. That revelation occurs in two spheres, and both are praised in the psalm. The first half of the poem (vss. 1-6) praises God's revelation in nature, while the second half (vss. 7-14) extols His glorious revelation of Himself in His law. Each half is itself divided into two units. Thus verses 1-4a are a song in praise of creation in general, while verses 4b to 6 are a hymn in praise of the sun. And, in the second half, verses 7 to 11 are a description of God's law, followed by a personal response and prayer in verses 12 to 14. Another structural principle in the poem consists of a gradual constriction, from the cosmic to the personal, from "the heavens" to "my heart."

The opening clause announces the theme of the first six verses: "The heavens are telling the glory of God." The poet's subject is the heavenly bodies, specifically what they tell us. The verb "are telling" calls attention to the ongoing nature of the heavens' revelation and conveys the idea that the message is perpetually available. The rest of the first verse completes the opening statement, the result being

---

[3] Ibid., p. 63.

synonymous parallelism: "and the firmament proclaims his handi-work." Implied even in this single statement is a whole cluster of statements that separate the passage from nonbiblical nature poetry: nature is a revelation, it is the product of God, it is different from God and yet bears the imprint of God's activity. The opening verse, being a lyric expression, is not objective. It conveys a sense of the speaker's emotional involvement in his subject, as evidenced by his evaluative descriptions.

The second verse is another example of parallelism: "Day to day pours forth speech, / and night to night declares knowledge." Both halves state that God's creation is telling a message. Within the pattern of recurrence, there is the pleasing antithesis of day and night. Another figure of speech used here and subsequently in the psalm is personification, or attributing human qualities to an inanimate object. Here the power of speech is given to the heavenly bodies. This organic view of nature, giving it a life and treating it like an organism, is characteristic of the ancient way of thinking. The verb "pours forth" implies strenuous activity and may itself be a nature image, evoking the picture of a gushing stream. The two phrases denoting day and night, by repeating the words ("day to day," "night to night"), make the process of natural revelation a perpetual, cyclic succession. The statement that the cosmos "declares knowledge" repeats the main theme of the poem, which is concerned with the knowledge that God has revealed about Himself in nature.

Verse 3 makes bold use of paradox: "There is no speech, nor are there words; / their voice is not heard." Despite the earlier assertion that the movement of the heavenly bodies "pours forth speech," there is now said to be "no speech." The resolution to the paradox lies in the fact that both day and night reveal, but they reveal while wrapped in silence. The heavenly bodies have movement, which implies such principles as order, power, intelligence, and providence, but their movement is silent. Hence their message or "speech" (since messages are usually spoken or at least conveyed through language) is communicated without language ("speech").

Verse 4 uses further parallelism and further play on the silent message paradox: "yet their voice goes out through all the earth, / and their words to the end of the world." Verse 3 has asserted that there are neither words nor voice, and here the words and voice of the heavens are said to be present in the whole earth. The "voice" and "words" are metaphors meaning "message, revelation, ideational content." The thought being expressed is the universality of God's revelation in nature, which exists "through all the earth" and "to the end of the world."

From the skies generally the focus narrows to the sun: "In them he has set a tent for the sun" (vs. 4), with the pronoun "them" referring to "the heavens" of the previous verses. We would expect the psalmist to accord a place of honor to the sun, which has played such a big role in primitive thinking and still evokes an archetypal human response. Unlike mythical thought, however, which equates God with the sun, the poet here maintains the view that creation is the product of God. *God* has set the sun in the heavens, the poet insists, and there is no confusion of creator and creation.

The course of the sun is then described in two similes, both overflowing with positive connotations and emotional overtones: the sun "comes forth like a bridegroom leaving his chamber, / and like a strong man runs its course with joy" (vs. 5). Both similes imply an occasion of excitement (a wedding and a competitive race), and both continue the process of the humanization of nature that had been introduced earlier.

Verse 6 is a descriptive verse:

> *Its rising is from the end of the heavens,*
> *and its circuit to the end of them;*
> *and there is nothing hid from its heat.*

The purpose of the poet is not to convey information about the movement of the sun but to express wonder at the mystery and majesty of the sun's daily circuit. The motifs of cyclic activity and universality are repeated in the description, and there is artistic balance in the phrases "from the end" and "to the end."

We would do well to summarize the concept of nature in the opening section of the poem. Nature is meaningful and intelligent. It tells us something. More specifically, nature is the revelation of God, revealing His glory, His creative craftsmanship, His universal presence, and His orderliness. Nature is both related to and separate from God. It is related to Him because He has made it and it therefore reflects His qualities. But nature is not God. Nature is an artistic phenomenon — something beautiful and meaningful to be contemplated but not (in this psalm) something to be used or subjected to human control. Finally, nature is both the object and vehicle of praise. On the one hand, the poet praises nature itself. But in that very act he is also praising God, for nature itself is engaged in constant praise of God and is God's achievement.

With verse 7 the subject shifts to God's revelation in His written Word, which in the psalmist's day was mainly the law. C. S. Lewis believes that the last clause of verse 6 is a transition from one topic to the other. He writes, "The key phrase on which the whole poem depends is 'there is nothing hid from the heat thereof.' It pierces everywhere with its strong, clean ardour. Then at once, in verse 7 he is talking of something else, which hardly seems to him something else because it is so like the all-piercing, all-detecting sunshine. The Law is 'undefiled,' the Law gives light, it is clean and everlasting, it is 'sweet.' No one can improve on this and nothing can more fully admit us to the old Jewish feeling about the Law; luminous, severe, disinfectant, exultant."[4] In short, the sun and the law are complementary parts of God's revelation and share much in common. All of this suggests, too, that there is a second point of unity in the psalm, for in addition to the theme of revelation there is the idea of law or ordinance, which is implied in the first half in the description of the movements of the heavenly bodies.

Verses 7 to 9 possess an intricate structure of artistic parallelism:

> *The law of the Lord is perfect, reviving the soul;*
> *the testimony of the Lord is sure, making wise the simple;*
> *the precepts of the Lord are right, rejoicing the heart;*
> *the commandment of the Lord is pure, enlightening the eyes;*
> *the fear of the Lord is clean, enduring for ever;*
> *the ordinances of the Lord are true, and righteous altogether.*

This is artistry of a very high and conscious order. There are six statements, each having generally the same number of words and each following an identical pattern, as follows: naming the law by a title, attributing a quality to it, and praising it for its results. The passage is thus a combination of recurrence (repetition of syntactical pattern and of the motif of the qualities and effects of the law) and variation (different synonyms for the law and different attributes and results). Describing the attributes and effects of the law is here an act of praise, as is evident from the favorable evaluative terms used in this subjective description. The important thoughts in the passage are that God's law is a revelation (it is the law "of the Lord," that is, belonging to Him and bearing His imprint), that it is a thing of perfect qualities, and that it evokes response and action.

Verse 10 continues to praise the law by asserting its value and desirability:

> *More to be desired are they than gold,*
> *even much fine gold;*
> *sweeter also than honey*
> *and drippings of the honeycomb.*

This technique of comparison is common in the poetry of praise. The poet in such an instance compares the object of praise (here, the law) to something highly desirable, to the latter's detriment. A

---

[4] Ibid., p. 64.

priority is thus established: the desirability of gold and honey is not denied, but moral rectitude is said to be even more desirable. In terms of tone, the poet is again subjective, taking sides in an act of praise.

Verse 11 completes the description of the laws of God: "Moreover by them is thy servant warned; / in keeping them there is great reward." This comment continues the emphasis on the effects that flow from the law. It also marks the point in the poem where the poet begins to address God directly.

The final verses in the poem move from praise to prayer and petition as the poet dramatizes the normative human response to the law of God (vss. 12-14) :

> *But who can discern his errors?*
>   *Clear thou me from hidden faults.*
> *Keep back thy servant also from presumptuous sins;*
>   *let them not have dominion over me!*
> *Then I shall be blameless,*
>   *and innocent of great transgression.*
> *Let the words of my mouth and the meditation of my heart*
>   *be acceptable in thy sight,*
>   *O Lord, my rock and my redeemer.*

This acknowledgment of sin and prayer for forgiveness grow out of the earlier description of God's moral law. The "hidden faults" that the speaker mentions are the faults that are hidden from himself. "Presumptuous sins" are sins done with a complacent attitude toward evil and lack of awe for the holy God who is injured by man's sin.

Psalm 19 evinces the true lyric spirit. The poet presents the fact of God's revelation largely in terms of his own emotional responses. The keynote of the opening descriptions of nature, for example, is marvel at the wonder of God's created universe. The poet describes the operations of the heavenly bodies, not as so many facts, but as phenomena so marvelous that he is led to exclaim their existence. As so often in the poetry of praise, a listing of facts is a way of praising and expressing excitement. Similarly, the section dealing with God's law dramatizes a variety of responses to it. The poet attaches evaluative descriptive words to it and names such responses as joy, desire, and remorse for sin. The psalm, then, is not a collection of facts about God's revelation but the presentation of a many-sided response to God's wonderful revelation.

Psalm 29, which Moulton terms "the Song of the Thunderstorm,"[5] praises God's presence and power as experienced in a storm. The

---

[5] Richard G. Moulton, *The Literary Study of the Bible*, 2nd ed. (Boston: D. C. Heath, 1900), p. 163.

poet is not primarily concerned with the storm itself, but with God's working in the storm. An index to this theocentric perspective is the fact that throughout the poem God is the subject of the verbs, so that the storm itself is viewed as a series of acts by God. The poem has a three-part structure and is shaped like a pyramid. There is a call to praise (vss. 1-2), a description of the progress of a storm (vss. 3-9), and a concluding comment on the character of God (vss. 10-11). There is a corresponding emotional sequence, moving from anticipation to awe to subdued calm and assurance. The storm itself is structured on the principle of movement eastward from the Mediterranean Sea over Palestine.

The call to praise evokes a mood of anticipation (vss. 1-2):

> *Ascribe to the Lord, O heavenly beings,*
> *ascribe to the Lord glory and strength.*
> *Ascribe to the Lord the glory of his name;*
> *worship the Lord in holy array.*

The opening lines are a good example of climactic parallelism, in which the second unit repeats part of the first unit and then completes it. The fact that angels, rather than men, are invoked to praise God is appropriate to the exalted nature of the subject of praise. The effect is to suggest that only an angelic host is qualified to ascribe appropriate praise to God.

Verses 3 to 9 describe the progress of the storm, which is viewed as a series of acts performed by God. In keeping with a similar emphasis elsewhere in biblical literature, there is a double plot — the physical event and the spiritual meaning or reality behind the event. The storm is pictured as rising in the western sea, and the emphasis is on the sounds of the storm (vs. 3):

> *The voice of the Lord is upon the waters;*
> *the God of glory thunders,*
> *the Lord, upon many waters.*

This piece of description is followed by commentary in which the poet conceptualizes the meaning of the storm at sea: "The voice of the Lord is powerful, / the voice of the Lord is full of majesty" (vs. 4).

In its second phase the storm moves eastward onto the land, breaking the branches of the trees in the forest: "The voice of the Lord breaks the cedars, / the Lord breaks the cedars of Lebanon" (vs. 5). In an imaginative stroke the poet also compares the waving of tree branches to the jumping of animals: "He makes Lebanon to skip like a calf, / and Sirion like a young wild ox" (vs. 6). In addition to the descriptions of the sound and the wind, there is a picture of lightning: "The voice of the Lord flashes forth flames of fire" (vs. 7).

As the storm progresses further it is pictured as moving beyond the forest regions to the wilderness: "The voice of the Lord shakes the wilderness, / the Lord shakes the wilderness of Kadesh" (vs. 8). The obscure ninth verse seems to be another reference to the forest, followed by a dramatization of the human response to God's glory as seen in the storm:

> *The voice of the Lord makes the oaks to whirl,*
> *and strips the forests bare;*
> *and in his temple all cry, "Glory!"*

Following the ecstasy of the thunderstorm, the poem subsides into quietness at its close. First there is a generalization that grows logically from the storm just described, namely, that God is king over nature: "The Lord sits enthroned over the flood; / the Lord sits enthroned as king for ever" (vs. 10). Then, in typical lyric fashion, the poet concludes his poem by expressing a wish or prayer: "May the Lord give strength to his people! / May the Lord bless his people with peace!" (vs. 11). This is the implication of God's kingship. If He is indeed enthroned over the earth, He is also the sovereign God who alone can bless His people.

The full meaning of Psalm 29 becomes clear when it is interpreted as a parody. In its general outlines the psalm is parallel to some Canaanite poetry on the same topic. Underlying the Canaanite poetry was a myth involving Baal, god of the storm and of fertility (since rain caused vegetation to grow). According to the myth, there was an annual battle between Baal and the god of death or of the salt sea. Baal always defeated his foe and brought rain to the land. In response he was enthroned as god over the earth, and in some versions Baal built a palace for himself on the land.

Psalm 29 is in some ways a parallel to this mythological theme of Canaanite poetry, though the parallel is not as close as is often claimed.[6] The geographic references in the psalm are not really Jewish, belonging instead to the region farther north. The direction of the storm corresponds to the stories involving Baal. There is also the conspicuous emphasis on the enthronement of God, who is said to be "enthroned over the flood." As a parody, Psalm 29 is argumentative in nature. It substitutes God for Baal and makes the point that what the pagans serve as Baal is really God. Jehovah, not Baal, is

---

[6] For a discussion of the similarities between Psalm 29 and pagan poetry, especially the Canaanite *Poem of Baal*, see Theodor H. Gaster, *Myth, Legend, and Custom in the Old Testament* (New York: Harper and Row, 1969), pp. 747-51. Further description of the Baal myth can be found in John Gray, *The Canaanites* (New York: Frederick A. Praeger, 1964), pp. 127-37.

the one who deserves to be enthroned and praised in song. It is important to note that the psalmist felt comfortable using a pagan literary form for the content of his own religious experience.

Psalm 104 is another of the exalted psalms that deserve the title of ode. Its organization has all the architectonic magnificence that a short poem can possess, unfolding according to the following sequence: the function of nature (vss. 1-4), the origin of nature (vss. 5-9), the provision of nature (vss. 10-30), and lyric response to the God of nature (vss. 31-35). The third section itself has a discernible movement from earth (vss. 10-18) to sky (vss. 19-23) to sea (vss. 24-26), followed by a summary (vss. 27-30).

The poet begins with commentary, praising God's qualities before praising His acts as seen in nature. In effect, the poet begins his nature poem by talking about God (vs. 1):

> *Bless the Lord, O my soul!*
> *O Lord my God, thou art very great!*
> *Thou art clothed with honor and majesty.*

The mention of God's clothing provides a transition to the description of nature that follows. Nature is described as serving God (vss. 2-4):

> *who coverest thyself with light as with a garment,*
> *who hast stretched out the heavens like a tent,*
> *who hast laid the beams of thy chambers on the waters,*
> *who makest the clouds thy chariot,*
> *who ridest on the wings of the wind,*
> *who makest the winds thy messengers,*
> *fire and flame thy ministers.*

This is poetic imagination of a very high order. The main technique is simile and metaphor, with the forces of nature being compared to a variety of phenomena in human experience. God is the main actor in the sequence. He is shown to be using nature for a garment, a tent, a chariot, a messenger. The meaning of the short narrative is that God controls nature and that nature is infused with spirit, being alive with God's activity. On a purely artistic level we respond to the appropriateness of the poet's comparisons — light covers an object like a garment, the overhead canopy of the sky is like a tent, the earth is like a building that stands on the expanse of the water of the seas, clouds move like a chariot, and wind moves like a bird.

Verses 5 to 9 describe the origin of nature. The passage is a creation story in miniature, replete with figurative descriptions. The creation of the earth is compared to the process of constructing a building: "Thou didst set the earth on its foundations, / so that it should never be shaken" (vs. 5). The particular quality of the earth that the poet is praising here is its permanence. Having created the earth, God is pictured as covering it with a garment, consisting of the sea: "Thou didst cover it with the deep as with a garment" (vs. 6). Subsequent lines amplify the act of creating the seas, which are personified and pictured as being engaged in vigorous activity (vss. 6-7):

> the waters stood above the mountains.
> At thy rebuke they fled;
> at the sound of thy thunder they took to flight.

The concluding phases of this creation drama describe the act of creation as an ordering process, much as early Genesis does (vss. 8-9):

> The mountains rose, the valleys sank down
> to the place which thou didst appoint for them.
> Thou didst set a bound which they should not pass,
> so that they might not again cover the earth.

It is not simply the fact of God's creation of nature that accounts for the power of verses 5 to 9. The passage achieves impact as poetry through the use of metaphor, action, and plot conflict between the forces of nature and God's controlling power.

The longest section of the poem (vss. 10-30) describes the provision that nature gives. The passage paints a whole series of word-pictures, as the poet-observer surveys the various phenomena of nature. He begins with a miscellany of scenes from earthly nature. For example, "Thou makest springs gush forth in the valleys; / they flow between the hills" (vs. 10). Or again, "... the birds of the air have their habitation; / they sing among the branches" (vs. 12). The imagery of this marvelous passage puts us at once into a world of elemental nature, replete with springs, valleys, hills, beasts, thirst, birds, air, branches, mountains, earth, fruit, grass, cattle, food, oil, bread, trees, and rocks.

Equally important is the functional attitude toward nature. For example, the streams are said to "give drink to every beast" (vs. 11), the grass grows "for the cattle" (vs. 14), the plants exist to give food, wine, oil, and bread to man (vs. 15), the trees supply a place for the birds to nest (vs. 16), the mountains "are for the wild goats" (vs. 18), and "the rocks are a refuge for the badgers" (vs. 18). The view of nature that emerges from all this is highly significant. Nature is a single, all-embracing organism, governed by God's providence. All aspects of nature are fellow dependents of God and of each other. Nature is orderly and purposeful, operating according to a divine plan that provides for the needs of every part.

From the earth the focus shifts to the sky (vss. 19-23). The poet makes the observation that the sun and moon, light and darkness, provide the world with time, or orderly progression. The heavenly bodies are accordingly described as the great ordering agency in the universe and in human experience:

> *Thou hast made the moon to mark the seasons;*
>   *the sun knows its time for setting.*
> *Thou makest darkness, and it is night,*
>   *when all the beasts of the forest creep forth....*
> *When the sun rises, they get them away*
>   *and lie down in their dens.*
> *Man goes forth to his work*
>   *and to his labor until the evening.*

Here is another of the provisions of nature — order that allows the natural creation to function according to a harmonious and mutually beneficial plan.

Following an exclamatory interlude (vs. 24), the poet completes his survey with a reference to the sea (vss. 25-26), thereby providing balance to the previously mentioned earth and sky:

> *Yonder is the sea, great and wide,*
>   *which teems with things innumerable,*
>   *living things both small and great.*
> *There go the ships,*
>   *and Leviathan which thou didst form to sport in it.*

The last verse, incidentally, combines the idea of nature's functional purpose with the notion that it provides enjoyment, or sport, for God's creatures.

Verses 27-30 summarize the point about nature's provision, in the meantime giving eloquent expression to the psalmist's God-centered conception of nature:

> *These all look to thee,*
>   *to give them their food in due season.*
> *When thou givest to them, they gather it up;*
>   *when thou openest thy hand, they are filled with good things.*
> *When thou hidest thy face, they are dismayed;*
>   *when thou takest away their breath, they die*
>   *and return to their dust.*
> *When thou sendest forth thy Spirit, they are created;*
>   *and thou renewest the face of the ground.*

God is clearly the actor, and nature is the agent of His provision.

The concluding phase of the poem is a lyric response to the God

who is revealed in nature. We get a miscellany of responses, unified
by the motif of glorifying God (vss. 31-35) :

> *May the glory of the Lord endure for ever,*
> > *may the Lord rejoice in his works,*
> *who looks on the earth and it trembles,*
> > *who touches the mountains and they smoke!*
> *I will sing to the Lord as long as I live;*
> > *I will sing praise to my God while I have being.*
> *May my meditation be pleasing to him,*
> > *for I rejoice in the Lord.*
> *Let sinners be consumed from the earth,*
> > *and let the wicked be no more!*
> *Bless the Lord, O my soul!*
> *Praise the Lord!*

It is a fitting conclusion for one of the greatest lyrics in the Psalter.

Psalm 148, another nature poem, makes the important point that
all of nature is unified in its obligation to praise God. The poem is
dramatic in structure, consisting of a series of direct addresses to
various parts of creation. The calls to praise are twice interrupted by
reasons for the calls (vss. 5b-6; 13b-14). In terms of structure, the
sequence of apostrophes shifts from heaven (vss. 1-6) to earth (vss.
7-10) to the human community (vss. 11-14).

The poem begins with a flurry of exhortations to praise God. The
general command is to "praise the Lord from the heavens" (vs. 1).
The subsequent apostrophes move from this generalization to a
catalog of more specific natural phenomena that reside in the sky
(vss. 2-4) :

> *Praise him, all his angels,*
> > *praise him, all his host!*
> *Praise him, sun and moon,*
> > *praise him, all you shining stars!*
> *Praise him, you highest heavens,*
> > *and you waters above the heavens!*

The emotional intensity of the speaker is communicated through the
imperative statements, the device of apostrophe, and the use of an
exclamatory idiom.

The section commanding the forces of nature to "praise the Lord
from the earth" (vs. 7) follows the same pattern as the opening
section, with the generalization filled out by naming some specific
objects of nature (vss. 7-10) :

> *you sea monsters and all deeps,*
> *fire and hail, snow and frost,*

stormy wind fulfilling his command!
Mountains and all hills,
fruit trees and all cedars!
Beasts and all cattle,
creeping things and flying birds!

The significant thing about the list is that it includes not only things beneficial to man but also natural forces that are indifferent or actively hostile to him. The explanation for this is that the Hebrews believed that God had created all of nature, with the result that all of nature was God's.

In the last movement the poet enjoins the human community to worship God, and here, too, he lists some of the varieties within the general heading (vss. 11-13):

Kings of the earth and all peoples,
princes and all rulers of the earth!
Young men and maidens together,
old men and children!
Let them praise the name of the Lord.

By placing mankind in this series the poet implies that man is a unified part of the natural creation.

Before leaving Psalm 148, we should consider the two sections that give the motivation or rationale for the praise that is commanded. The first passage draws attention to the fact that God created all of nature, which owes its existence to Him (vss. 5-6):

For he commanded and they were created.
And he established them for ever and ever;
he fixed their bounds which cannot be passed.

The second rationale, appearing in the section urging the human community to praise God, centers on God's exalted nature and His deliverance of the Jewish nation (vss. 13-14):

for his name alone is exalted;
his glory is above earth and heaven.
He has raised up a horn for his people,
praise for all his saints,
for the people of Israel who are near to him.
Praise the Lord!

If one attempts to relate the nature poetry of the Psalms to nature poetry in literature as a whole, some interesting generalizations emerge. Nature poetry generally has displayed two contradictory (or, in some instances, complementary) interpretations of nature. Nature has sometimes been equated with law, rule, order, and reason. In other ages and by other writers it has been identified with impulse, instinct, spontaneity, and energy. These two tendencies might be called the classical and romantic strains, respectively. It is much easier to relate biblical nature poetry to the first tradition. In the Psalms nature is repeatedly pictured as being orderly, law-bound, and operating according to God's purposeful plan. By implication some passages in the Psalms affirm nature to be instinctive, impulsive, and spontaneous, but there is very little of what we would call the typical romantic view of nature. It is not, of course, a question of enthusiasm for nature, since both views of nature can be equally appreciative of nature. The division results from different perceptions of what nature is.

The closer one scrutinizes the nature poetry of the Bible, the less similar it seems to either the classical or romantic traditions. The psalmists are preoccupied with God rather than nature. They certainly talk more about God's creation of nature and His revelation of Himself in nature than they do about either rule or energy, the common themes elsewhere. Poets who have written about nature outside the Hebraic-Christian tradition have tended to deify it. If they are what we call "nature poets," they have tended to treat nature as the highest value. They have been either naturalists (nature itself is the ultimate reality) or pantheists (nature is divine). The biblical poets are simply in another category. Their concern with nature is part of their broader concern with God. To them the nature poetry of other traditions would seem empty, as though the most important thing had been left out.

Praise is an integral part of the Psalms and other books in the biblical encomium. This is the spring at Ain Feshka, where David often led his sheep.

Biblical
Encomium

An encomium is a work of literature written in praise of someone or something. Although it can be a work in praise of a particular person, it is preferable to define the genre more precisely as a work that praises a generalized character type or an abstract quality. As a rhetorical form, encomium has a classical heritage and was discussed by such rhetoricians of antiquity as Quintilian, Hermogenes, and Aphthonius.[1] The conventional formulae used in an encomium include an introduction to the topic (the "exordium," in classical rhetoric), praise "by what kind he came of" (emphasis on the distinguished and ancient ancestry of the subject), praise by the acts and/or attributes of the subject, praise by declaring the indispensable or superior nature of the subject, and a conclusion urging the reader to emulate.

Psalm 1 is an encomium praising the godly person. The praise is conducted by describing the inner quality of the godly person and the overt manifestations of that inner character. The praise of the godly person is accentuated through the dispraise of the ungodly person, who is used as a foil.

The poem begins with a positive evaluation of the godly person, at once evoking favorable connotations toward the subject of praise: "Blessed is the man . . ." (vs. 1). In three parallel clauses the godly man is described negatively, in terms of what he avoids (vs. 1):

> *who walks not in the counsel of the wicked,*
> *nor stands in the way of sinners,*
> *nor sits in the seat of scoffers.*

Next the subject is praised by a description of his allegiance to God's law: "but his delight is in the law of the Lord, / and on his law he meditates day and night" (vs. 2). Verse 3 praises the godly person by picturing the productiveness of his life:

> *He is like a tree*
> *planted by streams of water,*

[1] For details, see Donald L. Clark, *John Milton at St. Paul's School* (New York: Columbia University Press, 1948), pp. 239-40.

> *that yields its fruit in its season,*
> *and its leaf does not wither.*
> *In all that he does, he prospers.*

In the remaining lines of the poem, the poet describes the misery of the ungodly as a way of heightening the praise that he has voiced for the godly person.

Psalm 15 is similar to Psalm 1, taking as its object of praise the holy person. It is not only an encomium but belongs also to an old literary kind known as "the character." In Greek literature the most famous practitioner of the genre was Theophrastus, and the form is sometimes called the Theophrastian character. A character is a brief descriptive sketch of a generalized character type who exemplifies some quality. The person is described not as an individualized personality but as a common type. The portrait can be either of a moral type (e.g., the proud man, the glutton), a social type (the young lover, the overdressed person), or a vocational type. The sketch can include both external appearance and inner qualities. The basic structure of a character is repetitive — we see a single principle maintained under a variety of different forms.

In Psalm 15, as perhaps also in Psalm 1, the character is turned to a spiritual use. The poet gives a generalized and idealized account of the holy person, in a specifically Hebraic-Christian sense. The encomium found in Psalm 15 is offered as an answer to a question of far-reaching importance, namely, Who can worship God acceptably? The question is addressed to God: "O Lord, who shall sojourn in thy tent? / Who shall dwell on thy holy hill?" (vs. 1).

The answer, which also constitutes the encomium, is a catalog of the acts of the holy person. The list alternates between positive and negative descriptions, beginning with a positive and generalized description of the integrity of the holy person: "He who walks blamelessly, and does what is right, / and speaks truth from his heart" (vs. 2). This is balanced by an account of the kinds of behavior that the holy person avoids (vs. 3):

> *who does not slander with his tongue,*
> *and does no evil to his friend,*
> *nor takes up a reproach against his neighbor.*

Another positive description emphasizes the consciousness of values that permeates the holy person's observation of reality: "in whose eyes a reprobate is despised, / but who honors those who fear the Lord" (vs. 4). There is a further reference to personal integrity in the holy person's unwillingness to go back on his word despite cost to himself: "who swears to his own hurt and does not change" (vs. 4).

The catalog concludes with another section that uses negative statements, this time to praise the generosity and honesty of the holy person: "who does not put out his money at interest, / and does not take a bribe against the innocent" (vs. 5). The last line of the poem is a concluding generalization that praises the holy person in comprehensive terms: "He who does these things shall never be moved" (vs. 5).

This encomium praising the holy person takes us to the heart of biblical religion. The portrait displays a vivid awareness of values, being based on the conviction that there is right and wrong and that these categories are ultimately of supreme importance. The alternation between positive and negative statements dramatizes the fact that holiness has two sides — positive action and refusal of wickedness. It also introduces an element of narrative conflict that conveys the impression that holiness requires active choice and discernment among opposing options. The poem implies that people do not drift into holiness but choose it by saying, "This, not that."

When we turn to Proverbs 31:10-31 we find another encomium that praises a generalized character type, this time a social type. This acrostic poem praises the good wife. The opening rhetorical question identifies the topic and asserts by implication the rarity and therefore the value of a good wife: "A good wife who can find?" (vs. 10). The next sentence continues the motif of worth by using a comparison: "She is far more precious than jewels" (vs. 10).

Verse 11 begins a list of the acts and qualities of the virtuous wife. The poet describes her first in relation to her husband, drawing attention to the primacy of the marital role of the good wife (vss. 11-12):

> The heart of her husband trusts in her,
>   and he will have no lack of gain.
> She does him good, and not harm,
>   all the days of her life.

The good wife is viewed next in a domestic role, with emphasis on her diligence in providing for the physical needs of her family (vss. 13-19):

> She seeks wool and flax,
>   and works with willing hands.
> She is like the ships of the merchant,
>   she brings her food from afar.
> She rises while it is yet night
>   and provides food for her household
>   and tasks for her maidens.
> She considers a field and buys it;
>   with the fruit of her hands she plants a vineyard.

She girds her loins with strength and makes her arms strong.
She perceives that her merchandise is profitable.
  Her lamp does not go out at night.
She puts her hands to the distaff,
  and her hands hold the spindle.

Verses 20 to 27 show the wife in more of a social role, in terms of her place in society as a whole. For example, her compassion for the oppressed segments of society is praised: "She opens her hand to the poor, / and reaches out her hands to the needy" (vs. 20). She is described as having concern for her appearance in public: "She makes herself coverings; / her clothing is fine linen and purple" (vs. 22). Her husband is described as a man of ability and social prominence, with the implication that the wife is partly responsible for this situation: "Her husband is known in the gates, / when he sits among the elders of the land" (vs. 23). The good wife's industry is not only a matter of providing for her family but also of being a productive contributor to society: "She makes linen garments and sells them; / she delivers girdles to the merchant" (vs. 24). There is also mention of her moral influence in society: "She opens her mouth with wisdom, / and the teaching of kindness is on her tongue" (vs. 26).

As the poem concludes, the climactic words of praise are put in the mouth of the wife's family, thus ending the poem with a domestic emphasis (vss. 28-29):

Her children rise up and call her blessed;
  her husband also, and he praises her:
"Many women have done excellently,
  but you surpass them all."

The narrator also establishes a hierarchy of values in which inner spiritual integrity is praised as being more worthy than external beauty: "Charm is deceitful, and beauty is vain, / but a woman who fears the Lord is to be praised" (vs. 30). And there is a final wish that the wife might be rewarded for her virtue: "Give her of the fruit of her hands, / and let her works praise her in the gates" (vs. 31).

There are several encomia embedded in New Testament writings. An example is the beginning of John's gospel (1:1-18), a poem in praise of the incarnate Christ. The emphasis is not on the incarnation (God's taking human form) as an abstraction, but on Christ as the incarnate God. It praises a specific role of Christ, in effect. The poem conveys the impression of having been written in a moment of intense emotion. Images, ideas, and feelings tumble out abruptly and in rapid succession. There is no attempt at a sustained and logically organized pattern of development. Like a true lyric poet, the writer does not argue but asserts, and he asserts as a way of praising. Several conventional formulae of the encomium are present in the poem, which can be divided into eight stanzas.

Stanza 1 praises the ancient and distinguished ancestry of the incarnate Christ:

> *In the beginning was the Word,*
> *and the Word was with God,*
> *and the Word was God.*
> *He was in the beginning with God.*

Whereas other gospel writers begin their accounts with a human genealogy of Christ, John begins with a divine genealogy. He also uses a technique of allusion by echoing the language of Genesis 1:1 ("In the beginning, God created..."), thus linking the incarnate Christ with the original act of God's creation. In this way the poet surrounds his topic with familiar associations of ancientness, since the primeval act of creation stands at the very beginning of antiquity. When the writer calls Jesus "the Word," he is using a metaphor that identifies Christ's status as a revelation from God to men. Also noteworthy is the strong sense of rhythmic repetition in the stanza, with the following phrases being stated more than once: "in the beginning," "the Word," "with God," "...was...." This creates a ritualistic effect and conveys a sense of emotional compulsion. Indeed, statements uttered under strong emotion often fall naturally into rhythmic patterns, achieving a kind of oracular effect in the process.

Stanza 2 praises the fact that Christ is indispensable to everything that exists, being the creator of all things:

> *All things were made through him,*
> *and without him was not anything made that was made.*

The poet here balances several opposite statements — "all things" against "not anything," and "through him" against "without him." The two lines are also an example of antithetic parallelism, in which the second unit states the truth of the first unit in negative terms, thus balancing the positive statement in the first unit.

The third stanza praises Christ's life-giving quality:

> *In him was life,*
> *and the life was the light of men.*
> *The light shines in the darkness,*
> *and the darkness has not overcome it.*

This, too, is a poetic utterance in which the writer uses the concrete images of light and darkness (which are also spiritual symbols) and pictures them as engaged in warfare. This stanza also employs the rhetorical device of gradation, in which successive clauses begin with the concept that the preceding clause used in its conclusion, as follows: "him . . . life," "life . . . light," "light . . . darkness," "darkness . . . it."

Stanza 4 exalts the dignity of the incarnate Christ by describing His forerunner, sent from God, no less:

> *There was a man sent from God,*
> *whose name was John.*
> *He came for testimony,*
> *to bear witness to the light,*
> *that all might believe through him.*
> *He was not the light,*
> *but came to bear witness to the light.*

The implied metaphor in this passage is that of kingship, since kings had heralds who went before them to proclaim their arrival. The passage also continues the motif of light imagery, which symbolizes spiritual truth and righteousness. These lines, like most others in the poem, produce the effect of an incantation or chant through the use of parallel clauses and repetition. Repeated words and phrases in this stanza include "to bear witness," "the light," and "he came."

The fifth stanza praises the incarnate Christ for His redemptive work in bringing to spiritual life all who receive Him and believe in His name. This is the greatest of the praiseworthy acts of the subject and accordingly is given the longest section of the poem:

> *The true light that enlightens every man was coming into the world.*
> *He was in the world,*
> *and the world was made through him,*
> *yet the world knew him not.*
> *He came to his own home,*
> *and his own people received him not.*
> *But to all who received him,*
> *who believed in his name,*
> *he gave power to become children of God;*
> *Who were born,*
> *not of blood nor of the will of the flesh*
> *nor of the will of man,*
> *but of God.*

The opening line of this passage, by calling Christ the "true" light, implies Christ's superiority to other lights. The allusion to Christ's creation of the world ("the world was made through him") is balanced by the extended description of His second great creative act, namely, bringing to spiritual life sinners who believe in Him. The birth imagery used to describe this redemptive act ("become children," "were born") reinforces the idea that it is a creative act.

Stanza 6 praises the fact of the incarnation itself:

> And the Word became flesh
> and dwelt among us,
> full of grace and truth;
> We have beheld his glory,
> glory as of the only Son from the Father.

This stanza praises the incarnate Christ by exalting the divine attributes that He manifested while living as a man.

The seventh stanza of the poem uses the words of John the Baptist to assert the superiority of Christ even to an illustrious prophet:

> (John bore witness to him, and cried,
> "This was he of whom I said,
> 'He who comes after me ranks before me,
> for he was before me.' ")

The statement that Christ "was before" John the Baptist is an allusion to Christ's eternal existence in His divine being. Like the earlier statement that Christ was "in the beginning" with God, it praises the ancient and divine ancestry of the incarnate Christ. It is noteworthy that the seventh stanza is a parenthetical sentence. As such it reinforces the impression that the poet is writing in the very intensity of thinking and feeling. He excitedly inserts thoughts when they occur instead of conducting a logically organized argument.

The last stanza of the encomium praises the acts of Christ in bringing to men the grace and knowledge of God:

> And from his fulness have we all received,
> grace upon grace.
> For the law was given through Moses;
> grace and truth came through Jesus Christ.
> No one has ever seen God;
> the only Son,
> who is in the bosom of the Father,
> he has made him known.

The first part of the stanza uses the familiar encomiastic device of comparison, praising Christ's revelation as being superior to the law, which was revealed through Moses. The second part of the passage employs the indispensability motif, asserting that Christ is the indispensable revealer of God to man.

Colossians 1:15-20 is a brief encomium that praises the person and work of Christ. It presents the Gospel in miniature. There is a structural principle of balance underlying the poem. Verses 15 to 17 praise the supremacy of Christ in the cosmos. Verses 18 to 20 balance this by praising His supremacy in the Church, the body of the redeemed. Further balance is achieved by emphasizing the theme of being first, or firstborn, in both spheres.

The poet begins his praise by declaring Christ's divinity, which makes Him supreme over the creation (vs. 15):

> *He is the image of the invisible God,*
> *the first-born of all creation.*

The fact that Christ is "first-born" denotes not only supremacy but also ancient ancestry, a conventional motif in an encomium. Verse 16 praises, by listing, Christ's acts of creation:

> *For in him all things were created,*
> *in heaven and on earth,*
> *visible and invisible,*
> *whether thrones or dominions or principalities or authorities —*
> *all things were created through him and for him.*

By describing Christ's acts of creation, the poet is praising Him as being both supreme over the creation and prior to it. The verse uses parallelism and balance to achieve its eloquence, as evidenced by such phrases as "in heaven and on earth," "visible and invisible," "thrones or dominions or principalities or authorities," and "through him and for him." Verse 17 climaxes the first movement of the poem by praising Christ for being indispensable to the existence of all things:

> *He is before all things,*
> *and in him all things hold together.*

With verse 18 the focus shifts to the Church, with the poet retaining the motifs of Christ's being first and therefore supreme:

> *He is the head of the body, the church;*
> *he is the beginning,*
> *the first-born from the dead,*
> *that in everything he might be pre-eminent.*

The statement that Christ is "the first-born from the dead" is a conscious parallel to the earlier statement that he is "the first-born of all creation." Furthermore, a sense of climax is conveyed by the statement that Christ is head of the church as well as the cosmos so that He might be supreme "in everything." The implication is that by adding the Church to the earlier topic of the world, the poet has now included the last remaining item of consideration.

Verses 19 and 20, which describe Christ's redemptive acts, praise the spiritual parallel to His creation of the physical world (the topic of verse 16) :

> *For in him all the fullness of God was pleased to dwell,*
> *and through him to reconcile to himself all things,*
> > *whether on earth or in heaven,*
> *making peace by the blood of his cross.*

The first half of the poem praises Christ for creating the world, while the second half praises Him for bringing it back to a restored state after it had been lost by the fall. The key term "reconcile" in verse 20 summarizes this theme. The parallel between the original act of creation and the restoration is accentuated by the balanced clauses "all things ... in heaven and on earth" (vs. 16) and "all things, whether on earth or in heaven" (vs. 20).

The keynote of the poem is the idea of supremacy. Christ is praised by being declared supreme over everything else. An index to this emphasis is the recurrence of the words "all" and "everything": "all creation" (vs. 15), "all things" (twice in vs. 16, twice in vs. 17, once in vs. 20), "in everything" (vs. 18), and "all the fulness" (vs. 19).

In 1 Corinthians 13 we find a prose encomium that praises an abstract quality. The subject of this discourse is love, which is praised by using some of the standard motifs of the encomium.[2]

The encomium begins by praising love as being the indispensable ingredient of the Christian life:

> 1 *If I speak in the tongues of men and of angels, but have not love, I am a noisy gong or a clanging cymbal.*
> 2 *And if I have prophetic powers, and understand all mysteries and all knowledge, and if I have all faith, so as to remove mountains, but have not love, I am nothing.*
> 3 *If I give away all I have, and if I deliver my body to be burned, but have not love, I gain nothing.*

The indispensability motif is heightened by the emphasis on "all" and "nothing": "all mysteries," "all knowledge," "all faith," become "nothing" in the absence of love, and giving away "all I have" gains "nothing" if not accompanied by love.

The next section of the discourse (vss. 4-7) praises love by listing its qualities and acts. Love is personified in the passage, which is permeated with parallelism:

---

[2] I have reserved for chapter 16 a discussion of the artistic pattern that pervades 1 Corinthians 13.

> 4 *Love is patient and kind; love is not jealous or boastful;*
> 5 *it is not arrogant or rude. Love does not insist on its own way; it is not irritable or resentful;*
> 6 *it does not rejoice at wrong, but rejoices in the right;*
> 7 *Love bears all things, believes all things, hopes all things, endures all things.*

There is an envelope structure underlying the passage, which moves from the description of positive acts to a description of things that love avoids, returning finally to an account of the positive acts of love. Thematically, there is an emphasis on the fact that love avoids as well as performs.

The concluding section (vss. 8-13) praises love by declaring its permanence, as opposed to the transience of three spiritual gifts. It is a variation of the superiority motif so common in encomia. The first sentence of the passage asserts the main theme to be developed: "Love never ends" (vs. 8). Paul develops this idea by contrasting love to three spiritual gifts that are not permanent: "as for prophecy, it will pass away; as for tongues, they will cease; as for knowledge, it will pass away" (vs. 8). In typical Pauline fashion, the writer goes on to analyze how it is that prophecy, tongues, and knowledge will pass away (vss. 9-12), emphasizing the process of maturation that makes earlier phenomena unnecessary.

Paul clinches his point with a concluding aphorism about the superiority of love. In contrast to the transience of prophecy, tongues, and knowledge, there are three spiritual qualities that endure: "So faith, hope, love abide" (vs. 13). Then, in the climax of the whole discourse, the writer singles out love as being the greatest of the illustrious group of three permanent qualities: "but the greatest of these is love" (vs. 13). The first sentence in the next chapter belongs with the encomium on love, since it represents the familiar conclusion found in many encomia, the command to emulate: "Make love your aim" (1 Cor. 14:1).

Faith is the subject of an encomium found in Hebrews 11–12:2. The encomium begins with a brief definition of exactly what quality will be praised: "Now faith is the assurance of things hoped for, the conviction of things not seen" (vs. 1). As this definition makes clear, the kind of faith being praised is that which enables a person to believe something in the absence of tangible, empirical proof. The second verse adds the idea that such faith has divine sanction: "For by it the men of old received divine approval." The motif of ancient and distinguished ancestry is latent in the idea that it is men "of old" who possessed this kind of faith.

The main part of the encomium, beginning with verse 3, is a

catalog of the mighty acts of faith. Part of the artistry of the list comes from the repeated formula used to introduce the illustrations: "By faith. . . ." The repetition of sentences beginning with this phrase has a tremendous cumulative effect as the catalog progresses. The structural principle underlying the list is historical chronology. We begin with an allusion to the creation of the world (vs. 3) and then march straight through Old Testament history: Abel (vs. 4), Enoch (vs. 5), Noah (vs. 7), Abraham (vss. 8-19), Isaac (vs. 20), Jacob (vs. 21), Joseph (vs. 22), Moses (vss. 23-28), the Israelites who lived through the exodus and conquest (vss. 29-31), the judges and kings (vs. 32). This means that the chief literary device used in the encomium is allusion, with the writer managing to evoke all kinds of positive responses to his subject (faith) by linking it to the high points of the national history of his Hebrew audience.

Several smaller effects should also be noted in the catalog of the acts of faith. The statement that despite Abel's death "through his faith he is still speaking" (vs. 4) introduces the important motif that these past examples of faith are living models for later generations. Verse 6 interrupts the catalog and employs the indispensability motif. There are also several places where the writer uses the conventional device of declaring the comparative superiority of his subject, as when he asserts that faith will lead to "a better country" (vs. 16), "greater wealth" (vs. 26), and "a better life" (vs. 35).

The catalog ends with a rhetorical flourish that carries the reader along by means of its sheer eloquence. The passage begins with the inexpressibility motif. The acts of faith are so numerous that the writer declines even to try to recount them all: "And what more shall I say? For time would fail me to tell of Gideon, Barak, Samson, Jephthah, of David and Samuel and the prophets" (vs. 32). Then, in a passage replete with parallelism, we get a whole barrage of mighty acts of faith (vss. 33-38):

33 who through faith conquered kingdoms, enforced justice, received promises, stopped the mouths of lions,

34 quenched raging fire, escaped the edge of the sword, won strength out of weakness, became mighty in war, put foreign armies to flight.

35 Women received their dead by resurrection. Some were tortured, refusing to accept release, that they might rise again to a better life.

36 Others suffered mocking and scourging, and even chains and imprisonment.

37 They were stoned, they were sawn in two, they were killed with the sword; they went about in skins of sheep and goats, destitute, afflicted, ill-treated —

38 of whom the world was not worthy — wandering over deserts and mountains, and in dens and caves of the earth.

As one looks back over the list of the acts of faith he cannot fail to notice the incongruous nature of the listing. There are rather commonplace acts, within the reach of any believer, such as believing the Genesis account of creation, blessing one's children on his deathbed, hiding fugitives from the law, and enforcing justice. Side by side with these are the extraordinary, spectacular accomplishments of faith. There is also an incongruous mingling of occasions when people were miraculously delivered from danger with occasions when people had to endure defeat on the physical, earthly plane.

The first two verses of Hebrews 12 complete the encomium with a conventional motif, the command to emulate:

> *Therefore, since we are surrounded by so great a cloud of witnesses,*
> *let us also lay aside every weight, and sin which clings so closely,*
> *and let us run with perseverance the race that is set before us,*
> *looking to Jesus the pioneer and perfecter of our faith, who for the*
> *joy that was set before him endured the cross, despising the shame,*
> *and is seated at the right hand of the throne of God.*

The writer, in a brilliant stroke, allows the reader to place himself in a long and distinguished line of heroes. To call the heroes of faith "witnesses" is to use a metaphor from the courtroom, conveying the idea that they testify to the reality and worthwhileness of faith in God. Calling these Old Testament characters a "cloud" of witnesses is a veiled allusion to the pillar of cloud used by God to guide the Israelites through the wilderness. The implication is significant: the heroes of faith listed in Hebrews 11 are intended to serve as a guide and model for believers of later ages. Appropriately, Jesus is held up as the crowning example of faith to whom the reader is urged to look for guidance and the very perfection of his own faith.

With the foregoing encomia serving as background, we are in a position to turn at last to the most unusual and paradoxical encomium ever written. The encomium found in the last part of Isaiah 52 (vss. 13-15) and in Isaiah 53 is a poem in praise of the suffering servant, the Messiah. The encomium both employs and inverts the usual conventions.

The main poetic mode in the discourse is parallelism, in which the poet tends to repeat every idea in two or more different expressions. The effect is to beautify the suffering that is described in the poem. Perhaps this is exactly the paradox underlying the encomium: the suffering of the servant is beautiful because it accomplishes the salvation of the believer.

The encomium opens with a paradox. The servant is said to be exalted and high (Isa. 52:13):

> *Behold, my servant shall prosper,*
> *he shall be exalted and lifted up,*
> *and shall be very high.*

The paradox is explicable on the ground that although the servant is of low social esteem, he is spiritually exalted. Verses 14 and 15 employ a simile to assert that just as many people were shocked by this anti-hero's marred appearance, so they will be shocked when they understand who he is, namely, God in human form:

> *As many were astonished at him —*
> *his appearance was so marred, beyond human semblance,*
> *and his form beyond that of the sons of men —*
> *so shall he startle many nations;*
> *kings shall shut their mouths because of him;*
> *for that which has not been told them they shall see,*
> *and that which they have not heard they shall understand.*

Verse 14 praises the subject for the unlikely reason that his body was mutilated, much as the book of Revelation praises the Lamb because He was slain.

The next section of the poem continues the idealization of the anti-hero by reversing the usual motif of distinguished ancestry (Isa. 53:1-3) :

> *Who has believed what we have heard?*
> *And to whom has the arm of the Lord been revealed?*
> *For he grew up before him like a young plant,*
> *and like a root out of dry ground;*
> *he had no form or comeliness that we should look at him,*
> *and no beauty that we should desire him.*
> *He was despised and rejected by men;*
> *a man of sorrows, and acquainted with grief;*
> *and as one from whom men hide their faces*
> *he was despised, and we esteemed him not.*

We might say that this literary protagonist is praised for the wrong reasons. Instead of coming from prominent social rank, he grew up by a very natural, unspectacular process ("like a young plant") and came from an unpromising source ("like a root out of dry ground"). Whereas the beauty of Odysseus and Telemachos and Aeneas is compared by their storyteller to the gods, this protagonist is explicitly denied any kind of impressive appearance. Instead of being socially exalted, he is despised. This is, indeed, the apotheosis of the anti-hero.

Verses 4 to 9 praise the suffering servant by listing his acts. Again we are forced to note how the acts reverse the usual standards of success. A typical example occurs in verses 4 and 5:

> *Surely he has borne our griefs*
> *and carried our sorrows;*
> *yet we esteemed him stricken,*
> *smitten by God, and afflicted.*
> *But he was wounded for our transgressions,*
> *he was bruised for our iniquities;*
> *upon him was the chastisement that made us whole,*
> *and with his stripes we are healed.*

To be wounded and bruised is not usually the kind of behavior that is said in literature to merit heroic status. Furthermore, whereas the conventional hero wins rewards for himself, the suffering servant inverts the formula by enduring pain for the benefit of others. The picture of how the suffering servant "was oppressed, and . . . afflicted, / yet he opened not his mouth" (vs. 7) is exactly the opposite of Achilles and the old heroic ideal. Similarly, to be led as "a lamb . . . to the slaughter" (vs. 7) and to be silent "like a sheep . . . before its shearers" (vs. 7) is to display a humility that is the antithesis of what the heroes of classical epic and medieval romance espouse. The fact that the suffering servant dies as a man condemned by the law and the courts of justice (vs. 8) should be an index to criminality, yet here it is one of the acts for which he is praised. The fact that "they made his grave with the wicked" (vs. 9) is similarly held up for praise, and the way in which his death was unnoticed by others (vs. 8) is in obvious contrast to the elaborate funeral rites of epic heroes.

The last section of the poem, verses 10 to 12, praises the suffering servant by listing the redemptive results that his suffering accomplished for sinners. Here, too, there are some paradoxical inversions of conventional literary expectations. God is recorded as saying (vs. 12) :

> *Therefore I will divide him a portion with the great,*
> *and he shall divide the spoil with the strong;*
> *because he poured out his soul to death,*
> *and was numbered with the transgressors;*
> *yet he bore the sin of many,*
> *and made intercession for the transgressors.*

The image of the hero dividing the spoils on the battlefield is straight from the heroic world of ancient literature, but the heroic values have been completely inverted. Conventional heroes divide the spoil because they have killed their enemies, for their own benefit. This anti-hero divides the spoil (that is, celebrates spiritual victory) because he has been killed for the sake of others, who are ignoble people at that.

"Let my beloved come to his garden, and eat its choicest fruits."

The Song
of Solomon

10

I

The Song of Solomon has evoked a variety of interpretations, in regard to both content and form. Its content has been viewed as an allegory of the love that God had for Israel and now has for His Church and the individual soul, as a fertility myth depicting the marriage of the sun with the mother earth goddess, and as romantic love between a man and a woman. The present discussion takes the view that the subject of the work is what it claims to be — the beauty of romantic love.

There has also been a variety of views regarding the form of the work. Many readers have regarded the work as a drama, and some editions contain elaborate stage directions. On the face of it, the poem is dramatic, at least in parts. There is dialogue, and a story underlying the dialogue. There are several objections to regarding the work as a play, however. A drama ordinarily follows a clearly discernible chronology. The stage is not a good place for flashbacks and abrupt shifts. Yet this is exactly what we get in the Song of Solomon. Moreover, if the Song of Solomon were staged it would consist of one passionate love scene after another, not a likely strategy for a dramatist. Drama is based on conflict and an easily grasped sequence of events. We get neither in the Song of Solomon, which is a celebration of happy love instead of a conflict, and which has a fragmented structure that would be confusing if staged. If the poem were a drama in any sense at all, the poet would have inserted names for the various speeches. Far too much — in fact, practically everything — has to be supplied in order to turn the work into a play.

A more tenable view is that the work is a collection of pastoral love lyrics dealing with a single romance. It is not a consecutive narrative, though certain events in the romance are alluded to. The fact that the work is a series of lyric moods accounts for the fragmentary structure, abrupt shifts in subject matter, and the essentially emotional nature of the work. The organization of the lyrics is similar to a stream-of-consciousness technique. The pastoral identity of the poem accounts for the rustic setting and imagery and the pastoral disguises of the characters. Some of the lyrics are sung by a man, some by a woman, and some by a chorus.

As C. S. Lewis has insisted, a collection of love lyrics is not a way of telling a story.[1] Accordingly, the Song of Solomon does not tell a story but instead alludes to one. There are two lovers, Solomon, called "the beloved," and a Shulamite girl, called "love." We can infer that Solomon met and fell in love with a beautiful rustic girl. Alternately, the rustic identity of the girl might be a fictional disguise, since Solomon's rustic identity in the work is obviously fictional and since such a technique is common in pastoral literature. Solomon invited the girl to the palace to be part of the royal harem. The love progressed and was consummated in marriage. Part of the poem describes the wedding.

Because of the shifting, stream-of-consciousness pattern of organization, one of the prerequisites for understanding the work is a firm grasp of its sequential structure. The following outline is offered as one explanation of how the work unfolds:

1. *Title of the book* (1:1).

2. *Expository lyrics:* the lady, with her companions at court and absent from her beloved, expresses her love for Solomon.
   (a) 1:2-4: the lady longs for her lover.
   (b) 1:5-6: the lady addresses the women of the palace, describing her own physical appearance and establishing her rustic identity.
   (c) 1:7: the lady expresses desire for Solomon's companionship, addressing him directly under the guise of a shepherd.
   (d) 1:8: choral response, reinforcing the pastoral atmosphere.

3. *The lovers' dialogue:* expression of mutual love.
   (a) 1:9-11: the lover praises the lady's beauty in figurative terms.
   (b) 1:12-14: the lady replies, praising the king as her beloved.
   (c) 1:15: the lover assures her of his delight in her loveliness.
   (d) 1:16-17: the lady praises Solomon and their pastoral surroundings.
   (e) 2:1-2: the lady compares herself to flowers and the lover repeats the image.

4. *The marriage lyrics:* an epithalamion (wedding song).
   (a) 2:3-7: the lady meditates, praising her beloved, recalling the past delights of their reciprocal love, and expressing her longing for their wedding.

---

[1] *English Literature in the Sixteenth Century Excluding Drama* (Oxford: Oxford University Press, 1954), p. 327.

- (b) 2:8-17: excitement over Solomon's arrival for the wedding.
- (c) 3:1-5: the lady's dream of anticipation; a wish fulfillment dream about what it will mean to be married.
- (d) 3:6-11: description of Solomon's appearance in the wedding procession.
- (e) 4:1-15: Solomon praises the beauty and virtue of his bride.
- (f) 4:16–5:1a: the lady expresses a wish to be desirable to her husband and issues an invitation for him to possess her, and the lover responds.
- (g) 5:1b: a choral celebration of the consummation of the love.
5. *Songs of separation and reunion.*
   - (a) 5:2-8: the lady's second dream, a vision of separation.
   - (b) 5:9–6:3: praise of the lover, ending with joyful reunion.
   - (c) 6:4-12: the lover's praise of his bride's beauty and uniqueness.
   - (d) 6:13–7:9: praise of the bride's beauty and erotic attractiveness.
6. *Courtship lyrics* (pre-marriage).
   - (a) 7:10-13: pastoral invitation to love and the good life.
   - (b) 8:1-4: the lady's wish that her lover's affection might be acknowledged in her parental home and that she might marry her lover.
   - (c) 8:5: the lover calls on the lady at her home.
   - (d) 8:6-7: a description of the lady's desire for unquenchable love.
   - (e) 8:8-10: the lady asserts her purity and maturity.
   - (f) 8:11-14: the lovers' dialogue: the lady expresses contentment with her lover (vss. 11-12), the lover asks to hear his beloved's voice (vs. 13), and the lady replies (vs. 14).

The view of love embodied in the Song of Solomon is one of the reasons for the importance of the work in biblical literature. To begin, the love described in the work is *eros,* with no mention of *agape.* The keynote of the work is "love because of," not "love in spite of." Although in modern usage the adjective "erotic" implies sexual lust, the word should be applied to the Song of Solomon with the neutral meaning "having to do with sexual love; amatory." The love in the poem is erotic in the sense that it exists between a man and a woman and has a strong physical dimension. The implication of the poem is that the mutual physical attractiveness of the sexes is God-ordained and that sex is meant to play a good and normal role within its God-ordained confines.

The love in the poem is also romantic. It is sentimentalized, highly refined, and conducted according to an elaborate social pattern. It is humanly refined and could not possibly be considered animalistic. This distinctly human identity of the love removes it from lust, which treats sex only as a physical appetite.

A third characteristic of the love depicted in the work is that it is idealized. It is held to be an ennobling human sentiment, involving such moral qualities as kindness, humility, modesty, high regard for another person, and loyalty in love. The idealization of romantic love removes the poem from asceticism, which holds that romantic love is never a good thing in itself.

Finally, the romantic love that is celebrated in the poem occurs within the context of marriage. As the love deepens it is directed toward marriage, and the physical consummation of the love is described as occurring after a wedding ceremony. In chapters 4 and 5 the lady is six times referred to as Solomon's "bride."

To summarize, we can say that the ideal that is celebrated in the work is wedded romantic love. What is somewhat surprising is that this love is not put into a spiritual context of faith in God. In fact, the name of God occurs only once in the poem, in passing. We know from other writings in the Bible that biblical writers do not believe that a successful marriage can be based only or even primarily on *eros*, yet *agape* is not a theme in the poem. The explanation is undoubtedly that a poet is under no obligation to write about everything in every poem he writes. This poem is a celebration of erotic love, and its scope is limited to that. The conclusion to be drawn is that in biblical literature something does not have to be spiritual in order to be sacred. The Song of Solomon establishes the principle that human romantic love can be a good and sacred thing, even though it is not something that belongs exclusively to adherents of the Hebraic-Christian religion. Once we have noted this, it is also important to be reminded that "Christianity has glorified marriage more than any other religion; and nearly all the greatest love poetry in the world has been produced by Christians."[2]

II

The inscription of the poem identifies it as "The Song of Songs, which is Solomon's" (1:1). The title is a Hebrew superlative meaning "the best song" or "the greatest song." The phrase "which is Solomon's" probably does not refer to authorship but to the fact that the poem is about Solomon and was perhaps written under the auspices of Solomon.

The first lyrics in the collection (1:2-8) are expository in nature and introduce us to the setting, characters, and style of the work as a whole. The two protagonists of the collection are identified as

---

[2] C. S. Lewis, *Mere Christianity* (New York: The Macmillan Company, 1958), p. 77.

lovers and as worthy persons. For example, the lady characterizes herself as being in love and her beloved as being romantically attractive when she states (vss. 2-3),

> *O that you would kiss me with the kisses of your mouth!*
> *For your love is better than wine,*
>   *your anointing oils are fragrant,*
> *your name is oil poured out;*
>   *therefore the maidens love you.*

Solomon's exalted status is established in similar terms when the lady says (vs. 4),

> *We will exult and rejoice in you;*
>   *we will extol your love more than wine;*
>   *rightly do they love you.*

The lady characterizes herself as being beautiful, rustic, and dark-complected (vss. 5-6):

> *I am very dark, but comely,*
>   *O daughters of Jerusalem. . . .*
> *Do not gaze at me because I am swarthy,*
>   *because the sun has scorched me.*
> *My mother's sons were angry with me,*
>   *they made me keeper of the vineyards;*
>   *but my own vineyard I have not kept!*

The setting to which we are introduced is also rustic. For example, the male lover is pictured as pasturing his flock in the countryside (vs. 7) and as being "beside the shepherds' tents" (vs. 8). Combined with the pastoral references, however, there are pictures of aristocratic court life. There is an allusion to the fact that Solomon has taken the Shulamite girl "into his chambers" (vs. 4) as part of the royal harem. A subsequent reference to the king's palace occurs when the lady compares her dark complexion to "the curtains of Solomon" (vs. 5). This paradoxical mingling of pastoral and courtly references is a staple in much pastoral literature. After all, most pastoral poetry has been written by city poets. All of this suggests that the pastoral setting and characterization are a disguise for historical people and events. The pastoral atmosphere also provides an idealized setting for the idealized romance.

Several stylistic techniques also strike us at once as we begin to read the poems. There is a kaleidoscopic shifting in the objects of address and in the pronouns that are used. The effect is to take us into the very consciousness of the speaker, and the fiction that is maintained is that we observe the speaker in the very process of thinking. Another feature of the style is its sensuousness ("having to do with sensory experience"). The romance is obviously a physical experience, replete with fragrant smells (vs. 3) and tingling kisses (vs. 2). As we continue to read, it becomes evident that the poetic style of the Song of Solomon is what C. S. Lewis has called, in another context, "golden poetry."[3] The main effort of such poetry is directed toward richness of imagery, metaphor, and emotion. Golden poetry uses words that invite sensory and emotional response. There is a delight in external nature, and the imagery is filled with references to flowers and trees, the moon and the sun. The golden subject matter that usually goes along with this golden style consists of ideally ardent lovers in an ideally flowery and fruitful landscape. This kind of poetry is obviously at the opposite end of the stylistic spectrum from realism. Golden poetry could never be mistaken for the ordinary speaking voice. It is a consciously poetic style, and one which the modern reader, conditioned to expect realism, is likely to have to learn to enjoy.

The second group of lyrics contains the lovers' dialogue on the subject of their mutual love. It is a rule of pastoral love poetry that the lovers praise each other in terms appropriate to the rustic setting. This is exactly what occurs in the dialogue. The man compliments the lady by comparing her to "a mare of Pharaoh's chariots" (1:9). The correspondence between the lady and the horse is not, of course, physical but is rather a matter of value, or desirability, though strength may also be implied. Just as a mare of Pharaoh's chariots is a recognized standard of excellence, so the beloved measures up to the lover's standard of worth.[4] Similarly, when the lady states, "My beloved is to me a bag of myrrh" (1:13), the primary meaning of the comparison involves a general transfer of value from one area of experience to another. Other images that must be understood in terms of the pastoral convention of praising the beloved in images that come from the rustic milieu include comparisons of one or the other of the two lovers to doves (1:15), a rose (2:1), a lily (2:1, 2), and an apple tree (2:3).

Such references to the rural setting keep in our minds the idealized setting in which the romance is pictured as occurring. So do descrip-

---

[3] *English Literature in the Sixteenth Century Excluding Drama*, pp. 64-65, 323.
[4] My remarks about the imagery of the Song of Solomon are based on what I regard as the definitive study of the subject by Israel Baroway, "The Imagery of Spenser and the Song of Songs," *The Journal of English and Germanic Philology*, XXXIII (1934), 23-45; conveniently reprinted in *Edmund Spenser: Epithalamion*, ed. Robert Beum (Columbus: Charles E. Merrill Publishing Company, 1968), pp. 81-103. Baroway's conclusions were, in turn, indebted to Richard G. Moulton, *The Modern Reader's Bible* (New York: The Macmillan Company, 1895), pp. 1448-50.

tive passages which are present solely to evoke a pastoral atmosphere. In many of these passages the pastoral atmosphere becomes transmuted into romantic feeling. The following passage is a typical example (1:16-17):

> Behold, you are beautiful, my beloved,
>   truly lovely,
> Our couch is green;
>   the beams of our house are cedar,
>   our rafters are pine.

We might well ask what the connection is between the loveliness of the beloved and the rustic setting. The answer is that we transfer our natural sentiment, evoked by the descriptions of nature, into romantic sentiment.

The middle section of lyrics is the marriage poems. The exact title for poetry that takes its origin not simply from a romance but from a single event, the wedding, is "epithalamion." The opening lyric of this section is an introspective meditation by the lady (2:3-7). She praises the superiority of her lover by using an analogy from nature: "As an apple tree among the trees of the wood, / so is my beloved among young men" (vs. 3). In keeping with this kind of figurative description, she compares the delight of their relationship to sitting in the shadow of a tree and eating its fruit: "With great delight I sat in his shadow, / and his fruit was sweet to my taste" (vs. 3). We get an island of narrative in the lyric sea when the lady recalls the past courtship: "He brought me to the banqueting house, / and his banner over me was love" (vs. 4). We return quickly to emotion as the lady expresses the excess of her passion (vs. 5):

> Sustain me with raisins,
>   refresh me with apples;
>   for I am sick with love.

The lady also expresses her strong desire to be present with her beloved: "O that his left hand were under my head, / and that his right hand embraced me!" (vs. 6).

In this context of strong anticipation we find the first occurrence of the refrain that will occur a total of three times in the work (2:7; 3:5; 8:4). The refrain states,

> I adjure you, O daughters of Jerusalem,
>   by the gazelles or the hinds of the field,
> that you stir not up nor awaken love
>   until it please.

This refrain appears in situations of overpowering anticipation and is a call for patient waiting. Its main point is that love must be allowed to take its course and should not be rushed. Gazelles and hinds are invoked because they were timid creatures, hence appropriate in a plea for nonaggressiveness.

The emotional pace of the work continues at a high pitch in the next poem, an expression of the lady's excitement over Solomon's arrival for the wedding (2:8-17). The picture of the groom "leaping upon the mountains, / bounding over the hills" (vs. 8) is hyperbolic, conveying the lover's emotional experience of the event rather than literal fact. Masculine vigor and attractiveness are conveyed by the comparison of the man to a gazelle and young stag (vs. 8). Upon his arrival the groom is pictured as uttering the conventional pastoral invitation to love (vss. 10ff.):

> *Arise, my love, my fair one,*
> *and come away;*
> *for lo, the winter is past,*
> *the rain is over and gone.*
> *The flowers appear on the earth,*
> *the time of singing has come,*
> *and the voice of the turtledove*
> *is heard in our land.*
> *The fig tree puts forth its figs,*
> *and the vines are in blossom;*
> *they give forth fragrance.*
> *Arise, my love, my fair one,*
> *and come away. . . .*

On the pastoral level this is simply an invitation to go for a walk, with the springtime setting serving as an allurement and the basis for the appeal. The real meaning of the invitation lies in the fact that it is a symbolic way of promising the lady fulfillment and a good life. The security of the lovers' relationship is expressed in the statement, "My beloved is mine and I am his, / he pastures his flock among the lilies" (vs. 16). And there is a concluding plea for the wedding day to come quickly (vs. 17):

> *Until the day breathes*
> *and the shadows flee,*
> *turn, my beloved, be like a gazelle,*
> *or a young stag upon rugged mountains.*

In another of the marriage lyrics the lady uses a vision to express her strong desire for the marriage (3:1-5). In the dream, the lady wanders about the city in search of her beloved. The climax of the brief narrative is the successful completion of her quest (vs. 4):

> *. . . I found him whom my soul loves.*
> *I held him, and would not let him go*
> *   until I had brought him into my mother's house,*
> *   and into the chamber of her that conceived me.*

To bring her lover into her mother's house would be to marry him (cf. Gen. 24:67). The dream, then, has been a wish-fulfillment dream in which the lady anticipates her marriage to Solomon. Since the marriage has not yet occurred, the dream appropriately concludes with a repetition of the refrain (3:5), which, as we have seen, occurs in contexts of intense anticipation and is a plea for patience while the love runs its natural progression.

Yet another of the wedding lyrics is the description of the wedding procession, a conventional feature of an epithalamion. In the Song of Solomon it takes the form of a description of Solomon (3:6-11), who is pictured "on the day of his wedding, / on the day of the gladness of his heart" (vs. 11). The style is pictorial, as in the following portrait (vss. 9-10):

> *King Solomon made himself a palanquin*
> *   from the wood of Lebanon.*
> *He made its posts of silver,*
> *   its back of gold, its seat of purple;*
> *it was lovingly wrought within,*
> *   by the daughters of Jerusalem.*

We might note in passing that although Solomon is usually given a pastoral identity in the work, his description in the wedding procession pictures him as he really was — a king with regal splendor. The pastoral paraphernalia, as so often in such literature, is a thinly veiled disguise for aristocratic persons.

Solomon's praise of the beauty and virtue of his bride (4:1-7) exemplifies a type of love lyric found three more times in the Song of Solomon (5:10-16; 6:4-10; 7:1-9). Since these poems are so similar in structure, we can profitably consider them together. They belong to a type that can best be called the emblematic blazon. A blazon is a poem that praises, by listing, the beautiful features or virtuous qualities of the beloved. An emblematic blazon compares the physical features of a person to objects (or "emblems") in nature. The resulting poem is figurative and symbolic. The following catalog of the lady's beautiful features is a typical example (4:1-5):

> *Behold, you are beautiful, my love,*
> *   behold, you are beautiful!*
> *Your eyes are doves*
> *   behind your veil.*

> Your hair is like a flock of goats,
>   moving down the slopes of Gilead.
> Your teeth are like a flock of shorn ewes
>   that have come up from the washing,
> all of which bear twins,
>   and not one among them is bereaved.
> Your lips are like a scarlet thread,
>   and your mouth is lovely.
> Your cheeks are like halves of a pomegranate
>   behind your veil.
> Your neck is like the tower of David,
>   built for an arsenal,
> whereon hang a thousand bucklers,
>   all of them shields of warriors.
> Your two breasts are like two fawns,
>   twins of a gazelle,
>   that feed among the lilies.

The important point about this blazon is that it is symbolic rather than pictorial. For his comparisons the poet is content with only a vague visual correspondence between the feature of the beloved and the object to which it is compared. The primary meaning of the comparison rests not in close visual correspondence but in the transferal of value. The poet is comparing his lady to supreme standards of excellence. The lady's neck, for example, is compared to the tower of David, which is described as an arsenal full of weapons. The visual correspondence is slight. If pressed very far, the effect is to make the lady appear ludicrous. The poet refers to the tower of David as a tower par excellence, surrounded by glorious associations of national history. It is the supreme value of the tower of defense that makes it like the lady's neck.

That the main point of the comparisons in these emblematic blazons is a general transference of value rather than close pictorial similarity is evident from other comparisons as well. The lady's hair is compared to a flock of goats moving down a slope of Gilead (4:1). This comparison may be original and imaginative, but it is not literal and precise. The movement of a flock of goats down a slope takes several minutes, whereas the waving of hair in the wind is a movement of one or two seconds. The flock of goats is primarily a symbol of what would be considered valuable to a shepherd. In a subsequent passage the hair of the man is said to be like "the finest gold" and "black as a raven" (5:11). Literally the man's hair cannot be both blond and black. The images used in the comparisons simply represent two examples of beauty. A similar transference of value occurs when various features of the beloved are compared to treasured minerals (5:14-15) and to fragrance (5:13).

What is true of the individual comparisons applies also to the catalog of comparisons in a blazon. The effect of such a grouping is a general one. The result is not a picture of the beloved but a general impression of value and desirability. As an attempt at a unified and coherent picture, these blazons are contradictory and unsuccessful, but as a combination of acknowledged standards of excellence they effectively evoke a feeling of worth.

The epithalamion that comprises the middle of the Song of Solomon reaches its climax with a figurative description of the lovers' consummation of their love. The groom compares the desirability of his bride to a fragrant garden (4:12-15):

> A garden locked is my sister, my bride,
>   a garden locked, a fountain sealed.
> Your shoots are an orchard of pomegranates
>   with all choicest fruits,
>   henna with nard,
> nard and saffron, calamus and cinnamon,
>   with all trees of frankincense,
>   myrrh and aloes,
>   with all chief spices —
> a garden fountain, a well of living water,
>   and flowing streams from Lebanon.

In this comparison the value of the garden is transferred to the bride. A second level of the meaning is sensuous or physical desirability and attractiveness. The lady responds to her lover's praise by expressing a wish to be desirable to her husband and extending an invitation for him to possess her. In expressing these things, she continues the figure of the garden (4:16):

> Awake, O north wind,
>   and come, O south wind!
> Blow upon my garden,
>   let its fragrance be wafted abroad.
> Let my beloved come to his garden,
>   and eat its choicest fruits.

The husband, continuing the same metaphor, claims his wife (5:1) with the words,

> I come to my garden, my sister, my bride,
> I gather my myrrh with my spice,
> I eat my honeycomb with my honey,
> I drink my wine with my milk.

The lyric concludes with a choral celebration of the consummation of the love: "Eat, O friends, and drink: / drink deeply, O lovers!" (5:1). This wealth of imagery is the means by which the poet conveys his conviction about the beauty and value of physical, sexual love within a context of marriage. In claiming the sexual love of his wife, the husband is shown to be claiming something of great value.

The fourth group of lyrics (5:2—7:9) consists of songs of separation and reunion, appropriate to any stage of the courtship or marriage. The section begins with the lady's second dream, which this time depicts her separation from her lover (5:2-8). The fact that the passage is intended to represent a dream is signalized by the statement, "I slept, but my heart was awake" (vs. 2). The lady pictures herself as going to open the door to her beloved: "...my hands dripped with myrrh, / my fingers with liquid myrrh" (vs. 5). As elsewhere in the Song of Solomon, the sensuous density of such a description is meant to be translated into an impression of emotional intensity. In contrast to the earlier vision, the lady's quest through the city ends without her finding her lover (vss. 6-7). The dream, in short, has been a narrative way of presenting the feelings and frustrations of separated lovers. A subsequent narrative fragment pictures the reunion of the lovers in an idealized pastoral setting (6:1-3).

A blazon in chapter 6 (vss. 4-12) makes use of some conventional motifs found elsewhere in love poetry. One of these consists of turning a biographical fact into a compliment. In this case the lover cites the fact that his lady is the only daughter of her mother as evidence of her uniqueness (vs. 9):

> *My dove, my perfect one, is only one,*
> *the darling of her mother,*
> *flawless to her that bore her.*

A second passage uses the common technique of comparing the lady to some resplendent object in nature, with the lady said to be "like the dawn, / fair as the moon, bright as the sun" (vs. 10). Yet another motif in classical and Petrarchan love poetry is the comparison of the lady's hair to a net that captures her lover. The motif appears in the Song of Solomon in the statement "...your flowing locks are like purple; / a king is held captive in the tresses" (7:5).

It is usually assumed that the concluding lyrics in the Song of Solomon express sentiments that occur after the wedding. This reading is based on the assumption that the work follows a chronological principle. The last series of lyrics, however, conveys thoughts and feelings that are consistently appropriate to the courtship phase of the romance. It is one evidence among many that the Song of Solomon is a loosely structured collection of lyrics, not a story that follows a chronological arrangement from beginning to end.

The last group of lyrics begins with a pastoral invitation to love that epitomizes the technique used in the collection as a whole (7:10-13):

> *I am my beloved's,*
> *and his desire is for me.*

Come, my beloved,
let us go forth into the fields,
and lodge in the villages;
let us go out early to the vineyards,
and see whether the vines have budded,
whether the grape blossoms have opened
and the pomegranates are in bloom.
There I will give you my love.
The mandrakes give forth fragrance,
and over our doors are all choice fruits,
new as well as old,
which I have laid up for you, O my beloved.

This is golden poetry at its most typical. The mode is metaphoric, with the delights and fulfillment of mutual love compared to a journey through a rustic landscape. The imagery evokes a series of pleasant associations, with our sentiment for nature being transmuted into romantic emotion. The usual subject matter of golden poetry, ideally ardent lovers in an ideally flowery and fruitful landscape, is present.

A lyric containing the lady's plea for permanence in love (8:6-7) is not only a high point in the emotional progress of the Song of Solomon but also one of the most eloquent descriptions of love ever written. The lady first requests permanence by using the legal terminology of setting a seal on something as a mark of possession: "Set me as a seal upon your heart, / as a seal upon your arm" (vs. 6). She then gives the reason for her request: "for love is strong as death, / jealousy is cruel as the grave" (vs. 6). The comparison of love's strength to death is a way of asserting that it cannot be conquered or combated. The second clause is probably intended to be parallel in meaning, as it is in the New English Bible: "passion is cruel as the grave." Another comparison draws upon the archetypal association of romantic emotion with fire: "Its flashes are flashes of fire, / a most vehement flame" (vs. 6). An element of narrative conflict between warring forces of nature is introduced when the fire image is amplified and given the quality of permanence: "Many waters cannot quench love, / neither can floods drown it" (vs. 7). A final statement asserts the supreme value of true love (vs. 7):

If a man offered for love
all the wealth of his house,
it would be utterly scorned.

Another lyric sequence asserts the lady's maturity and sexual purity (8:8-10). In the initial part of the passage, the lady's brothers are pictured as speaking while their sister is yet immature (vs. 8). The brothers' first comment is that if their sister has been chaste when she reaches marriageable age, they will arrange a marriage and dowry for her: "If she is a wall, / we will build upon her a battlement of silver" (vs. 9). If, however, their sister has been morally loose ("a door" instead of "a wall"), they will take measures to guard her sexual purity: "but if she is a door, / we will enclose her with boards of cedar" (vs. 9). Recalling these earlier sentiments of her brothers, the lady asserts that she is both mature and chaste, and that she has found a lover (vs. 10):

> I was a wall,
>> and my breasts were like towers;
> then I was in his eyes
>> as one who brings peace.

In another lyric fragment the lady states that her whole wealth is contained in Solomon, her "vineyard." The multiplicity of Solomon's vineyards serves as a foil to the lady's single vineyard (8:11-12):

> Solomon had a vineyard at Baalhamon;
>> he let out the vineyard to keepers;
>> each one was to bring for its fruit a thousand pieces of silver.
> My vineyard, my very own, is for myself;
>> you, O Solomon, may have the thousand,
>> and the keepers of the fruit two hundred.

Solomon responds to the lady's expression of love by referring to her metaphor of the vineyard while stating his desire to hear her voice (8:13):

> O you who dwell in the gardens,
>> my companions are listening for your voice;
>> let me hear it.

In answering the king's request, the lady expresses her desire for her lover's presence (8:14):

> Make haste, my beloved,
>> and be like a gazelle
> or a young stag
>> upon the mountains of spices.

The Song of Solomon is a notable example of how one love poet solved the problem of depicting romantic, sexual love in literature. On the one hand, the poet avoids the pitfall of allowing the love to evaporate into an abstraction by continually making physical attractiveness the main ingredient of the romantic relationship. On the other hand, the poet avoids pornography by consistently choosing to portray the sexual love that is his subject through the use of symbolism. The result is that we get a strong impression of the sexual attractiveness of the lovers and the value of their physical love without being asked to picture the physical details of their relationship.

Bethlehem as seen from the Shepherd's Fields.

Biblical
Pastoral

11

I

Pastoral literature is literature in which the characters are shepherds or rustics, the setting is rural, and the actions are those customarily done by shepherds. There is often a great deal of emphasis on the country setting, resulting in much description. There is relatively little action. In pastoral literature the shepherds can be treated realistically, with the pastoral world presented with at least superficial resemblances to actual rustic conditions, or the poet can present the pastoral world as an idealized never-never land — a golden world of wish fulfillment far removed from burdensome realities.

What does pastoral literature really mean? In answering this question we must be careful not to confuse the symbol with the thing symbolized. To regard pastoral literature as simple because it tells of a simple life is to misunderstand it. Pastoral literature is not ordinarily escape literature but is rather concerned with reality. It is a serious criticism of life, to use Matthew Arnold's definition of literature.

As a criticism of life, pastoral literature falls into three main categories. It has been used to portray the experience of love, to depict the good life, or perfection, and as a vehicle for talking about the issues and problems of real life. We shall take a closer look at these categories later.

The figure of the shepherd became, in pastoral literature, a symbol. Simply by using a shepherd as a character, a pastoral writer implied certain values. Most broadly, the shepherd was an idealized figure. He was the humble rustic, exempt from the vices of civilized life. In biblical literature, for example, the early life of man in Paradise was a pastoral, rural existence and was a model of moral perfection. In Genesis 4:2 we read that "Abel was a keeper of sheep," and he is depicted there as a symbol of the man of spiritual integrity, approved by God. David was a shepherd who in Hebrew literature was said to be "a man after [God's own] heart" (1 Sam. 13:14; Acts 13:22).

The birth of Jesus was first announced to humble shepherds, further idealizing them.

Furthermore, just as the shepherd exercised leadership over his sheep, so the shepherd in pastoral literature became a ready symbol for the person of spiritual leadership. In biblical pastoral this spiritual leader might be either a king or priest, or God Himself. Psalm 78:52, in talking about God's leading Israel out of Egypt, states, "Then he led forth his people like sheep, and guided them in the wilderness like a flock." Psalm 100:3 uses the same metaphor when it states, "We are his people, and the sheep of his pasture" (see also Ps. 95:7). Jeremiah castigates corrupt religious leaders with these words: " 'Woe to the shepherds who destroy and scatter the sheep of my pasture!' says the Lord. . . .'I will set shepherds over them who will care for them, and they shall fear no more, nor be dismayed' " (Jer. 23:1, 4). Isaiah predicted regarding the coming Messiah, "He will feed his flock like a shepherd, he will gather the lambs in his arms, he will carry them in his bosom, and gently lead those that are with young" (Isa. 40:11). On one occasion Jesus defined His ministry with the statement that He "was sent only to the lost sheep of the house of Israel" (Matt. 15:24), and in commissioning Peter to the task of the ministry, Jesus said, "Feed my lambs" (John 21:15), "Tend my sheep" (John 21:16), and "Feed my sheep" (John 21:17). Jesus is often associated with pastoral symbolism, as when He is called "the great shepherd of the sheep" (Heb. 13:20) and "the chief Shepherd" (I Pet. 5:4).

Finally, in classical literature the shepherd was also a poet — a maker of songs. Usually, of course, this was only a metaphor, but it became a part of the symbolic meaning of the shepherd in pastoral literature. This motif receives less attention in the biblical pastoral tradition. The chief exceptions are David, the sweet singer of Israel who was literally a shepherd-poet, and the lover in the Song of Solomon, who likewise combines the roles of shepherd and poet.

To sum up, in pastoral literature the shepherd was an idealized figure, a model of virtue, a spiritual or religious leader, and, on occasion, a poet.

II

One of the biggest categories of pastoral literature is that which uses pastoral as a vehicle for writing about the experience of love. In this kind of literature, the pastoral setting provides an idealized atmosphere for the idealized love that is the topic of the work.

Pastoral love poetry can also be a way of writing autobiographical or biographical romance.

Within the general category of pastoral love poetry, there are several well-established forms. One is the pastoral invitation to love, in which a lover invites his beloved to the good life, a life of mutual love and fulfillment, in terms appropriate to the pastoral world. Examples include two poems in the Song of Solomon (2:10-15; 7:10-13). Another form is the pastoral blazon, a poem praising the beauty and virtue of the beloved, using images that are rustic or natural. There are numerous illustrations of the technique in the Song of Solomon, including 2:1-3a; 4:1-5, 12-15; 5:12-13; 7:1-9. Yet a third kind is simply the description of the delights of the love, using rural images and metaphors (see Song of Solomon 1:14, 16-17; 2:3b, 16; 4:16; 5:1; 6:2-3). Finally, there is the pastoral complaint or lament; an example is the lady's complaint over the slowness of her love to culminate in marriage in the Song of Solomon 8:1-4.

Why did poets for many centuries use pastoral as a way of writing about love, and why do pastoral motifs continue to appear in love poetry? There are several answers. Pastoral is a ready-made vehicle. A poet writing about love has rather limited possibilities from which to choose. He can write direct, personal lyric poetry; he can tell a story; or he can project the sentiments of love onto fictional characters. Pastoral is a way of doing the latter. Secondly, the pastoral mode is a way to distance and objectify an experience that may be too personal to write about directly. In the third place, the pastoral mode, being conventional and surrounded with rich traditional associations, is a way of giving dignity and status to one's love poetry. Finally, the pastoral setting provides an idealized context for the sentiments of romantic love. Pastoral poetry presents a world in which love can flourish without the pressures that exist in ordinary life. The positive qualities of the natural environment reinforce the beauty of the love that is depicted, and sensory delight in nature is transmuted into romantic sentiment.

Another major branch of pastoral literature is that which uses pastoral to praise the good life. The rural image may be the literal conception of the good life, with the poet equating virtue with the life of nature. Or the rural image may be a metaphor for qualities that appeal to the human imagination, such as contentment or peacefulness or perfection generally.

The example par excellence of the pastoral poem in praise of the good life is Psalm 23. It primarily uses the pastoral world of sheep and shepherd and countryside to celebrate the provision that God exercises in the life of his creatures. It is the good life — that is, the life of God's provision — that the poem is primarily celebrating. Beneath the ostensible theme of providence, however, there lies the experience of nature and the shepherd's life. The poem implicitly praises the simple rural life of the shepherd and holds it up as a model of virtue. For example, the poet writes about the supply of daily necessities, thereby establishing the simple life as the norm by which unnecessary luxury is dispraised. Similarly, the reference to green pastures and still waters is a way of evoking our instinct for nature, as opposed to civilization. In short, the allusions to the activities of the shepherd are not only a vehicle for talking about provision but are also an indirect way of celebrating this type of rural existence.

In terms of strategy, the writer of Psalm 23 has chosen to treat the pastoral world realistically. For contrast, one has only to go to the Song of Solomon, which treats the pastoral world strictly as a convention and paints an idealized picture of shepherds leading sheep among lilies instead of attempting to describe the actual conditions of shepherding. Psalm 23, on the other hand, is not highly conventional but realistic. It is primitive poetry, with folk literature characteristics. This can be explained by a simple fact — the poet was himself a shepherd. This cannot be overemphasized. It makes David's pastoral poetry virtually a *sui generis*. David could not have been more original if he had tried.

Psalm 23 happens to belong to a particular category of pastoral poetry known as the pastoral day. Such a poem is structured on the chronology of the day and catalogs the typical activities of the ideal day. Examples in English poetry include Milton's poems *L'Allegro* and *Il Penseroso*. Psalm 23 follows this pattern also, for it describes the shepherd leading his sheep along a path to noontime rest, and then progresses to activities associated with caring for the sheep at the end of the day.

Another category of biblical pastoral, a subtype of the "good life" class, consists of those passages in the prophets where future restoration to God's favor and blessing is pictured in pastoral or rural images. A typical instance of this archetype of the green world used to symbolize God's blessing is Hosea 14:4-7:

> *I will heal their faithlessness;*
> *I will love them freely,*
> *for my anger has turned from them.*
> *I will be as the dew to Israel;*
> *he shall blossom as the lily,*
> *he shall strike root as the poplar;*

> *his shoots shall spread out;*
> > *his beauty shall be like the olive,*
> > *and his fragrance like Lebanon.*
> *They shall return and dwell beneath my shadow,*
> > *they shall flourish as a garden;*
> *they shall blossom as the vine,*
> > *their fragrance shall be like the wine of Lebanon.*

God's words in Isaiah 41:18-19 likewise describe His deliverance of His people in nature images that would appeal to the rural or pastoral background of the Israelites:

> *I will open rivers on the bare heights,*
> > *and fountains in the midst of the valleys;*
> *I will make the wilderness a pool of water,*
> > *and the dry land springs of water.*
> *I will put in the wilderness the cedar,*
> > *the acacia, the myrtle, and the olive;*
> *I will set in the desert the cypress,*
> > *the plane and the pine together.*

This type of future golden age, pictured in pastoral terms, is unique to biblical literature. By contrast, pagan literature pictured the golden age as having existed in the distant past, with no reference to a coming millennium of bliss.

Narrowly defined, pastoral literature depicts characters who are shepherds or shepherdesses. But the term can be extended to include rural poetry in general. The earthly paradise, whether populated by shepherds or not, is pastoral poetry, belonging to the green world archetype. The description of Paradise in early Genesis is the biblical version of the earthly paradise, which has numerous analogues in nonbiblical literature. According to the Bible, the picture of Paradise in early Genesis describes something that did once exist and which continues to be part of human consciousness. To use the words of C. S. Lewis, it depicts an experience "that does exist and should be visited often."[1]

The description given in Genesis 2 is extremely brief, giving only the outline and evoking within the reader his own vision of what the details were like. There is emphasis on the fact that Paradise was a garden (vss. 8-10, 15-16). Other pastoral motifs are also hinted at. It is a place of sensory delight in the natural environment, as evidenced by the statement that "out of the ground the Lord God made to grow every tree that is pleasant to the sight and good for food" (vs. 9). It is a place where, as in most pastoral literature, the human

---

[1] *The Allegory of Love* (New York: Oxford University Press, 1936), p. 352. Lewis is here talking about pastoral literature in general.

diet consists of vegetation (Gen. 1:30; 2:16). It is a way of life in which man's vocation involves caring for the natural environment (2:15, 19-20). Paradise is a simple, self-contained world, stripped of all the complexities of civilized life and the vices of fallen human experience. It is a place where, before the fall, man experienced spiritual rapport with God as well as rapport with his natural environment, as suggested by the picture of "the Lord God walking in the garden in the cool of the day" (3:8). The pastoral version of kingship appears in the form of Adam's dominion over the natural surroundings (1:28).

There is an element of parody in the significance that the Bible attributes to the pastoral story of Adam and Eve's life in the garden. Literature as a whole, especially ancient literature, has celebrated a heroic scale of values in which significant action is held to involve such motifs as kingship and empire and civilization. The story of early Genesis inverts these values by idealizing instead a simple life free from ordinary civilized concerns. Instead of picturing monarchs who in their public role rule nations, early Genesis praises a man and woman in their private role as keepers of a garden. Whereas heroic narrative ordinarily makes the battlefield the scene of decisive historical activity, early Genesis makes a small garden the setting for the choice that determined the whole destiny of the human history, suggesting at the same time that the truly decisive events of history are not external and physical but rather inner and spiritual. In short, the Bible holds up early Genesis as "a moral center against which traditional assumptions about heroism and the proper end of human activities are tested."[2]

Perhaps Genesis also parodies (that is, parallels but also inverts) pastoral literature itself. In much pastoral literature the rustic life described is obviously a symbol for the absence of all that civilized poets and readers find distressing about contemporary life. Pastoral literature of this type is a kind of solemn joke. By contrast, early Genesis insists that we accept its pastoral image with complete seriousness — as historical truth and "not as a kind of literary balm for minds bruised by the contentions" of ordinary civilized existence.[3]

IV

The third broad category of pastoral is the allegorical tradition.

---

[2] John R. Knott, *Milton's Pastoral Vision: An Approach to Paradise Lost* (Chicago: University of Chicago Press, 1971), p. xv, makes this comment about Paradise as it is portrayed in Milton's *Paradise Lost*.

[3] The quoted phrase comes from Knott, *Milton's Pastoral Vision*, p. 6.

It uses the pastoral image as a vehicle for talking about the problems and concerns of real life. It takes the complex and puts it into the simple. Biblical pastoral does not make extensive use of this form, unless one includes pastoral in which God's relationship to people is described metaphorically as the relationship of shepherd to sheep. One branch of the allegorical category is ecclesiastical pastoral. Since one meaning of the shepherd figure was the idea of spiritual or religious leadership, pastoral was a logical form to use when writing about the religious scene. One member of this pastoral family, in turn, is ecclesiastical satire, which uses the pastoral mode as a means of attacking abuses among religious leaders.

Ezekiel 34 is an example of allegorical pastoral turned mainly to a satiric purpose. The prophecy "against the shepherds of Israel" (vs. 2) is really a satiric attack on Israel's religious leaders, whether political or priestly. The charges are couched in the pastoral mode and must be translated into their appropriate human counterpart. Thus the charge that the shepherds feed themselves instead of the sheep (vss. 2-3) is a comment on the selfishness and greed of the religious leaders, and the description of the shepherds' failure to care for wounded sheep (vs. 4) refers to the leaders' neglect in meeting the needs of the people. The scattering of the flock, which falls prey to "wild beasts" (vss. 5-8), is an indictment of the irresponsibility of the religious leaders of Israel, with the image of the ideal shepherd (as described, for example, in Psalm 23) the implied norm by which the bad shepherds are judged. God's spiritual deliverance of His people is described as the care of a shepherd over his flock (vss. 11-16), with the imagery remaining consistently pastoral in its references. The effect of such a passage is to make God's deliverance realistic, homey, immediate, and tender. The description of good and bad sheep to refer to good and evil people (vss. 17-23) is very unconventional in pastoral literature, which usually uses only the figure of the bad shepherd to symbolize corrupt people. The concluding section of the chapter (vss. 25-31) pictures spiritual fulfillment and security in images that come from the pastoral world of sheep and woods and pasture and showers of rain. This is pastoral used to image forth the good life. The last verse of the chapter, which identifies the Israelites as the sheep and God as the shepherd, makes clear the essentially allegorical use to which pastoral has been put in this passage.

The well-known parable of the lost sheep (Luke 15:3-7) is also based on the pastoral convention. The picture of the good shepherd seeking the one lost sheep has had a hold over the human imagination all out of proportion to the length of the parable, which is very brief. In fact, the image epitomizes the Christian Gospel, which is based on the fact that God does for the creature what the creature cannot do for himself. As in the other parables, the story of the shepherd rescuing the lost sheep secures a positive response on its literal level and then asks the reader to transfer that response to a spiritual level. Jesus makes the allegorical meaning of the pastoral story explicit when He states, "Even so, I tell you, there will be more joy in heaven over one sinner who repents than over ninety-nine righteous persons who need no repentance" (vs. 7).

Jesus' discourse on the good shepherd (John 10:1-18) brings to a climax the class of biblical pastoral that pictures God's spiritual provision for His people as a shepherd's care for his sheep. The literary form is allegory, with the shepherd's relationship to his sheep symbolizing certain things about God's relationship to His people. This kind of pastoral literature communicates at levels that defy logical analysis or propositional statement. It touches people at unconscious as well as conscious levels. The discourse begins (vss. 1-5) with a descriptive contrast between true and false shepherds, thereby focusing on the question of spiritual leadership and allegiance to a worthy authority. The statement that the good shepherd "calls his own sheep by name and leads them out" (vs. 3) stresses the intimacy between the shepherd and his sheep, Christ and the believer, while the statement that "the sheep follow him, for they know his voice" (vs. 4) draws attention to the guidance that Christ gives to the believer. Throughout the discourse, references to the hireling or bad shepherd keep the theme of religious satire before the reader.

When Jesus' listeners did not understand the meaning of his pastoral narrative (John 10:6), Christ responded by allegorizing the story He had just told. He compares Himself to the door of the sheepfold and thus makes the sheepfold a symbol for salvation (vss. 7-9). The life into which the shepherd leads his sheep is allegorized as meaning the abundant life that Christ, the Good Shepherd, gives to His followers (vss. 10-11). In keeping with the pastoral context, the false shepherd who runs and leaves the sheep (vss. 12-13) is the ultimate traitor, just as "the wolf" (vs. 12) is the great terror. By describing the good shepherd as one who lays down his life for his sheep (vss. 11, 15, 17-18) Jesus uses the pastoral mode to describe His own substitutionary atonement on the cross. The emphasis on *"one* flock, *one* shepherd" (vs. 16) is something that recurs in literature as an apocalyptic image of perfection, just as heaven is described as one city or one mansion. In summary, it is partly the pastoral form that makes a passage such as John 10 so meaningful and appealing to the reader who understands the experience that Christ is here describing.

In Wisdom Literature, the narrator is often elderly—a father figure and an authority figure.

Wisdom
Literature

12

I

Wisdom literature is a somewhat amorphous category of biblical literature. There would appear to be two main criteria for placing a work in this classification. Wisdom literature is characterized first of all by the stance of the narrator, who pictures himself as the wise man declaring his observations about human experience. He is elderly — a father figure and an authority figure. Whereas the prophet was the proclaimed spokesman from God, the writer of wisdom literature is the more ordinary person who bases his comments on what he has observed in life around him. In Hebrew culture there were three main classes of spiritual leaders — the priests, the prophets, and the wise men (Jer. 18:18 refers to all three groups). The wise man's role was a relatively humble one but had the appeal of human experience behind it. To sum up, the wise men were seekers of the good life and earnest teachers of what they felt to be true, based on their observation of reality.

Wisdom literature also denotes literature that makes extensive use of the proverb and other related short literary units. The proverb can best be defined as a concise statement of a general truth. Attempts are often made to distinguish among proverb, epigram, maxim, aphorism, and similar terms, but when applied to biblical literature the attempt results in arbitrary definitions that are not very helpful. Some proverbs are more concise than others, but this is the only real distinction.

The proverb represents literature at its most rudimentary level. Its unit is the smallest possible one. The proverb can be regarded as folk literature. Its real environment is not a collection, where it forms one fragment among hundreds, but by itself in the everyday situations of life. The individual proverb is a self-contained unit, "bounded by its own horizon, without any connection with anything else."[1]

It is possible to trace the evolution of the single proverb into a more complex form of literature. The first step in such an evolution is the proverb cluster — a series of individual proverbs on a common theme. Examples from the biblical book of Proverbs include a series of maxims on the king (25:2-7), on the fool (26:1-12), on the sluggard (26:13-16), and on various social pests (26:17-28). A further stage of development in the direction of literary sophistication consists of the collection of proverbs with a unifying theme, a single narrator, and a unified structure and poetic texture. The classic example is Proverbs 1-9, which will be discussed in a subsequent section of this chapter.

The proverb uses a wide range of literary techniques. One is antithesis, which Moulton calls "the very life blood of the proverb."[2] Usually the antithesis takes the form of antithetic parallelism (the same truth stated in positive and negative ways), as illustrated from two proverbs appearing in Proverbs 12:1-2:

> *Whoever loves discipline loves knowledge,*
> *but he who hates reproof is stupid.*
> *A good man obtains favor from the Lord,*
> *but a man of evil devices he condemns.*

Synonymous parallelism is also sometimes used: "From the fruit of his words a man is satisfied with good, / and the work of a man's hand comes back to him" (12:14); "when the wicked dies, his hope perishes, / and the expectation of the godless comes to nought" (11:7). Comparison is likewise a fairly regular feature in wisdom literature: "Better is a man of humble standing who works for himself than one who plays the great man but lacks bread" (12:9). Metaphor and simile are also recurrent: "the root of the righteous will never be moved" (vs. 3); "she who brings shame is like rottenness in his bones" (vs. 4). Occasionally paradox is used, as when the wise man comments that "the mercy of the wicked is cruel" (vs. 10).

There are several additional, more extended literary techniques. One of these is the portrait. For example, Proverbs 23:29-35 is a descriptive portrait of the drunkard, while Proverbs 30:11-14 is a brief portrait of an evil society. The dramatized speech sometimes appears, as when the sluggard is quoted as saying, "There is a lion in the road!" (26:13), and the drunkard is described as stating,

---

[1] Richard G. Moulton, *The Modern Reader's Bible* (New York: The Macmillan Company, 1966; originally published 1895), p. 1457.
[2] Moulton, *Modern Reader's Bible*, p. 1455.

"They struck me,...but I was not hurt;...When shall I awake? I will seek another drink" (23:35). Another possibility for the writer of proverbs is the brief narrative, illustrated in the book of Proverbs by the story of a harlot seducing a young man (7:6-23) and the account of how wisdom prepares a feast (9:1-6). The vignette, or brief sketch, is exemplified in the picture of farming found in Proverbs 27:23-27.

As this survey of techniques suggests, there is abundant evidence of a literary imagination at work in wisdom literature. Yet there is little attempt to construct anything more than the very smallest literary unit. It is an example of literary artistry at its simplest level. Because of its brevity, the proverb suffers more from appearing in a collection than any other literary form. A proverb is an isolated fragment, and the reading of one such fragment after another produces monotony, especially when the basic structure of nearly every proverb is antithesis.

II

The first nine chapters of Proverbs clearly represent a more complex kind of artistic design than the rest of the book. There is much more reliance on bigger units. Equally refreshing is the variety of literary devices used to convey the wisdom theme. And there is a unifying theme, poetic texture, narrative viewpoint, and structure to this block of chapters. Although it would be accurate to call these chapters a miscellany, or collection of separate poems, it is a miscellany possessing a high degree of unity.

These nine chapters are carefully structured as a series of corresponding conflicts. The effect is that of a plot. The conflicts include wisdom (a lady) against the harlot, the good man against the evil man, life against death, wisdom against folly, and wisdom against evil. This series of conflicts sets up the necessity of choice between the competing sets of values. The "son" of the series, and by extension the reader, is constantly enjoined to choose one thing over another. Choice between conflicting forces thus lends plot structure to the piece. It is another chapter in the overriding plot of the Bible — the conflict between good and evil.

The group of chapters has its own unifying topic — wisdom. Within this single subject, various subordinate themes appear, including the origin of wisdom, the benefits of wisdom, the tragic results of rejecting wisdom for folly (an indirect way of praising wisdom), the necessity to choose wisdom, and the characteristics and acts of wisdom.

There is also a unifying viewpoint and tone. The repeated addresses to "my son" give these chapters a single viewpoint. We have a strong sense of a single narrator throughout the chapters, something we do not have in the rest of the book or in the typical collection of proverbs. The narrator is always depicted as a wise authority figure. He speaks frequently in the imperative mood, giving instructions and advice. There are also repeated formulae, usually stating in one way or another the need to be attentive. Many sections begin, for example, with a formula that echoes the ideas present in this call to be attentive: "My son, do not forget my teaching, / but let your heart keep my commandments" (Prov. 3:1). The effect is to support the impression of a father addressing a son with urgently needed information. Unity of tone comes from the repeated imperative statements, which serve to stress the authority of the speaker, the necessity for choice, or the urgency of the situation.

Unity of poetic texture is achieved through the use of recurrent images and symbols, which bind the various smaller units into an artistic whole. These repeated images include the woman (Wisdom and the harlot), the son, jewel imagery, the path or way, and wisdom, whether as a conceptual image or a personified quality.

In the midst of all this unity, the writer has incorporated a diversity of literary techniques. In fact, the artistry of the author is seen as much in his ability to handle a variety of forms as it is in his achievement of unity. There is synonymous parallelism as well as the antithetical proverb. Other forms include the lyric poem, the dramatic monologue, the encomium, narrative, and the dramatized scene. The writer seldom relies solely on the sentence proverb, usually managing to present a larger poetic unit.

Both the variety and unity of the work are implied in the following outline:

1. 1:1-7: prologue (introduction to the author, purpose, and theme)
2. 1:8-19: dramatic monologue — the father's advice to avoid getting gain by violence
3. 1:20–33: dramatic monologue — Wisdom's cry of warning against the neglect of wisdom
4. 2:1–3:12: dramatic monologue — the father's advice to follow wisdom and a description of the rewards of doing so
5. 3:13-20: an encomium in praise of wisdom
6. 3:21–4:27: dramatic monologue — the father's advice to follow wisdom and his description of the rewards of doing so. Within the monologue, 4:10-19 constitutes a descriptive poem contrasting the way of the righteous and the way of the wicked.

7. Ch. 5: dramatic monologue — a warning against unchastity and a call to married sexual love

8. 6:1-19: miscellaneous instructions

9. 6:20–7:27: dramatic monologue — the father's warning against adultery

10. Ch. 8: the speech of Wisdom

11. Ch. 9: a poem contrasting the feasts of Wisdom and Folly

The prologue (Prov. 1:1-7) introduces us to the important elements of the whole section. It identifies the work as a collection of proverbs and its purpose as the instruction of people in the ways of wisdom. It also states that the writer is "Solomon, son of David, king of Israel." Most biblical scholars agree that this may be a persona and that Proverbs is not literally the work of Solomon.[3] Within the logic of the work, though, the narrator is given the characteristics of King Solomon. If this is a fictitious persona, it may be an example of satire against Solomon, since the references to the dangers of strange women would indict the folly of Solomon in this regard. Verse 7 serves as a motto or superscription for the opening chapters and beyond them for the entire book: "The fear of the Lord is the beginning of knowledge; / fools despise wisdom and instruction." This passage places wisdom in a supernatural context and asserts that the search for wisdom begins with religious reverence for God. The contrast between wisdom and folly in this verse establishes the main narrative conflict for the succeeding sections.

The first dramatic monologue (Prov. 1:8-19) is typical of the technique used in the other dramatic monologues. A dramatic monologue is a work in which a single speaker addresses a mute audience whose reactions are sometimes implied. In the present monologue, references to "my son" (vss. 8, 10, 15) keep alive the reader's awareness of the dramatic situation. The monologue thus becomes a way of characterizing the speaker as a father figure who is qualified to speak because of his age and experience. On yet another level of meaning, the father is a symbol for God, revealing His will to His creatures. Within the monologue, there is emphasis on the self-destructive nature of getting gain by violence (vss. 16-19), making such activity an example of folly. There is also an interesting use of extended parallelism in verses 10 to 15. Verses 11 to 14 are an extended parallel to the first half of verse 10, and verse 15 constitutes the parallel to the second half of verse 10. The principles involved

---

[3] Biblical scholars come to this conclusion on the basis of the language of the work, which suggests a later date. For a summary of this view, see Samuel J. Schultz, *The Old Testament Speaks* (New York: Harper and Row, 1960), p. 289.

are the same as in a two-line parallel construction, but the units are much longer in what Moulton calls "higher parallelism."

Wisdom, a personified abstraction pictured as a lady, is one of two main characters in the opening chapters of Proverbs. She is the grand antagonist to the harlot or the strange woman, thus providing part of the narrative conflict of the work. She is usually pictured as calling people, especially "the son," to pursue wisdom. Examples include her monologue warning people against the neglect of wisdom (1: 20-33) and her call to seek wisdom (Prov. 8).

The other woman who is vying for the allegiance of "the son" is "the loose woman," also called "the harlot" and "the strange woman." There is an ambiguity about the identity of the loose woman in these chapters. Some references describe her quite literally as a source of sexual temptation, while others seem to suggest that she is a symbol for all types of sin and folly, as the figure of the harlot often is in biblical literature. Many of these passages have a double meaning, referring to sin in general and to sexual infidelity or promiscuity in particular. For example, when the father states that "her feet go down to death" (5:5) and that "she does not take heed to the path of life" (5:6), the woman is symbolic of the effects of sin in general. But when the son is warned not to "go near the door of her house" (5:8), the father evokes the picture of a literal prostitute. Proverbs 5:15-23 contrasts the immoral woman to the ideal of faithful wedded love in a passage that sums up much of the biblical teaching about the beauty and privacy of sexual love in its God-ordained state. Other monologues in which the father warns against sexual and spiritual adultery include Proverbs 6:20-35 and Proverbs 7:6-23, a story of temptation and seduction which is the most elaborate narrative in the book of Proverbs.

The lady named Wisdom is also sometimes described in terms appropriate to romantic love, thereby maintaining the balance and contrast of the work. The following passage, for example, urges the young man to seek wisdom in images suggesting romantic devotion (4:6, 8-9):

> Do not forsake her, and she will keep you;
> love her, and she will guard you. . . .
> Prize her highly, and she will exalt you;
> she will honor you if you embrace her.
> She will place on your head a fair garland;
> she will bestow on you a beautiful crown.

In a similar passage the son is enjoined to "call insight your intimate friend; to preserve you from the loose woman" (7:4-5).

The conflict between Wisdom and the foolish woman reaches its climax in chapter 9. The first six verses describe the feast that Wisdom prepares for the people of the town. The invitation to the feast of Wisdom is dramatized and uses the same images that have been used earlier in the seductions of the loose woman (Prov. 9:4-5):

> *Whoever is simple, let him turn in here!* ...
> *Come, eat of my bread*
> *and drink of the wine I have mixed.*

Verses 13 to 18 balance the feast of Wisdom with a description of the feast that "a foolish woman" prepares for the people of the town. She, too, extends an alluring invitation to passers-by from "the high places of the town," just as the maids of Wisdom had done (vs. 3). Part of her invitation is a verbatim repetition of the invitation uttered by the maids of Wisdom: "Whoever is simple, let him turn in here!" (vs. 16). The speech also repeats the images of bread and drink, but this time the addition of modifying words makes the feast a perversion of the feast of wisdom: "Stolen water is sweet, and bread eaten in secret is pleasant" (vs. 17). The bold juxtaposition of the two feasts and the accompanying invitations concludes this unit on a note of vivid conflict and reinforces the theme that moral choice between wisdom and folly is a basic reality of life.

This discussion of the literary artistry of Proverbs 1-9 would be incomplete without mention of some additional literary effects achieved in individual passages. The image of the way or path is the most recurrent metaphor in these chapters (especially in 2:12-20, where it appears nine times) and conveys the ideas that wisdom and folly are habitual and long-term in nature and lead in the end to consequences, just as a journey leads to a destination. Proverbs 3:1-10 is a tightly woven passage in which a pattern of command followed by reward occurs five times. Proverbs 3:13-20 is an encomium, praising the supreme value of wisdom (vss. 13-15), the qualities of wisdom (vss. 16-18), and the antiquity of wisdom (vss. 19-20). Proverbs 4:10-19 is a descriptive lyric that contrasts the way of wisdom and uprightness (vss. 11-13, 18) with the way of wickedness (vss. 14-17, 19). The command for the sluggard, or lazy person, to consider the industriousness of the ant (6:6-8) is a short vignette from nature, while the portrait of the "worthless person" (6:12-15) belongs to the genre known as the character. The catalog of seven sins (6:16-19) is a conventional form in Old Testament wisdom literature. The seduction scene of Proverbs 7:6-23 is an elaborate temptation story, and the animal similes used to describe the doom of the foolish young man (7:21-23) evoke the impression that sexual temptation is like a trap. The speech of Wisdom in chapter 8, although not a conventional encomium (since it is self-praise), employs several of the usual encomiastic formulae, including a listing of the qualities and acts of wisdom (8:5-21), the ancient and distinguished ancestry of wisdom (vss. 22-31), and a call to emulate the quality being praised (vss. 32-36).

What, finally, is the nature of the wisdom that is praised in these chapters? It is a highly spiritualized quality that goes far beyond worldly expediency. Its origin is "the fear of the Lord" (1:7). To hate knowledge is equivalent to not choosing the fear of the Lord (1:29). The divine source of wisdom is further indicated by the statement that "the Lord gives wisdom; from his mouth come knowledge and understanding" (2:6). The antithesis of wisdom is not simply folly but also evil (2:12-15). To follow this kind of wisdom is nothing less than to lead a God-centered life: "Trust in the Lord with all your heart.... In all your ways acknowledge him, and he will make straight your paths" (3:5-6). To be foolish involves not simply worldly disadvantage. The real burden of these chapters is that the lack of wisdom is destructive of inner character, as evidenced by the assertion that the foolish person "destroys himself" (6:32).

The book of Ecclesiastes adheres to the two criteria of wisdom literature. Its narrator pictures himself as a wise man who has observed human experience. This stance is well summarized near the end of the work when the narrator writes, "Besides being wise, the Preacher also taught the people knowledge, weighing and studying and arranging proverbs with great care" (Eccles. 12:9). Secondly, the writer's basic literary unit falls into the general category of the proverb — not only the sentence proverb but such devices as the brief narrative, the portrait, the description, and the command to the reader.

Ecclesiastes might well be the most misunderstood book in the Bible. Most commentators have found the theme of the book to be inconsistent with the rest of biblical teaching. How such a view of the book arose is baffling. It is no exaggeration to say that this book espouses the most basic theme of biblical literature — that life lived by purely earthly or human values, without faith in God and supernatural values, is meaningless and futile. The key term in the book is the phrase "under the sun." This phrase, or its equivalent "under the heaven," occurs thirty times in the book and denotes that which is only earthly. To be "under the sun" is to be earth-bound, cut off from the supernatural order.

In developing his theme, the writer has chosen a common literary device. He demonstrates at length the inadequacy of any world view other than a theocentric one, and he combines with this demonstration an affirmation of an alternate world view. This means that the individual passages must be placed carefully in their contexts. If we read every passage as being equally indicative of the writer's settled philosophic position, we are left with a meaningless collection of contradictory statements, for it is indisputable that the views of some passages contradict those of others. Actually the contradiction is part of a meaningful pattern in which the writer's negative comments are understood to be the conclusions that emerge when he limits his gaze to the earthly scene. When the narrator voices despair over the futility of life under the sun, he is not affirming this as his final answer to life's existence.

The matter of the theme of Ecclesiastes is closely tied to the question of the work's structure. Typical statements about the structure of the book are that it "is without formal structure" or is "a miscellany of wisdom literature" or "a miscellaneous collection of proverbs." In fact, however, Ecclesiastes is one of the most rigidly structured books in the Bible. The principle of organization is dialectical, that is, based on a conflict between opposites. Passages of negation and affirmation follow each other from the beginning of the work to the end. The narrative conflict underlying the dialectical structure is the contrast between a God-centered world view and all the other world views.

One of the significant things about the juxtaposition of negative and positive passages is that the phrase "under the sun," or an equivalent, occurs in thirteen of the fifteen passages that are wholly negative in theme. The phrase is found in only four of the twelve affirmative passages. Furthermore, emphasis on God and the divine perspective to earthly life is the main theme in nearly all of the positive passages. The obvious conclusion is that the work is structured in such a way as to espouse the God-centered life and expose the varieties of earth-centered existence.

The device of antithesis appears on a smaller scale in individual passages, reinforcing the dialectical nature of the book. Youth and age, wisdom and folly, expectation and disappointment, toil and pleasure, heaven and earth, change and permanence are examples of these local tensions in the texture of the work. The famous lyric on the theme of "a time for everything" (3:1-8) takes antithesis as its chief structural principle.

In addition to giving his work a dialectical structure, the author has seized upon one of the oldest of all literary devices, the quest motif. He pictures himself as a wise man in search of the good life.

His approach to the quest is partly narrative, in which he describes his quest as a series of actions, and partly lyric, in which he praises the good life and dispraises the varieties of inadequate world views.

The book does not have a chronological or narrative unity. It does have unity of other kinds, however. Both the quest motif and the dialectical juxtaposition of positive and negative passages provide unity, as does the stylistic device of antithesis. The recurrence of stock words and phrases is perhaps the most discernible element of unity. The phrases "under the sun," "eat and drink," "vanity of vanities," "this also is vanity" recur, giving a unity of poetic texture.

Two features of the imagery of the book are worthy of note. For one thing, the imagery of the book does much to give it an elemental quality. There are constant references to the sun, to eating and drinking, to the cycles of nature, to death, and to God. A second feature of the imagery is its comprehensiveness. The narrator mentions virtually all of the activities of men. There are references to the city, cultivated fields, gardens, the temple, a house, a bedchamber, courts of justice, seats of power, and battle. The preacher is concerned with all of the main areas of life — wealth, power, religion, social relationships, work, and pleasure.

The popular view of the book is that it is mainly negative, with a ray of hope at the end. This is hardly accurate. There are fifteen negative passages, twelve positive ones, and three passages combining positive and negative elements. The following outline of the book puts it into its constituent parts and shows how the author has structured his work on a dialectical principle.

1. 1:1-3: introduction to the narrator and theme (negative)
2. 1:4-11: description of the meaningless cycle of life under the sun (negative)
3. 1:12-18: the futile quest for meaning in human wisdom (negative)
4. 2:1-11: the futile quest for meaning in pleasure and wealth (negative)
5. 2:12-23: the futile quest for meaning in human attainment that survives one's death (negative)
6. 2:24–3:22: man's quest satisfied:
   (a) 2:24-26: enjoyment of life as a gift from God (positive)
   (b) 3:1-9: further recognition of the order and purpose underlying life (positive)
   (c) 3:10-15: God's provision for the satisfaction of man's quest for meaning (positive)
   (d) 3:16-22: reinforcement of two earlier themes — the necessity for a divine perspective (vss. 16-17) and the

legitimacy of enjoying earthly life during our lifetime (vss. 18-22) (positive)

7. 4:1-16: description of the misery and futility of life under the sun (negative)

8. 5:1-7: description of the proper worship of God — another alternative to life under the sun (positive)

9. 5:8-17: the futile quest for meaning in wealth (negative)

10. 5:18-20: man's quest satisfied by the enjoyment of life as God's gift to man (positive)

11. 6:1-12: the futile quest for meaning in life and earthly endeavor by themselves (negative)

12. 7:1-8: description of the sorrow of human existence and an assertion of the wisdom of viewing life as tragic (negative)

13. 7:9-14: the wisdom of accepting life's sorrows and adversity (positive)

14. 7:15-17: disillusionment with life (negative)

15. 7:18-19: the fear of God and the exercise of wisdom as the escape from disillusionment (positive)

16. 7:20-29: comment on the evil that men and women do apart from God (negative)

17. 8:1-9: description of how man is subject to earthly authorities and limitations (mixed: mainly neutral but concluding with a pessimistic comment on social hierarchy)

18. 8:10-13: assertion of the ultimate benefits of fearing God and a statement about the ultimate judgment of the wicked (positive)

19. 8:14-15: assertion of the ultimate meaninglessness of life under the sun (negative)

20. 8:16-17: a summary of the inability of purely human wisdom, limited by an earthly perspective, to perceive God's pattern in the universe (negative)

21. 9:1-6: description of the futility that stems from the inevitability of death (negative)

22. 9:7-10: a command to enjoy earthly life with zest (mixed, since the positive command to enjoy life is based on the view that life has no ultimate goal beyond life itself)

23. 9:11-12: description of the seeming fickleness of men's fortunes (negative)

24. 9:13–10:15: praise of wisdom (positive)

25. 10:16–11:8: a catalog of miscellaneous maxims and sayings (positive)

26. 11:9–12:8: a call for righteous and purposeful living in the time of youth, with the decay of old age serving as the background that adds urgency to the command (mixed, since

the specter of old age dominates the section, despite the
positive note of righteous living in one's youth)
27. 12:9-14: conclusion (positive)

Instead of attempting to explicate the entire book, I have chosen
to look at some representative negative passages, some significant
positive sections, and a few of the most poetic parts of the work.

The introduction to the entire work sets the keynote for most of
what follows. It identifies the narrator as a preacher (a man of
wisdom and spiritual insight) and a king (a man who has observed
life from the privileged end of the social spectrum and is qualified
to comment on life at its best). The brief second verse names the
concept of vanity five times:

> *Vanity of vanities, says the Preacher,*
> *vanity of vanities! All is vanity.*

The third verse completes the theme of futility by defining it as a
futility that occurs when man "toils under the sun," that is, when he
lives life on a purely earthly or naturalistic level.

If one puts the negative passages together, he finds that they constitute a rather comprehensive summary of the various world views
by which people have lived throughout the centuries. These sections,
usually based on the quest motif, picture the narrator as living for
such things as wisdom, pleasure, wealth, achievement that lives after
a man's death, and life itelf. The typical formulae used to introduce
the activity in these sections stress the quest idea: "I applied my
mind to seek and to search out by wisdom" (1:13); "I said to myself, 'Come now, I will make a test of pleasure' " (2:1); "I turned to
consider wisdom and madness and folly" (2:12); "I turned about
and gave my heart up to despair" (2:20); "I turned my mind to
know and to search out and to seek wisdom and the sum of things"
(7:25). The supernatural perspective is as conspicuously absent from
these passages as the phrase "under the sun" is conspicuously present.
Together these units comprise a vision of the futility of life bound
by earthly perspective.

Other negative passages simply describe the misery of human
existence apart from a supernatural basis. The poem on the meaningless cycle of life (1:4-11), for example, paints a vivid picture of the
endless cycle of natural and human life as events repeat themselves
without leading to a goal. The passage in 2:12-23 is a lament on
how death comes equally to the good and the evil, thereby robbing
life of any ultimate purpose. Another poetic passage, 7:1-8, is based
on the theme that it is best to view life as tragic; a wise person will

sorrow because such an attitude conforms to the truth about reality under the sun. There is also an antifeminist note (7:26-29), in which the narrator complains about the unreliability of women. Elsewhere the poet laments the fickleness that seems to prevail in the world (9:11-12). Social injustice is yet another cause for despair (4:1-2). These passages add up to a tremendous protest against life, in a manner very similar to modern naturalistic or nihilistic works of literature. Unlike most modern literature, however, Ecclesiastes does not offer this pessimistic assessment of earthly life as the whole truth about man's potential. It repeatedly contrasts the futility of life under the sun to a better alternative.

The first positive passage is an extended one that begins with Ecclesiastes 2:24, after the pessimistic note has been clearly sounded. The concluding verses of chapter 2 at once bring in a supernatural dimension that the negative passages lack. The speaker states that the enjoyment of life "is from the hand of God" (vs. 24). Enjoying life as a gift from God is far different from giving one's heart to life, as though this were the ultimately valuable thing in itself. The God-centered emphasis is also evident when the narrator asks regarding God, "For apart from him who can eat or who can have enjoyment?" (vs. 25). He also makes the far-reaching claim that "to the man who pleases him God gives wisdom and knowledge and joy" (vs. 26). This is a way of asserting that life's meaning does not exist independent of obedience to God, and it locates the source of meaning outside of the earthly sphere, in distinction from the negative passages of the work.

A supernatural alternative to life under the sun also dominates the section found in 3:10-15. Instead of the earlier pessimism, we find the optimistic conclusion that God "has made everything beautiful in its time" (vs. 11), with the last phrase tying this section to the "time for everything" poem just preceding. The next statement of the narrator is one of the key assertions in the entire work: "also he has put eternity into man's mind" (vs. 11). In other words, God has given man a supernatural faculty and an awareness of something above the sun. Verse 14 advances the thought still further by claiming that God has created reality in such a way that meaning cannot be found in the merely earthly sphere, with the result that people will be drawn to God: "I know that whatever God does endures for ever . . . ; God has made it so, in order that men should fear before him" (vs. 14). The meaning here is close to Augustine's aphorism that man's soul is restless until it rests in God. Life under the sun is futile for the very good reason that this fact will lead people to place their highest devotion in a greater rather than a lesser good.

Whenever we reach one of the positive sections of the work, we are likely to find two themes that are absent elsewhere. They are the idea that life can be enjoyed and the pervasive consciousness of God. By bringing in a supernatural basis for his views, the preacher is free to affirm the goodness of earthly existence, something he cannot do when he is limiting his focus to the purely natural. Chapter 5:18-20 is typical in this regard. The writer concludes here that it is "fitting to eat and drink and find enjoyment in all the toil with which one toils under the sun" (vs. 18). This affirmation of life is closely related to God: "Every man also to whom God has given wealth and possessions and power to enjoy them, and to accept his lot and find enjoyment in his toil — this is the gift of God" (vs. 19). Verse 20 takes us again to the very heart of Ecclesiastes: "For he will not much remember the days of his life because God keeps him occupied with joy in his heart." That is, the person who recognizes God as the center of life is free to enjoy life as a gift precisely because he has not given his heart to something less than God. The capacity to enjoy is here declared to come from putting first things first and to be God-given.

The positive thread of the book's argument reaches its climax at the end of the work. First there is an eloquent call for young people to live a righteous and purposeful and enjoyable life (11:9–12:1). This type of life is defined in terms of a supernatural orientation — in awareness "that for all these things God will bring you into judgment" (11:9) and in remembrance of "your Creator" (12:1). And then, with the whole weight of the preceding quest behind it, the preacher concludes with a magnificent summing up of his plea for a God-centered life: "The end of the matter; all has been heard. Fear God, and keep his commandments; for this is the whole duty of man. For God will bring every deed into judgment, with every secret thing, whether good or evil" (12:13-14). The emphasis on "the end" brings the quest motif to its final goal. The stress on obeying God is nothing less than a summary of Hebraic-Christian religion, just as the concluding mention of good and evil ties the book to the overriding biblical plot involving spiritual conflict. A note of finality is achieved with such phrases as "the end," "all has been heard," "this is the whole duty of man," and "every deed." Rarely has a conclusion achieved greater impact.

Before leaving this discussion of Ecclesiastes, we should look briefly at some of the great lyric poems embedded in the work. The lament on the meaningless cycle of life (1:4-11) is one such poem. The lyric has a repetitive form in which we see a single principle — cyclic meaninglessness — maintained under various guises. The imagery of the poem evokes a sense of elemental human experience, with references to the sun, the wind, stream, the sea, seeing, hearing. The poem describes man as living against the background of a timeless natural cycle, setting up a picture of earthbound man that is memorable in itself and which is a preamble to a similar emphasis all through the book of Ecclesiastes. Balance and antithesis underlie most of the verses in the poem. For example, "A generation goes" is balanced by the statement that "a generation comes" (1:4). The passing generations, in turn, are together contrasted to the earth, which "remains for ever" (vs. 4). Meaninglessness on the natural level (vss. 4-7) is balanced by meaninglessness on the human level (vss. 8-11). To sum up, the poem does a magnificent job of capturing a pervasive longing evident throughout the history of Western thought — the desire to transcend the transient and cyclic nature of earthly existence.

The poem based on the theme that there is a time for everything (3:1-8) is one of the world's most famous descriptive lyrics. The poem begins with a generalization announcing the theme: "For everything there is a season, and a time for every matter under heaven" (vs. 1). The rest of the poem makes the generalization concrete by listing particular examples of things for which there is an appropriate time. Strict parallelism underlies the passage, with each statement constructed on the scheme of "a time to . . . , and a time to. . . ." Antithesis is equally pervasive, with each statement naming a pair of opposites. This poem, like others in Ecclesiastes, evokes elemental human responses, since the experiences described are universal and basic in human experience. The overall tone of the poem is positive, based on the confidence that everything is good in its proper place. The poem implies an order and a purpose to life.

The description of old age and advancing death (12:1-8) is the most amazing poetic performance in the whole work. The poem belongs to the genre known as the character and is here a generalized and figurative description of old age in its physical manifestations. The portrait begins with a generalized description of old age as a time of "evil days" and a loss of the desire for living (vs. 1). The description of how "the sun and the light, and the moon, and the stars are darkened" (vs. 2) refers either to weak eyesight or to a loss of sensitivity to the ordinary flow of events in the external world. Similarly, the account of the clouds returning after the rain (vs. 2) suggests either tears from eyestrain or the inability of old people to rally back after a crisis, whether physical or emotional. Subsequent references are clearly physiological. The trembling of "the keepers of the house" (vs. 3) describes the shaking of the hands and arms, while the reference to "strong men" that "are bent" (vs. 3) depicts stooping shoulders. The loss of teeth is figuratively described in the statement that "the grinders cease because they are few" (vs. 3), and weak eyes are pictured in the figure of "the windows" that "are dimmed" (vs. 3). Weak hearing is evoked by "the doors on the street" that "are shut" (vs. 4). Three successive details illustrate, respectively, the loss of appetite, of sleep, and of ability to speak: "the sound of the grinding is low, and one rises up at the voice of a bird, and all the daughters of song are brought low" (vs. 4). Fear of high places and walking is pictured in the account of how "they are afraid also of what is high, and terrors are in the way" (vs. 5). The picture of "the almond tree" that "blossoms" (vs. 5) refers to the presence of white hair, while the account of how "the grasshopper drags itself along" (vs. 5) is probably a reference to the loss of sprightliness in walking. The physical portrait is summarized in conceptual fashion by the statement that "desire fails" (vs. 5). After the failure of physical powers, death itself is pictured, again through concrete symbols of cessation of activity and dissolution (vs. 6): "the silver cord is snapped," probably a picture of the silver cord from which a house lamp was suspended; "the golden bowl," an object of great value, "is broken"; "the pitcher is broken at the fountain," and "the wheel" is "broken at the cistern." As Moulton comments, "The poetic beauty of the passage is marvellous."[4]

---

[4] Moulton, *Modern Reader's Bible,* p. 1645.

The ruins of Tekoa, birthplace of the prophet Amos. His prophecy is an example of biblical satire.

Biblical
Satire

13

I

Satire is the exposure, through ridicule or rebuke, of human vice or folly. Satire by itself is not literary, since the exposure of vice or folly can occur in expository and persuasive writing as well as literary writing. Satire becomes literary when the controlling purpose of exposure is combined with a literary method (fiction, action, characters, etc.). The satirist's aim is positive (the reform of mankind), but his technique is mainly negative, since he is always busy attacking someone or something. Satire may appear in any literary genre (drama, lyric, narrative, etc.) and may be either a minor part of a work or the main point of an entire work. Although satire usually has one main object of attack, satiric works often make a number of jabs in various directions, a feature that can be called "satiric ripples." A satirist is dependent on the agreement of his readers. The satirist, moreover, may distort and oversimplify and exaggerate in order to make his satiric point.

Edward Rosenheim has defined satire as "an attack by means of a manifest fiction upon discernible historical particulars."[1] I would suggest two modifications to this definition, especially as applied to biblical literature. Instead of speaking of a "manifest fiction," it is preferable to define the matter more broadly as a "recognizable literary device." Secondly, although satire usually attacks historical people and situations, it is possible for a satirist to attack a general moral vice, such as greed, pride, or sensuality, without turning the attack on specific people. As the foregoing definition suggests, the basic ingredient of satire is an object of attack. Usually this means that the reader of satire must have some knowledge of contemporary economic, political, religious, and social conditions. Satire is thus a topical form of literature, but if it is to survive in later generations

---

[1] Edward W. Rosenheim, *Swift and the Satirist's Art* (Chicago: University of Chicago Press, 1963), p. 31.

it must rise above topicality and must include enough details within it to relieve the reader of the burden of reading extensive footnotes before he can understand the object of attack.

Satire falls into two categories on the basis of tone. One type, traditionally known as Horatian satire, is gentle, urbane, and smiling. It aims to correct folly or vice by gentle and sympathetic laughter. The other type, known as Juvenalian satire, is biting, bitter, and angry. It points with contempt and moral indignation at the corruptness and evil of men and institutions.

Satire always states or implies certain norms by which folly and vice are judged to be folly and vice. To criticize implies some standard by which the criticism is made. Usually satire will explicitly suggest solutions as well as attacking problems. In the disorderly scene of satire there is usually some hint of the ideal.

Satire also falls into two classes on the basis of form. The two categories can be called sophisticated and informal satire. Sophisticated satire is a polished work of literature. The style is accomplished and the work of a craftsman. The satire is embodied in a distinct literary form, such as narrative or fable. The satirist is more than a person denouncing vice in direct rebuke. He is also the maker of a literary object, through which the satire is indirectly conveyed. The sophisticated satirist is a private observer of society, not the spokesman for a cause or a social group. The tone of sophisticated satire is more likely to be light than bitter, though this is not uniformly true. Generally the impression that it leaves is that the satirist believes in ridiculing rather than loathing.

The writer of informal satire is much less of a literary craftsman, being preoccupied with content. He is much less likely to tell a well-designed story, for example, than to employ direct rebuke and invective. His form is often loose in structure, his style is direct and simple, and his work may approach something unliterary. This literary naivete corresponds to the moral and social naivete of the informal satirist, whose stance is that of a plain-spoken man of simple piety, humility, and poverty. He is much more likely to be the spokesman or representative for a whole cause than simply a private person observing society. His satire is motivated by a sense of urgent involvement. He is not the detached observer reflecting philosophically on what he sees around him. The result is what can be called religious or social protest. The object of attack is likely to be public evil or a corrupt social group, not the private evil of a single person. The tone of informal satire is rather consistently serious, moralistic, and sharply condemnatory, not light and humorous. To use Alvin Kernan's formula, the writer of informal satire is "the plain man with plain morals addressing plain people in plain terms on plain matters."[2]

II

The satiric discourses of Jesus illustrate both the sophisticated and informal kinds of satire. The sophisticated satire appears in Jesus' satiric parables. Here we find a carefully designed story, presumably fictional, in which the satiric attack is embodied. The satirist is not only the one who denounces but also the one who makes a literary object.

In the parable of the rich fool (Luke 12:13-21), for example, Jesus tells a fictional story about a farmer to make an attack on a generalized moral category — covetous greed for material things. Jesus begins His discourse by establishing the satiric norm: "Take heed, and beware of all covetousness; for a man's life does not consist in the abundance of his possessions" (vs. 15). There follows the story of a successful farmer who tore down his barns and built bigger ones in which to store his grain. The real object of attack is the attitude of soul that materialism engenders, namely, a trust in material things. This spiritual vice is dramatized in the statement of the farmer, "Soul, you have ample goods laid up for many years; take your ease, eat, drink, be merry" (vs. 19). God's judgment of the man is also dramatized: "Fool! This night your soul is required of you; and the things you have prepared, whose will they be?" (vs. 20). God's indictment exposes the folly of placing one's trust in something that is transient. Having completed the parable, Jesus contrasts physical and spiritual wealth, thereby making explicit the standard by which the farmer's error is judged to be error: "So is he who lays up treasure for himself, and is not rich toward God" (vs. 21).

The parable of the rich man and Lazarus (Luke 16:19-31) is occasional in nature. After Jesus had warned that people "cannot serve God and mammon" (vs. 13), the Pharisees, "who were lovers of money, heard all this, and they scoffed at him" (vs. 14). In reply, Jesus attacked their love of money in a satiric parable involving two characters. The characterization is polarized, with the rich man embodying the object of attack. The parable turns out to have a dual thrust, being an indictment of rich people who show no compassion toward the poor and of people who discount the sufficiency of what God has revealed in His Scripture. The attack on the Pharisee's lack of compassion is embodied in the sending of the rich man to a place

---

[2] *The Cankered Muse: Satire of the English Renaissance* (New Haven: Yale University Press, 1959), p. 43.

of punishment after he has died, while Lazarus goes to a place of bliss after death. In other words, the concept of justice is the satiric norm, as implied by Abraham's words, "Son, remember that you in your lifetime received your good things, and Lazarus in like manner evil things; but now he is comforted here, and you are in anguish" (vs. 25).

The parable of the Pharisee and tax collector (Luke 18:9-14) is another attack on a historical particular, this time the self-righteousness of the Pharisees. Jesus repeats the technique of using a story involving two characters, one a satiric norm and the other a villain. The Pharisee's "prayer," actually a rehearsing of his righteous acts for his own benefit, is a speech dramatizing unadulterated pride: "God, I thank thee that I am not like other men, extortioners, unjust, adulterers, or even like this tax collector. I fast twice a week, I give tithes of all that I get" (vss. 11-12). The tax collector, who recognizes his spiritual poverty and is humble in confessing his sins before God, serves as the ideal. Jesus comments that the tax collector "went down to his house justified rather than the other" (vs. 14), thereby focusing on the theological issue involved in the parable, the question of how a person can be justified in God's sight. Jesus concludes this carefully designed satiric story with a moral aphorism: "every one who exalts himself will be humbled, but he who humbles himself will be exalted" (vs. 14).

For an example of Christ's use of informal satire, the best known passage is Matthew 23, a discourse in which Jesus lashes out against the Pharisees. It is a discourse delivered by the founder of the Christian faith and carries with it an unusual sense of authority. The fact that the discourse is directed toward "the crowds and to his disciples" (vs. 1) confirms that satire ordinarily appeals to people who already share the satirist's convictions. The object of attack is the gap between the Pharisees' doctrine and practice, as Jesus makes clear at the outset: "The scribes and the Pharisees sit on Moses' seat; so practice and observe whatever they tell you, but not what they do; for they preach, but do not practice" (vss. 2-3). What follows is a very loosely structured series of attacks on the practices of the Pharisees. There is no carefully designed literary object, as in the parables. In verses 5-7 Jesus simply narrates or describes customary vices of the Pharisees, following His narrative with an explanation of the norm by which their actions are blameworthy (vss. 8-11). Beginning with verse 13, Jesus pronounces a series of woes against the Pharisees. The "woe formula" is a standard device in informal satire of the Bible and represents a relatively unliterary mode of satire. Jesus uses satiric exaggeration, as when He pictures the Pharisees "straining out a gnat and swallowing a camel" (Matt. 23:24).

He also uses vivid metaphor, claiming that the Pharisees "are like whitewashed tombs, which outwardly appear beautiful, but within they are full of dead men's bones and all uncleanness" (vs. 27). Elsewhere Christ uses direct personal attack: "You serpents, you brood of vipers, how are you to escape being sentenced to hell?" (vs. 33). Corresponding to this random sequence of satiric devices is the constantly shifting objects of attack, which include the Pharisees' religious ostentatiousness (vss. 5-7), unbiblical distinctions regarding oaths (vss. 16-19), neglect of the important moral issues (vss. 23-24), hypocrisy (throughout the discourse), and hostility to God's prophets (vss. 29-36). It has been noted that the informal satirist is not a detached observer of society but is deeply moved by the vice that he attacks. Jesus' moving lament over Jerusalem (vss. 37-39) concludes His satiric discourse and illustrates His sense of personal involvement in the issues that His satire has discussed.

To read the enigmatic book of Jonah as a satire will not account for every detail in it, but it will account for more than any other approach to the story.[3] The protagonist of the story embodies attitudes that the writer wishes to attack. Jonah himself is the main vehicle of satiric attack. The story of Jonah belongs to the sophisticated, literary type of satire. The satirist has completely incarnated his satire in his narrative, which is skillfully told. The satirist is not the plain-spoken man who thinly veils his indignation. He is instead completely submerged in the story and does not emerge as an identifiable persona.

The object of satiric attack is the kind of nationalistic zeal that made God the exclusive property of Israel and refused to accept the universality of God's grace. Jonah's basic problem is theological — he refuses to accept the fact of God's universal love. The story thus stands as a corrective to followers of God who view pagans only as objects of God's wrath and not also as sinners eligible for God's salvation.

The satirist uses narrative as his satiric device. The simple story,

---

[3] Considering the book of Jonah a satire implies nothing about the question of the historicity of the book. Satire is always to some extent historical by virtue of its attack on historical persons and situations. As for the historicity of the story of Jonah, Jesus' comparison of His own burial to the descent of Jonah into the whale (Matt. 12:40) has traditionally been regarded as evidence of the historicity of Jonah, since it is unlikely that Christ would compare His actual burial to a fictitious event.

clear in outline, has two main characters. Jonah is the embodiment of the attitudes being attacked. God functions in the story as the satiric norm who exposes what is wrong with Jonah's attitude. Since He is God, He is the absolute standard against which there can be no argument. The picture of God that emerges from this satire is one of the most positive and beautiful portraits in all of biblical literature. He is depicted as a God of both judgment and mercy, with the latter the dominant motif.

As is typical in satire, there is not so much a plot as an anti-plot to the story. Various things happen to Jonah, but there is no real progress. Jonah merely becomes hardened in his ill-tempered bigotry and nationalism. The scope of God's saving love serves as a foil to Jonah's hatred of everything non-Jewish, without initiating any kind of character development.

In terms of satiric tone, the satire is light rather than biting. Jonah is held up to scorn by being rendered ridiculous. He is a small man who thinks he can run away from God and a rancorous man who is so sadistic and irascible that he is laughable. He perpetrates no vast evil but is rather the outsider who pouts like a child when he fails to get his way.

The action of the story is initiated by God, whose command for Jonah to go to "Nineveh, that great city" (Jonah 1:2) is likely to lose its impact on a modern reader. Nineveh was a world capital (of the Assyrians), a center of pagan worship, a military threat to Israel, and the embodiment of everything that the Israelites detested. Since the message that God gives to Jonah is one of judgment, we might expect that Jonah would respond to the call with eagerness. We learn later that his act of running away from the commission is motivated by his awareness that God is "a gracious God and merciful, slow to anger, and abounding in steadfast love" (4:2). Jonah's attempt to flee "from the presence of the Lord" (1:3) makes him the memorable and archetypal example of man trying to run away from God. The fact that he is a prophet makes his rebellion doubly satiric, since he should have been eager to serve God in both a private role and a prophetic role. His failure to live up to the obligations of his position as a prophet results in ecclesiastical satire in much the same way that Chaucer's irreligious clerics do.

The second paragraph of the story (1:4-6) captures the elemental conflict of man against his environment. The image of the men toiling to escape drowning evokes instinctive feelings of dread. The satiric denigration of Jonah continues when he is pictured as escaping to "the inner part of the ship" and sleeping while the sailors toil to save the ship (vss. 5-6).

The second half of the opening chapter relies heavily on dialogue, thus providing variety and balance to the first half, where narrative summary prevails. This mingling of narrative and dialogue recurs throughout the story. During the course of the dialogue, the sailors discover that Jonah's God is "the Lord, the God of heaven, who made the sea and the dry land" (1:9). There is satire in the narrator's comment that "the men knew that he was fleeing from the presence of the Lord, because he had told them" (vs. 10); this conveys the impression that Jonah is so deficient as a prophet that the only thing others know about him is that he is trying to run away from his God.

The opening chapter of exposition concludes with the casting of Jonah into the sea and a consequent calm. The chapter is a tremendous opening scene. It is like a sudden flurry of intense action, followed by an equally sudden calm. The chapter is filled with action and the sounds of men engaged in a struggle against the sea.

Chapter 2 is the part of the story that is somewhat extraneous to the satiric intention of the story. Instead of attacking Jonah, as the rest of the story does, this chapter implicitly idealizes him by giving him a moving prayer and showing him in a repentant frame of mind. God's deliverance likewise places a kind of sanction on him. The lyric interlude does contribute to the satire, however. By making Jonah such an obvious and miraculous recipient of God's mercy and salvation, the episode serves to render inexcusable and repulsive his later rejection of God's salvation when it is extended to others. Of all people, Jonah should have rejoiced at God's deliverance of Nineveh. The temporary nature of Jonah's repentance and godliness is also a sign that he is a crisis believer who repudiates God until it becomes personally feasible to submit to God. Jonah represents the kind of religious person for whom obedience to God is not a way of life but rather an escape valve when difficulty arises.

The main theme of the beautiful poetic prayer voiced by Jonah from the fish is God's deliverance from watery death. Lyric, instead of narrative, is used to describe Jonah's experience in the great fish. This is a masterful stroke because it takes us into the inner consciousness of the protagonist during his crisis. The archetypal pattern underlying the chapter is important. It is a well-known version of the death-rebirth archetype. Images of descent and suffocation vividly describe the death-like experience, and the archetypal image of ascent from the depths is used to depict the rebirth phase of the action. Even the pattern of three days in the subterranean depths is an archetype, as Jesus recognized (Matt. 12:39-40).

Chapter 4 of the book of Jonah contains the main thrust of the satire. It dramatizes Jonah's antagonistic response to God's mercy. Jonah's bigotry, nationalism, sadism, and distorted view of God are weighed in the balance of God's universal mercy and are found to be wanting. The satire remains implicit; the narrator does not intrude into the story to make his point explicit but allows the story to reveal its satiric meaning. Jonah's cantankerous personality comes out when, after God removes the plant that had shaded Jonah, Jonah is consumed with rage and concludes that "it is better for me to die than to live" (vs. 8). Not only is his reaction ridiculous in its intensity — it is also a standard by which his unconcern for the people of Nineveh is shown to be illogical. As God says to Jonah, if Jonah can have such concern for a plant, God should naturally have concern for a city of "more than a hundred and twenty thousand persons . . . , and also much cattle" (vs. 11). The story concludes on the note of God's loving compassion for all His creatures, thus reinforcing the positive norm of the satire at its close.

It is in its conclusion that the book of Jonah shows itself to be most clearly a satire. The portrait of Jonah in chapters 1-3, while mainly unsympathetic, has not been wholly negative. The conclusion of the story could turn Jonah into a heroic protagonist and an exemplary character by showing his repentance from earlier vices. But instead of doing this, the conclusion leaves the protagonist in the most unfavorable light of all. He is a pouting infant and a sadistic bigot, all in one. There is no attempt to idealize him, but rather to denigrate him. The conclusion is truncated if the story is viewed as heroic narrative, since the protagonist is not shown to be exemplary. The last chapter is the expected and appropriate conclusion if the story is regarded as a satire.

If the aim of the satirist is to move the reader to an acceptance of the truth, no satirist has succeeded more splendidly than the writer of Jonah. The satirist not only attacks bigotry, sadism, and poor theology, but he also evokes a positive response to his beautiful presentation of the God whose mercy and concern extend to all nations. Most satirists make vice appear ugly but are powerless to make the good appear beautiful. A lesser satirist than the one who penned Jonah would have obscured the positive aspect of the story by spilling his own rancor against Jonah's attitude into the story. The writer of Jonah maintains an objective, urbane tone and is at pains to give as much attention to the positive norm as to the abuses he is attacking.

IV

If Jonah is the obvious example of sophisticated literary satire, the book of Amos fulfills all of the expectations of the informal tradition.

Its satirist is not the completely submerged narrator but rather the plain-spoken, naive satirist. He is a man of simple piety, humility, and social obscurity (see Amos 1:1 and 7:12-15). He is not even a professional prophet. He is a farmer, without social prominence and sophistication. The fact that he is a shepherd evokes the innocent associations of the pastoral figure. Amos, like most informal satirists, is a man of religious indignation and prophetic zeal. In tone, the satire of Amos, like that of the typical plain-spoken satirist, is serious, moralistic, and practical. His satire is fired by a spirit of religious outrage, and it uses invective, abuse, and rebuke to convey this tone.

If we turn to the object of attack, it is apparent that the concern of Amos is not with human folly but with religious, social, and political vice. Amos champions the cause of a whole group (the socially oppressed) and of God. He is especially concerned with the avarice, social injustice, luxury, and moral callousness of those who professed to be models of righteousness. His focus is on public evils, in contrast to Jonah, which satirizes the private bigotry and sadism of a single person. Political and ecclesiastical satire is recurrent in Amos.

In terms of satiric form, Amos is also typical of its kind. Instead of a unified, carefully designed story such as we find in the book of Jonah and in Jesus' parables, we find in Amos an encyclopedic accumulation of fragments, loosely structured and somewhat unliterary in development. This absence of form gives the satirist a literary naivete corresponding to his social lack of sophistication. The book of Amos contains elements of the "saying," narrative, predictive prophecy, vision, dialogue, dramatic monologue, lyric, and pronouncement of woe. Its plot is similar to what Alvin Kernan describes as the usual kind of satiric plot: "It is clear that satire never offers that direct, linear progression which is ordinarily taken as plot. Instead, we get collections of loosely related scenes and busyness which curls back on itself. . . . Disjunctiveness and the absence of change" are the chief ingredients of the satiric plot.[4] Like the medieval English poem *Piers Plowman,* the book of Amos displays evidence of literary imagination not in its structure, which is random, but in the use of such devices as imagery, metaphor, simile, epithet, parallelism, rhetorical questions, paradox, sarcasm, climax, and conflict. The artistry of the work is not in its large effects but in the individual fragments. A few passages will illustrate the kind of literary quality that the book of Amos possesses.

Chapter 4 begins with direct and vicious attack on the wealthy women of Israel and uses animal imagery to convey vituperation: "Hear this word, you cows of Bashan, who are in the mountain of

---

[4] *The Plot of Satire* (New Haven: Yale University Press, 1965), p. 100.

Samaria" (vs. 1). The women are rebuked for their oppression of the poor and their self-indulgence, the typical satiric theme of Amos: "who oppress the poor, who crush the needy, who say to their husbands, 'Bring, that we may drink!'" (vs. 1). Verse 2 combines a description of the satiric norm (God's holiness and sense of justice) with a prediction of coming judgment, another recurrent motif: "The Lord God has sworn by his holiness that, behold, the days are coming upon you, when they shall take you away with hooks, even the last of you with fishhooks." Amos is also capable of using paradox for shocking and sarcastic effect, as when he begins a sentence with a priestly exhortation to worship God and concludes it with an attack on the hypocrisy involved in the Israelites' worship: "Come to Bethel, and transgress; to Gilgal, and multiply transgression" (vs. 4). Amos 4:6-11 is a narrative section in which God describes His futile attempts to bring Israel to repentance through adverse circumstances. The passage is a catalog of disasters and is a parody of many of the Psalms, which also treat history as the unfolding of God's acts but make it a history of prosperity, whereas this catalog makes history the unfolding of God's judgments upon Israel. Amos 4:13 is one of several passages in the book which simply attribute exalted epithets to God as a means of evoking an impression of the sovereign power of the God who is calling His people to judgment:

> *For lo, he who forms the mountains, and creates the wind,*
> *and declares to man what is his thought;*
> *who makes the morning darkness,*
> *and treads on the heights of the earth —*
> *the Lord, the God of hosts, is his name!*

As this survey of Chapter 4 has suggested, the structure of Amos is a constantly shifting sequence of topics and techniques. It is this way from the beginning of the book to the end, although there is a discernible five-part structure to the work.[5] A piecemeal explication of the book is beyond the scope of this study, but such an explication would reveal the richness of the writer's literary imagination in the mastery of small literary units and techniques, and a corresponding lack of concern for large structural unity.

---

[5] The overall movement of the book of Amos is as follows: (1) introduction to the book (1:1-2); (2) oracles against the nations (1:3-ch. 2); (3) denunciation of Israel (3-6); (4) the five visions (7-9:10); (5) the oracle of salvation (9:11-15).

The Sea of Galilee seen from the traditional Mount of Beatitudes, where the Sermon on the Mount may have been given.

The Gospel As a
Literary Form

14

I

The writers of the New Testament, and especially of the gospels, display an overpowering conviction that the incarnation of Jesus represented a unique and unprecedented event. The uniqueness of God's disclosure in Christ is summarized by the writer of Hebrews when he states, "In many and various ways God spoke of old to our fathers by the prophets; but in these last days he has spoken to us by a Son, whom he appointed the heir of all things, through whom also he created the world" (Heb. 1:1-2). The uniqueness of their subject matter led the New Testament writers to create unique forms that can be categorized as gospel, acts, epistle, and apocalypse.[1]

The uniqueness of the form known as the gospel ("good news") is obvious at once when we reflect that the form has no real parallel outside of the New Testament writings. Furthermore, none of the usual literary categories does justice to the gospels, although of course they have affinities to a number of conventional forms.

The relationship between heroic narrative and gospel illustrates the difficulty of identifying this New Testament genre. Like heroic narrative, the gospel centers in the life and exploits of the heroic protagonist. The gospel, however, is structured differently from the Old Testament heroic narratives, which are more unified as stories. The story of Abraham, for example, is unified at every point by such overriding plot motifs as the quest and the progressive revelation of the covenant. Similarly, the stories of Joseph, Gideon, Samson, Ruth, and Esther are structured around a single chain of related events. Equally important is the fact that in these stories approximately the same cast of characters is present from the beginning of the story to the end. Even when characters appear only temporarily, they usually make some contribution to a causally related chain of events that

---

[1] The definitive study of the uniqueness of the New Testament forms is Amos Wilder's book *Early Christian Rhetoric: The Language of the Gospel* (Cambridge: Harvard University Press, 1971).

constitutes the plot. In a word, Old Testament heroic narratives are single plots. By contrast, the gospels are collections of stories. They are, accordingly, more fragmented in structure than the heroic narratives. The synoptic gospels, in particular, are very episodic. A given fragment in the gospels can usually be rearranged or omitted without affecting the overall movement of the narrative. Many of the characters who encounter Christ in the gospels appear only once and then drop out of the story. Compared to the unified Old Testament literary narratives (I omit what I consider to be historical chronicles), the gospels are kaleidoscopic in their ever-changing, episodic account of the life of Christ.

It is true that there is another category of Old Testament narratives that are less unified than the stories I have just described. Many of these stories, such as the stories of Moses, David and other kings, Samuel, Elijah, and Elisha, have the episodic and fragmented structure I have claimed for the gospels. A look at these more diffuse narratives will show, however, that they are usually intertwined with other historical material. This material suggests that the writer's motive was not the biography of an individual but the history of a nation or an era. In these instances the story of the individual is not self-contained, as in heroic narrative, but is part of the larger historical survey. By contrast, the gospels keep the focus on Jesus, whose story is continuous instead of being interrupted by extraneous historical material. This sustained devotion by the gospel writers to a single person rather than a historical period makes the gospels different in narrative structure from the diffuse biographies of the Old Testament. The gospels, in short, are both more episodic than Old Testament heroic narrative and more concentrated than the biographies embedded in historical surveys.

The characterization of the protagonist also makes the gospels a unique genre. While the protagonist of heroic narrative is merely exemplary, the protagonist of the gospels, Jesus, calls people to belief in Himself as their divine Savior. Other literary heroes do not forgive sins or devote a major part of their lives to performing miracles. Equally distinctive is the emphasis on the teachings of the protagonist. Other literary heroes may be given semidivine status, but this status is either understood to be a literary fiction or is distanced by the placing of the protagonist in a mythic world outside of ordinary history. By contrast, the protagonist of the gospels is presented as being both fully human and fully divine, and He is situated in a historical setting. Like most other parts of biblical literature, the gospels record historical events. These events were written down and circulated at a time when contemporaries of Jesus and the writers would have exposed the gospels as fraudulent if they had been anything other than historical. The inadequacy of the term "heroic narrative" to describe the gospels is also evident when we consider the many ways in which Jesus was an anti-hero — a figure who reversed conventional conceptions of the hero. Instead of ruling as a political king, Jesus was the suffering servant, and instead of triumphing over His enemies by military force, He was executed as a criminal.

The protagonist of the gospels is unique in the claims He makes regarding Himself. The conventional literary hero is an idealized human held up as a model to be admired and emulated. The gospel writers do not allow the reader the option of concluding that the protagonist is merely an idealized human being. As presented in the gospels, Jesus made claims about Himself that make Him either fraudulent or divine, either a lunatic or God. A merely human hero who claims to forgive sins or who calls people to believe in him as Savior is not an admirable person. As C. S. Lewis has commented, "Either this man was, and is, the Son of God: or else a madman or something worse.... Let us not come with any patronising nonsense about His being a great human teacher. He has not left that open to us."[2] With the gospels, in short, we reach the climax of a tendency found elsewhere in biblical literature — the unavoidability of responsive choice to the God of the Bible.

The gospel differs not only from heroic narrative but from other conventional categories as well. The gospels lack the detailed reconstruction of the subject's life that is customary in biography, although Old Testament biography furnishes a partial model. The account of the life of Jesus cannot be considered a tragedy because His suffering and death accomplished the salvation of the world and ended in resurrection. The gospels also lack a systematic codification of thought that might merit the title of theological treatise, while the insistent narrative thread makes them something different from an essay.

What, then, are the essential features of the gospel as a literary kind? The gospels are collections of stories, far more packed with action than is customary in narrative. The overriding purpose of the gospel stories is to explain and praise the person and work of Jesus, who is always the moving force behind the writers' presentation. The impulse to get the facts of Jesus' life and meaning before the reader is combined with the impulse to celebrate what is recorded. The person and work of Jesus are presented through several familiar narrative devices — through His actions, through His words, and through the responses of other people to Him.

The gospels are encyclopedic forms in the sense that they are

---

[2] *Mere Christianity* (New York: The Macmillan Company, 1958), p. 41.

compilations of a number of individual segments that existed independently, in either written or oral form, before being brought together in a single written book. The gospels are encyclopedic also by virtue of the variety of different literary forms that they include. One form is the brief narrative, which itself can be separated into several categories. We should picture the brief narratives of the gospels as existing on a continuum that ranges from simple narrative on the one end to embellished narrative on the other. By "simple narrative" I mean a story that gives only the bare outline of an event, while "embellished narrative" refers to a story that fills out the event in relative detail. Another recurrent form in the gospels is dialogue. Also important are the utterances of Jesus, which range on a spectrum similar to the narratives. At one end of the spectrum is the brief saying of Jesus, and at the other end is the extended discourse (such as we find in the Sermon on the Mount and some of the discourses in John's gospel). Yet another form is the parable of Jesus, prominent in the synoptic gospels. The somewhat random combination of these varied ingredients probably reflects the fact that the content of the gospels existed as separate units before being brought together in a single work. The diversity of forms also sets the gospels apart from Old Testament narratives, which share the emphasis on dialogue and summarized narrative but generally lack the interspersed discourses, parables, and proclamations.

Miracle stories are so prominent in the gospels that the reader must come to grips with their interpretation. Although biblical literature is consistently supernatural in its orientation, the actual miracles recorded in the Bible tend to cluster in four eras — the Exodus, the Babylonian captivity of Judah, the earthly life of Jesus, and the period of the early New Testament church. My concern is with reading the miracle stories in a way that preserves their literary integrity. To read any work of literature with understanding, the reader must allow the storyteller to be the authority of his story. To attempt a naturalistic explanation of miracles in biblical literature is an indefensible type of literary criticism. Literary critics do not find it necessary to explain away the supernatural events in Homer or Virgil or Spenser. In the same way, the miracle stories of the Bible can be read as literature only by accepting what the narrator tells us.

II

To illustrate the characteristic features of the gospel as a literary form I have selected for comment the gospel of John. A literary approach to the gospel will concern itself, among other things, with the narrative unity and design of the work. The impact of any long narrative depends in part on the overriding structure that the writer is able to impose on his details. The gospel of John is built on several unifying principles that span the work as a whole.

The general outline of the book follows the chronology of the protagonist's career. The gospel thus begins with an account of Jesus' divine origin. It then proceeds through the preparatory ministry of John the Baptist, the early events of Jesus' public ministry, some main incidents of His career as an itinerant religious teacher, and finally, His trial, death, and resurrection. This is clearly a story with a beginning, middle, and end. In fact, the self-conscious shaping by Jesus of His own life has all the shapeliness of a carefully constructed story. At every stage it is evident that Jesus was controlling His life according to a plan. The climax toward which His entire life was slanted was His death and resurrection. This movement toward a climax can be traced through the successive references to the "hour" of Jesus, an allusion to the time of His death and resurrection. Early in the book there are references to the fact that Jesus' hour had not yet come (2:4; 7:30; 8:20). There are also statements that "the hour is coming" (4:21 and 5:28). Late in the narrative there are reminders that Christ's hour has definitely arrived (12:23; 13:1; 17:1). As the final confrontation with the Jews approaches, Jesus begins to speak more openly of His coming death, and in His last public discourse He defines His whole purpose on earth as being His death as the Savior of the world (12:20-36).

Another element of narrative structure is the progressive intensification of plot conflict and a corresponding movement toward the climax of the story. The writer begins his story with events that evoked no conflict (the miracle at Cana, the discourses with Nicodemus and the Samaritan woman, the healing of the official's son), and then moves to acts of Jesus that elicited extreme conflict (the healing on the Sabbath, the argument over Christ's claims to be the bread of life, the controversy at the Feast of Tabernacles, and so forth). Finally there is the overt conspiracy to kill Jesus and at last the crucifixion itself. The only exception to this pattern of increasing hostility is the cleansing of the temple (2:13-16), a scene of violent conflict that appears early and serves the narrative function of foreshadowing the eventual struggle between Jesus and the Jews and the ultimate victory of Jesus in this struggle. It is important to note, too, that in the cleansing of the temple Jesus was the one who initiated the conflict, whereas later episodes of the struggle show the antagonism of the Jews against Jesus.

The gospel of John is structured on the principle of expansion followed by constriction. The action begins with an account of Jesus' relations with a small circle of believers, including John the Baptist, the disciples whom He called to follow Him, and His family and friends, seen with Jesus at the wedding of an acquaintance in Cana. From this intimate circle of friends, Jesus' public ministry quickly expands throughout Palestine and encompasses huge crowds of people, as Jesus becomes one of the most talked about public figures of His time. As the conspiracy to kill Jesus grows, His contacts again become constricted. During the last week of His life, He spends His time with the disciples, and His post-resurrection appearances likewise involve the small circle of inner friends.

Yet another aspect of the structural unity of the gospel of John is the overriding conflict between belief and unbelief. Keeping Jesus always in the center of the focus, the writer presents a series of responses by people who come into contact with the protagonist. At root, these responses show either belief or unbelief in the saving work of Christ. In John's gospel the unbelief is concentrated in "the Jews," that is, the religious leaders. Many individual episodes are specifically tied to this ongoing struggle, which is based on the clash of Jesus with His environment. In the words of G. Wilson Knight, the gospel pictures "Jesus silhouetted against a world of formalized religion, hypocrisy, envy, evil and suffering."[3] The writer's purpose in presenting this conflict between belief and unbelief is to instill belief in the reader, as he makes clear at the end of the book: "Now Jesus did many other signs in the presence of the disciples, which are not written in this book; but these are written that you may believe that Jesus is the Christ, the Son of God, and that believing you may have life in his name" (20:30-31).

The writer's narrative skill is seen not only in his management of large narrative patterns but also in his construction of smaller units. One of these elements of design consists of the combining of an event involving Jesus with a discourse that interprets the meaning of the event. Typical examples include Jesus' request for a drink from the Samaritan woman followed by His statements about the water of life (ch. 4), the healing on the sabbath linked to Christ's words about His divine authority (ch. 5), the feeding of the five thousand related to the discourse on the bread of life (ch. 6), and the raising of Lazarus accompanied by Jesus' remarks about His being the resurrection and the life (ch. 11). An elaboration of this narrative technique is the linking of a single discourse to two events. For example, the discourse on Christ as the light of the world (ch. 8) is flanked by a reference to attendance at the Feast of Tabernacles, where the burning of huge torches was part of the ritual

---

[3] *The Christian Renaissance* (New York: W. W. Norton and Company, 1962), p. 169.

(ch. 7), and the giving of sight to the blind man (ch. 9). The same pattern occurs with the discourse on the bread of heaven, which is placed in the context of both the Passover Feast and the feeding of the five thousand (ch. 6). Yet another variation of the pattern is the relation of a single event to two discourses. For example, the healing of the blind man (ch. 9) illustrates Jesus' preceding discourse about the light of the world (ch. 8), while the expulsion of the healed man from the synagogue leads immediately into Jesus' discourse about the good shepherd and bad shepherds (ch. 10). The author's sensitivity to symbolism is obvious in all this, since the events that he describes are external symbols or illustrations of the theological truths that Christ proclaims in His discourses.

A similar type of narrative pattern that underlies a number of individual episodes is the motif of the misunderstood statement. These dramas in miniature unfold in three stages: Jesus makes a pronouncement, a bystander expresses a misunderstanding of the utterance, and Jesus proceeds to explain the meaning of His original statement. This narrative pattern occurs no fewer than nine times in the book.[4] Usually the misunderstanding arises when Jesus' statement calls for a figurative or symbolic interpretation and is given a literal meaning by the bystander, a fact whose significance for biblical exegesis should not be overlooked.

The writer of the fourth gospel makes much use of number pattern, in a manner similar to that which pervades the book of Revelation. There is repeated use of sets of three. The narrator, for example, records three Passovers and three other feasts that Jesus attended. Early in the book John the Baptist three times states his witness to Christ's messiahship. Late in the narrative Jesus is three times condemned. He also speaks three times from the cross and makes three appearances after His resurrection. There are three denials by Peter and three stages in Christ's restoration of Peter.

There is a similar use of the number seven. The writer structures the central part of his narrative around seven great miracles or "signs" that Jesus performed. The list includes the turning of the water into wine (2:1-11), the healing of the official's son (4:46-54), the cure of the paralytic (5:1-18), the feeding of the five thousand (6:5-13), walking on the water (6:16-21), the healing of the blind man (9:1-7), and the raising of Lazarus (11:1-44). Equally important is the pattern of seven statements by Jesus beginning with the formula "I am" and followed by a metaphoric description of Jesus' person and work: the bread of life (6:35), the light of the world

---

[4] The passages are as follows: 3:3-8; 4:10-15; 4:31-38; 6:47-58; 7:33-36; 8:21-30; 8:31-47; 8:56-58; 11:11-15. The pattern appears with slight modification in 2:17-22.

(8:12), the door of the sheep (10:7), the good shepherd (10:11), the resurrection and the life (11:25), the way, and the truth, and the life (14:6), and the true vine (15:1). There is also a sevenfold witness to Christ: the witness of the Father (5:37; 8:18); the witness of the Son (8:14; 18:37); the witness of Christ's works (10:25; 5:36); the witness of Scripture (5:39-46); the witness of the forerunner, John the Baptist (1:7; 5:35); the witness of the disciples (15:27; 19:35); and the witness of the Spirit (15:26; 16:14).

A literary approach to the gospels is concerned not only with elements of narrative pattern and design but also with the sequential unfolding of the story. The linear structure of a story is not of primary concern to a theologian, whose study may even depend on his rearrangement of the material according to his own theological framework. By contrast, the progress of the book from beginning to end, the sequential order of the material, is of prime importance if we look at the work as a story. For this reason the following survey of the gospel of John will remain closely tied to the linear development of the story.

I have already explained (in chapter 9) the lyric prologue to the gospel of John (1:1-18) as an example of the conventional form known as the encomium. More needs to be said, however, about its place in the overall design of the gospel. The prologue is the reader's introduction to the protagonist of the Gospel story. In terms of character, He is declared to be the incarnate God — both divine and human, both heavenly and earthly. In terms of His meaning, Christ is said to be the revelation of God to man and the bringer of spiritual life.

The prologue also introduces some leading literary techniques that will be characteristic of the style of the gospel. Already we see the reliance on symbol and metaphor as the form through which the nature of God's unprecedented disclosure in Christ is conveyed. Thus Christ is presented as "the Word" and as "the light" that "shines in the darkness" and "enlightens every man." Also evident is the inclination toward antithesis and plot conflict, seen in the contrasting pairs of light and darkness, being in the world and yet rejected by the world, coming to His own home and not being received there.

The remainder of the first chapter is devoted to a few brief narratives that introduce us to the protagonist by showing His impact on other people. One of these people is John the Baptist, who regards his successful ministry as only the prelude to the even greater ministry of the coming Messiah (1:19-34). These early references to Christ's fulfillment of both Old Testament prophecies and the preparatory ministry of John the Baptist are similar in function to the narrative device of the delayed entrance of the hero, whose initial appearance comes with greater impact because of what has preceded. The unique status of the divine hero of the story is also dramatized in the short narrative of the baptism of Jesus, which was accompanied by the supernatural sign of the descent of the Spirit in the form of a dove (vss. 29-34).

The unelaborated stories that depict Christ's call of several of His disciples (1:35-51) characterize the hero indirectly by showing His power to elicit the loyalty of others. These brief stories give us a vivid glimpse of the unique and mysterious attraction that Jesus held over many persons who met Him during His lifetime. The stories become, in fact, a narrative way of praising the desirability and worthiness of Christ. Dialogue pervades these brief stories, the appropriate form for capturing the element of encounter that Jesus brought into the lives of the persons around Him.

Having indirectly dramatized the unique identity of the protagonist, the writer moves to a more direct presentation of Him by narrating the first of Christ's seven great miracles. It is the well-known story of the turning of water into wine at a wedding in Cana (2:1-11). In terms of narrative technique, the storyteller combines summarized narrative and dialogue. The author treats the event as an initiation by emphasizing that it was "the first of his signs" (vs. 11). The precise term "sign" should not escape our attention. It is John's way of describing the significance inherent in Christ's miracles, which were specific illustrations or symbols that embodied great spiritual principles. This fusion of event and symbolic meaning is, in fact, one of the most distinctive features of the narrative style of John's Gospel.

What meaning, then, did the first great sign embody? John himself makes one meaning explicit when he states that Christ's miracle "manifested his glory" in such a way that "his disciples believed in him" (vs. 11). Another meaning is also implicit in this parabolic miracle of Jesus. The six stone jars contained water that was used for the ceremonial rituals that would have accompanied a Jewish wedding. By turning this water into wine Jesus was announcing, through a symbolic act, that He had come to fulfill and supercede the ceremonial laws of the Old Testament religion. In the background there is also the biblical motif of the messianic banquet, in which the Kingdom of God is compared to a feast. The large quantity of the water changed to wine is symbolic of the abundance of the messianic banquet, a fact that the narrator himself makes explicit by emphasizing that each of the jars held "twenty or thirty gallons" (vs. 6).

Up to this point in the narrative, Jesus has been shown in His relations to a small circle of friends and relatives. With the episode of the cleansing of the temple (2:13-25), the scope of the action is broadened, as Jesus enters the public spotlight. The story also introduces into the gospel the note of intense conflict, which is vividly and visually presented. In terms of the characterization of the protagonist, this event brings out for the first time in the narrative the judgmental side of his nature. The event shows his authority as He challenges the religious establishment of His day on the basis of His own claims to power. It also shows the revolutionary nature of His ministry, as He singlehandedly uses physical force to drive the moneychangers out of the temple. Because of the unique identity of Jesus, it is best to interpret the act of cleansing the temple not as a private campaign but as a messianic gesture in which God Himself enters His temple with divine authority to cleanse it. Yet another narrative feature that is introduced into the gospel with this event is the pattern of a figurative statement made by Jesus and misinterpreted by those who hear it (2:18-22).

Jesus' discourse with Nicodemus about the new birth (3:1-15) is typical of the self-contained nature of the narrative pieces that were compiled by the writers of the Gospels. In such narratives a character enters the life of Jesus, encounters the claims of Christ, and then drops out of the story. In most of these episodes dialogue is the means of encounter, as it is in this instance. Yet another feature that many of these stories share is their portrayal of Christ in the role of a teacher.

The dialogue with Nicodemus dramatizes one of the misunderstood utterances of Jesus that recur throughout John's Gospel. Jesus' statement that "unless one is born anew, he cannot see the kingdom of God" (3:3) is misunderstood by Nicodemus when he interprets the statement literally and asks, "How can a man be born when he is old? Can he enter a second time into his mother's womb and be born?" (3:4). Jesus then replies by interpreting His original statement in a spiritual manner. His reply about being spiritually born through the work of the Holy Spirit contains the Gospel in miniature and concludes, as we would expect in John's gospel, by stressing the centrality of belief: ". . . that whoever believes in him may have eternal life" (3:15). As we read such a narrative, which illuminates the Gospel so clearly, we should keep in mind that the stories and sayings of Jesus that were preserved in the gospels were originally the content of the disciples' early proclamation about Jesus. No doubt the stories about Jesus that were used most in the preaching of the disciples were those that could most easily be used to teach the basic outlines of the Christian faith.

The writers who compiled the stories and put them into the collections known as the gospels molded their material according to their purposes as a writer. They kept their history about Jesus in a clearly discernible interpretive framework. This is well illustrated when the narrative account of Christ's discussion with Nicodemus is followed by the narrator's commentary that elaborates the statements made by Jesus (3:16-21). These verses, beginning with the famous Gospel statement that "God so loved the world that he gave his only Son," are not only a statement of the theological truth of the Gospel but take on the nature of personal testimony by the writer. John's statement in these verses relates the preceding episode to the over-riding plot conflict of his gospel as he several times speaks of the conflict between believing and not believing and, on the symbolic level, between light and darkness.

Jesus' conversation with the Samaritan woman (4:1-30) is a master-piece of narrative art. The writer begins with a brief exposition in which he explains Christ's presence at the well and describes the physical setting of the encounter (vss. 3-6). Dialogue again carries the burden of the meeting. Jesus initiates the action with a request for a drink. As elsewhere, Jesus' use of a physical phenomenon (water) as a symbol for spiritual truth evokes bewilderment and misunderstanding, as conveyed by the woman's comment, "Sir, you have nothing to draw with, and the well is deep; where do you get that living water?" (vs. 11).

When the woman continues to misunderstand Jesus' statement (vs. 15), Christ uses his omniscience about the woman's marital history (vss. 16-18) to lead her to a deeper level of insight. Psycho-logical realism is evident as the woman tries to shift the topic from the issue of her own adultery to an impersonal theological question about the proper mode of worship (vss. 19-20). Refusing to allow the woman to escape his claims as Savior, Jesus replies to the woman's question about worship by revealing Himself to her as the Messiah who has come to establish God's spiritual kingdom (vss. 21-26). The climax of the encounter is the belief of the woman (vss. 28-30), a belief that radiates outward from the woman to many Samaritans (as described in the postscript in verses 39 to 42). The astonishment of the disciples when they arrive on the scene (vs. 27) heightens the drama of the situation.

Several things account for the greatness of this embellished gospel narrative. One is the masterful use of realistic dialogue to capture the drama of Christ's encounter with an outcast woman. Pervading the story is the momentousness that always attaches to the spiritual quest of the individual soul to attain belief in Jesus. The story has an overpowering sense of onward pressure, with one detail leading in progressive fashion to a further development and then another. The narrative shapeliness of the story is evident in its structuring on the principle of a beginning (Jesus' apparently casual request for a drink), a middle (the progressive revelation of Christ's messianic status as the Savior), and an end (the woman's belief and testimony). In terms of the narrative spectrum, this is one of the longer stories, told with a leisurely pace and including realistic details.

With the healing of the official's son (4:46-54), the narrative returns to a miracle story. It shows Christ's supernatural power, His compassion for the physical needs of people, and the way in which those who realized His divine power were brought to belief. The story is an example of simple narrative, existing for the sole purpose of informing the reader what Jesus did. We might say that the simple narrative answers the basic narrative question, "What happened?" By comparison, embellished narrative answers as well a second question, equally recurrent in storytelling, namely, "How did it happen?"

The healing of the paralytic man at Bethesda on the sabbath (ch. 5) is another story of miraculous healing, but its differences from the preceding story of the official's son show the variety of adventure that the writer is at pains to give his narrative. Instead of brief narrative, we get an elaborated story. Whereas the healing of the official's son led to belief, this miracle ends in conflict with the Pharisees over the issue of whether the healing had violated the sabbath and over Christ's claims of authority (5:10-18). In the healing of the official's son, the account of the miracle was followed by a one-sentence summary of the belief of those who witnessed the miracle; here the description of the miracle is accompanied by the extended discourse of Jesus about His divine authority (vss. 19-47). This fusion of act and discourse, event and spiritual significance, is characteristic of the gospel writers' technique. In this instance the discourse is the protagonist's self-characterization, a self-characterization that is without parallel anywhere else in literature.

The miraculous feeding of five thousand people (6:1-14) continues the pattern of variety of adventure. It introduces a new kind of miracle after two healing miracles, and it encompasses a huge crowd of people after miracles involving single persons. The miracle of the feeding is another chapter in the gospel motif of the messianic banquet. The common pattern in the gospel of John is for belief to be the result, not the cause, of a miracle. This pattern is illustrated in the story of the feeding of the crowd when the people respond to the miracle by exclaiming, "This is indeed the prophet who is to come into the world!" (vs. 14).

As elsewhere in John's gospel, the miracle of the feeding of the crowd is a sign that reaches its culmination in an interpretive discourse, in this case Jesus' famous discourse on His status as the bread of life (6:22-40). In keeping with Christ's everpresent tendency, a physical analogue — bread — is used as a symbol for a spiritual reality.

Also characteristic of Jesus' discourses in the gospels is His way of taking commonplace terms and transforming their meaning in ways that go beyond the ordinary reach of words: "food which endures to eternal life" (vs. 27); "the true bread from heaven" (vs. 32); "the bread of life" (vs. 35); and "the living bread which came down from heaven" (vs. 51).

The story of the miracle is embellished not only by Jesus' discourse but also by the description of the varied responses by Jesus' listeners to His statements. Plot conflict enters with the murmuring of the Jews (vs. 41) and continues throughout the subsequent debate between them and Jesus (vss. 41-59). The questioning of the disciples (vss. 60-71) also contributes to the conflict between belief and unbelief, bringing the conflict within the inner circle of the disciples. On one side are the disciples who "drew back and no longer went about with him" (vs. 66) and Judas Iscariot, whose future betrayal is foreshadowed (vss. 70-71). The contrasting belief of other disciples is captured in Peter's great affirmation, "Lord, to whom shall we go? You have the words of eternal life; and we have believed, and have come to know, that you are the Holy One of God" (vss. 68-69).

In summary, the long sixth chapter illustrates the typical structure of the embellished stories found in the gospels. The storyteller's impulse in these stories is to linger on the event, not simply to give the bare outline. In the center of the story are the person and activity of Jesus. The story begins with a miracle and is elaborated by a discourse. Then both become transmuted into a conflict between belief and unbelief. This is the recurrent structural principle of many stories in the gospels, where Jesus' claims as Savior are always the still center around which activity revolves.

The gospels use two main means of characterizing the protagonist. One is Jesus' self-characterization through deed and word. This is balanced by the response of others to His self-characterization. The account of Christ's appearance at the Feast of Tabernacles (ch. 7) illustrates the interplay of these two types of characterization, as we witness a variety of responses to Jesus' claims about Himself. One response is the hostility of the Jewish leaders. In keeping with the plot structure of increasing antagonism against Jesus, the earlier intellectual debate now intensifies into a conspiracy to kill Jesus (vss. 1, 25) and an unsuccessful attempt to arrest Him (vs. 32). Uncertainty about the claims of Jesus is another common response, as captured in the following vivid picture: "And there was much muttering about him among the people. While some said, 'He is a good man,' others said, 'No, he is leading the people astray'" (vs. 12). A third response is belief in Jesus as Savior, as evidenced by the report that "many of the people believed in him" (vs. 31). Behind this pattern of varied response is the clear call of Jesus for people to believe in Him: "If any one thirst, let him come to me and drink" (vs. 37). Like so many other chapters in the gospels, this one is full of voices — voices arguing and voices expressing perplexity, hostility, and belief.

Debate is also the mode of chapter 8, where Jesus continues the defense of His claims against the Pharisees. The verbal exchange concludes with the Pharisees' taking up stones to throw at Jesus (vs. 59), keeping the intensity of the plot conflict very much in the reader's consciousness.

The narrator returns to the narrative mode in chapter 9, another miracle story and another account of healing, this time of a man born blind. The story is an outstanding example of embellished gospel narrative. It begins with the disciples' question about whether the man's blindness could be attributed to the man or his parents (vs. 2). Jesus' reply that the blindness of the man was intended solely that "the works of God might be made manifest in him" (vs. 3) is itself a commentary on the meaning of the miracle. In keeping with the writer's tendency toward circumstantial narrative, even the process of the healing is described (vss. 6-7). The varied response of the neighbors is made vivid by the storyteller's reportage of their utterances (vss. 8-12).

The elaboration of the sign follows a now familiar pattern. The actual miracle is only the force that initiates an ever-widening series of ripples. From the neighbors the action moves outward to the unbelieving Jews (vss. 13-34). There is a pervasive humor as well as pathos in the dialogue that ensues the miracle, with the Pharisees inflexibly denying the obvious healing of the man and the equally obvious divinity of Jesus. The narrative concludes on a note that several other stories in John's gospel also do — the belief of the few. In this case Jesus befriends the man who had been healed only to find Himself cast out of the synagogue. Jesus reveals Himself as Savior (vss. 36-37), and the man responds with belief and worship (vs. 38). Once again faith is shown to be the goal of Jesus' miracles. In keeping with the essentially narrative mode of the gospels, even this drama of belief is not concluded without a reminder of the conflict between belief and unbelief, with Christ's satiric attack on the Pharisees (vss. 40-41) keeping the plot conflict at a point of high tension.

Miracle is again combined with discourse when Jesus follows His healing of the blind man with His allegory about the good shepherd (10:1-18). Jesus' discourse is the climax of the whole biblical tradition of pastoral literature. It is the apotheosis of the idealized shepherd of the pastoral tradition. It also shows us the poetic Jesus, using the pastoral metaphor as a way of defining His intimate relationship to those who believe in Him, His superiority to false religious teachers, and His voluntary atonement for His followers.

The account of Jesus' appearance at the Feast of Dedication (10:22-42) is a parallel to the earlier appearance at the Feast of Tabernacles (ch. 7). In the six references in the gospel of John to Christ's attendance at Jewish religious festivals, we are to see an extension of the writer's use of symbolism to describe Christ's ministry. In each case we are reminded of how Jesus was the ultimate fulfillment of the Old Testament ceremonial laws. As at the Feast of Tabernacles, Jesus is again the center of controversy when He attends the Feast of Dedication. Again His claim to divinity is the stimulus for both doubt and intense hatred, and again His method of defense against His enemies is verbal.

The raising of Lazarus from death (ch. 11) comes in the middle of the book and is a climactic event in John's gospel. It is, accordingly, one of the embellished narratives in the gospel, told in circumstantial detail. Before Jesus performs the miracle He makes it clear that the death of Lazarus is the occasion for bringing glory to God and to the Son of God (vs. 4). Having established this interpretive framework, the narrator goes on to describe the mighty sign, depending heavily on dialogue as his narrative mode.

This death-rebirth story is structured partly on the motif of the misunderstood statement by Jesus. Jesus' statement to His disciples that "our friend Lazarus has fallen asleep, but I go to awake him out of sleep" (vs. 11) constitutes a puzzle that the subsequent miracle will solve. Evident in this pattern is the archetypal narrative rhythm that is by now virtually inevitable in John's gospel — the movement from event to meaning, from misunderstanding to perception, from question to answer. The episode involving the raising of Lazarus conforms to two other narrative patterns in the gospel — the linking of an event to a spiritual reality of which the event is a symbol and the relation of an "I am" self-characterization by Jesus to a particular event. In the present instance, Christ's statement, "I am the resurrection and the life" (vs. 25), is the spiritual parallel to the physical raising of Lazarus from the grave.

The story is structured like a suspense story. First Jesus delays for two days His trip to Bethany. Jesus' mysterious comments that Lazarus is only sleeping likewise seem to raise doubt that He plans to do anything about the death. As Jesus approaches the village, the friends and relatives of Lazarus are pictured as coming out to meet Him. The narrator takes time to record the conversations of Jesus with both Martha (vss. 20-27) and Mary (vss. 28-34). There is the memorable brief picture of Jesus' weeping (vs. 35). The actual miracle is narrated with attention to the precise way in which it was accomplished and in such a way as to allow the reader to visualize the suspenseful moment when the stone is rolled away from the tomb and Lazarus comes forth (vss. 38-44).

As in the case of previous signs recorded in the gospel, Jesus' raising of Lazarus generates conflicting responses. As always, the overriding contrast is between belief and unbelief, and between Jesus and the Jews (vss. 45-47). The normal narrative function of these epilogues to the events is to tie the given episode to the larger plot of the story.

The story of Mary of Bethany's anointing of Jesus (12:1-8) is a simple narrative, complementing the series of embellished stories that John has narrated in the middle chapters of his book. Mary's act is a symbolic gesture, capturing as with a camera click the leading gospel theme of the supreme worthiness of Jesus. The episode also reenacts the usual narrative pattern of event leading to conflict, as Judas Iscariot and Jesus disagree on the appropriateness of the anointing (vss. 4-8). From another perspective, the contrast is between the responses of Mary and Judas to the person of Jesus.

The triumphal entry into Jerusalem (12:12-19) is another example of simple narrative. It is evident that the narrator's choice to use simple or embellished narrative does not depend on the significance of an event in the life of Jesus. The gospel of Luke, for example, treats the same event with much more narrative detail. The decision regarding the length of an episode seems to have been a storyteller's rather than a theologian's decision. John uses the event of the triumphal entry to embody two themes — the imperfect understanding that the disciples had of the event until after Christ's glorification (vss. 14-16) and the popularity that Jesus enjoyed from the crowd at the height of His earthly career (vss. 17-19). The latter motif is continued in the ensuing brief narrative about the Greeks who came to hear Jesus (vss. 20-22).

In terms of the dynamics of plot, the gospel writers succeed splendidly in moving their narratives inexorably and progressively toward a climactic conflict between Jesus and His enemies. We can trace, step by step, the development from early debates with Jesus to a general plan to kill Him. In the latter phases of the story the threat to Jesus is so imminent that He travels secretly (11:54). As noted earlier, the same movement toward the climactic encounter can be seen in the references to the coming "hour" and to the actual arrival of the "hour."

As the story of the Gospel of John approaches the events of Christ's death, the focus becomes constricted from Jesus' ministry in the

world to His last days with His loyal disciples. Accompanying narrative details reflect this constriction. Instead of miraculous signs that
produce belief for the first time, Jesus now performs the equally
significant but less spectacular act of washing the feet of His disciples,
who already believe in Him but need a lesson on the meaning of
humble discipleship (13:1-20). The foot washing is another of Jesus'
parabolic acts, combining action and meaning to teach spiritual truth
in a manner similar to that used in the miracles and parables of
Jesus. The sin of unbelief, which had earlier involved large numbers
of Jews, now becomes narrowed to unbelief within the disciples, as
embodied in the dismissal of the traitor Judas Iscariot (vss. 21-30)
and the prediction of Peter's denial (vss. 36-38). And in contrast to
the earlier public discourses, we now get a private address in the
upper room to the inner circle of disciples (chapters 14-16).

The discourse in the upper room belongs to the Hebraic literary
form of the farewell address by an important person on the eve of
his death to his children or followers.[5] Jesus' farewell address includes
the following conventional motifs: the speaker's announcement of
His imminent departure, the listeners' sorrow and the accompanying
words of comfort from the speaker, the directive to keep God's commandments, a command to the listeners to love one another, a
prediction of what will happen to the listeners in the future, the
invocation of peace upon the listeners, the naming of a successor
(the Holy Spirit), and a concluding prayer for the listeners. The
tone of Jesus' farewell address is intimate, loving, and full of compassionate concern for the disciples. In the background is the initiation motif, as the disciples are being introduced to the mission they
will carry out in the absence of their master. The symbolic "I am"
pronouncements that Jesus makes in John's Gospel here reach their
culmination in the discourse about the true vine (15:1-6).

As is true of the other gospels, the gospel of John devotes a pro-
portionately large amount of space to the events surrounding the
death of Jesus. In terms of narrative structure, the passion story in
the gospel of John unfolds in three stages — the betrayal (18:1-11),
the trial (18:12–19:16), and the crucifixion (19:17-42). The betrayal
is narrated summarily, while the trial is described very circum-
stantially. The trial scene is virtually staged, as in a drama, and it is

---

[5] For a discussion of how the last discourse adheres to the literary form of
the farewell address as found in Old Testament and intertestamental literature, see Raymond E. Brown, *The Anchor Bible: The Gospel According to John*
(Garden City: Doubleday and Company, 1970), II, 597-601. Old Testament
examples include the discourses of Jacob (Gen. 48-49), Moses (the book of
Deuteronomy), Joshua (Josh. 23-24), and David (1 Chron. 28-29). 2 Peter
shows some of the same motifs.

accordingly full of voices — voices questioning, accusing, denying, and demanding crucifixion.

The passion story of Jesus is the climax not only of the individual gospels but of the whole story of the Bible. It is the center toward which the rest of biblical literature points either forward or backward. It is the fulfillment of the Old Testament ceremonial laws and prophecies, of Old Testament types (foreshadowings), and of the biblical archetype of the suffering servant. The substitutionary atonement represented by Jesus' death on the cross is also the basis for the "good news" that pervades the New Testament and is the foundation for the whole edifice of New Testament theology.

The resurrection of Jesus from the grave (ch. 20) is the climax of John's gospel, as it is of the others. It is the ultimate triumph of the protagonist, proof of His uniqueness and divinity. It is also the ultimate fulfillment of the literary archetype of movement through death to renewed life. In terms of plot structure, the resurrection is the final phase of the U-shaped comic plot of the gospel. The gradual isolation of the protagonist which prevailed in the tragic phase of the story is now followed by the gradual reintegration of the hero into His society. It is evident that the inherent form of the New Testament gospels is comedy, not tragedy, as is sometimes claimed. If the plot did not end in triumph, the term "gospel" would be a misnomer.

The post-resurrection appearances of Jesus are all structured as encounters with individuals. These stories reach their climax through the use of dialogue that leads to a recognition of the risen Christ. Mary Magdalene's moment of surprised recognition is captured by her exclamation "Rabboni!" (20:16). The story of the appearance to Thomas (20:24-29) follows a similar pattern, moving from initial skepticism to the exclamation of recognition and adoration, "My Lord and my God!" (vs. 28). The encounter with Thomas, incidentally, is the last phase of the prolonged conflict between belief and unbelief.

The post-resurrection appearance that is most fully elaborated in the gospel of John is the dialogue between Peter and Jesus (21:1-19). Mystery pervades this appearance of Jesus on the beach at daybreak. The appearance is accompanied by the miraculous haul of fishes and by the apparently instantaneous provision of a fire and food when the disciples land on the shore. These reminders of Christ's earlier miracles are merely preliminary to the restoration of Peter, which gains its dramatic impact because of its use of repetition and its powerful parallels to the threefold denial of Peter on the evening of Christ's arrest.

As one looks back over the entire gospel, he might well ask what principle of organization accounts for the arrangement of the individual parts in their final form. If the gospel writers were compilers of stories and sayings already in circulation, what pattern did they follow in weaving the individual parts into the completed fabric? Although the general outline of events is chronological, the writers do not claim that each event is strictly chronological in its relation to other details. The gospel of John, in particular, may deliberately dislocate chronology in order to achieve its ends. The arrangement of parts is not determined by theological considerations, since the theology would remain unchanged with any other arrangement.

The organization of the gospel of John is based on narrative principles. One of these is variety of episode. With a storyteller's instinct, the writer mingles long and short episodes, as well as mighty acts and spoken discourses. Events that carry their own meaning are interspersed with acts that are accompanied by interpretive discourses. Jesus' encounters with individuals are balanced by appearances to large crowds. Stories that end in belief are juxtaposed to episodes that lead to conflict and unbelief.

In addition to the narrative principle of variety, the gospel of John is structured as a series of progressions. These patterns include the progressive intensification of plot conflict, the movement toward the climax of Christ's execution, an expansion of Jesus' career followed by a constriction, and the continuing plot conflict between belief and unbelief.

One of the leading literary features of the gospels is the account they give of the literary genius of Jesus. Jesus is one of the world's most famous poets. If we are unaccustomed to regarding Him as such, it is because His poetry is so natural and apparently artless that it enters our consciousness without striking us as being poetic. Upon analysis, His speech shows total mastery of poetic forms.

Jesus' speech is saturated with metaphors and symbols. Using the resources of the poetic imagination, He repeatedly drew upon one area of human experience to shed light on another. According to Jesus, calling people to belief in God was like gathering a harvest (Matt. 9:37-38). Sending the disciples to minister in a hostile world was similar to sending "sheep in the midst of wolves" (Matt. 10:16). Living a life of self-sacrifice for the sake of Christ called to Jesus' mind the picture of picking up a cross and bearing it (Matt. 10:38), while the ordeal of His own death was a cup whose contents had to be drunk (Matt. 26:39). Jesus compared the hypocritical Pharisees to "whitewashed tombs, which outwardly appear beautiful, but within they are full of dead men's bones and all uncleanness" (Matt. 23:27), and to "graves which are not seen, and men walk over them without knowing it" (Luke 11:44). By contrast, Jesus compared His own followers to a flock (Luke 12:32). His desire to save Jerusalem was like a hen that "gathers her brood under her wings" (Luke 13:34). Many of Jesus' comparisons drew upon archetypal images, as when He spoke about living water (John 4:10), the bread of life (John 6:35), the light of the world (John 8:12), and the good shepherd (John 10:11). Jesus' reliance on analogy as the most effective way of explaining His saving ministry reaches its climax in the parables, where the kingdom of God is compared to a field, a mustard seed, a treasure, a pearl, a vineyard, a banquet, and a wedding.

Jesus also used paradox. He asserted, for example, "My yoke is easy, and my burden is light" (Matt. 11:30). The effect of paradox depends, of course, on the listener's resolution of the apparent contradiction. In this case, Jesus is making the claim that submission to Him, symbolized by the yoke and burden, brings freedom and salvation to a person. In stressing the need for his followers to deny themselves as a condition for gaining eternal life, Jesus made the paradoxical statement, "For whoever would save his life will lose it, and whoever loses his life for my sake will find it" (Matt. 16:25). The ideal of service to others is captured in Christ's statement that "whoever would be great among you must be your servant, and whoever would be first among you must be your slave" (Matt. 20:26-27), while the biblical commonplace that God's standards of judgment run counter to the world's evaluation of success was made memorable in Jesus' remark that "many that are first will be last, and the last first" (Mark 10:31). On another occasion Jesus told His disciples, "If any one would be first, he must be last of all" (Mark 9:35). It becomes evident that paradox was rooted in the nature of Christ's message, which challenged conventional attitudes at so many points.

Jesus was equally adept at using hyperbole. There is obvious exaggeration in the statement that "it is easier for a camel to go through the eye of a needle than for a rich man to enter the kingdom of God" (Matt. 19:24),[6] and in the satiric comment that the Pharisees

---

[6] The hyperbole of this saying is denied by many commentators who point out that there is an actual gate in Jerusalem known as "the eye of the needle," through which a camel could pass with great difficulty. This interpretation overlooks the context of Jesus' saying, which informs us that Jesus' disciples accepted His statement as an impossibility, as evidenced by the statement that they "were greatly astonished, saying, 'Who then can be saved?'" (Matt. 19:25). Jesus' reply affirms that he was using hyperbole rather than literal fact when he talked about a camel passing through the eye of a needle: "With men this is impossible . . ." (vs. 26).

are guilty of "straining out a gnat and swallowing a camel" (Matt. 23:24). Another of Jesus' humorous exaggerations occurs in His satire against self-righteous judgment: "How can you say to your brother, 'Brother, let me take out the speck that is in your eye,' when you yourself do not see the log that is in your own eye?" (Luke 6:42). Some of Jesus' hyperbolic statements will be misinterpreted if they are taken literally. For example, Jesus was not stating a reasoned ethical position when He said that "if any one comes to me and does not hate his own father and mother and wife and children and brothers and sisters, yes, and even his own life, he cannot be my disciple" (Luke 14:26). Rather, He was using hyperbole to assert the priority that a person must give to God over other relationships.

The literary genius of Jesus is seen not only in His mastery of poetic figures, but also in His oratorical ability. The best illustration is the Sermon on the Mount (Matt. 5-7), which has affinities to several literary forms. It is similar in tone to Old Testament wisdom literature, in which a wise authority figure sits in the middle of his disciples and instructs them. Much of the discourse is a satiric attack on religious abuses. In its composite picture of the Christian, the sermon resembles the genre known as "the character." The discourse is sometimes considered an example of utopian literature, an appropriate designation for the work because it outlines the general principles for the conduct of the perfect spiritual kingdom that Christ came to establish and of which this sermon is a kind of inaugural address.

The beatitudes that begin the discourse are one of the most famous passages in the literature of the world. They are one of the most patterned passages in the Bible:

3 *Blessed are the poor in spirit, for theirs is the kingdom of heaven.*
4 *Blessed are those who mourn, for they shall be comforted.*
5 *Blessed are the meek, for they shall inherit the earth.*
6 *Blessed are those who hunger and thirst for righteousness, for they shall be satisfied.*
7 *Blessed are the merciful, for they shall obtain mercy.*
8 *Blessed are the pure in heart, for they shall see God.*
9 *Blessed are the peacemakers, for they shall be called sons of God.*
10 *Blessed are those who are persecuted for righteousness' sake, for theirs is the kingdom of heaven.*
11 *Blessed are you when men revile you and persecute you and utter all kinds of evil against you falsely on my account.*
12 *Rejoice and be glad, for your reward is great in heaven, for so men persecuted the prophets who were before you.*

Much of the memorable quality of the beatitudes, like that of the Ten Commandments, stems from the artistic form in which they are cast. The overall literary genre is the character, in this case a composite portrait of the blessed person. The various beatitudes are organized around a central theme — the qualities of character that make for blessedness. Recurrence underlies the whole series, with each beatitude following the same pattern, based on a balancing of blessing with the reason for the blessing. The formula consists of three parts — an initial statement beginning with the clause "Blessed are," the naming of a character type, and a rationale for the pronouncement of blessing, starting with the statement "for they shall" or "for theirs is." This parallelism of expression, which comes straight from the Hebraic poetry with which Jesus was so familiar, lends an aphoristic quality to the individual beatitudes and links them with the proverbs of Hebrew wisdom literature. Since these principles are not intended only for the individual but are a shorthand outline for a whole society, the beatitudes also have affinities to utopian literature.

One of the most striking features of the beatitudes is their status as parody. The passage parallels other literature by embodying human values in an artistic form. It is on the level of values that the beatitudes completely invert what most literature has espoused. The beatitudes assign blessedness to character types that are generally slighted in literature as a whole, and they base the contradictory definition of blessedness on a spiritual reality that runs counter to what is praised elsewhere. Most literature holds up as models of happiness the courageous (especially on the battlefield), the aristocratic, the self-sufficient, the famous, and the successful. By contrast, the beatitudes hold up for emulation the poor in spirit, the mourners, the meek, the seekers after righteousness, the pure in heart, the peacemakers, and the persecuted. The rewards that Jesus outlines as the motivation for following His ethical standards also contradict what we find elsewhere in literature. Instead of offering an earthly kingdom, Jesus speaks of the kingdom of heaven. Instead of accepting the conventional view that mankind's deepest longings will be satisfied by fame, possessions, and romance, Jesus asserts that the way to fulfillment is found in spiritual righteousness. Instead of offering a reward that is earthly and material, Jesus holds out the possibility of seeing God, being called the son of God, and receiving a reward in heaven. It is obvious that Jesus is setting up ideals that differ from those commonly espoused in literature. He calls people to order their lives by an unseen spiritual reality rather than the realities of empirical demonstration. Not only does His formula for blessedness run counter to the conventional formulae, but the rewards that it offers are for the most part deliberately defiant of the tangible rewards that motivate other literary protagonists.

The next main section of the Sermon on the Mount, Jesus' discourse about the law (5:17-48), is mainly satiric in form. Jesus begins by stating the norm by which He will attack the Pharisees (vs. 17-19). That norm turns out to be the Old Testament law, which the Pharisees had distorted. The actual attack falls into a very patterned sequence. In each case Jesus begins with the formula, "You have heard that it was said. . . ." Balancing this formula is the repeated refrain that begins Jesus' own teaching: "But I say unto you. . . ." Underlying this pattern is the principle of antithesis that Jesus will use in other sections of the sermon as well.

Satiric attack and positive advice continue in the next section (6:1-16), where Jesus takes up the topic of religious observances. In the areas of giving alms, prayer, and fasting, Jesus conducts a satiric attack on those who are ostentatious in their religious practices. In each instance the positive norm is shown to be something inner and spiritual rather than external. Here, too, Jesus' speech falls into rhetorical patterns. All three sections are based on a principle of antithesis in which Jesus states, in effect, "Do not observe this religious practice ostentatiously but rather practice it in secrecy." In all three instances, the satiric description of the abuse is concluded with the refrain, "Truly, I say to you, they have their reward" (6:2, 5, 16). The three passages of positive instruction also end with a refrain that stresses the motif of reward: "and your Father who sees in secret will reward you" (vss. 4, 6, 18). A memorable instance of hyperbole is Christ's advice that in giving alms, "do not let your left hand know what your right hand is doing" (vs. 3).

The three pieces of advice on religious observances are balanced by a threefold exhortation on the theme of choosing heavenly or spiritual values over earthly values (6:19-24). Antithesis underlies the contrasts between earthly and heavenly treasures, light and darkness (or sound and unsound eyes), and the two masters, God and mammon. Here, indeed, we find the very epitome of the choice between opposites that pervades the plot of biblical literature. Each of the contrasts ends with an aphorism that clinches the point: "For where your treasure is, there will your heart be also"; "If then the light in you is darkness, how great is the darkness"; "you cannot serve God and mammon."

One of the most eloquent passages in the Sermon on the Mount is the section in which Jesus dispraises anxiety (6:25-34). The unit is structured like an argument, as Jesus gives reasons against being anxious. Like any good persuasive speech, it mingles evidence and direct appeal to the listener. Jesus begins by stating his thesis, using the balanced headings of "life" and "body" and employing three parallel "what" clauses as a further element of pattern:

> *Therefore I tell you,*
> *do not be anxious about your life,*
> *what you shall eat or*
> *what you shall drink,*
> *nor about your body,*
> *what you shall put on.*

A twofold rhetorical question repeats the pair of headings that have been introduced:

> *Is not life more than food,*
> *and the body more than clothing?*

Jesus first discusses the topic of food, basing His argument on an analogy from nature and clinching the point with the persuasive use of rhetorical question:

> *Look at the birds of the air:*
> *they neither sow nor reap nor gather into barns,*
> *and yet your heavenly Father feeds them.*
> *Are you not of more value than they?*

The rhetorical question that follows forces the listener to acknowledge the ineffectualness of worry: "And which of you by being anxious can add one cubit to his span of life?"

Having disposed of any supposed reasons for worrying about food, Jesus proceeds to discuss the second topic, clothing. Again He uses an analogy from nature, saying, in effect, "Take a look around you and observe God's providence":

> *And why are you anxious about clothing?*
> *Consider the lilies of the field, how they grow;*
> *they neither toil nor spin.*

Not only are the lilies clothed without effort on their part, but the beauty of their clothing is said to be even greater than that of Solomon, the Old Testament touchstone for magnificence:

> *yet I tell you,*
> *even Solomon in all his glory*
> *was not arrayed like one of these.*

Jesus then proceeds to apply a second analogy, also taken from nature:

> *But if God so clothes the grass of the field,*
> *which today is alive*
> *and tomorrow is thrown into the oven,*

will he not much more clothe you,
O men of little faith?

In a summary statement, Jesus returns to the categories of experience in which, as He has proved, worry is useless:

Therefore do not be anxious, saying,
"What shall we eat?" or
"What shall we drink?" or
"What shall we wear?"

Two further reasons explain why these questions are so ignominious:

For the Gentiles seek all these things;
and your heavenly Father knows that you need them all.

Jesus expresses the antidote to anxiety about material provision in a famous aphorism:

But seek his kingdom and his righteousness,
and all these things shall be yours as well.

Having refuted all possible counter arguments, Jesus states with finality the conclusion toward which His argument has been pointing:

Therefore do not be anxious about tomorrow,
for tomorrow will be anxious for itself.

In Jesus' concluding aphorism there is a note of gentle cynicism and compassionate realism about what life in a fallen world is like: "Let the day's own trouble be sufficient for the day."

The parallelism of the Hebraic poetry that Jesus knew and loved pervades the next section of His discourse (7:1-12):

with the judgment you pronounce you will be judged,
and the measure you give will be the measure you get.

Do not give dogs what is holy;
and do not throw your pearls before swine.

Ask, and it will be given you;
seek, and you will find;
knock, and it will be opened to you.
For every one who asks receives,
and he who seeks finds,
and to him who knocks it will be opened.

As He concludes His discourse (7:13-27), Jesus sharpens the issues and begins to force a response from His listeners. He leaves His audience with a challenge, urging them to make sure that they are members of God's kingdom. In order to make His point with impact, Jesus uses three memorable contrasts — the narrow gate that leads to life vs. the wide gate that leads to destruction (vss. 13-14), true prophets vs. false prophets (vss. 15-23), and the wise man who builds his house on a rock vs. the foolish man who builds on the sand (vss. 24-27). Jesus' masterful use of metaphor is much in evidence at the finish of His most famous public speech: life is a path with a gate at the entrance, false prophets are ravenous wolves in sheep's clothing, prophets are like fruit trees that can be judged by their fruit, and hearing or rejecting the words of Jesus is like building a house. The persuasive function of the last illustration is clear: having addressed His listeners, Christ now calls them to hear and do His words (vss. 24-25), and utters a warning about what will happen to anyone who does not respond (vss. 26-27). The narrator's concluding framework editorializes the impressiveness of the sermon: "And when Jesus finished these sayings, the crowds were astonished at his teaching, for he taught them as one who had authority" (vss. 28-29).

Many of the parables of Jesus had a rural setting. "And other fell on good ground, and did yield fruit that sprang up and increased; and brought forth, some thirty, and some sixty, and some an hundred fold" (Mark 4:8). This is a field of wheat in Palestine.

Biblical
Parable

15

I

The parables of Jesus belong to the literary family known as allegory. By "allegory" I do not here mean the arbitrary allegorizing of medieval exegesis.[1] A responsible approach to the allegorical nature of Christ's parables begins with an awareness that all literature is allegorical in the ordinary definition — a work in which the details have a conceptual meaning. As Northrop Frye has written, "It is not often realized that all commentary is allegorical interpretation, an attaching of ideas to the structure of poetic imagery. The instant that any critic permits himself to make a genuine comment about a poem (e.g., 'In *Hamlet* Shakespeare appears to be portraying the tragedy of irresolution') he has begun to allegorize."[2]

What is needed, then, is a critical tool that will allow us to differentiate degrees of allegorical explicitness in works of literature. This is exactly what Frye has provided with his viewpoint that all literature exists somewhere on an allegorical continuum ranging from the most explicitly allegorical at one end to the most elusive, anti-explicit at the other. At one end theme is dominant, at the other end image or story is dominant. At one end we have explicit, conceptual allegory in which the details of the story represent in obvious fashion a corresponding set of concepts or allegorical meanings. Frye calls this "continuous allegory." Other points on the spectrum include literature with an insistent doctrinal interest, literature that combines theme and image in roughly equal degrees, and literature that approaches realistic reportage, with little thematic implication. Traditionally the term "allegory" has been applied to works that exist

---

[1] For a typical example of this kind of allegorical interpretation, see Augustine's interpretation of the parable of the good Samaritan, quoted in C. H. Dodd, *The Parables of the Kingdom* (New York: Charles Scribner's Sons, 1956; first published 1935), pp. 11-12; also quoted by William Barclay, *And Jesus Said: A Handbook on the Parables of Jesus* (Philadelphia: Westminster Press, 1970), pp. 15-16.

[2] *Anatomy of Criticism* (Princeton: Princeton University Press, 1957), p. 89.

near the explicit end of the spectrum, where Christ's parables obviously belong. If anyone doubts this, he has only to turn to Jesus' interpretations of His parables of the sower and the tares (Matt. 13:18-23, 36-43), where He translates virtually all of the details in the stories into corresponding conceptual meanings.

The parables are oral literature. They were apparently composed by Jesus on the spur of the moment. They were responses to an immediate situation and often arose out of some kind of conflict. As one commentator states, "In its most characteristic use the parable is a weapon of controversy, not shaped like a sonnet in undisputed concentration but improvised to meet the unpremeditated situation."[3]

Another characteristic of the parables is that they rely heavily on the technique of realism. They draw upon the familiar experience of the listeners. They are experiential, so simple in detail that a child can usually grasp them. Part of their realism is that they do not violate rules of plausibility. There is an absence of unreality, and we find no talking animals or marvelous adventures. Being realistic, the parables appeal to the unsophisticated literary taste. They are folk literature, easily grasped on at least one level of meaning and universally understood. This is not to say that they are not at the same time profound, nor to deny that they lend themselves to almost indefinite explication and application.

The parables as a whole illustrate a wide range of literary sophistication. At their most rudimentary they are no more than a brief analogy between the topic Jesus is discussing and some object or event in the world of familiar experience. At its most refined, the parable is a short story with a skillfully designed plot, a somewhat detailed setting, dialogue, and careful characterization.

Some of the parables are satiric. Virtually all of them serve an obvious rhetorical purpose. They are addressed to a specific audience and are the means of persuasion used by Jesus to move His audience. In fact, the gospel accounts of the parables often give a description of the context that occasioned the parables.

The parables tend to deal with the basic doctrines and ethical beliefs of the Christian faith — salvation, the kingdom of God, judgment, service, and the second coming of Jesus. Many of the parables were used by Jesus to teach an unpopular or little understood truth. In particular, many were designed to teach an unconventional view of the kingdom of God and the unpopular truth that God will punish unrepentant sinners.

The parables show the interrelationship of this world and the

---

[3] A. T. Cadoux, *The Parables of Jesus: Their Art and Use* (London: James Clarke and Company, 1930), p. 13.

spiritual realm. The experiences of life point to the other world. By the same token, the great spiritual truths of the Christian faith are domesticated and made commonplace, in the manner of the English poet George Herbert.

In one sense the parables are a very sophisticated literary form — they work by indirection instead of direct statement. They force people to make a judgment on some commonplace situation and then to transfer that judgment to a spiritual plane. As Cadoux states, "The parable elicits a judgment in one sphere in order to transfer it to another."[4]

II

Jesus' parable of the sower (Matt. 13:1-9, 18-23), more accurately called the parable of the soils, is typical of many of the parables. The story draws upon a rural situation and no doubt struck a responsive note in the lives of Christ's audience. In this respect it illustrates the realism of the parables. On the narrative level there are three main ingredients in the parable — a sower, seed, and soil. The action of the plot is negligible: a farmer sows seed in four kinds of soil, only one of which proves productive. This means that of the three elements in the story, the sower and seed are constant, while the types of soil are variable. Despite the paucity of action, the plot does contain conflict. A certain amount of struggle is conveyed by the description of how the birds "devoured" the seeds (Matt. 13:4) and how the thorns "choked" them (vs. 7), as well as by the statement that the sun "scorched" some of the shoots (vs. 6).

The story becomes a parable when Jesus allegorizes the event of the sower and his seed. The seed is God's message of salvation and righteous living. The sower is the evangelist, or even Christ Himself. The kinds of soil are the responses of hearers to the Word of God. Since it is the kinds of soil that are variable, this is where the emphasis of the parable falls.

There are several themes inherent in this allegorical story. The preaching of the Gospel is shown to occur in a context of spiritual warfare, with the result that the proclamation of the Word will inevitably meet resistance. The story also suggests that one cannot expect uniformly positive results from the preaching of the Gospel. The parable shows that salvation involves the responses of the people who hear the Word of God. And there is the assurance that Christ's Gospel will produce positive results in the lives of some people.

---

[4] Cadoux, *Parables of Jesus*, p. 56.

What application might this classification of responses to the Gospel have had in Christ's day? For one thing, the analogies of the types of soils would have helped Jesus' followers to understand what happened when the Word was preached. It helped to organize their observation of reality. It would have been no small thing for the founder of the Christian faith to state in definitive terms what the expectations of His followers ought to be. Jesus here calls His workers to a platform of realism.

Most interpreters of the parable believe that Jesus intended it as an encouragement to His disillusioned disciples. When the disciples saw the resistance that Jesus encountered, this theory states, they became discouraged and doubtful. Jesus told a parable that had the concept of fruitfulness and success as its climax in order to counteract their disillusionment.

This emphasis is somewhat misleading. Matthew 13:2 makes it clear that Jesus was speaking to a huge crowd of people, not simply to His disciples. The parable, moreover, concentrates on the kinds of soil, not the sower. The whole interest is with the soil, that is, the hearers of the Gospel. It would appear that the parable was a challenge to those who were listening to the claims of the Gospel. Jesus delineates three inadequate responses to His message of the kingdom. It is a warning to His listeners to avoid these errors. The fourth response provides the opportunity to choose a better way. Even here there are varieties of fruitfulness, thereby providing a challenge to the listeners to be as responsive as they possibly could. To sum up, the parable of the sower stresses human responsiveness to God's message of salvation. It sets up options from which the listener must choose.

The parable of the wheat and the tares (Matt. 13:24-30, 36-43) is another rural story. The parable tells about a farmer who sowed wheat in his field, only to find as the wheat grew that an enemy had planted a semipoisonous weed called bearded darnel in his field. When asked by his servants if they should pull up the darnel, the farmer instructed them to allow the weeds to grow until the harvest time, lest they also pluck the wheat plants out of the ground. There is realism in this parable, for in fact the tares of the parable were indistinguishable from the wheat until later stages of growth, when the roots of the weeds had become intertwined with the roots of the wheat.

Again a simple story succeeds as a story because of the element of conflict. Intense character conflict is present in the feud between the farmer and his enemy. The conflict between the wheat and the tares extends the sense of elemental struggle even farther. The motif of deceptiveness, present in the fact that the enemy sows the weeds

"while men were sleeping" (Matt. 13:25) and in the similarity between the wheat and the darnel, also gives tension to the narrative.

As Christ's interpretation of the parable indicates (Matt. 13:36-43),
this story, too, achieves its parabolic intention through the allegorical
nature of the narrative. The sower is Christ, the field is the world
(not the church, incidentally), the good seed is the community of
believers in God, the enemy is the devil, the weeds are unbelievers,
the burning of the weeds at harvest time is the punishment in hell of
unbelievers, and the gathering of the wheat into barns is the entrance
of believers into heaven at the end of history. This is obviously continuous, explicit allegory, with virtually every detail in the story
having a corresponding conceptual meaning.

Several themes emerge from this allegorical story. The narrative
establishes the fact of spiritual conflict. Indeed, a whole set of opposites underlies the story: good seed and bad seed, wheat and tares,
the sower and the enemy, storage in barns and burning. The story
suggests that the good in the world is the work of God; evil comes
from Satan. Satan is shown to be a reality, as is the certainty of divine
judgment at the end of history. The main thrust of the parable is to
teach the necessary mixture of good and evil persons in history. Men
are incapable of carrying out final judgment, which is left to God.

When we turn to application, we discover two traditional interpretations of the parable. According to one view, the parable was a
lesson to the disciples not to be overly confident in their own ability
to distinguish between good and evil. The parable is in effect a
plea for tolerance. A second traditional interpretation is that the
parable was an attack on the Pharisees, with their judgmental and
exclusivist tendencies.

A close reading of the allegory should lead us to question these
traditional interpretations. The sower in the parable does not say
that the servants are wrong in judging between wheat and tares. He
does not encourage tolerance and unconcern about the poisonous
tares. What he does is prevent the servants from destroying the tares.
The interpretation given by Jesus later in the chapter (vss. 36-43)
does not concentrate on the attitudes of the servants but on the
certainty and nature of the final judgment of evildoers. The emphasis
of the parable is eschatalogical, that is, concerned with the end of
history. The parable calls for believers to live in an awareness of the
final judgment and to be patient as they live in a hostile world. As
a plea for patient waiting, the parable may have been Jesus' reply
to the Zealots, who demanded revolution as a means of combating
evil. The parable pictures the church in relation to the world and
prohibits persecution of unbelievers. It is often claimed that the
parable is talking about the relation between believers and un-

believers within the church. This interpretation equates the field with the church, but Christ's interpretation shows that the field is not the church but the world. The tares are not unbelievers within the church but in the world at large.

The parable of the generous employer (Matt. 20:1-16) is a good illustration of how the typical parable secures a judgment in one sphere of experience and then asks the audience to transfer that judgment to a spiritual plane. This rural story tells how in the pressure of grape harvesting the owner of a vineyard presses all available men into service. He recruits workers at various hours of the day and then pays all the workers an equal wage. On the narrative level the main interest is the character of the owner of the vineyard, and the story turns upon the question of the justness of the employer's practice. The workers complain to the employer because the equal payment does not reflect the differences in effort on the part of the workers.

The success of the story as a parable depends on the integrity of the employer, who represents God on the allegorical level. The employer offers several explanations that show him to be, within the logic of the story, a just and generous man. He points out that the workers hired earlier in the day have received the amount for which they were contracted (Matt. 20:13). He also asserts that as employer he is master of his own pay scale (vss. 14-15). The crucial point in his exoneration, however, is his observation that he is not guilty of skimping on the payment of the early workers but is simply more generous than might be expected with the late workers. Since a denarius was equivalent to a living wage, there may even be the suggestion that the employer showed a humanitarian concern that all his workers have enough to live. Everything considered, the employer emerges as a generous man within the logic of the story.

Once we have grasped the main point of the surface narrative, we are in a position to transfer our judgment about the employer's generosity to a spiritual level of meaning. Again it is the allegory of the story that will unfold its intended themes. The owner of the vineyard is God. The vineyard is the world, or human life. The reward is eternal salvation, especially as consummated at the end of history. The servants who agree to work in the vineyard are believers who respond to God's call. The equality of payment signifies that all believers will receive salvation and glorification, despite obvious differences in effort and spiritual service.

The application to Jesus' audience is fairly obvious. The parable was an explanation to the Jews that they were not the victims of injustice simply because the Gentiles were saved without all the encumbrances that the Jews had accepted as part of their religious experience for many centuries. The dissatisfaction of Jewish Christians over the exemption of Gentile believers from the Jewish ceremonial laws would eventually precipitate *the* great conflict in the early New Testament church. The application of the parable is more general than the first century situation, however. Throughout history there has always been a great deal of disparity in the spiritual exertion of members of any typical group of Christians. Both Christian doctrine and this parable teach that anyone who believes in Christ will be saved and glorified in heaven. The explanation of the equality of reward despite differences in effort is that salvation depends on God's grace (the employer's generosity), not on human merit (the work of the laborers in the vineyard).

The parable of the talents (Matt. 25:14-30) dispenses with the rustic setting of so many parables and takes us instead into a commercial world of money and finances. The story tells how a wealthy man, before going on a distant journey, distributes his wealth to three servants. Two of the servants invest their master's money and double the amount by the time their employer returns. The third servant hides his weight of money in the ground. In terms of underlying idea, the parable is concerned with stewardship, or management of a master's entrusted possessions.

As a story, the parable depends on several narrative motifs. One is the motif of testing. The entrusted wealth becomes a test of the ability and stewardship of the servants, with the delayed return of the master intensifying the suspense of the testing. A second narrative device is poetic justice, which here takes the form of rewarding the virtuous servants (Matt. 25:21, 23) and punishing the slothful servant (vss. 26-30). A third narrative strand is the character conflict between the unprofitable servant and his master. Faced with his own lack of activity and productiveness, the servant attacks the character of his master (vs. 24). The master meets the servant on his own terms and, instead of defending his character, makes an assault on the integrity of the servant with the words, "You wicked and slothful servant!" (vs. 26). A final narrative motif, common in folk stories, is the use of a pattern of three, with stress on the third instance.

The parable is an example of continuous allegory. Many details in the story have a meaning on the spiritual level. The master is God, and the three servants represent people. The entrusted talents, literally weights of money (probably worth about a thousand dollars each), symbolize people's abilities and opportunities to serve God. The return after a long journey is Christ's coming at the end of history, the reward and punishment are the final judgment, the outer darkness is hell, and the joy of the lord is the joy of heaven.

Several themes are implicit in this allegory. The story shows that

God gives abilities and opportunities to people and that He demands that His creatures use their opportunities in productive service for Him. There will be ultimate reward for service and punishment for sloth. The story is an indictment of people who do not try, who do not develop and progress, and who use their lives as an occasion for repudiating God instead of serving Him. The fact that the master gives different amounts of wealth to his servants suggests a hierarchy of abilities and opportunities in human experience. Regardless of how much one has been given, the expectation is the same — a person must serve God with what he has. Nothing should be made of the fact, incidentally, that it is the servant who received the least wealth who failed to achieve. The narrative states clearly that the master gave "to each according to his ability" (vs. 15); if the servant who received one talent could not manage even that amount, obviously he would not have succeeded with a greater amount. The important thing is not how much one is given but rather what he does with what he has been given.

When we consider the matter of the parable's application, it is essential to realize that it occurs in Jesus' Olivet Discourse, in which He answered the disciples' question regarding what it would be like at the end of the age (Matt. 24:3). The parable fits into this eschatalogical context on several levels. It asserts that despite a long delay (the master returns "after a long time" — vs. 19), Jesus will come again. It is a call for endurance over the long haul, since final reward and punishment will not come quickly. The emphasis of the story is on reward and judgment. The parable teaches that heaven or hell is the destination of all people. It is a motivation for believers to serve God with diligence while He delays His return, and for unbelievers to repent while there is still time. Above all, the parable stresses the need to be responsible stewards of what God has given, for judgment will be partly on the basis of works. Like many another of Jesus' parables, this one impresses the hearer with the seriousness of God's kingdom. It also takes its place with many parables that teach people to order their lives by an awareness of what the end of history and eternity will be like. Eschatology is never theoretic in the parables; it is the basis for life and action.

The parable of the good Samaritan (Luke 10:25-37) is a contrast to the parables considered thus far. It is not explicit or continuous allegory. It is near the middle of the allegorical spectrum. The details of the story do not have a corresponding conceptual meaning, and we do not transfer the meaning of the story to another level. The surface meaning is here the real meaning.

The story uses several narrative techniques. There is conflict between the robbers and the victim, and contrast between the priest and Levite on the one hand and the Samaritan on the other. The motif of testing enters the story when the injured man in the middle of the road becomes a test of the humanitarian compassion of all who travel over the road. There is climax in the story, based on the folktale motif of threefold repetition. In this case, the Samaritan's actions assume greater force because of the two previous refusals of aid. Also, the appearance of the Samaritan in the third position on the list may have reversed the expectations of Christ's audience, which was accustomed to thinking in the categories of priest, Levite, and Israelite instead of (as in the parable) priest, Levite, and Samaritan. Yet another literary ingredient of the story is satire, here an attack on the ecclesiastical elite of Jesus' day.

The parable is not concerned with doctrine but with ethics — with practical Christian living as it touches upon relations with other people. We might call the story an exemplum, in the medieval definition of a story in which a character displays ideal behavior that serves as a model for others to follow. It is designed to move the listener to moral action.

Since the story depends for its effect on the sequential unfolding of the action, its explication should be closely tied to the forward progress of the narrative. As in the case of many other recorded parables, the context in which Jesus told the parable of the good Samaritan explains a great deal. We read that "a lawyer stood up to put him to the test, saying, 'Teacher, what shall I do to inherit eternal life?'" (Luke 10:25). This frame shows that the parable arose from the heat of controversy. When Jesus tells the story of the Samaritan, He answers the exact question of the lawyer very precisely, for the parable does, in fact, emphasize doing.

Jesus responds to the lawyer's question by affirming the efficacy of the Old Testament moral law as the right way to attain spiritual life (Luke 10:26-28). The significance of this affirmation is that it shows that Christ's real attack was not on the theory of the religious leaders of His day but on their faulty application of the law. We read further that the lawyer desired "to justify himself" (vs. 29). The most likely inference is that the lawyer was trying to justify his racism before his own conscience. His further question is the one that prompts the parable: "And who is my neighbor?" (vs. 29). The parable that follows is a literary definition of "neighbor."

Precise realism underlies the story. The violent action with which the narrative begins would not have been unexpected in Jesus' day, since lone travelers from Jerusalem to Jericho were easy victims for robbers. There is even a touch of geographic realism in the statement that the man went "down" from Jerusalem to Jericho (Luke 10:30), since the trip did involve a literal descent in altitude. Similar realism underlies the account of a priest going down the same route as the victim had taken. In Christ's day many priests who served in Jerusalem actually lived in Jericho. We are not told why the priest passed by on the other side. He may have simply lacked compassion. In the background of the parable was the fact that robbers sometimes used supposedly wounded people as decoys, putting travelers at a disadvantage if they stooped over the decoy to investigate. Whatever the reason for the priest's action, he becomes the object of satiric attack, with his high religious standing increasing his condemnation.

The Levite who passes by reinforces the ecclesiastical satire against the religious elite. Levites were also ministers in the temple. There was a Jewish ceremonial law (Num. 19:11) that made anyone who touched a dead body unclean for seven days. If the Levite was enroute to a stint of service in Jerusalem, he may have been deterred from helping the wounded man by the fact that he would have been unable to carry out his religious function for a whole week. If this is the situation, the parable becomes an interesting conflict between established religious rules and moral compassion for people in need.

In the final phase of the action, moral behavior comes from the least likely person, a Samaritan. Given the prevailing Jewish attitude, to speak of a good Samaritan would have been a contradiction in terms. It is significant that the Samaritan is first said to have "had compassion" (Luke 10:33) and then to have cared for the physical needs of the wounded man. This detail focuses attention on the inner attitude that leads to good moral action. The compassionate acts of provision that the Samaritan undertakes for the injured person are told in such detail (vss. 34-35) that they heighten the contrast between the Samaritan and the two religious officials.

Jesus clinches the point of the parable by returning to the context out of which the story grew. He asks the lawyer, "Which of these three, do you think, proved neighbor to the man who fell among the robbers?" (vs. 36). The bigoted Jewish lawyer cannot bring himself to use the despised word "Samaritan," so he replies, "The one who showed mercy on him" (vs. 37). Recalling that the lawyer's original question had concerned what he must *do* to inherit eternal life, Jesus concludes His discussion by saying, "Go and *do* likewise" (vs. 37). This command shows that the parable has been an exemplum in which a model character has been held up as a pattern for others to follow.

The primary application of the parable is that it answers the immediate question, "Who is my neighbor?" Jesus uses the narrative to show that our neighbor is anyone whom we encounter in need. But the parable has a broader application than this. It also answers the question, "What is my duty toward my neighbor?" by indicating that our duty is to go out of our way to help those in need, even at risk to our own safety and comfort. The parable, furthermore, is an attack on the religious establishment of Jesus' day, on the hypocrisy of the ecclesiastical elite, and on the racism of the Jews in general. The parable remains to this day a touchstone for Christian ethics. It shows that the real test of religion is service to others. In its clarity and emphasis on practical moral action it cuts through abstract theological speculation and leaves the reader with the challenge to put his ethical principles to work.

The parable of the forgiving father (Luke 15:11-32), popularly known by the somewhat misleading title of the parable of the prodigal son, represents the technique of the parable at its most sophisticated and intricate. It is a fairly long story with complication of action and subtlety of characterization. The three-phase story emphasizes differentiation of characters and the relationships among them, with particular attention given to child rebellion, parental love, and sibling rivalry. The story also draws upon several archetypal plot patterns, including the journey (here a circular withdrawal-return journey, common in literature), the death-rebirth motif, and the initiation motif (initiation into sin and its consequences, into adulthood, into the hardships and suffering of life). The prodigal or wastrel is an archetypal character type. The story is constructed around the emotional climax of the reconciliation of father and son, and there is effective use of dialogue and realistic detail to evoke an explicit picture of what takes place.

This parable, like most of Jesus' parables, is Jesus' half of an argument in which He found Himself. We read that "the Pharisees and the scribes murmured, saying, 'This man receives sinners and eats with them'" (vs. 2). In replying, Jesus told two short parables, the parables of the lost sheep and the lost coin, both of which stress God's joy in receiving repentant sinners into fellowship. The story involving the lost son, the forgiving father, and the belligerent older son is the third parable in this series of parables on the common theme of God's restoration of repentant sinners.

The opening of the parable is delightfully conventional, even to the point of being childlike: "There was a man who had two sons" (vs. 11). The action begins with the younger son's demand, "Father, give me the share of property that falls to me" (vs. 12). In view of the son's later confession that he had sinned against his father (vs. 18), his act of requesting the inheritance must be viewed in a negative light. His attitude is callous and calculating, as though the inheritance was his right rather than a gift. The father surprisingly takes it all in stride, giving the foolish son his share of the inheritance, which would have been one-third of the estate (the elder son received a double portion in Jewish custom).

The picture of the prodigal son wasting his money in immoral indulgence is told with stark simplicity: "Not many days later, the younger son gathered all he had and took his journey into a far country, and there he squandered his property in loose living" (vs. 13). As in many another work of literature, it is human suffering that contributes to the character development of the son. We read that "when he had spent everything, a great famine arose in that country, and he began to be in want" (vs. 14). A few vivid details portray the depths to which the son falls as he is initiated into the world of adulthood and moral consequences: "So he went and joined himself to one of the citizens of that country, who sent him into his fields to feed swine. And he would gladly have fed on the pods that the swine ate; and no one gave him anything" (vss. 15-16). In the background is the fact that swine were unclean animals to the Jew (Lev. 11:7). To eat the food of the pigs would reduce one to a sub-human level; even this is denied to the younger son.

The turning point in the son's development comes when he reaches moral perception. His recognition of his moral failing to date is conveyed by the statement that "when he came to himself" he decided to return to his father (Luke 15:17). The son's reasoning that many of his father's "hired servants have bread enough and to spare" (vs. 17) must be understood in terms of the three kinds of employees in the Jewish culture of the day. Hired servants were the lowest of three categories of servants. The categories were bondmen (slaves with good family standing), servants (subordinates of the slaves), and hired servants (hired for the occasion). That the parable intends to picture the spiritual act of confession is evident from the words in which the son couches his resolution to return to his father: "I will arise and go to my father, and I will say to him, 'Father, I have sinned against heaven and before you; I am no longer worthy to be called your son; treat me as one of your hired servants'" (vss. 18-19).

In the second phase of the action, the character of the father becomes the focus of interest. The father reverses our expectations of disapproval by having compassion on his returning son and embracing him (vs. 20). The father also rejects the son's offer to be accepted as a hired servant and instead commands, "Bring quickly the best robe, and put it on him; and put a ring on his hand, and shoes on his feet; and bring the fatted calf and kill it, and let us eat and make merry" (vss. 22-23). The command communicates its meaning through symbols. The robe would symbolize the honor with which the son was being received into family fellowship. The ring, if it was a signet ring, would signify great status for the son, who was being granted the rights and authority of a member of the ruling family instead of being subordinated as a slave. The shoes would also represent his status as a son, since slaves went barefoot. Yet another index to the exalted nature of the son's reception is the fatted calf, which in biblical times was reserved for occasions when a host entertained a special guest. The reason given by the father for the honor accorded to the returning son links the plot to the death-rebirth archetype: "for this my son was dead, and is alive again; he was lost, and is found" (vs. 24). This language is appropriate on the literal, narrative level, but in a biblical context it also has theological meanings, making it clear that on an allegorical level the parable is depicting the spiritual conversion or repentance of a sinner.

In the third act of the drama, Jesus turns the story into a satiric attack on the scribes and Pharisees. The stimulus to the parable, we must remember, had been the complaint of the scribes and Pharisees that Jesus associated with sinners. This attitude is embodied in the elder son of the parable. As a literary character the elder son belongs to the familiar archetype of the refuser of festivities. In response to his father's entreaty to join the celebration, the son replies, "Lo, these many years I have served you, and I never disobeyed your command; yet you never gave me a kid, that I might make merry with my friends" (vs. 29). Although there may be a note of self-righteousness in these words, this is not the crucial issue in the case against the elder brother. Surely it was nothing less than admirable for the son to have been so conscientious in fulfilling his family duties toward his father.

The thing that makes the elder so unattractive is his unwillingness to rejoice in the repentance of his brother. This comes out when he states, "But when this son of yours came, who has devoured your living with harlots, you killed for him the fatted calf!" (vs. 30). The elder son does not understand the nature of either repentance or forgiveness. He does not perceive the new nature of his brother, seeing him only as the prodigal of the past. And instead of understanding that forgiveness involves foregoing the penalty for sin, he thinks only in terms of the punishment that his brother should receive. He is even unwilling to accept the younger son as his brother, as evidenced by his reference to "this son of yours," rather than "my brother." These aspects of the story stand as an exposure of the unforgiving attitudes of the Pharisees.

The response of the father to the elder son is an important comment on both sons. The father states, "Son, you are always with me, and all that is mine is yours. It was fitting to make merry and be glad, for this your brother was dead, and is alive; he was lost, and is found" (vss. 31-32). This is the satiric norm by which the elder son's attitude is shown to be deficient. He himself is rich in inheritance, so that he is inexcusable in begrudging his brother the festal reception. Furthermore, the celebration is shown to be appropriate because of the reclamation of the younger son. But if the father's statement is a rebuke of the elder son's inability to get beyond himself, it is also an interesting comment on the final state of the younger son. The father's statement that "all that is mine is yours" (vs. 31) shows that the prodigal son's sin had permanent consequences in his life. He did not receive compensation for his squandered inheritance.

The parable has several themes and applications. For one thing, it depicts the Gospel in its essence. Surely the focus of the story is on God's forgiving love toward the sinner. It shows that God loves sinners as well as the righteous. The emphasis is on the joy that accompanies God's forgiveness of the penitent sinner. The application of this central thrust of the parable is perpetually relevant to man and answers the most basic of all religious questions, namely, What is God like? The parable also emphasizes the human responsibility in the divine-human relationship. Misery is shown to result from the creature's sinful acts. The younger son would have been better off if he had never left his father in the first place. His sin is self-assertion — a declaration of independence from his father. The parable also shows the human responsibility to seek forgiveness through confession and repentance. Finally, the parable is an exposure of the ugly attitudes of people who refuse to share the joy of others and who do not understand the true nature of forgiveness.

The parable was one of the commonest forms used by Jesus — so common, in fact, that Mark comments that Jesus "did not speak to them without a parable" (Mark 4:34). It is evident that Jesus did not share the bias against fiction that has existed in Western thought. We might profitably ask why Jesus used fiction as His medium.

Makers of literature, including Jesus, use fiction partly because it appeals to a deep-seated human capacity to enjoy an imaginative story. Like the other human faculties, the imagination asks to be exercised. By using fictional stories, an author satisfies this unconscious as well as conscious capacity for imaginative narrative.

A second function served by fiction is that it is often the best or even the only medium by which a writer can express his vision. Makers of fiction have something true to say about life, but they can say it only by embodying it in an imaginative projection of life. The imagined world of fiction, rather than the real world of fact, is sometimes the world where the issues can be seen in greatest clarity. It is evident that Jesus often looked upon fiction as the most accurate form for expressing His teachings.

The "Marble Street" of Ephesus.

Epistle and Oratory in the New Testament

16

I

The letter is on the periphery of what most literary critics would consider to be literature. As a form of written discourse it ranges on a continuum from the expository to the literary. At the former end of the spectrum is the letter whose main purpose is simply to convey information. Letters that merit the literary title of epistle have several distinguishing features. Some epistles, especially those written with publication in mind, can be considered artistic by virtue of their mastery of rhetorical forms and eloquence of style. Epistles also sometimes constitute a branch of autobiography and are considered literary because of the emergence of the writer as a protagonist or because of the experiential view they give of an era. The epistolary form can be a matter of literary artifice, providing a framework for what is really a general treatise on a subject.

In general, the New Testament epistles do not conform closely to any existing models. For one thing, they show an unusual mixture of the personal letter and the more formalized literary epistle. They contain the personal notes, salutations, and news that informal letters contain, and they are addressed, for the most part, to specific readers (in contrast to literary epistles intended for publication, which assume a generalized audience and lack specific addresses to a reader). But along with this informality, there is much that is obviously formalized in the epistles. Their tone is more public than intimate. The personality of the writers is much less important than the religious content of their letters. The writers, indeed, do not write primarily as individual persons but in their role as apostles — as the conveyors of divine truth in a manner reminiscent of the Hebrew prophets. The destination of the epistles is usually the believing community, either a local church or a group of churches. Everything considered, the New Testament epistles are an extension of the Gospels. Both were written by authoritative Christian leaders and both existed to explain the life and teachings of Jesus.

II

The most important of the New Testament letter writers was Paul. His epistle to the Ephesians is exemplary of some typical features of the New Testament epistle. Written during Paul's imprisonment, the letter was intended for general circulation among several churches and therefore has the public tone that the epistles generally display. Although it omits the customary section of thanksgiving, the epistle otherwise follows the structure that is characteristic of Paul's epistles: a salutation (1:1-2), an exposition of Christian doctrine (1:3–3:21), a section of practical exhortations (4:1–6:20), and a section of personal messages and salutations (6:21-24).

The epistle to the Ephesians is closely unified around the controlling theme of the church. With this as the focal point, Paul develops a series of related themes — the divine origin of the church (1:3-14), Christ's salvation of the church (2:1-10), the unity and concord of the church (2:11-22), and the calling or purpose of the church (ch. 3). Following these doctrinal affirmations, Paul articulates the practical implications, which include unity among church members (4:1-16), moral standards for believers (4:17–5:20), and rules for the Christian household (5:21–6:9).

This outline of the epistle hardly hints at its literary qualities. The life of the New Testament epistles is in the words themselves. Their literary mastery is evident when we pay attention to the more minute aspects of stylistics. The Ephesian letter, for example, is full of Paul's typical long, suspended sentences (whose meaning is left incomplete over a number of phrases). These sentences are filled to overflowing with evocative words and build gradually to a climax of eloquence. A single illustration, the prayer in 1:15-23, will have to suffice:

For this reason,
  because I have heard of your faith in the Lord Jesus and
                 your love toward all the saints,
I do not cease to give thanks for you,
  remembering you in my prayers,
  that the God of our Lord Jesus Christ,
      the Father of glory,
  may give you a spirit of wisdom and
                     of revelation in the knowledge of him,
                         having the eyes of your hearts enlightened,
    that you may know what is the hope to which he has called you,
                     what are the riches of his glorious inheritance
                     in the saints,
                     what is the immeasurable greatness of his power
                     in us who believe,

> according to the working of his great might
>> which he accomplished in Christ
>> when he raised him from the dead and
>>> made him sit at his right hand in the heavenly places,
>>>> far above all rule
>>>>> and authority
>>>>> and power
>>>>> and dominion, and
>>>> above every name that is
>>>> named,
>>>>> not only in this age
>>>>> but also in that which
>>>>> is to come;
>>> and he has put all things under his feet and
>>>> has made him the head over all things for the church,
>>>>> which is his body,
>>>>>> the fulness of him who fills all in all.

The literary effects are achieved here through the controlled movement of a succession of related clauses, the use of parallel clauses, the inclusion of evocative words and images (God, glory, wisdom, hope, light, riches, power, heavenly places, fulness), the use of stately epithets ("the Lord Jesus," "the God of our Lord Jesus Christ," "the Father of glory," "him who fills all in all"), and allusions to events in the redemptive life of Jesus.

Paul was a master of the eloquent climax, known in ancient rhetoric as the "peroration." In the letter to the Ephesians, this eloquent summary (6:10-17) consists of an extended metaphor that compares the Christian life to a military battle and the Christian's resources to a set of armor. The passage gains its forcefulness through the vividness and aptness of the metaphors, the underlying plot conflict, and the use of parallelism:

> Finally, be strong in the Lord and
>> in the strength of his might.
>> Put on the whole armor of God,
>>> that you may be able to stand against the wiles of the devil.
>>> For we are not contending against flesh and blood, but
>>>> against the principalities,
>>>> against the powers,
>>>> against the world rulers of this
>>>> present darkness,
>>>> against the spiritual hosts of wicked-
>>>> ness in the heavenly places.
>> Therefore take the whole armor of God,
>>> that you may be able to withstand in the evil day,
>>> and having done all, to stand.
>> Stand therefore, having girded your loins with truth, and
>>> having put on the breastplate of righteousness, and

> *having shod your feet with the equipment of the*
>   *gospel of peace;*
> *above all taking the shield of faith,*
>   *with which you can quench all the flaming darts*
>   *of the evil one.*
> *And take the helmet of salvation, and*
>   *the sword of the Spirit,*
>   *which is the word of God.*

III

As I have suggested, the literary genius of the New Testament epistles is seen not so much in the features of the epistle as a written form but in the stylistic richness that confronts the reader everywhere. Again and again we find in the epistles mastery of the high style, of rhetorical technique, and of figures of speech. The best known examples come from Paul but are by no means limited to him.

Even a salutation in Paul's letters is likely to be fired with the exaltation of the high style. The opening of his letter to the Romans is an example:

> *Paul, a servant of Jesus Christ,*
>   *called to be an apostle,*
>   *set apart for the gospel of God*
>   *which he promised beforehand through his prophets*
>   *in the holy scriptures,*
>   *the gospel concerning his Son,*
>   *who was descended from David according to the flesh and*
>   *designated Son of God in power according to the Spirit of*
>   *holiness by his resurrection from the dead,*
>   *Jesus Christ our Lord,*
>   *through whom we have received grace and apostleship*
>   *to bring about the obedience to the faith*
>   *for the sake of his name*
>   *among all the nations,*
>   *including yourselves who are called to belong to Jesus Christ;*
> *To all God's beloved in Rome,*
>   *who are called to be saints:*
> *Grace to you and peace from God our Father and*
>   *the Lord Jesus Christ.*

A suspended sentence such as this, with its series of clauses moving ever forward to the end, is like a great stream on which we embark as we begin to read.

Embedded in Paul's expository writing are a number of lyric passages, some of which may have existed independently as hymns or creeds:

320

There is one body and one Spirit,
just as you were called to the one hope that belongs to your call,
   one Lord,
   one faith,
   one baptism,
   one God and Father of us all,
   who is above all and
       through all and
       in all.
                 (Eph. 4:4-6)

Great indeed, we confess, is the mystery of our religion:
He was manifested in the flesh,
     vindicated in the Spirit,
     seen by angels,
     preached among the nations,
     believed on in the world,
     taken up in glory.
                 (1 Tim. 3:16)

The saying is true:
   If we have died with him, we shall also live with him;
   if we endure, we shall also reign with him;
   if we deny him, he also will deny us;
   if we are faithless, he remains faithful —
      for he cannot deny himself.
              (2 Tim. 2:11-13)

Paul's skill at writing a magnificent conclusion is well illustrated from Romans 8:31-39, where he ends a long theological discussion about justification with his famous peroration in praise of Christ's inseparable love. The passage begins with a series of rhetorical questions, all of them constituting reasons not to be fearful:

What then shall we say to this?
   If God is for us, who is against us?
   He who did not spare his own Son but gave him up for us all,
     will he not also give us all things with him?
   Who shall bring any charge against God's elect?
   It is God who justifies; who is to condemn?
   Is it Christ Jesus, who died, yes,
              who was raised from the dead,
              who is at the right hand of God,
              who indeed intercedes for us?
Who shall separate us from the love of Christ?
Shall tribulation,
   or distress,
   or persecution,
   or famine,
   or nakedness,
   or peril,
   or sword?

An allusion to a Psalm (44:22) furnishes a brief interlude in the onward sweep (8:36). Then Paul moves from the rhetorical questions to a great declaration. He first states a generalization in reply to the earlier list of questions: "No, in all these things we are more than conquerors through him who loved us." Paul fills out his thesis by listing the obstacles that cannot separate the believer from the love of God:

For I am sure that neither death,
>*nor life,*
>*nor angels,*
>*nor principalities,*
>*nor things present,*
>*nor things to come,*
>*nor powers,*
>*nor height,*
>*nor depth,*
>*nor anything else in all creation,*

will be able to separate us from the love of God in Christ Jesus our Lord.

In addition to the parallelism, Paul has used balance and antithesis to add vigor to his assertion.

We do well to ask what the high style adds to the meaning of such an utterance. What does Paul communicate that is not conveyed in the bare statement, "I am persuaded that nothing can separate us from the love of God"? Is the exalted style only an embellishment? In passages such as this, the form is part of the meaning. Paul's statement conveys an ecstasy and an emotional conviction that is an important part of his meaning and that would be lacking in an unadorned style.

Another illustration of the deeper meanings that Paul is able to convey through his use of rhetorical forms is his concluding exhortation to the Philippians (4:8):

>*Finally, brethren, whatever is true,*
>>*whatever is honorable,*
>>*whatever is just,*
>>*whatever is pure,*
>>*whatever is lovely,*
>>*whatever is gracious,*
>>>*if there is any excellence,*
>>>*if there is anything worthy of praise,*
>>>>*think about these things.*

This is one of the most evocative passages in the Bible. It overflows with positive connotations, thereby serving the persuasive function of instilling a desire to follow the injunction that Paul expresses in the passage.

The persuasive use of the exalted style is equally evident when Paul uses parallel listings to convince the Philippians that unity is a possibility in the believing community (Phil. 2:1-2):

> *So if there is any encouragement in Christ,*
> *any incentive of love,*
> *any participation in the Spirit,*
> *any affection and sympathy,*
> *complete my joy by being of the same mind,*
> *having the same love,*
> *being in full accord and of one mind.*

Although Paul was not a narrative writer, he frequently uses the antithesis of opposing forces to make his utterances compelling. One thinks at once of his famous contrasts between the flesh and the Spirit (Rom. 8:2-11), the physical body and the spiritual body (1 Cor. 15:42-54), the works of the flesh and the fruits of the Spirit (Gal. 5:19-23). In describing his ministry to the Corinthians, Paul lends his utterance the vigor of plot conflict through his use of antithesis (2 Cor. 4:8-9):

> *We are afflicted in every way, but not crushed;*
> *perplexed, but not driven to despair;*
> *persecuted, but not forsaken;*
> *struck down, but not destroyed.*

Often the memorable oppositions of Paul merge into paradox, as the following passage (2 Cor. 6:8-10) illustrates:

> *We are treated as imposters, and yet are true;*
> *as unknown, and yet well known;*
> *as dying, and behold we live;*
> *as punished, and yet not killed;*
> *as sorrowful, yet always rejoicing;*
> *as poor, yet making many rich;*
> *as having nothing, and yet possessing everything.*

Paul's mastery of literary style reaches a high point in his discourse about the certainty and nature of the resurrection of the body (1 Cor. 15). Parallelism, repetition, balance, and antithesis pervade the conclusion of the discourse:

What is sown is perishable, what is raised is imperishable.
It is sown in dishonor, it is raised in glory.
It is sown in weakness, it is raised in power.

It is sown a physical body, it is raised a spiritual body.
If there is a physical body, there is also a spiritual body. . . .
The first man was from the earth, a man of dust;
    the second man is from heaven.
As was the man of dust, so are those who are of the dust;
and as we have borne the image of the man of dust,
    we shall also bear the image of the man of heaven. . . .
Lo! I tell you a mystery.
We shall not all sleep, but we shall all be changed,
    in a moment,
    in the twinkling of an eye,
    at the last trumpet.
For the trumpet will sound,
    and the dead will be raised imperishable,
    and we shall be changed.
For this perishable nature must put on the imperishable,
    and this mortal nature must put on immortality.
When the perishable puts on the imperishable,
    and the mortal puts on immortality,
then shall come to pass the saying that is written:
    'Death is swallowed up in victory.'
'O death, where is thy victory?
O death, where is thy sting?'
The sting of death is sin,
    and the power of sin is the law.
But thanks be to God,
    who gives us the victory through our Lord Jesus Christ.
Therefore, my beloved brethren, be steadfast,
                            immovable,
                            always abounding in the work of the Lord,
                            knowing that in the Lord your labor is
                                not in vain.

In addition to the larger elements of pattern in this passage, we can note several instances of clauses arranged in triplet form, the metaphoric comparison of death to sleep, the taunting apostrophes to death, and the personification of death.

The most artistic discourse of Paul is probably 1 Corinthians 13, which I have already discussed in terms of the conventions of the encomium. Balance, parallelism, and contrast are the basic rhetorical forms used in the discourse, with many of the smaller units falling into threefold patterns.

The first triad comes at the very beginning. In three successive verses, Paul uses the threefold formula, "If I . . . , but have not love, . . . nothing." Within this formalized structure, Paul makes use of further repetition and contrast:

> *1 If I speak in the tongues of men and*
>   *of angels,*

> but have not love,
> I am a noisy gong or
> a clanging cymbal.
> 2 And if I have prophetic powers, and
> understand all mysteries and
> all knowledge,
> and if I have all faith,
> so as to remove mountains,
> but have not love,
> I am nothing.
> 3 If I give away all I have, and
> if I deliver my body to be burned,
> but have not love,
> I gain nothing.

The subsequent passage is also a triplet, as the list of the acts of love consists of three successive clauses that have the word "love" as the subject of the verbs that follow:[1]

> 4 Love is longsuffering,
> is kind;
> love envieth not;
> love vaunteth not itself,
> is not puffed up,
> 5 doth not behave itself unseemly,
> seeketh not its own,
> is not easily provoked,
> imputeth not the evil;
> 6 rejoiceth not at unrighteousness, but
> rejoiceth with the truth;
> 7 beareth all things,
> believeth all things,
> hopeth all things,
> endureth all things.

The passage is replete with parallelism and contains an example of antithesis in verse 6.

Verse 8 is based on a contrast between the permanence of love and the transience of three spiritual gifts, with the latter group falling again into the pattern of a triplet:

> Love never ends;
> as for prophecy, it will pass away;
> as for tongues, they will cease;
> as for knowledge, it will pass away.

The triad pattern continues in verses 9 and 10, which use the word

---

[1] English translations tend to obscure Paul's rhetorical pattern in verses 4 to 7. My quotation of the passage is based on Henry Alford, *The New Testament for English Readers* (Chicago: Moody Press, no date).

"imperfect" three times and also contain a contrast between the concepts of "imperfect" and "perfect":

> 9 For our knowledge is imperfect and
>   our prophecy is imperfect;
> 10 But when the perfect comes,
>   the imperfect will pass away.

Repetition and contrast pervade the next verses, where Paul uses analogy to explain the reason for the transience of the three spiritual gifts. The figure of childhood immaturity falls into another triplet of clauses:

> 11 When I was a child, I spoke like a child,
>   I thought like a child,
>   I reasoned like a child.

The next clause introduces a contrast: "when I became a man, I gave up childish ways." Verse 12 continues the antithetical mode, mentioning contrasts between "now" and "then," "dimly" and "face to face," "in part" and "fully":

> For now we see in a mirror dimly,
>   but then face to face.
> Now I know in part;
>   then I shall understand fully,
>   even as I have been fully understood.

The threefold pattern reaches its climax in the famous aphorism that concludes the discourse:

> 13 So faith, hope, love abide, these three;
>   but the greatest of these is love.

It would be misleading to leave the impression that the stylistic brilliance of New Testament epistolary literature is the exclusive property of Paul. The style of the epistles is continuously great. For a concluding example, we can observe the metaphoric richness, the argument from analogy, the antithesis and rhetorical questions of the following passage from James (3:6-12):

> And the tongue is a fire.
> The tongue is an unrighteous world among our members,
>   staining the whole body,
>   setting on fire the cycle of nature,
>   and set on fire by hell.
> For every kind of beast and bird,
>   of reptile and sea creature,

can be tamed and has been tamed by humankind,
but no human being can tame the tongue —
 a restless evil,
 full of deadly poison.
  With it we bless the Lord and Father, and
  with it we curse men, who are made in the likeness of God.
  From the same mouth come blessing and cursing.
   my brethren, this ought not to be so.
Does a spring pour forth from the same opening fresh water and brackish?
Can a fig tree, my brethren, yield olives,
 or a grapevine figs?
No more can salt water yield fresh.

IV

There is a close relationship between the New Testament epistles and oratory. Most of the epistles were written with a view toward their being read aloud in congregational meetings. Paul, moreover, composed most of his letters orally while dictating them to a secretary. As a result, New Testament epistles and oratories show great similarity of style.

The oratorical ability of Paul is attested both by the examples of his speeches that are included in the New Testament and by the narrative accounts of the effect of his speaking on various audiences. At Lystra the listeners honored Paul as Mercury, god of eloquence. After his first recorded sermon (Acts 13:16-41) the people of Antioch were so impressed that "the next sabbath almost the whole city gathered together to hear the word of God" (Acts 13:44). At Jerusalem Paul temporarily controlled an enraged mob with his eloquence (Acts 21:17–22:24). His address before Felix filled his listener with conviction (Acts 24:25).

Of all the addresses of Paul recorded in the New Testament, his oration before the Areopagus in Athens (Acts 17:16-33) is the one that is surrounded with the most drama. The Athenian oration has evoked a great amount of commentary and disagreement. In particular, scholars have been troubled by the need to reconcile Paul's seeming approval of the pagan assumptions of his audience with the uncompromising Christian witness that is customary in his preaching. I believe that the key to the interpretation of the Athenian address lies in a literary approach, that is, one which pays close attention to the narrative details given in Acts 17 and which places the oration in the context of the rules of classical rhetoric and oratory.

The narrative tells us what we need to know about the circumstances surrounding the oration. We learn, for example, that the thing that prompted Paul to speak was his horror at the idolatry that he saw around him: "Now while Paul was waiting ... at Athens, his spirit was provoked within him as he saw that the city was full of idols" (vs. 16). The people who cleared the way for him to speak were "the Epicurean and Stoic philosophers" (vs. 18). This means that Paul was addressing an intellectual audience, not the man on the street with his crude idolatry. There has been disagreement about what is meant by the statement that Paul was brought "to the Areopagus" (vs. 19) to deliver his address. The Areopagus was both a hill and a council of men who exercised control over the public speaking that went on in Athens. There would seem to be good evidence for concluding that Paul spoke before this council or court, having been asked to demonstrate his credentials as a speaker in the market place. We read that Paul stood "in the middle of the Areopagus" (vs. 22) and that at the end "Paul went out from among them" (vs. 33), indicating that Paul stood before a group of men known as "the Areopagus." If we realize that the address was delivered to a dignified council, we are in a better position to understand the drama of the occasion and the reason for the dignity of Paul's address, which adheres to the best form of classical oration and is replete with allusions to Homer, Plato, and other Greek writers.

The narrative framework also informs us that the oration is a truncated address, cut short by the interruption of the audience. It is often claimed that the address as it has been recorded in Acts is a summary of a much longer address. If we look closely at the text, however, this conclusion appears very doubtful. The dignified opening of the address shows no sign of being condensed. The style is leisurely and drawn out. There are relatively long sentences and the inclusion of parallel constructions (vss. 24-25, 29). The account given in Acts even includes the quotations that Paul made of several Greek poets. Furthermore, verse 32 states clearly that "when they heard of the resurrection of the dead, some mocked," indicating that at a specific point in the address the audience made it impossible for Paul to continue.

The narrative context, when combined with an awareness of the structure of a classical oration, gives us the key to the interpretation of the Athenian address. According to classical rhetoric, the first part of an address was the "exordium." This was the introduction to the main part of the speech. According to Quintilian, a contemporary of Paul, the aim of the exordium was "to prepare the hearer to listen to us more readily in the subsequent parts of our pleading. This object, as is agreed among most authors, is principally effected by three means, by securing his good will and attention, and by rendering him desirous of further information."[2] The introduction, in short, was designed to ingratiate the speaker with his audience. A common way of gaining the attention of the listeners was to cite some anecdote that would interest them.

The recorded oration of Paul to the Areopagus is virtually all exordium. In it Paul's whole purpose is to establish rapport with his listeners, to say things with which they will agree, to find a common base, to make his audience feel that they have begun their quest for God with the right conception and *then* to add the Christian distinctives in the main part of the message.

Paul begins his dignified oration with the formula that the famous Athenian orator Demosthenes used to open his addresses — "Men of Athens" (vs. 22). He then gives an assessment of the character of the Athenians, appealing to the interest that any audience has in how a visitor views them: "I perceive that in every way you are very religious" (vs. 22). This is a commendation and an attempt to find common ground between Paul and his audience. The word translated "religious" could mean either "superstitious," with negative connotations, or "religious," with positive connotations. Obviously Paul is using it in the favorable sense as part of his strategy to gain a sympathetic hearing.

Paul next uses the time-honored technique of recounting an anecdote, in this case one that involved the listeners themselves: "For as I passed along, and observed the objects of your worship, I found also an altar with this inscription, 'To an unknown God' " (vs. 23). In the second half of the verse, Paul announces his topic: "What therefore you worship as unknown, this I proclaim to you." Paul is here defining his audience very carefully. He is not appealing to the crass worshiper of physical idols. He is addressing philosophers or anyone else for whom the altar to the unknown god summed up their religious state of mind. An altar to an unknown god implies people who have religious sensitivity, who believe that there is a god, but who have not yet found this god. The inscription would appeal to someone dissatisfied with, and skeptical of, the existing religious climate. Paul is appealing to such people, playing on their dissatisfaction and building upon it.

As Paul proceeds to talk about the God whom he and his audience agree exists, he first stresses something with which his intelligent audience would agree — that God cannot be confined in physical idols: "The God who made the world and everything in it, being Lord of heaven and earth, does not live in shrines made by man, nor is he served by human hands, as though he needed anything,

---

[2] Quoted from Kenneth Myrick, *Sir Philip Sidney as a Literary Craftsman* (Lincoln: University of Nebraska Press, 1965), p. 55.

since he himself gives to all men life and breath and everything" (vss. 24-25). We must bear in mind that Paul is addressing persons who are dissatisfied with the existing idol worship, as evidenced by their declaration that their god is still an unknown god.

Verses 26 and 27 simply continue Paul's very general remarks about universal theism. He claims that there is a universal divine being, that man has a religious consciousness, and that men who seek God can find Him: "And he made from one every nation of men to live on all the face of the earth, having determined allotted periods and the boundaries of their habitation, that they should seek God, in the hope that they might feel after him and find him. Yet he is not far from each one of us." As developed by Paul in his exordium, there is nothing distinctively Christian about this. Paul is simply closing ranks with his audience, assuring them that they share with him an awareness that there is a God and that together they can know this God. The word translated "feel after" may have struck a familiar note in Paul's Greek audience, since Homer had used the word to describe the groping of the blinded Cyclops Polyphemus as he sought the entrance of his cave and Plato had used it in the *Phaedo* to describe man's guesses at the truth.[3]

Paul proceeds (vs. 28) to emphasize the common nature of the theism of his audience and himself by quoting with approval from several Stoic poets who had expressed the same idea: "For 'In him we live and move and have our being'; as even some of your poets have said, 'For we are indeed his offspring.' " One source to which Paul may be alluding here is Cleanthes, who had written, "Thou, Zeus, art praised above all gods. . . . The origin of the world was from thee: and by law thou rulest over all things. Unto thee may all flesh speak, for we are thy offspring." The poet Aratus had written, "Always we have need of Zeus. For we are also his offspring. . . ." And the poet Epimenides had written about Zeus, "For in thee we live and are moved and have our being." The fact that the brief exordium of Paul's oration contains so many echoes of Greek authors is testimony to Paul's Greek education and to the dignity of the occasion.

In verse 29 Paul simply summarizes the general points that he has made in his introduction: "Being then God's offspring, we ought not to think that the Deity is like gold, or silver, or stone, a representation by the art and imagination of man." The style of the speech up to this point has been exalted, leisurely, allusive, and repetitive — the opposite of what it would be if the speech as recorded in Acts were a condensation.

---

[3] Based on E. M. Blaiklock, *The Acts of the Apostles: An Historical Commentary* (Grand Rapids: Eerdmans Publishing Company, 1959), pp. 144-45. My subsequent references to the sources of Paul's allusions come from the same source.

Having completed the exordium, Paul moves to the part of his oration that Latin rhetoricians would have called the "propositio" — the statement of thesis. It is here, at last, that Paul begins to declare the distinctives of the Christian faith — things such as repentance, judgment, Jesus, and eternal life. The first clause of verse 30 is Paul's final statement of agreement with his pagan audience and serves as a transition: "The times of ignorance God overlooked." Paul then makes sure that he will leave his listeners with a vital challenge by declaring how his views differ from theirs: "but now he commands all men everywhere to repent" (vs. 30). The next verse continues the statement of the thesis that Paul hopes to develop: "because he has fixed a day on which he will judge the world in righteousness by a man whom he has appointed, and of this he has given assurance to all men by raising him from the dead." Paul has now warmed to the occasion and is ready to develop his Christian message. And what happens? He is interrupted and cannot continue: "Now when they heard of the resurrection of the dead, some mocked; but others said, 'We will hear you again about this'" (vs. 32). The subsequent verse states, "So Paul went out from among them," with the connective word "so" relating Paul's departure to the interruption of his speech.

Verse 34 is an epilogue that suggests that Paul's interrupted address was not a total failure. One of Paul's converts in Athens was "Dionysius the Areopagite," a member of the Areopagus who became a famous mystic of the early Christian church.

How did Paul evaluate his oratorical performance before the Areopagus? There is evidence that he may have been disillusioned with his attempt to impress his listeners with his high-flown address that never got beyond the introduction. Paul's next stop on his missionary journey was Corinth (Acts 18:1). In a letter that he was eventually to write to the Corinthian church, Paul described two kinds of preaching: "When I came to you, brethren, I did not come proclaiming to you the testimony of God in lofty words or wisdom. For I decided to know nothing among you except Jesus Christ and him crucified" (1 Cor. 2:1-2). Although we cannot be dogmatic about the point, Paul might well be alluding to his address before the Areopagus. He describes how "when" he came to Corinth he made a conscious decision not to preach in "lofty words or wisdom" (that is, the wisdom of men) and not to preach about anything except the distinctively Christian subject of "Jesus Christ and him crucified." Regardless of whether we accept the view that Paul intends a reference to the Athenian address, it is indisputable that the style of preaching that Paul rejected when he came to Corinth accurately describes his oration before the Areopagus.

"Worship him who made . . . the sea and the fountains of water." (Rev. 14:7)

The Book
of Revelation

17

I

From a literary point of view, the book of Revelation is a fitting climax to the study of biblical literature. It is the most thoroughly literary work in the Bible, and also the book that biblical commentators have devoted the most energy to translating out of its given literary mode into an expository mode. A legitimate commentary on the work is one that preserves its literary integrity — that makes the reader aware of the literary devices and their meaning without taking him away from the literary forms that are present. Commentary that translates the literary mode into an expository one, in effect substituting itself for what John wrote, is an invalid type of commentary.

The book of Revelation is the most carefully structured long work in the Bible. It does not have a unified narrative structure. In fact, as a story it is one of the most disjointed works in the Bible. The main element of structure is the vast system of contrasts that underlies the whole work. The overriding conflict is a spiritual struggle between good and evil. This results in character conflicts — God and Christ against Satan, the saints against the followers of the beast, Israel and the virginal bride of Christ against the whore of Babylon, the Lamb against the dragon, the holy Trinity against the demonic parody of the Trinity (the dragon, the beast from the sea, and the beast from the earth), and Michael's angels against the dragon's angels. There are corresponding scenic conflicts between heaven on the one hand and earth and the bottomless pit on the other, and between the city of God, new Jerusalem, and Babylon, "the great city" of evil. Contrasting actions include the establishment of the new Jerusalem vs. the destruction of Babylon, and the sealing of the saints vs. the receiving of the beast's mark. There is also a temporal contrast between timeless eternity, associated with deliverance for believers, and temporal history, associated with misery of various types.

A second structural principle is the recurrent use of the number seven. There are so many details in Revelation that we might well despair of finding unity and of being able to keep it in our mind as a single entity. Upon close study, however, the work turns out to have a simple and very manageable sequential structure. There is a prologue, a series of six sevenfold units, and an epilogue, as the following outline demonstrates.

1. Prologue (ch. 1).
2. Letters to the seven churches, climaxed by a vision of heaven (2-4).
3. The seven seals:
   a. prologue (5).
   b. warrior on a white horse (6:1-2).
   c. warrior on a red horse (6:3-4).
   d. rider on a black horse (6:5-6).
   e. Death riding on a pale horse (6:7-8).
   f. martyrs in heaven (6:9-11).
   g. cosmic dissolution, associated with judgment (6:12-17).
   h. interlude: sealing of the 144,000; picture of the glorified saints (7:1-17).
   i. silence (8:1).
4. the seven trumpets:
   a. prologue (8:2-6).
   b. hail, fire, blood on the earth (8:7).
   c. the sea becomes blood, destruction at sea (8:8-9).
   d. the falling star, bringing bitter water (8:10-11).
   e. darkening of sun, moon, stars (8:12).
   f. locusts from the pit (8:13–9:12).
   g. the cavalry of judgment (9:13-20).
   h. interlude: John eats the scroll; the two witnesses, persecuted and triumphant (10:1–11:14).
   i. judgment and glorification of believers in heaven (11:15-19).
5. The seven great signs:
   a. the dragon's war against the Son, the woman, and the woman's offspring (ch. 12).
   b. the beast from the sea (13:1-10).
   c. the beast from the earth (13:11-18).
   d. the Lamb on Mount Zion (14:1-5).
   e. angelic messages of judgment (14:6-13).
   f. the reaping of the earth (14:14-16).
   g. reaping and judgment of the wicked (14:17-20).
6. The seven bowls of wrath:
   a. prologue (ch. 15).
   b. sores on men (16:1-2).
   c. sea becomes blood (16:3).

      d. rivers become blood (16:4-7).

      e. fierce heat of the sun (16:8-9).

      f. darkness (16:10-11).

      g. the foul spirits prepare for Armageddon (16:12-16).

      h. earthquake and final judgment against evil (16:17-21).

  7. The seven events of final judgment and consummation:

      a. judgment of Babylon (chs. 17-18).

      b. marriage supper of the Lamb (19:1-10).

      c. Christ defeats the beast and false prophet (19:11-21).

      d. the binding of Satan and the millennial reign of Christ (20:1-6).

      e. the loosing of Satan and his defeat (20:7-10).

      f. final judgment (20:11-15).

      g. description of the new heaven and the new earth (21:1–22:5).

  8. Epilogue (22:6-21).

Each of the sevenfold units is composed of two basic ingredients — fallen human history, closely associated with evil and judgment, and the consummation of history, often linked particularly with the glorification of believers in heaven. Generally, each of the units shows a general progress from fallen human history, associated with evil and misery, to either the glorification of the saints or the events surrounding the end of history. An awareness of this structural principle makes the work as a whole easy to remember and allows the reader to pick up the flow of action at any point and have a general grasp of what is happening.

The third element of structure is simply the linear sequence of visions, images, and events. There are few works of literature that have such a strong onward pressure, with the reader being propelled ever forward. The linear movement is not a smooth narrative flow from one event to the next. Instead, the sequential structure is exactly like that of modern cinema — a kaleidoscopic sequence of visions, pictures, sounds, images, and events, ever shifting and never in focus for very long. The lack of a smooth narrative sweep, combined with the repetitive structure of the book, makes it impossible to arrange the book according to a rigid chronology in which each event is regarded as following in time the preceding event or scene. Although the book as a whole lacks the sustained movement of a single narrative, each small unit will be most easily grasped if it is approached with the usual narrative question, as follows: (1) What is the setting? (2) Who are the characters? (3) What action occurs? (4) What are the consequences?

To say that the book itself does not follow a firm chronological progression is not to say that the events and images in the book cannot be put into some kind of chronological sequence. It is the old distinction between plot (the events as arranged in the story by the storyteller) and the story (the chronology of the events, quite apart from any rearrangement the storyteller may have constructed). For the order of events that underlies the work, we can go to the Olivet Discourse of Jesus on the topic of the destruction of Jerusalem and His second coming at the end of history (Matt. 24-25). Jesus here speaks of a sequence of five main events, as follows: (1) wars and rumors of war, conflict among nations, earthquakes and famines, and false teachers; (2) great persecution for Christ's followers, including the destruction of Jerusalem; (3) the appearance of false Christs and false prophets; (4) great natural disasters, the appearance of the Son of man, and the dispatch of the angels to harvest the elect from the earth; (5) a final judgment, pictured in Matthew's account by several parables and a description of God's judgment between the good and evil. Revelation follows this general outline, which provides structure for the individual units and the whole, and which should be firmly fixed in the reader's mind as he reads each of the sevenfold units. John adds details to the outline provided by Jesus, especially between the fourth and fifth phases. For example, Jesus did not speak, as John does, about a great and final confrontation between the forces of good and evil, or the binding of Satan, or a millennial reign of Christ ushered in by His second coming.

The book of Revelation is the most archetypal piece of literature in the Bible. One notices at once the presence of terms and images that name the elemental, universal aspects of human experience — life, death, blood, lamb, dragon, beast, light, darkness, earth, heaven, water, sea, sun, war, harvest, white, scarlet, bride, throne, jewels, and gold. There are many references to rising, usually associated with spiritual goodness, and falling, associated with spiritual evil. Heaven is high and light, while the bottomless pit is low and dark. There are also several archetypal plot patterns. The last half of the book (chapters 12-22) is a spiritualized version of several common fairy tale motifs, including a lady in distress who is marvelously delivered, a hero who kills a dragon, a wicked witch who is finally exposed, the marriage of the triumphant hero to his bride, the celebration of the wedding with a feast, and the description of a palace glittering with jewels in which the hero and his bride live happily ever after. The journey of a human character, sometimes the narrator, to supernatural realms, where he encounters spiritual beings and returns to human life newly equipped, is an archetype of literature (examples include Odysseus, Aeneas, Moses, Dante, and the Red Cross Knight). The use of the vision as a way of narrating supernatural events is itself an archetypal plot device.

The book of Revelation belongs to a category of literature known as apocalyptic writing. This genre has a number of identifying characteristics. The world of an apocalyptic work is dualistic in the sense of being clearly divided into good and evil. Apocalyptic writing is also eschatological, being primarily concerned with future events. Pseudonymity is a frequent trait, as is the presence of visions as a means of expressing the content of the work. Biblical apocalypse tends to be messianic, centering in the appearance and work of a divine Messiah. Spiritism, in the form of angels and demons, is prevalent. There is also animal symbolism and numerology (the recurrent use of certain numbers, sometimes with symbolic intent). Apocalyptic writing also tends to be judgmental, with the writer predicting woes. The book of Revelation manifests all of these typical qualities of apocalyptic writing, with the exception of pseudonymity.

The work also makes use of two timeless and popular literary devices — animal characters and color symbolism. The first convention is readily apparent in the presence of "living creatures" around the throne in heaven, the divine Lamb, horses of various colors, locusts, a dragon, and terrifying "beasts" from the sea and earth. Color symbolism is less prevalent but still noteworthy. The color white is associated with Christ (1:14), the saints of God (3:18; 4:4; 7:9, 14; 19:8), the armies of heaven (19:14), and God's throne of judgment (20:11). Red, by contrast, appears in contexts of evil — warfare (6:4), the appearance of the satanic dragon (12:3), and the whore of Babylon and her beast (17:3-4).

The basic literary mode used in Revelation is symbolism. This means that concrete images are constantly used to represent something else. Instead of Christ being pictured as a spirit or a man, for example, He is depicted as a lion or a lamb. This is not unusual in literature, but this kind of imaginative rendering of experience and history is an obstacle to a reader who responds only to literal fact.

To insist that the mode is symbolic is not to deny that Revelation describes historical events that really happen. The question is not, Are the events historical? but rather, How does the writer go about describing history? Fortunately we have in chapter 12 a recognizable series of historical events. The passage therefore affords a glimpse into the writer's characteristic way of describing historical events that really happen but do not happen in a literal manner. The series of events describes the incarnation of Christ, Satan's attempt to destroy Christ during His earthly life, the eventual triumph of Christ and His ascent to heaven, and the subsequent attack of Satan on the church during the rest of human history. These events are not described literally. Instead we read about an unusual woman giving birth to a son, a red dragon of epic size, a great battle between two groups of warring angels, and the dragon's descent from heaven to earth, where he makes war upon the descendants of the woman. The chapter thus suggests that the imagery of Revelation tends to be symbolic rather than literal.

This kind of symbolic description is common in biblical prophecy. Daniel 2 describes the figure of a person composed of various minerals. There never was a literal fulfillment of the vision; instead, it is a symbolic image in which the various minerals must be translated into political empires. Isaiah 8:5-8 describes a river that is predicted as overflowing Judah; in fact the river was a symbol for the Assyrian army. Even an image such as the one that pictures those who wait upon the Lord mounting up with wings like eagles (Isa. 40:31) does not describe what literally happens to people who trust in God. Similarly, Isaiah 13:10-13, in predicting the fall of Babylon, describes the sun and moon being darkened, the heavens trembling, and the earth being shaken. There is no evidence to suggest that this picture of cosmic dissolution is anything other than a symbolic account of the military destruction of Babylon. Revelation, being a work of prophecy, uses the conventional symbolic devices of this genre.

How does one know what a given image symbolizes? This is perhaps the central problem in the interpretation of Revelation. The best equipment is a wide acquaintance with literature as a whole, since literary symbolism is to a remarkable degree a conventional language. The second prerequisite is contact with everyday experience and a keen eye for the obvious. It is important to remember that literary symbols are a universal language whose meaning is usually intended to be readily accessible to most readers. The purpose of the symbols in Revelation is not to conceal but to reveal in an easily grasped, universal form of communication. John's first-century readers knew the Old Testament well. They did not have copious commentaries on the book. Knowing Old Testament symbolism is an obvious prerequisite for understanding a book in which there are approximately 350 allusions to the Old Testament. A modern reader may need some help in interpreting the symbols, but mainly he must be sensitive to the obvious connotations of images. We must be on our guard against allegorizing every image. A symbol usually has a general meaning or nexus of meanings; it must not be turned into an esoteric historical reference. Wherever a somewhat esoteric meaning is intended, the book of Revelation makes the allegorical meaning clear.[1] For the rest, we must be content with a general reading of the symbols. Images and symbols are of course less precise and more elusive than propositional language. They thus preserve a sense of mystery

---

[1] For examples of passages where somewhat esoteric allegorical meanings are made explicit, see 1:20; 4:5; 17:7-18; and 19:8.

appropriate to a work that depicts spiritual realities that transcend ordinary reality.

What kind of historical events does Revelation depict? There have been four major approaches to the book. One approach regards the book as arising out of the situation of the first-century church and interprets the events as having occurred in the early centuries of history after Christ. A second interpretation considers the book as forecasting the whole of human history from the time of Christ to His return. Thirdly, the futurist approach takes the view that, except for the first few chapters, the book is exclusively concerned with happenings at the end of the age. Finally, the idealist view minimizes any historical dimension to the book and holds that the book is concerned with depicting the principles and theological ideas on which God operates throughout history.

Without going into a detailed critique of these four approaches, let me simply suggest that the best approach to Revelation is a pluralistic one, combining elements from all of these approaches. We must always begin with the situation of the church to which the book was written. However, because of the literary form of the book, which is filled with symbolic and archetypal images and patterns, its relevance extends throughout the history of the world. Babylon, for example, may have been the Roman empire for John's first-century audience, but in Old Testament times it was literally Babylon, and in history since John's time it has taken many forms. In short, the literary mode of symbolism allows the visions of Revelation to say many things simultaneously. The images and events in Revelation are perpetually relevant and will be ultimately relevant at the end of history.

There are several leading ideas that constitute the controlling themes of Revelation. The work asserts that God is sovereign. He is a God of judgment whose ultimate purpose is to destroy all forms of evil. He is also a God of salvation who glorifies those who believe in Him. The work repeatedly asserts the necessity for patient endurance as God's followers live in a hostile world. The ultimate security of the saints is their assurance that God is in control of history, which He is directing toward a goal. The book conveys a sense of the heavenly reality that transcends the tribulation of earthly existence. Finally, the book is filled with pictures of the worship and adoration of God in heaven. These glimpses of heavenly worship are a model or pattern of the response that people experience whenever they acknowledge the character and worthiness of God.

The book of Revelation does not assume full literary significance by itself. It is the climax of biblical literature as a whole, and this is part of its significance. The whole Bible builds toward it and provides a context for understanding it.

In the first place, Revelation is the concluding phase of the biblical pattern of history. It brings to a conclusion the plot of biblical literature, whose beginning is the creation of the world and the fall of man and whose middle is the pilgrimage through fallen human history. In the book of Revelation the great spiritual conflict between good and evil is finally resolved and eternity finally ushered in. Revelation not only closes biblical literature, but provides a comic conclusion to it. To use Northrop Frye's definition of a comic plot, comedy presents a U-shaped sequence of events that begins in prosperity, descends into potentially tragic action, and ends happily. The usual comic ending in literature is a marriage or a feast, or both. Revelation concludes the Bible with both a feast and a marriage, after the forces of evil have been destroyed. It is in connection with the comic ending that we see the real importance of such fairy tale motifs as the marvelous deliverance of a lady in distress, the hero's conquest of the dragon, the exposure of the wicked witch, and the marriage of the triumphant hero and his bride, who live happily ever after. These literary motifs give expression to man's longings and represent human wish fulfillment. Revelation transmutes this wish fulfillment into a spiritual mode and declares it to be a reality — to be, in fact, the ultimate reality.

A second way in which Revelation rests for its full effect on biblical literature as a whole concerns the fact that it is a virtual compendium of biblical literary forms. Apocalyptic writing, prophecy, vision, epistle, pastoral, satire, encomium, lyric, heroic narrative, and epic all find their place in this encyclopedic work.

Finally, Revelation depends on previous biblical literature because of its abundant use of allusion.[2] Most of the allusions are to Old Testament literature and include, in addition to specific references, such general allusions as the trumpet, the tree of life, the temple, the sacrificial lamb, the twelve tribes of Israel, Babylon, Jerusalem, Mount Zion, and the prostitute. The usual practice is to use these Old Testament phenomena to symbolize spiritual or heavenly realities. The burden of proof is on those who treat Babylon and the prostitute symbolically but insist that references to Jerusalem and Israel are literal.

The book of Revelation is not an epic, but it has many epic characteristics, the recognition of which will enhance one's understanding and enjoyment of the work. The book contains many scenes

[2] For further comment on Old Testament allusions in Revelation, see Merrill G. Tenney, *Interpreting Revelation* (Grand Rapids: Eerdmans Publishing Company, 1957), pp. 101-116.

set in heaven, where decisions are made that will affect what occurs on earth. These scenes resemble, both in construction and function, the epic councils of the gods. The story is an epic story of great and heightened conflict among spiritual beings using supernatural means of warfare. The setting of the action is cosmic, including (as in epic) heaven as well as earth and hell. References to the earth often extend to the whole earth, not just a localized part of it, reinforcing the epic expansiveness of the work. Epic often deals with the establishment of an empire through conquest of enemies. Revelation depicts Christ's establishment of His eternal kingdom by defeating the forces of evil. Epic is constructed around a heroic leader, much as Revelation is a record of the mighty acts of Christ. Epics are often structured on the principle of the quest. The frequently repeated pattern underlying Revelation is the believer's quest for heaven and the movement of history toward its consummation and goal.

In epic the narrator is an important character in the story, mediating between the reader and the events, and directing reader response. John's presence in Revelation is typical of the epic narrator's role and is reminiscent especially of *The Divine Comedy* and *Paradise Lost*. Revelation also has the epic emphasis on the poet's inspiration by a divine source, for whom he acts as a spokesman. The book opens, in fact, with the conventional epic formula of announcing the theme and identifying the divine source of the work.

Two stylistic features of epic are prominent in Revelation. One is simile, used by the writer to compare the great and supernatural events of the story to known earthly experience. In Revelation, as in some epics, the similes function to assert both a similarity and disparity between the events being described and known experience. The disparity occurs when the narrator suggests the impossibility of finding adequate earthly parallels, or when he hints at the fact of only the relative accuracy of an analogy. Examples include such statements as "I heard what seemed to be a voice" (6:6) and "I saw what appeared to be a sea of glass mingled with fire" (15:2).

The second feature of epic style that recurs throughout Revelation is the use of epithets (titles for people or things). These epithets are an important element of form and require careful attention. They are a way of raising the importance or magnitude of the thing being described, as when God is called "the living God" or "the Lord God Almighty." Epithets are also a chief means of characterization. Thus when Christ is called "the Lion," attention is called to His power and headship, while the title "the Lamb" evokes an impression of His status as the sacrificial sinbearer. Thirdly, epithets are often appropriate to a certain stage in the action and serve to draw attention to a given quality or role of a character at a particular point in the story. For example, when God's eternity and sovereignty are being described, He is called "the Lord God Almighty, who was and is and is to come" (4:8); when His kingship is the relevant consideration, He is called "Lord of lords and King of kings" (17:14); and when the justness of His judgments is described, He is called "Holy One" (16:5).

II

The opening of Revelation closely resembles the conventional opening of an epic poem. The writer begins in epic fashion by announcing his theme or topic, which is said to be "the revelation of Jesus Christ" (1:1). The phrase "of Jesus Christ" has multiple meanings. The revelation concerns Jesus, who constitutes the content of the work, but it is also a revelation given by Jesus, who is the source or origin of the work. By calling his work a "revelation" or "apocalypse," John identifies his work as belonging to the category known as apocalyptic literature. The word denotes an uncovering of spiritual realities hidden from ordinary human view but here made plain. This at once sets up a dual expectation: the work will be both supernatural and earthly. Spiritual phenomena will be depicted in terms that are understandable to the human mind. Mystery and realism, heaven and earth will be combined. Any reading that denies the importance of either of these qualities will be an impoverished reading. Not everything has to have an identifiable earthly meaning. Many images are there for the very purpose of retaining a sense of mystery. What is meant to be uncovered will be easily uncovered.

Epic poets also begin their poems by invoking the muse (the goddess who inspires the epic poet) to help and inspire them. John does not invoke God but does, like the epic poet, begin by identifying the divine source of his work. The revelation that he is writing is a "revelation of Jesus Christ, which God gave him to show to his servants" (1:1), and John is the mediator who bears "witness to the word of God and to the testimony of Jesus Christ" (1:2). Like the epic poet, John here places himself in relation both to his work and to his divine source. He is only an agent or spokesman.

Verse three, containing the first of seven beatitudes scattered throughout the book, is also reminiscent of epic. John pronounces a blessing on the person "who reads aloud the words of the prophecy." The emphasis on oral reading indicates John's intention that the prophecy would be read publically in the churches. Epic poetry, too, was originally oral poetry, chanted to a roomful of nobles in a courtly setting. Verse three also makes clear a didactic purpose, something that is also characteristic of epic: "Blessed . . . are those who hear, and who keep what is written therein." John obviously wishes his readers to believe the doctrine contained in his apocalypse and to practice what is revealed. In short, he wishes to influence the lives of his readers, alerting us to the fact that his message is more practical and less theoretical than it is often given credit for being. When John calls his work a "prophecy" (vs. 3), he again draws attention to its divine source, since a prophet in biblical times was primarily a person who spoke forth what God had revealed.

Verses 4 to 8 of the first chapter are part of the general prologue and give the impression of having been written with intense emotion. The thoughts and images tumble out abruptly in kaleidoscopic fashion much as in the opening lyric of John's gospel. There are several long epithets for God and Christ, and the interspersed "Amen" by the narrator shows his subjective involvement in his subject matter.

The most notable feature of the prologue is the picture of Christ (1:12-16). The vision of the transcendent Christ is like an introduction to an epic hero, and it sets the tone for the whole work, which has as its focal point the mighty acts of Christ. We must remember that John was writing to a small, persecuted church, and that for such an audience the image of the transcendent Christ would have been a source of comfort and encouragement. The vision of Christ is not intended to allow us to envision a single composite figure. It mingles images so as to create a general sense of splendor and otherworldliness.

The variety of techniques used in the description of Christ is typical of the apocalyptic style of the whole book. When John describes himself as turning "to see the voice that was speaking to me" (vs. 12), he conveys a sense of God's presence without localizing and visualizing Him. Christ is described as "one like a son of man" (vs. 13), a deliberately vague image. The "long robe" (vs. 13) is a symbol indicating a person of distinction (the associations are either priestly or kingly), and it, too, is an image that veils a figure from direct view. The white head and hair ("white as white wool, white as snow" — vs. 14) suggest ancientness, since the image is modeled on the picture of the "Ancient of Days" in Daniel 7:9. The images of the eyes "like a flame of fire" (vs. 14) and feet "like burnished bronze, refined as in a furnace" (vs. 15) are the first of many examples of what I shall call enameled imagery. Such imagery combines hardness of texture (usually minerals or jewels are involved) and brilliance of light, evoking an impression of supernatural brilliance and suggesting a realm of transcendent permanence, in contrast to the cyclic vegetative world that we experience. The voice, earlier said to be "like a trumpet" (vs. 10), is now said to be "like the sound of many waters" (vs. 15). Obviously the narrator is groping for earthly analogies that will somehow do justice to his supernatural vision. The picture of Christ holding seven stars in His hand (vs. 15) suggests hugeness of size and mystery, since it is not easily imagined how someone could hold stars in his hand. When we read that "from his mouth issued a sharp two-edged sword" (1:16), we are not intended to visualize the picture, which is grotesque. The imagery here, as is customary in Revelation, is symbolic rather than pictorial, conveying the sense of Christ's judgment. The face "like the sun shining in full strength" (vs. 16) is simply the climactic bit of splendor in this fragmented figure of Christ. The vision has conveyed a general impression of Christ rather than a sharply visualized picture, and it has symbolized such qualities as awesomeness, ancientness, splendor, power, judgment, and mystery.

Chapters 2 and 3 contain the letters to the seven churches. The letters follow an elaborate pattern of parallels, with the general outline of each consisting of seven parts, as follows:

1. a greeting ("To the angel of the church in . . .")
2. a title for Christ (with all but the last taking some detail from the description of Christ in chapter 1).
3. a commendation of the church (beginning, "I know . . .")
4. a criticism of the church (omitted in the cases of Smyrna and Philadelphia).
5. a warning.
6. an exhortation to be attentive (beginning with the statement, "He that hath an ear, let him hear . . .")
7. a promise (beginning with a formula to the effect that "to him that overcometh I will give . . .")

In the last four letters, the order of items 6 and 7 is reversed, introducing an element of variety into the overall pattern of recurrence.

Although the letters are addressed to particular churches, their relevance extends to Christian believers of all times and places. Together the letters embody certain themes that are important to the book of Revelation as a whole. The letters indicate that there is a great spiritual conflict going on in the world. Everyone is involved. The forms of evil differ from one church to another, but they are very much in evidence. In one way or another, some kind of positive choice for Christ is demanded in every letter. People's response to the call to godly living is a matter of momentous importance, with a person's eternal welfare at stake. Another theme in the letters is that God is the sovereign judge who is concerned about what people are doing in the world. Man is urged to live in an awareness of God's presence, and the certainty of God's judgment is constantly offered as the rationale for repentance while there is time. There is, finally, repeated emphasis on the fact that Christ is coming again. The important matter is not when He is coming but that He is coming. Christians are enjoined to live in an eschatalogical awareness, ordering their lives around the certainty of Christ's return. Because life has a goal, patient endurance becomes a chief mark of the Christian in these letters.

Taken together, the letters speak of the same kinds of events that Jesus mentioned in His Olivet Discourse. There are references to persecution of believers, false teachers within the churches, the return of Christ, and final judgment. I have noted earlier that each of the sevenfold units in Revelation shows a general movement from history to the spiritual realities that will be ushered in at the end of history. Chapter 4, often considered to be an independent interlude, completes this twofold movement. That it belongs with the letters to the seven churches is suggested by the statement that the voice "will show ... what must take place after this" (vs. 1), that is, after the historical process just described in the letters.

Chapter 4 is one of many apocalyptic visions of the believers in heaven. The transcendental nature of the experience is suggested by John's statement that he saw the vision while "in the Spirit" (vs. 2). After two chapters set on earth, the scene now suddenly shifts to heaven. There is a deliberate visual vagueness in the statement that "a throne stood in heaven, and one seated on the throne" (vs. 2). The supernatural splendor of God is conveyed through the enameled images of jasper, carnelian, and emerald (vs. 3), and the image of the rainbow, identical to a passage in Ezekiel 1:27-28, is used to convey the impression of an encircling brightness around the throne. The twenty-four elders seated on thrones are not identified, leaving the reader with a sense of the mystery surrounding the heavenly court. Lightning and thunder, archetypally associated with God's presence and activity in biblical literature, find their expected place in this vision of God (vs. 5), while the seven torches of fire, symbolic of spirit, are allegorized as meaning "the seven spirits of God" (vs. 5). The simile that describes the splendor of heaven as being "as it were a sea of glass, like crystal" (vs. 6) conveys a sense of both the similarity of the brightness to known earthly phenomena and a sense of the disparity between heaven and earth. The "four living creatures" (vs. 6), whose watchfulness and omniscience are symbolized by the fact that they are "full of eyes in front and behind" (vs. 6), are also vague images that defy realistic detail. Into this heavenly scene praise of God is introduced (vss. 8-11). The description as a whole has done two things: it has admitted the reader into a new mode of experience (spiritual reality), and it has celebrated (in its picture of God's greatness and the worship of God by His creatures) Christian experience as a Christian reader has known it.

Chapter 5 is a prelude to the sequence of the seven seals. It is a self-contained unit with a single setting, the heavenly court, and an overriding theme, the worthiness of the Lamb. This scene set in heaven resembles the epic convention of the council of the gods, where action is first decreed in a heavenly council and then put into action on earth. The episode is initiated by the question of who is worthy to open a scroll sealed with seven seals. The scroll represents the events of the future. The unworthiness of any creature to open the seal becomes a narrative way of praising Christ's worthiness. Christ is first pictured as a lion (vs. 5) and then as a lamb (vss. 6 ff.). The mode is symbolism, or emblem, with Christ being pictured not as a man or spirit but as an animal. There is no intention of consistency in the images used to refer to Christ. The emphasis on the lamb not only draws upon the idealized pastoral tradition but also centers attention on Christ's status as the sacrificial atonement. The heavenly scene reaches a crescendo of praise as the encomium praising the worthiness of the Lamb moves from the four creatures and twenty-four elders around the throne (vs. 8) to all the heavenly hosts of angels and saints (vs. 11) and finally to "every creature in heaven and on earth and under the earth and in the sea" (vs. 13).

Chapter 6 introduces the reader to the first of several closely related groups of seven visions. The seven seals, structured as a procession, are roughly parallel to the seven trumpets, seven great signs, and seven bowls with the seven last plagues. These groups of seven events follow the same general sequence, moving from the earthly scene, which is shown in misery, to the consummation of history and the reality of heaven. In following this movement the sections also adhere generally to the arrangement of eschatological events outlined in Jesus' Olivet Discourse. Further pattern emerges from the fact that several of the units begin with four visions that belong together.

The seven seals begin with four visions involving horses. The four visions should be taken as different stages in a single process. The picture of a crowned conqueror on a white horse symbolizes the spirit of military conquest. By itself the picture is an attractive one, but this attractiveness is ironic because its connotations become transformed into something sinister in the three subsequent visions. An important theme to note in these visions and indeed throughout the book of Revelation is the control that God exercises over the events that are depicted, as evidenced by such statements as that a crown "was given" to the warrior (6:2), that the next rider "was permitted to take peace from the earth" (vs. 4), and that in the fourth vision Death and Hades "were given power over a fourth of the earth" (vs. 8).

The next three visions employ the device of climax, with the misery on earth becoming progressively intensified. The second horse is bright red, more sinister than the white horse. Its warrior, also, is more threatening, taking peace from the earth and carrying a sword (vs. 4). The negative connotations become even stronger with the vision of a black horse (vs. 5) and a warrior carrying not military equipment but a scale. This is a symbol for famine, as the prices of the weighted grain suggest (vs. 6) and as parallel references to the weighing of grain mean in Ezekiel 4:9-10 and Leviticus 26:26. The fourth horse, said to be pale, literally yellowish-green (vs. 8), is the most terrifying of all. The allegorical characters Death and Hades reinforce the image of dread, as does the description of how they have "power over a fourth of the earth, to kill with sword and with famine and with pestilence and by wild beasts of the earth" (vs. 8).

From this demonic vision of catastrophe on earth, the focus suddenly shifts to heaven, where the martyrs are pictured awaiting God's vengeance against the forces of evil (vss. 9-11). The vision has a dual thrust, characteristic of the whole book. On the one hand, we are given a pessimistic view of history in which there is a prediction of hostility toward God's followers throughout history. It must be remembered that the book was written to a persecuted group of Christian believers and that to ignore the reality of persecution would have been irrelevant to the first readers of the work. To balance the pessimistic view of history, there is a picture of the martyrs receiving a white robe, symbolic of the victory that is theirs in heaven. This brief scene epitomizes the whole book of Revelation in its balance between optimism and pessimism, hope and despair, triumph and tragedy.

The sixth vision returns to the theme of destruction on earth. The picture of cosmic dissolution (vss. 12-14) draws upon archetypal images for the end of time in biblical literature, while the scene of unbelievers trying to flee the wrath of Christ (vss. 15-17) echoes a prediction made by Jesus in Luke 23:30. The image of people fearing "the wrath of the Lamb" (vs. 16) is particularly striking, since ordinarily a lamb is gentle. Revelation consistently pictures God as being both loving and angry or judgmental. The fact that the wrath of God is predicted so often and so plainly in the book confirms the didactic intent of the writer and the providential concern of God, who gives these warnings before the occurrence of judgment so that men may repent while there is time.

There is an important interlude between the sixth and seventh seals, just as there will be an interruption between the sixth and seventh trumpets. The sealing of the believers (ch. 7) is a symbolic action that identifies these persons as belonging to God. It is the great opposite of the receiving of the mark of the beast by unbelievers (13:16). The sealing occurs in two stages, with John first hearing the number of the sealed (7:4) and then looking and beholding the multitude of the redeemed (vs. 9). The number of the sealed is symbolic of the completeness and large number of the redeemed. All of the twelve tribes are present, with the four-square symbolism of 12 x 12 reinforcing the sense of completeness that we feel in connection with the number 144,000. The symbolic number of a thousand conveys a sense of the vastness of the multitude. When John looks at the multitude he sees people "from every nation" (vs. 9), including Jews as well as Gentiles and emphasizing the motif of the universality of the Christian faith. The white robes and palm branches of the saints (vs. 9) are symbols of victory, and the various songs of praise are encomia exalting the Lamb. The apocalyptic vision of heavenly perfection that concludes the chapter (vss. 15-17) includes the techniques of describing heaven as the absence of ordinary fallen reality (no thirst, no hunger, no scorching heat, no tears) and pastoral idealization, with heavenly experience described in the images of the shepherd's life. This scene of heavenly bliss completes the movement within this section from earthly misery to heavenly victory, and it provides an anticipation of subsequent scenes of triumph in heaven.

The seven trumpets (chs. 8-11) follow the same general pattern as the seven seals, emphasizing the repetitive, cyclic structure of the book as a whole. Again there is a preliminary scene set in heaven, where God's judgment against the evil earth is decreed (8:3-6). The four visions of horses have their parallel in four visions involving the elemental aspects of nature — earth, sea, rivers, sun, moon, and stars (vss. 7-12). These elemental forces are used to convey the impression that something basic is happening in the earthly sphere of things. The sense of calamity is increased over the seven seals, for the fourth part of the earth affected there (6:8) is now replaced by destruction of a third part of the earth (8:7), the sea (vs. 8), the rivers (vss. 10-11), and the sun, moon, and stars (vs. 12).

The fifth trumpet (9:1-11), involving the opening of the bottomless pit, is the most terrifying image of evil yet to appear in the unfolding drama of Revelation. This pit, with its archetypal associations of descent (it is bottomless), smoke and intense heat (vs. 2), and darkness (vs. 9), is an image evoking instinctive feelings of horror and revulsion. Pictured as an abyss with a narrow opening at the top, the pit is a hell-like place, if not a picture of hell itself. The locusts that ascend from the pit symbolize God's judgment against unbelievers (vs. 4) and are a biblical archetype, recalling similar judgments of God in the eighth plague against the Egyptians and against Israel in the prophecy of Joel. In one of the most amazing poetic passages in the entire book (vss. 7-11), the terror of the locusts is greatly amplified in a description that compares various features of the locusts to other threatening aspects of human experience. Two interpretations of the description are possible: either the locusts that are described are imagined, apocalyptic locusts that exist, like the dragon, only in the literary world of the imagination, or they are literal locusts whose destructiveness is described by comparing them to other, bigger forces in known reality. The second interpretation is probably preferable. Thus the locusts are like horses (vs. 7), not in size, but because they literally come in great force and numbers, like war horses. Similarly, the pictures of heads with crowns, faces like human faces (intent on destruction, giving the impression of malicious intention), hair like women's hair, mouths that devour as a lion does, scales like iron breastplates, and wings that sound like horse-drawn chariots might all be based on a real locust.

The sixth trumpet (9:13-21) is one of the most mysterious episodes in the book. It pictures a cavalry of warriors who execute God's judgment on a third of mankind. In this regard the episode fits into the overall plot of spiritual conflict. The troops of the cavalry are introduced abruptly in verse 16, as if they had already been mentioned, but in fact the reader has not been told whether they are human or angelic warriors. What is clear is that they have been reserved for judgment at a particular time and according to a fixed plan by God (vss. 14-15). The war horses, whose mouths eject fire, smoke, and sulfur (vss. 17-18), and whose tails are like serpents with heads (vs. 19), are probably apocalyptic beasts, imagined in a vision and having no basis in real life. The picture of unrepentant mankind (vss. 20-21) throws the burden on the reader to respond in a manner appropriate to the logic of the situation instead of following the incredible callousness of the characters in the work, who do not heed God's warnings.

The interlude in this unit of chapters (10:1–12:13) is important for several reasons. By delaying the climactic seventh vision, the writer creates suspense and dramatizes the theme that repentance is possible while God withholds His final judgment. The mighty angel who descends from heaven (10:1-2) is one of many epic figures in this expansive work. The prophet's eating of the scroll that contains his predictions (vss. 8-11) has a parallel in the Old Testament prophecies of Jeremiah (15:16) and Ezekiel (3:1-3). The simultaneous bitterness and sweetness of the scroll underscores the dual nature of John's prophecy, which is comforting to believers but bitter in its pronouncement of judgment upon evil.

The story of the two witnesses (11:1-13), also part of the interlude, is itself a reenactment of the history of believers that occurs elsewhere in Revelation. These two figures, symbolizing the believing church, are given the task of proclaiming God's Word in a degenerate time of history. They are associated with the images of olive trees (see Zechariah 4:14 for the source of the symbol), symbolizing life in the midst of death, and lampstands, symbolizing light in the midst of darkness. The two figures are linked by way of allusion with Moses and Elijah, as evidenced by their ability to prevent rainfall, to turn water into blood, and to bring about plagues (11:6). The symbolism of all this is clear: the church in persecution has the same resources available to it as the Old Testament prophets had. The two witnesses are given power to finish their epic feat of proclaiming God's Word (vs. 7). Following an epic-like battle in which the beast kills the two witnesses (vs. 7), there is a scene of exultant evil followed by the miraculous rescue of the witnesses. This sequence of events either pictures a single event that will occur near the end of history, or it is a vision of the archetypal pattern of what happens whenever the defeated church revives. In either case, the story of the two witnesses has reenacted the basic motif of Revelation — persecution of the church in a corrupt world followed by its eventual triumph. In the words of Austin Farrer, the interlude of chapter 11 "is a foreshortened and premature conclusion, cancelled, and yet permitted to stand by way of interlude."[3]

The seventh trumpet (11:15-19) brings this section of the book to an expected climax, modeled along the lines of earlier climaxes. History is consummated when "the kingdom of the world has become the kingdom of our Lord and of his Christ" (vs. 15). The coming of Christ to establish His kingdom is also accompanied by the judgment of all the dead, good and evil (vs. 18), in the manner predicted by Jesus in His Olivet Discourse and His eschatalogical parables. A riot of sensation forms the conclusion of the episode: "Then God's temple in heaven was opened, and the ark of his covenant was seen within his temple; and there were flashes of lightning, loud noises, peals of thunder, an earthquake, and heavy hail" (vs. 19).

Chapter 12, which initiates the section of the seven great signs, is in several ways a representative summary of the whole book of Revelation. It opens with a symbolic account of the birth of Christ (vss. 1-5) and a description of how a great red dragon (symbolizing Satan) attempts to destroy Him. The child's miraculous ascension into heaven (vs. 5) is a symbolic way of depicting Satan's inability to destroy Christ during His earthly ministry. The picture of war in

3 Austin Farrer, *A Rebirth of Images: The Making of St. John's Apocalypse* (London: Dacre Press, 1949), p. 44.

heaven, "Michael and his angels fighting against the dragon" (vs. 7), is a magnificent epitome of the overriding plot of the Bible. The basis of the victory of Christ's followers is "the blood of the Lamb and ... the word of their testimony" (vs. 11), suggesting that the battle is not physical but a spiritual struggle, of which the physical image is a fitting symbol. The vision of the earth opening to swallow the river that proceeded from the dragon (vss. 15-16) is a variation of a favorite literary motif through the centuries — the miraculous deliverance of a woman in distress. The concluding event in the chapter, picturing the dragon going off "to make war on the rest of her offspring, on those who keep the commandments of God and bear testimony to Jesus" (vs. 17), shows that in history after Christ's earthly life the spiritual battle takes the form of warfare between Satan and the believing community. This is what the book of Revelation as a whole describes. Chapter 12 thus uses symbolic narrative to explain what lies behind the great conflict described elsewhere in the book.

Chapter 13 is devoted to a description of two terrifying beasts which are demonic parodies of the Lamb and which, together with the dragon, constitute the demonic counterpart of the holy Trinity. There are other elements of parody as well. One of the heads of the beast from the sea "seemed to have a mortal wound, but its mortal wound was healed, and the whole earth followed the beast with wonder" (vs. 3). This is the demonic counterfeit of the dying and reviving Christ. Similarly, the beast from the earth "had two horns like a lamb" (vs. 11), giving it a resemblance to the Lamb of God. In addition, the mark that is put on the right hand or the forehead of the beast's followers (vs. 16) echoes the earlier sealing of the believers as a mark of their possession by God. The fact that the beast from the sea "was allowed to make war on the saints and to conquer them" (vs. 7) corresponds to the second phase outlined by Jesus in the Olivet Discourse, just as the "great signs" with which the beast from the earth "deceives those who dwell on earth" (vss. 13-14) corresponds exactly to Jesus' prediction that in the third phase "false prophets will arise and show great signs and wonders, so as to lead astray, if possible, even the elect" (Matt. 24:24).

As the reader has by this time been led to expect, the sequence of the seven great signs moves from what will happen on earth to a vision of ultimate victory for believers in heaven. Thus chapter 14 opens with a vision of the Lamb on Mount Zion, symbolic of heaven. The body of the redeemed, the mighty opposite of the followers who bear the mark of the beast, are described by means of two symbols. They are compared to chaste men "who have not defiled themselves with women" (vs. 4). This male image complements the more familiar image of the church as a bride. Like the bride image, it uses sexual purity as a way of symbolizing that believers are pure in their devotion to Christ. The believers in heaven are also described as those who have been "redeemed from mankind as first fruits for God and the Lamb" (vs. 4). In Hebrew sacrifices the firstfruits were the choicest part of a harvest set aside as a special offering to God. The body of the redeemed is said to be set aside to God in a similar manner.

The remaining parts of chapter 14 are devoted to scenes connected with the end of history. In verse 8 we are introduced to what will become a leading figure in the work — the whore of Babylon, symbol of evil, whose fall is predicted (vs. 8). There are archetypal pictures of judgment, such as the wine of God's wrath (vs. 10), the fire and brimstone that torment the evildoers (vs. 10), and the smoke of torment (vs. 11). The destruction of the wicked is balanced by the reward of the righteous (vs. 13), with comfort following judgment as it does elsewhere in the book. In the two concluding visions, the writer draws upon the archetypal image of Christ harvesting the earth, suggesting the end of history.

Chapters 12 to 14, beginning with the incarnation of Christ and concluding with His second coming, "provide a complete apocalypse."[4] Like the sections of the book dealing with the letters, the seals, and the trumpets, these chapters display a movement from the flow of history to events that will culminate history and bring triumph to believers. It is evidence of the rhythmic structure of Revelation — of its tendency to repeat common themes and patterns in new ways. It also shows the writer's mastery of foreshadowing, with several anticipated conclusions preceding the ultimate sequence of judgment and salvation.

The seven bowls of wrath are prefaced with a heavenly council (ch. 15), just as the visions of the seals and trumpets were. As in the earlier sequences, the seven plagues cover a whole range of judgments. This time, however, there is an emphasis on the finality of the judgments, as evidenced by the statement that the seven plagues "are the last, for with them the wrath of God is ended" (vs. 1). The first five bowls picture God's judgment on earth, with the plagues of sores on men, water turned into blood, and darkness resembling some of the ten plagues against Egypt in the book of Exodus. The sixth bowl (16:12-16) describes, without giving details, a climactic battle between good and evil that will occur at Armageddon. This, too, is part of the ever-present theme of the Bible and keeps the epic identity of Revelation alive. The seventh bowl shows

---

[4] Farrer, *Rebirth of Images*, p. 53.

the dissolution of the earthly order of things and is replete with such eschatalogical archetypes as an earthquake of unprecedented magnitude (vs. 18), the draining of the cup of God's fury (vs. 19), and the removal of islands and mountains (vs. 20).

Chapters 17 to 22 bring to a conclusion all of the smaller, tentative cycles that have preceded. The first of seven events that constitute the final phase of the plot involves the judgment of the whore of Babylon. The harlot is described in 17:1-6a, her significance is explained in the remainder of the chapter, and her punishment is predicted in chapter 18. The whore of Babylon is another of the great symbols of Revelation. On the literal level she is described as being "seated upon many waters" (17:1). Since in the Old Testament Jeremiah had addressed the city of Babylon as "you who dwell by many waters" (Jer. 51:13), it is evident that John is modeling his symbolic Babylon along the lines of the Babylon of ancient times. The symbolic value of Babylon is what is important, however. The color symbolism of the scarlet beast on which the woman sits (17:3) is one of the things that makes the harlot a symbol. Furthermore, her status as a prostitute carries primarily spiritual rather than sexual connotations. The additional fact that Babylon is said to be "mother . . . of earth's abominations" (17:5) serves to establish her as a general image of evil, just as the fact that she is said to contain the blood of *all* who had been slain on the earth (18:24) makes it clear that Babylon is more than a single, literal city.

The symbolic meanings of the harlot are explicated at some length by an angel who speaks to the narrator (17:7-18). She is closely associated with Satan, as evidenced by the fact that the beast on which she rides is identified as Satan (vs. 8). She is also connected with Rome by virtue of the fact that "the seven heads are seven hills on which the woman is seated" (vs. 9). This was undoubtedly the chief contemporary significance of the symbol. By making the heads and horns symbolic of political kings (vss. 10-12), the angelic interpreter gives this image of evil an ever-expanding set of meanings. And when we finally learn that the various kings symbolized by the harlot and the beast "will make war on the Lamb" (17:14), it becomes clear that the image is intended to be a universal embodiment of the principle of evil. What, then, is represented by the woman, who is also said to be "the great city" (17:18)? She is man in community in rebellion against God. In the Old Testament era one form of such evil was Babylon. In John's day it was Rome. It has taken many forms since then, and it will assume an ultimate form at the end of history.

The entire eighteenth chapter announces the coming doom of Babylon. It is an example of a familiar type of satire found in Old

Testament prophecy — the doom song. The lament of the world over Babylon (vss. 9-19) describes her as a worldwide commercial empire. The references to contemporary Rome are unmistakable in the description. The rejoicing in heaven over Babylon's fall (vs. 20) is the antithesis to the lament of the evil world over her destruction.

The destruction of evil is balanced by a picture of the marriage supper of the Lamb in heaven (19:1-10), which connotes the positive values appropriate to the union of the believing church with Christ. The marriage feast is also the conventional conclusion to a comic plot. Following the description of the feast, Christ suddenly appears, not as a bridegroom, as we might expect, but as a warrior (vs. 11). It is typical of the kaleidoscopic mingling of images that goes to make up the book of Revelation. Christ is said to judge and make war (vs. 11), in the conventional manner of an epic hero establishing his empire through conquest. Accompanying the conquest of the beast and false prophet are several events treated summarily by the writer, including the binding of Satan for a thousand years, a corresponding millennial reign of Christ, the loosing of Satan, a climactic battle between the forces of good and evil, and the final judgment of the dead.

The final climax, culminating many other climaxes in Revelation, is the description of the new heaven and the new earth (chapters 21 and 22). The description is filled with apocalyptic archetypes. The church is called a bride (21:2). God is pictured as giving "water without price from the fountain of the water of life" (vs. 6). There is emphasis on the completeness implied by the number twelve (vss. 12-14), and more completeness is conveyed by the symbolism of four-square (vs. 16). There is a barrage of enameled jewel images (vss. 18-21), as well as an abundance of light (vss. 23-24). There is "the river of the water of life" (22:1) and an allusion to Paradise in the image of the tree of life (vs. 2). It is the most appropriate conclusion that one could imagine for biblical literature as a whole.

Glossary

The following glossary provides definitions of the technical terms that appear in the text. Parenthetical page numbers that accompany some of the definitions refer to the pages in the text where a more complete definition appears.

acrostic, a poem in which the successive units begin with the consecutive letters of the Hebrew alphabet (p. 153)

allegory, a work of literature in which the details have a corresponding conceptual meaning or set of conceptual meanings (p. 301)

allusion, a reference to past history or literature

anti-hero, a literary protagonist who exhibits an absence of the character traits that are conventionally associated with literary heroes

anti-romance, a work of literature, or part of a work of literature, that presents unideal experience; a literary world of total bondage and the absence of anything ideal (pp. 23-25)

antithetic parallelism, a two-line poetic pattern in which the second unit states the truth of the first in a negative way or introduces a contrast (p. 122)

apocalyptic literature, a branch of Hebrew literature whose distinguishing characteristics include dualism, eschatological orienta-tion, pseudonymity, the use of visions, emphasis on messianic intervention in history, spiritism, animal symbolism, numerology, and prediction of judgment (p. 339)

apostrophe, a figure of speech in which the writer addresses someone absent or something nonhuman as if it were present and human and could respond to the address

archetype, an image, plot motif, or character type that recurs throughout literature and whose meaning is universally understood (pp. 22-25)

blazon, a lyric poem of romantic love in which a lover praises the beloved by listing the beautiful features or virtuous qualities of the beloved (pp. 223-225)

comedy, a work of literature in which the plot structure is U-shaped, with the action beginning in prosperity, descending into potentially tragic events, and ending happily (pp. 23, 24)

denouement, the last phase of a story, consisting of the events that follow the climax

didactic, having the intention or impulse to teach

dramatic irony, a situation in a story where the reader knows more about what is happening than do some characters in the story

dramatic monologue, a work of literature in which a single speaker addresses an implied though mute listener and in which various details keep this dramatic situation alive in the reader's consciousness

embellished narrative, a story in the gospels in which an event is narrated in relatively great detail

emblem, a symbolic and sometimes pictorial image to which a person or thing is compared

encomium, a work of literature that praises an abstract quality or a generalized character type (p. 201)

epic, a long narrative having a number of conventional characteristics (p. 81)

epithalamion (also spelled "epithalamium"), a lyric poem that celebrates a wedding

epithet, an exalted title for a person or thing; a feature of the high style, especially as found in epic

exordium, in classical rhetoric and oratory, the introduction to a speech or composition (pp. 328-329)

exposition, the opening phase of a story, in which the writer presents the background information that the reader needs in order to understand the plot

that will subsequently unfold

expository writing, writing whose main purpose is to convey information and which therefore tends to be denotative

foil, a contrast, either a character or an action, that clarifies or heightens the effect of another character or another action

genre, a literary kind or type

gospel, a narrative form of the New Testament (pp. 273-276)

heroic narrative, a story built around the character and exploits of the protagonist, who is usually considered exemplary or representative (pp. 45-46)

hyperbole, a figure of speech in which a writer uses conscious exaggeration for the sake of effect; a standard way of expressing strong feeling in poetry

idyl, a short work of literature that describes a simple, pleasant aspect of rural, pastoral, or domestic life

irony. There are three types of irony. (1) Dramatic irony occurs when a reader knows more about what is happening than do some of the characters in a story. (2) Verbal irony occurs when a writer states something but means exactly the opposite. (3) Irony of situation occurs when a situation is the opposite of what is expected or appropriate.

lyric, a short poem containing the thoughts and especially the feelings of a single speaker (pp. 121-124)

metaphor, a figure of speech in which the writer makes an implied comparison between two phenomena (as when Jesus called His followers "the light of the world")

monomyth, the generalized, composite narrative that encompasses in a single, circular pattern the whole body of literature (pp. 22, 23)

motif, a discernible pattern composed of individual units, either in a single work or in literature generally

multiple meanings, a situation in which a word or image or phrase has several complementary meanings at the same time

narrative, a story; a series of events

narrator, the character or "voice" of the writer as he exists in a work of literature; even when the narrator is recognizably the author, he must be granted literary status as a character in his work.

occasional literature, a work of literature that takes its origin from a particular historical event or a particular event in the life of the writer

ode, an exalted lyric poem that celebrates a dignified subject in a lofty style; the gravest and loftiest kind of lyric, as epic is in the narrative family.

parable, a brief narrative that explicitly embodies one or more themes (pp. 301-303)

paradox, an apparent contradiction which, upon reflection, is seen to express a genuine truth

parallelism. The most general definition is a poetic or rhetorical pattern in which two or more successive clauses follow a discernible form or design, based on a principle of repetition or recurrence. For a discussion of the more technical types of parallelism found in Hebrew poetry, see page 122.

parody, a work of literature that parallels but inverts the usual meaning of the conventions of a literary genre or a specific earlier work of literature

pastoral, literature in which the setting is rustic, the characters are shepherds and shepherdesses, and the action consists of activities ordinarily done by shepherds (pp. 233-234)

peroration, in classical rhetoric and oratory, the eloquent climax that concludes a speech or composition

personification, a figure of speech in which human attributes are attached to an animal, an object, or an abstract quality or idea

plot, the sequence of events in a story, based on a central conflict; according to Aristotle, a sequence of events that are causally related and that have a beginning, a middle, and an end

poetic justice, a narrative technique in which good characters are rewarded for their virtue and evil characters are punished for their vice.

protagonist, the leading character in a story, whether sympathetic or unsympathetic

proverb, a concise expression of a moral truth

rhetorical question, a figure of speech in which the writer asks a question whose answer is obvious — so obvious that it is left unstated; a question asked for the sake of effect, not to elicit information

romance, a work of literature, or part of a work of literature, that presents ideal experience; wish-fulfillment literature (p. 23)

satire, the exposure, through ridicule or rebuke, of human vice or folly (pp. 261-263)

simile, a figure of speech in which the writer compares two phenomena, using the explicit formula "like" or "as" to introduce the comparison (An illustration is the statement in Psalm 1 that the godly person "is like a tree planted by streams of water.")

simple narrative, a story in the gospels that narrates only the bare outline of an event

story of origins, a story in which the narrative is designed to explain the origin of various features of human experience

symbol, any detail in a work of literature which, in addition to having its own identity in the work, also stands for something else; a symbol can represent or suggest a cluster of meanings.

synonymous parallelism, a poetic construction in which successive lines state the same truth in different words but using roughly the same grammatical form (p. 122)

theme, a generalization about life that is embodied in a work of literature

tragedy, a narrative form of literature in which a protagonist of high degree and greatness of spirit undertakes an action (makes a choice) within a given tragic world and as a result inevitably falls from prosperity to a state of physical and spiritual suffering, sometimes attaining perception (pp. 95-96)

well-made plot, a plot that unfolds according to the following pattern: exposition (background information), inciting moment (or inciting force), rising action, turning point (at which time the reader can begin to see how the conflict will be resolved), further complication, climax, and denouement (tying up of loose ends)

wisdom literature, a branch of Hebrew literature in which the writer depends on short literary units as the form for expressing his wise observations about human experience (pp. 243-245)

Indexes

SUBJECT INDEX

SCRIPTURE INDEX